Narendra Modi

Vision and Accomplishments

K.R. Gupta

ATLANTIC

PUBLISHERS & DISTRIBUTORS (P) LTD

Published by
ATLANTIC
PUBLISHERS & DISTRIBUTORS (P) LTD
7/22, Ansari Road, Darya Ganj, New Delhi-110002
Phones : +91-11-40775252, 23273880, 23275880, 23280451
Fax : +91-11-23285873
Web : www.atlanticbooks.com
E-mail : orders@atlanticbooks.com

Branch Office
5, Nallathambi Street, Wallajah Road, Chennai-600002
Phones : +91-44-48531784, 28411383
E-mail : chennai@atlanticbooks.com

Printed in India at Nice Printing Press, A-33/3A, Site-IV, Industrial Area, Sahibabad, Ghaziabad, U.P.

Preface

After serving continuously for more than 12 years, from 7 October 2009 to 22 May 2014, as Chief Minister of Gujarat, during which he not only hard-sold 'Gujarat Model of Development' but also got himself nominated as BJP's prime ministerial candidate for 2014 Lok Sabha election, Narendra Modi emerged strongly on the national scene influencing the national politics of India. Mesmerized by his dynamism, speeches, and poll promises, the voters gave him and his party an overwhelming support, and the Congress and its allies crashed to their worst ever defeat. Modi took oath as India's 15th Prime Minister on 26 May 2014. He is the first ever PM to be born after India attained Independence. Dynamic, dedicated, and determined, Narendra Modi reflects the hopes and aspirations of over a billion Indians.

Ever since assuming office, Narendra Modi has embarked on a journey of all-round and inclusive development in which all the people of India can live in peace and prosperity. He believes in the principle of 'Antyodaya', i.e., serving the last person in the queue. Through a number of innovative ideas and initiatives, his government has been trying to ensure that India achieves fast socio-economic progress and gets a high place in the comity of nations. Making governance open, easier and transparent is one of his goals.

Narendra Modi and his government have focused on reforming and modernizing India's infrastructure and governance, reducing bureaucracy, encouraging increased foreign direct investment, improving national standards of health and sanitation, and improving India's relations with other countries. He has announced several measures to speed up the efficiency of India's economy and reform the red tape that had traditionally hindered Indian business, streamlining the bureaucratic requirements on companies such as a complex permit and inspection system and numerous regulations, so as to make business easier. He has also initiated reform among the bureaucrats of the Indian Administrative Service to ensure a more efficient government bureaucracy.

The book is a delineation of Narendra Modi as a politician, as India's Prime Minister, and as a dynamic personality. It also assesses his policies, achievements, and the degree of success he and his government have achieved in bringing the desired transformation in India's economy, society, and work culture, and how far they have fulfilled the promises made to the people during 2014 election campaigns.

The subject matter is divided into 12 chapters, each dealing with a particular aspect of Narendra Modi's life, commitments, initiatives, and policies. Chapter 1 describes Modi's early life and his family. It states how as a child Narendra Modi helped his father sell tea at the Vadnagar railway station, and on trains. Despite poverty, Narendra continued and completed his education against all odds and adversities. The views of Modi's teachers and school time friends have been included and they reflect a great deal about his values as a child and his activities as a student. The chapter describes that the two persons who had an indelible impression on Narendra Modi's life and personality are: his mother Heeraben and Swami Vivekananda.

Narendra Modi was drawn to politics in his early teens, and during his college days he acted as a *pracharak* of the Rashtriya Swayamsevak Sangh (RSS). Modi was also a campaigner in the RSS during his college years and took on the task of encouraging the party members. Partnering with Shankersinh Vaghela, Modi formed a strong cadre base in Gujarat. All these form part of the chapter.

Chapter 2 deals with misconceptions about Hindutva in Narendra Modi. Modi was inducted into RSS at an early age and started going to *shakha* regularly. At the age of 21 he was made preacher of Gujarat RSS and was influenced by Savarkar's radical view of Hindu school and political consciousness. But, unfortunately, some people regarded this as an implied criticism of minorities like Christians and Muslims. His association with RSS and its associated bodies has confused many people. This chapter makes it clear that Modi is not biased against any community. That's why he has been able to maintain a balance between his affinities and responsibilities.

Chapter 3 is an assessment of Modi's terms as the Chief Minister of Gujarat. His first stint (2001-02) started in turbulent times in Gujarat as the allegations of corruption and poor governance were doing the rounds. The party was looking for a new leader for the state, so Modi was made the CM in October 2001. A terrible incident occurred in 2002 in Gujarat. On 27 February 2002, a train with several hundred passengers, including a large number of Hindu pilgrims returning from Ayodhya after a religious ceremony at the site of the demolished Babri Masjid, was burned near Godhra in which about 60 people were killed.

There were rumours that the fire was set by Muslim arsonists, due to which anti-Muslim violence spread throughout Gujarat. According to an estimate, death toll ranged from 900 to over 2,000, with several thousand injured. The Modi government imposed curfew in major cities, issued shoot-at-sight orders, and called for the army to prevent the violence from escalating. However, some human rights organizations, opposition parties, and some media accused the Gujarat government of taking insufficient action against the rioters. But, most people and organizations gave him the benefit of doubt. The court did not find any evidence against him. A major effect of the incident was the polarization of Hindu voters, which suited Modi well. The book briefly traverses through all those incidents and describes how Modi was instrumental in bringing socio-economic development at a fast pace in the state. All sections of society were benefited due to good policies and effective implementation thereof. The Gujarat Model of Development received praises from India and abroad.

Narendra Modi made important changes during his second term (2002-07) as the CM of Gujarat, which led to Gujarat being called an attractive investment destination. He started financial and technology parks in the state. During the 2007 Vibrant Gujarat Summit, real estate investment deals worth ₹ 6.6 trillion were signed in Gujarat. In his third term as CM (2007-12), Gujarat became a state of dynamic development, economic growth, and prosperity. He also facilitated the ease of doing business and ended bureaucratic logjam, which made investment in Gujarat easy and rewarding. Gujarat also became the top-ranked Indian state in terms of economic freedom.

In March 2012, when Modi was serving his fourth term as CM of Gujarat, he appeared on the cover of the Asian edition of the *Time* magazine, one of India's few politicians to have achieve this honour. His leadership was described as being strong and businesslike; one that could guide India towards honesty and efficiency.

Chapter 4 is on Modi's vision of Digital India, having a larger aim of transforming the country into a digitally empowered society. It accentuates the necessity of digitizing India and the benefits of connecting it with Skill India. Mapping the global needs, digitizing transport and road safety, knowledge portal for railways, empowerment and livelihood through digitization, promoting informal sector, and information and communication revolution in India, are the areas of focus in this chapter.

Chapter 5 explains in detail, Narendra Modi's vision of Make in India. The major components and the focus of the initiative, as well as the key parameters of considerations have been explained in the chapter. Ease of doing business in which many formalities have been done away with, and international acceptance of Make in India, have been included. The details of agreements with countries like Japan, France, Australia, South Korea, Canada, Russia, and Brazil have been given.

Chapter 6 is about Startup India—a campaign based on an action plan aimed at promoting bank financing for startup ventures to boost entrepreneurship and encourage startups with jobs creation in the country. The main features of the programme and investment by many foreign based companies have been explained. Standup India for boosting entrepreneurship, standup for smart city, and infrastructure elements in smart city have been explained.

Chapter 7 discusses in the detail, Narendra Modi's Skill India Programme and explains how it will enhance employability and generate more employment. The features of the programme, the functions of National Skill Development Agency (NSDA) which was created with the mandate to coordinate and harmonise skill development activities, India Skill Report, Skill Loan Scheme, and Prime Minister's Kaushal Vikas Yojana (PMKVY)—a skill training scheme that aims to incentivize skill training by providing financial rewards to candidates who successfully complete approved skill training programmes—form part of the chapter.

Chapter 8 describes in detail all the schemes and programmes brought by Prime Minister Modi. Included in it are Pradhan Mantri Jan-Dhan Yojana, Swachh Bharat Abhiyan, Prime Minister's Employment Generation Programme (PMEGP), Beti Bachao Beti Padhao Yojana, Atal Pension Yojana (APY), Pradhan Mantri Awas Yojana (PMAY), and Pradhan Mantri Kaushal Vikas Yojana (PMKVY), among others.

Modi has paid visit to a number of countries after becoming India's Prime Minister. In 2015 he visited as many as 26 countries. In 2016 too he visited several countries holding discussions with the respective state heads and other important people. He addressed the Indian people settled abroad. His visits have not only strengthened India's relationships with other countries, but also endeavored to build a common consensus on issues of concern like terrorism, environmental pollution, slow trade, inadequate energy sources, hindrances in the way of peaceful use of nuclear energy, and disputes in sharing water, among others. Entering into important agreements with other countries, signing the Memorandums of Understanding (MOUs) and issuing joint statements, Narendra Modi has exhibited a high level of active diplomacy not hitherto reached by any earlier Indian Prime Minister. Chapter 9 deliberates on the foreign visits of Narendra Modi.

There have been some changes in India's foreign policy under the prime ministership of Narendra Modi since May 2014. The broad focus of his foreign policy has been on improving relations with neighbouring countries in South Asia, and engaging the extended neighbourhood in Southeast Asia and the major global powers. He made official visits to Bhutan, Nepal, and Japan followed by his visits to the United States, Myanmar, Australia, and Fiji. Foreign Affairs Minister Sushma Swaraj has also made official visits to Bangladesh, Bhutan, Nepal, Myanmar, Singapore, Vietnam, Bahrain, Afghanistan, Tajikistan, United States, United Kingdom, Mauritius, Maldives, United Arab Emirates, South Korea, China, Oman, and Sri Lanka. Chapter 10 discusses Narendra Modi's foreign policy. Modi's Act East Policy, Neighbourhood First Policy, closer ties with the United States and other major powers of the world, and alliances to form a strong deterrent against the rising might of China, have been included in the chapter. Chapter 11 deals with Narendra Modi's crackdown on black money through demonetization of currencies in the denominations of ₹ 500 and ₹ 1000. The immediate impact of the move in terms of inconvenience to public and scope of the move as regards long-term benefits have been explained.

Chapter 12 deals with an assessment of Modi Government's achievements. Various parameters have been used to make this assessment. Some of the achievements of Modi and his government have been highlighted. For example, Modi has been doing his best to stop corruption at lower level by introducing technology and removing middlemen. E-auction of coal mines has ruled out any scams that had brought the downfall of UPA government. Some of the areas in which the government has not done well have also been discussed. For example, inflation has persisted all along and the level of pollution in big cities continues to be high. Cleaning of Ganga remains a distant dream despite huge spending by the government.

The book throws ample light on the personality, vision, and achievements of Narendra Modi, India's most dynamic Prime Minister so far. It will apprise the readers about the governance of Modi and his determination to transform India into a modern and prosperous country. It will also serve as a source of inspiration for people who want to emulate him.

I am thankful to all the sources and sites that have been drawn upon to prepare the book.

K.R. Gupta

Contents

CHAPTER 1

Narendra Modi—Early Life

Birth, Early Life and Interest in Politics

Narendra Damodardas Modi hails from a middle-class family of grocers living in a town called Vadnagar in the northern Mehsana district, in the then Bombay state, now in Gujarat. (Vadnagar is 112 km away from Ahmedabad and 34 km from Mehsana.) He was born on 17 September 1950 to Shri Damodardas Mulchand Modi and Smt. Heeraben. They were six siblings, among whom he is the third. Somabhai Modi is Narendra Modi's eldest brother. He was an officer in the Health Department, and is now retired, and is managing a home for the old. Amritbhai Modi is Narendra Modi's elder brother. Modi's sister named Vasantiben is a housewife. She is a lady of noble and pious thoughts. Modi's younger brother, Prahaladbhai, owns a shop in Ahmedabad. He takes active part in the welfare of those running the ration shops. The youngest brother, Pankajbhai, is a clerk in the Information Department of Gujarat government in Gandhinagar.

As a child, Narandra Modi helped his father in selling tea at Vadnagar railway station, and on trains. It is appreciable how despite poverty Narendra continued and completed his education against all odds and adversities. He received his primary education from Govt. Primary School, Vadnagar. Then he went to Bhagwatcharaya Narayanchari High School, a few kilometer from his village. As no transportation was available at that time, he had to walk to and from school each day. He was very fond of reading, and spent many hours in the library every day. One of his school teachers had described him as an average student but a brilliant debater. In 1967, he completed his matriculation from this school. Social Science was his favourite subject. Then he sought admission in Visnagar College, about 29 km away from Vadnagar. After completing Intermediate education from this college, he obtained a bachelor's degree in Political Science through distance education from Delhi University. Since he was active in politics, Modi faced many problems in his higher education. But on the advice of a lawyer he took admission in Gujarat University to pursue his Masters in Political Science. This degree played an important role in polishing his personality further at a later stage during the 1990s when Modi was serving in New Delhi as the official spokesperson of the Bharatiya Janata Party (BJP). In this way, fighting against the odds and facing the problems of poverty, along with lack of resources and infrastructure, Narendra Modi completed his education and laid the foundation of his mercurial career, taking part in politics alongside his studies. He has also completed a three-month long course in the US on public relations and image management.

Vadnagar Railway Station

Views of Teachers and Friends of Modi about Him

The views of Modi's teachers and his school-time friends reflect a great deal about his values and activities as a student. Since they come from people who spent a lot of time with him and watched him grow, they provide an understanding about his nature and aspirations. Given below are some of such views.

1. Jasood Khan, a friend of Narendra Modi, is now in his seventies. He states that he does not remember if ever there had been a quarrel between them. Caste and religion had never been an issue in their friendship. After school, Narendra Damodardas Modi used to help his father in his tea shop. Narendra Modi had two main hobbies—reading books and swimming. His spare time was spent in the library. Narendra Modi also used to help his mother at home. He loved animals, especially the cow. The family reared a cow, and Modi used to look after it very well. In the religious-cultural environment, he inherited many great qualities.

2. Dr. Prahaladbhai Patel was Narendra Modi's schoolteacher. He says that Narendra Modi was a keen competitor in debates. He had great willpower and he focused on everything. For this he always got appreciation from his companions. He had a great sense of the good and the bad from the very beginning. He always fought against what he thought was not right. Once he was given a homework of writing an essay on the "Forms of Rivers". All the students were asked to show their essays to the class monitor. Narendra Modi refused to show it to the monitor saying that only teacher is the appropriate person to be shown the essay, as monitor is himself a student.

3. Goverdhan Bhai Patel was also Narendra Modi's teacher. He recounts as:

Those were hot summer days. All the students of the school had gone to the NCC camp. Everyone knows about the discipline of an NCC camp. The students were not allowed to go out of the compound. I saw that Narendra Modi had climbed up a pole. I was enraged to see this. But, when he found that Narendra Modi had climbed up the pole to save a bird which had got entangled there, my anger vanished. When Narendra Modi came down with the bird safe in his hands, I patted his back in appreciation.[1]

Love for nature and taking pity on animals are there in Modi's heart since his childhood.

4. Acharya Rasbihari Maniyar was another teacher of Narendra Modi. He recalls as follows:

Narendra Modi has been service-oriented and sensitive since childhood. He took an active part in NCC activities. Discipline, punctuality and helping others were in his nature. Despite living in poor financial condition, there was always self-respect in his eyes. He also took part in extra-curricular activities. As a student, he was known for a good memory and public speaking. He has a knack of finding solutions to different problems quickly.[2]

5. The fact that Modi was a creative student and a lover of drama has also been established. According to *Commonman: Narendra Modi,* "This student of 8th standard also took part in drama. This shows that he had a deep understanding of social injustice and this was his perspective of highlighting it. This sense which he had since his childhood later led to the acts of social development in Gujarat under his leadership."[3]

In school, he once staged a one-act play, *Peela Phool* (*Yellow Flower*). This play was unique in that Modi himself was the writer, director, and actor of this play. The story of the play was like this:

There is a dalit family in a village. In the family there are a mother and her son. The son falls ill. The mother takes the son to hakim, vaid, etc. (different types of doctors) in the village, but because of being a dalit child no one is ready to treat his illness. In the absence of cure, the child's condition becomes serious. Someone tells his mother that, instead of going here and there, she should go to the village temple, take one of the dedicated flowers offered to the deity and touch it to the ailing child, and he would be cured. Poor mother runs towards the temple, but she is not allowed to enter the temple precinct. She begs for the life of her child to the priest. The priest takes pity and gives a yellow flower to the mother. She reaches home with the flower, but by that time the child has breathed his last.

Narendra Modi as a student of 8th standard stated that all have equal right on the yellow flower offered in the temple to God.[4]

6. Dr. Sudhir Joshi, who was Narendra Modi's school mate, recalls those days and says:

Narendra Modi was full of confidence even then. He was not afraid of anyone. He faced each problem with courage and tried to find appropriate solution to it. His rationality was outstanding. He was fully determined, fearless, and courageous. He remained enthusiastic about leadership conferences. With his skill he once defeated a strong candidate in a school election. He was keen to complete whatever task he took in his hands. Today whatever Modi has been able to achieve, his nature is the same as it was when he was a child.[5]

Modi's qualities of strong willpower, discipline, courage, belief in the equality of all irrespective of caste and creed, and readiness to help others observed by his teachers and friends were an indication that he would do a lot for society, though no one could predict that he will rise to become a Chief Minister of a state and the Prime Minister of the country. However, these qualities have stayed with him since his childhood.

Interest in Politics

Narendra Modi was drawn to politics in his early teens, and during his college days he acted as a pracharak or propagandist of Rashtriya Swayamsevak Sangh (RSS). During the India-Pakistan war of 1965, he volunteered to serve soldiers travelling through railway stations. As a youth, he became a member of Akhil Bharatiya Vidyarthi Parishad (ABVP)—a student body involved in anti-corruption. His diligence and dedication towards the party hardly ebbed despite the fact that he was simultaneously pursuing a master's degree in Political Science. The idea of struggle was never very distant for Modi. With whatever minimal training he received from the party's associates, he surged ahead and exhibited enough capability to be given the charge of the ABVP. After having worked full time with it, he was nominated as its representative in the BJP. Modi was also a campaigner for the RSS during his college years and took on the task of encouraging the party members. Along with Shankersingh Vaghela, Modi created a strong cadre base in Gujarat.

BJP began getting political attention and formed a coalition government in Gujarat in April 1990. After this, the party came to power in Gujarat in 1995. During this period, Modi was responsible for the Somnath to Ayodhya Rath Yatra and a similar trek from Kanyakumari in Southern India all the way up to Kashmir in the north. A careful observation of his rise to the national podium would evince how he remained glued to his fundamentals—continuing agitations during the nationwide Emergency, organizing Murli Manohar Joshi's Ekta yatra (journey for unity), and impressing everyone with electoral strategy ahead of the 1995 state elections. As BJP tasted victory, Modi relished his newly-ordained post of the party's General Secretary. The workaholic and loyal 'sevak' moved to New Delhi to take up the new responsibility of managing the party's activities in Haryana and Himachal Pradesh. Three summers whizzed past and Modi already had the post of National Secretary of the BJP under his kitty.

Narendra Modi's Married Life

Narendra Modi's married life has been the subject of some controversy. It is known that he has been mentioned as a bachelor in some official documents. Modi acknowledged his marriage to Jashodaben for the first time in his affidavit filed on 9 April 2014 along with his nomination papers for Vadodara constituency in the Lok Sabha election. This declaration invited derisive remarks from different political parties.

He had left the column blank in the last four state assembly elections in 2001, 2002, 2007, and 2012. This was first openly challenged by Congress in January 2001 when Modi contested the by-election for Rajkot-2 assembly seat, three months after becoming the Chief Minister of Gujarat.

The acknowledgement of marriage drew attention of people from the entire country, and the supporters of political parties, other than those of the BJP, tried to tarnish Modi's image and make it a socio-political issue.

Modi's opponents hoped that this disclosure will dent his popularity among women who might empathize with Jashodaben, whom he never returned to after two weeks of their nuptials. The declaration was reported to have come after strict legal advice that he should come clean on the marriage which, his family members said, was never consummated.

As per the Representation of the People Act, 1951, every candidate is required to declare even assets held in the name of the spouse. In his nomination form, Modi said that he had no information about Jashodaben's income, IT returns, and PAN details.

Modi ended the speculation over his marital status perhaps because the Congress had run a smear campaign against him in the earlier Vidhan Sabha elections and had tried to project Jashodaben as a spurned wife and a victim of Modi's exploitation.

It is pertinent to mention here that in November 2013, the Supreme Court of India had refused to entertain a PIL accusing Modi of leaving the column on marital status blank in the nomination papers for the Maninagar assembly seat in 2012.

Modi's wife too clarified in an interview:

I, Jashodaben, am the wife of Narendra Damodardas Modi, the son of Damodardas Mulchand Modi, a resident of Kala Vasudev Ni Chali, Vadnagar.[6]

Jashodaben stated further,

I am working in Rajosana Primary School. We were married in 1968. I have been keeping safe the book gifted to me by him. The title of the book is *Sangharsh Ma Gujarat.* I have also kept his photograph. When he was twenty-two to twenty-five, he took his photograph back. Although my husband has gone away from me, yet by keeping the book given by him, I feel that he is with me. He tore all the photographs of our marriage, because he never wanted even a single photo of marriage to remain with me.

A day after BJP's Prime Ministerial nominee Narendra Modi declared in his poll affidavit filed in Vadodara that he was a married man and that his wife's name is Jashodaben, his elder brother Somabhai Modi issued a statement to explain that the marriage was forced on Narendra who was a teenager at that time. He said that the marriage was forced on Modi by his parents in his young age in keeping with the old orthodox tradition of fixing marriages between children and that it was never consummated as Modi walked out of the marriage soon after it was solemnised. Somabhai further said that young Modi did it in response to an inner call to work for the nation and the society inspired by the teachings of Swami Vivekanand. In his press statement, he appealed to the people to see the marriage in the backdrop of these facts. He said that Narendra Modi's current status should not be evaluated on the basis of "an incident" that had occurred 45 to 50 years ago. Praising his younger brother, he said, "Narendrabhai was different amongst the six siblings. His interest in the service to the nation was quite apparent to us. But nobody could have estimated the intensity of his idea of service to the nation." It was perhaps this intensity that forced Modi to relinquish the life of a normal married man, and put him on the path of pursuing his goal of serving the nation wholeheartedly.

According to Somabhai, Modi's family members did not know much about him as he had never maintained active contact with them after he left the house. In his affidavit, Modi had stated that he has no information about the assets and liabilities of his wife, and that is quite true, given the fact that they have been living apart since the time Modi had left her. Modi's other brother, Prahaladbhai said that Modi had never denied that he was a married man, and in the earlier election forms he had kept the column of wife blank.

Narendra's friends say that he was reluctant to get married. Nagji Desai, 64, an ayurvedic practitioner, who was his classmate at B.N. High School in Vadnagar, says that Narendra was engaged to Jashodaben a year before the marriage, but unlike other teenagers, he never spoke about her. He kept telling us that he wanted to serve the country and was not interested in marriage. But the marriage took place on the fixed date.

The next dawn, however, broke with a shocking news. "Narendra took the 6 a.m. train to Ahmedabad," says Desai. "He returned only after some 30 years." It came as a shock to Narendra's friends too, as he had not told them about his plan. "He gave in to parental pressure to get married," says Jasud Khan Pathan, 64, a retired bank manager who was also Modi's classmate at Shri B.N. High School. He says further, "That he has been married is true. But the fact is that they never lived together."

According to Desai, Jashodaben went to her parents' home after a few days, which was customary. When she returned to Vadnagar, Narendra's parents were said to have told her that she could stay with them as long as she wanted to. It is said that she stayed at the in-laws' place for a few months and then went back to her parents' home. She continued her studies as her husband had asked her to and became a school teacher.

Now retired, Jashodaben lives with her brother Ashok and his wife in Brahmanwada village of Unjha town of Mehsana district. And now that Narendra Modi has become India's Prime Minister, Jashodaben has been given round-the-clock police protection. One armed guard and four other unarmed policemen of police HQ have been deployed for her security. They remain stationed near her house 24×7 and move wherever she goes.

According to Daksha, Jashodaben regularly follows Modi on television and in the newspapers, and had prayed for him to become the Prime Minister. She does not like anyone criticizing him. Daksha is sure that Jashodaben will not say a word against Modi even if she is offered a fortune.

Despite all the media attentions, very little is known about Jashodaben. The many photos of Hindu deities that crowd the walls of her house indicate that she is as religious as her relatives. Students of the Rajosana Primary School near Brahmanwada, from where she has retired in 2010, recall her as an affectionate and popular teacher who used to teach social sciences, elementary maths, and Gujarati language.

School photographs show her surrounded by students, most of them Muslim, and villagers speak of her in tones bordering on reverence. "She used to rise very early and feed the cows chapattis and jaggery before leaving for school," said a villager. "She was very religious but was fond of all her students, irrespective of their differences", he continued.

Sheela Bhatt (National Editor for Politics in Indian Express) writes as under:

> If 17-year-old Modi wanted to get out of the marriage, which was imposed on him by a socially backward society and his family, it's not only ethical but his right to walk out of the forced marriage. Jashodaben, a highly conservative woman who understandably, by the social standards of India of the 1960s, opted to remain confined to the marriage instead of keeping Modi out from her life for not starting the marriage in the real sense. In spite of media pressure, if she does not speak against Modi, it suggests that Modi has not ill-treated her or exploited her after parting ways.[7]

It seems to be a fair judgement on the issue, because it points out to three major points: One that Indian society was backward at that time, and Modi had the right to live a life free from orthodox views imposed on him by means of marriage. Second, if Modi's wife continued to remain conservative, it was her own choice. Third, Modi never ill-treated her after walking away. Moreover, if Modi chose to serve the nation wholeheartedly, and felt that he could not do so living a life of a normal, married man, nothing should stop him.

Politicization of Modi's Marriage Issue

One of the problems of the present Indian society is that almost every issue is politicalized. People, especially politicians and their supporters, invariably try to get political mileage out of every situation. They use the ever eager media to blow things out of proportion so that the common man is influenced the way they want to. And though the supporters of other parties are also invited to offer their comments on various issues of actual or perceived importance, each tries to see things in his/her own perspective. The ultimate influence in the minds of the views depends on many things, but things get highlighted, given more public attention than they probably deserve.

No wonder, therefore, that Narendra Modi's rather-late-in-the-day public acceptance that he is married to Jashodaben created an uproar in political quarters. Ignoring the fact that he had never denied his marriage but only maintained a stoic silence over it, Congressmen and others from the rival groups attacked Modi over the issue. Congress's Digvijaya Singh, the party's pan-India machinery, and women activists raged against Modi.

But there has also been defence for Modi from people who, instead of getting carried away analyze it from various perspectives. One of them is Vikram Vakil, a Surat-based senior journalist. According to him, "The self-confessed strong man doesn't deserve any sympathy for inviting attacks, personal or political, but the fact of Modi's child marriage is more of a tragedy than a scandal that his critics are portraying." Vakil's comments are objective and forthright. They are neither appreciative of Modi, nor side with his rivals, because walking out the day after marriage is not something to be proud of, if not something for others to make an issue of it. Vakil adds, "By liberal standards, all individuals are free to have their own choice of partner. The family or the society can't impose their choice on a teenage son or daughter as it happened in the Modi-Jashodaben case. Modi's marriage was an accident of destiny. It was a kind of Shakespearean tragedy where neither the man nor woman can be blamed. Both can be judged as right or wrong. It depends on what is your premise to judge him and her. The external factor worked against them when their lives were not in their hands."

This best sums up the issue. In politics as in life, there are things which can be viewed both ways—positive and negative—just like the glass which is half full can also be called half empty. Giving up the comforts of a normal married man for serving the nation without any loss of focus has taken Modi to the position of Gujarat's Chief Minister and now India's Prime Minister, and more importantly, one of the country's most popular leaders. The controversy regarding his marriage, therefore, has every right to die down.

Is Modi Close to His Family?

We cannot say that Modi is close to his family, because he left his family at the age of 17 or 18. After that, he has never ever got involved with them, nor met them socially unless they happened to meet him accidentally. However, there is no discordant note within his family.

Modi is a kind of person who is so devoted to his goal of serving the nation that he finds little time to meet his family members. We must also give credit to his family that they have never tried to impose themselves on him.

Modi has deep love and respect for his mother, Heeraben. When he meets her, the impression is clear: You might be a big man, but that doesn't mean we have to follow you or even flaunt our connection. She is transparent and she is sure of the values that she has given to him. When asked, when Modi was the Chief Minister of Gujarat, "Don't you want to go and stay with him in the Chief Minister's bungalow?" She replied, "Me? Why should I go? I'll go mad.... What am I going to do there? He will be busy all day."

Inspirations for Modi

Two persons have an indelible impression on Narendra Modi's life and personality—his mother Heeraben and Swami Vivekananda. In a TV interview in 2014, with tears in his eyes, he said: "If there is anyone dear to me in this world, it is my mother. The love that I have for my mother in my heart cannot be expressed in words. It is something to be felt, not expressed. When I was a child, the financial condition of our family was not good. It was difficult to arrange meal for two times for the day. My father used to sell tea at the railway station but income was small, not enough to run the family. In order to support the family, my mother worked as helper in the neighbourhood. Cleaning the utensils, mopping the floor, and filling water for household were the daily activities of my mother."

Narendra Modi realized that his parents spared no effort to arrange food, clothing and education for the family. More than he himself, his mother took interest in his studies. The result was that after completing school education, Modi went to college, and received graduation and then post-graduation degrees. Modi says though he spends little time with his mother, yet wherever he remains, there is infinite love for her in his heart.

In an interview on Zee TV on 20/21 April 2014, he narrated a childhood incident. One day he caught a baby alligator from a pond and brought it to home. When his mother saw it, she asked him to take it from where he brought it. When he asked his mother why, she replied with a choked voice that the baby should not be separated from its mother. Hearing this, tears came in his eyes, and he took the baby alligator to the pond from where he had brought it. He realized how much love a mother carried in her heart for her baby. He says, wherever he is, her mother stays in his heart. I greet my mother from wherever I am from her. I think about my mother before starting any work. He says that now his father is no more and his mother lives with Somabhai and Pankajbhai Modi. Whenever he goes home he touches his mother's feet and takes her blessings.

As BJP registered a victory in the Lok Sabha election in 2014, its Prime Ministerial nominee Narendra Modi sought blessings of his mother Heeraben and clicked a 'selfie' of it and posted it on his twitter handle.

Selfie of Modi with his Mother

The 'selfie' by Modi shows his mother smiling while blessing him by putting her right hand on his head. Modi also posted on micro blogging website twitter: "Sought blessings from my mother."

Heeraben is a simple lady with pious thoughts. She says that her son is not against anybody. "For him love of the nation is more important than anything else in life," she said to a reporter. She also answers questions. When told that the Muslims dislike her son, she said "Ask the Muslims of Vadnagar. They will never say anything against my son. He is not against Muslims." Heeraben also tells about Modi's love for his country: "He always used to tell me that if there is one person who is ready to die for the country, it is him."

Heeraben says she doesn't resent the fact that her son never helps her financially. "My son is a man of principles. He will only help if people at large are benefited. Our whole family believes in simple living. In fact, we always taught Narendra to live honestly. So why should I feel bad if he does not help us financially," she says.

Heeraben is in her late eighties and cannot walk without the help of a cane. She wears thick spectacles and dresses up in a simple white sari. Though her elder sons are settled in Ahmedabad, she says she will not move away from Vadnagar. "I love my motherland very much and I cannot move to Ahmedabad because I don't like that place so much."

Heeraben also speaks about Modi's helpful nature. She reminisces: "Once he found a one-rupee coin on the road.... I told him to spend it on himself. But instead he gave that coin to a poor man's daughter in our village, who needed money to buy books and pencils."

Like all mothers, Heeraben misses her son very much. "After all I am his mother. But luckily, now I see him on television every day and give him blessings. I feel very proud of him."

Heeraben's simplicity can be judged from the fact that she travelled in an auto-rickshaw even when her son Narendra Modi was the Chief Minister of Gujarat.

Vivekananda

Narendra Modi, the Prime Minister of India, is an ardent admirer of Vivekananda. He visited Belur Math and meditated at the room of Vivekananda in April 2013, when he was Chief Minister of Gujarat and again in May 2015, as the Prime Minister of India.

Narendra Modi calls himself an admirer and follower of Swami Vivekananda. As the Chief Minister of Gujarat, Modi used to post one quote of Vivekananda every day on social networking sites for some time. He celebrated Swami Vivekananda's 150th birth anniversary by bringing 'Modi's Yatra', covering the entire Gujarat State, spreading the message of Vivekananda among the youth. Gujarat Government, under Modi's leadership, also organized events like Swami Vivekananda Youth Employment Week (9th to 15th April 2012), where they handed job appointment letters to 65,000 youths.

Modi's detractors do not accept that his party and its people, especially of the Sangh, are following what Vivekananda preached. He had a broad spectrum of Hinduism. His vision was not just one of Hindu ideals, but also one of Indian identity. It included an India unified, not just within the Hindu community, but one that also embraced other religions, including Islam.[8]

Many consider Modi's background with the Rashtriya Swayamsevak Sangh (RSS) to be indicative that he believes in the primacy of Hindus and Hindu culture and the suppression of minorities. It has been stated by some people that Modi is anti-Muslim or that he favours Hindus. But that is hardly true. During his tenures as the Chief Minister of Gujarat, not just Hindus, but people of all other communities prospered. There are a number of Muslims who love and trust him and his leadership. He himself is a Hindu and follows Hindu ideals and ways of life, but that doesn't make him against others in any way.

On entering Narendra Modi's home or office, one can see pictures of Swami Vivekananda and some gurus—and Spartan living quarters. It is believed that the teachings of Vivekananda have shaped the perspective and career of Narendra Modi.

The other and more inborn influence on Narendra Modi's world view comes from the fact that he was born a Ghanchi, a mid-level trading caste of oil pressers and grain sellers in Gujarat. Humble though his family may have been, the Gujarati trading castes have had a long history of international links with Rome, Persia, and China. At one time during the Mauryan Empire, a Persian/Parsi was appointed governor of Saurashtra (part of today's Gujarat).[9]

In a brief speech made at the time of filing his election papers on 24 April 2014, Narendra Modi mentioned the name of Chinese traveler, Hsuan Tsang, who had visited Modi's birthplace of Vadnagar (which was called Anandapur at that time) twice during his visit to India (from 627 to 643 CE.) His visits were aimed at finding relics and original Buddhist scriptures in India to find the origin of Buddhism. Hsuan Tsang followed the regular international land routes through Central Asia over the Himalayas into India. It appears that Modi's birthplace was an important Buddhist monastic centre for Tsang to have visited it not once but twice during his 14-year travel in India.

Narendra Modi's mention of Hsuan Tsang's name was an acknowledgment of India's international trade links, as well a reference to Swami Vivekananda's view of the central role of Buddhism in his universalist movement's thought, as exemplified by Vivekananda's lecture, "Buddhism, the Fulfillment of Hinduism" in Chicago on December 26, 1893.

It has been stated by his rivals that mentioning Hsuan Tsang's name was a political move to woo Buddhist voters, but considering the fact that the number of Buddhist voters is too small to influence election results, the charge seems unfair.

Modi's thoughts, and dreams went way beyond a conventional life. He wanted to go out and make a difference to society, to wipe tears and assuage suffering of the common people, and he did exactly that. At a young age, he developed an inclination towards renunciation and asceticism. He gave up eating salt, chilies, oil, and jaggery. He read the works of Swami Vivekananda, which took Modi to a journey of spiritualism. This also laid the foundation for his own mission to fulfill

Swami Vivekananda's dream of a Jagad Guru Bharat. He even sacrificed the comforts of married life to serve the country and society wholeheartedly.

If there is one word that characterized Narendra Modi's childhood and stayed with him for the rest of his life, it is service. When floods wreaked havoc in the Tapi River, Modi, who was just 9 years old, and his friends started a food stall to donate the proceeds for relief work. When a war broke out between India and Pakistan in 1965, he set out on the railway station and served tea to the Jawans who were going and coming from the border. This was a small step but it displayed his firm resolve to answer the call of Mother India, even at a remarkably young age. Doing all this, he never ignored his studies, and ultimately obtained a postgraduation in Political Science.

Modi's early life teaches us hard work, renunciation, service to the humanity and to the nation. It is a lesson on how to overcome the problems that come our way and pursue the dreams that we envision for ourselves.

Notes

1. Kishore Makwana's *Commonman Narendra Modi* (Prabhat Prakashan).
2. *Ibid.*
3. *Ibid.*
4. *Ibid.*
5. *Ibid.*
6. An Interview published on Youtube.
7. Sheela Bhatt, National Editor for Politics in Indian Express.
8. Vivekananda delivered lectures at the Parliament of World Religions and ecumenical gathering in Chicago in 1893, showing his respect for all religions.
9. Farok J. Contractor, What Drives Narendra Modi?—Swami Vivekananda and Hsuan Tsang...http://globalbusiness.me/2014/06/

CHAPTER 2

Misconceptions About Hindutva in Narendra Modi

Modi as a Sangh Pracharak

Narendra Modi was inducted into RSS as a balswayamsevak (junior cadet) by Lakshmanrao Inamdar (popularly known as Vakil Saheb) in the tender age of only eight, and became a child self-servant and he started going to *shakha*[1] regularly. It is clearly mentioned in *Namo Vani*[2] that he started leading a very disciplined life. His daily routine was difficult, but he followed this routine happily and zealously. In 1970, he became the propagandist (pracharak) of RSS and decided to devote his life to the cause of Hindutva without having anything in his mind to get in return. Such was his resoluteness and devotion. In 1978, he became an RSS regional organiser (sambhag pracharak).

Influences of Eminent People on Modi

Working as a pracharak of RSS, Modi got an opportunity to meet with some great devoted personalities whose influences he carried along to develop his own vision. He says,

> I worked as Sangh Pracharak. I received help and cooperation from many people. I received help from Lakshmanrao Inamdar. Apart from him, I had regular discussions with Balasaheb Deoras and Bhaurao Deoras.

He also came in contact with Vasant Gajendragadkar and Nathalal Jagda, leaders of the Jan Sangh, who were instrumental in laying the foundation of BJP in Gujarat in 1980. This contact also brought a change in Modi's vision. There was a political predilection in his vision.

It has been stated in *Namo Vani* that seeing Narendra Modi's management and his style of doing work, it was decided to give him a higher responsibility. At the age of 21, after taking training from the Nagpur Head Office, he was made the pracharak of Gujarat RSS unit. During this period, he met prominent people like Dattopant Thengadi and Eknath Ranade. After some time, at the insistence of Lakshmanrao Inamdar, he completed his post-graduation in Political Science.

It has been stated by many that there was a deep influence of Maharishi Arvind, Ramakrishna Paramahamsa and Swami Vivekananda's life of sacrifice on Narendra Modi. The influence of these great men shaped Narendra Modi's life of sacrifice, austerity and asceticism. He was a staunch follower of Swami Vivekananda and fully devoted to his philosophy and ideologies. The centenary of Vivekananda's historic lecture in Chicago was celebrated there in 1993. Narendra Modi went there as a special invitee.

There has been a deep influence of revolutionaries like Shivaji, Sardar Patel, Bhagat Singh, Chandrashekhar Azad, and Khudiram Bose on Narendra Modi's life. He read literature on these revolutionaries in the library. Veer Savarkar's writings were his favourite. He was as much influenced by Savarkar as by Vivekananda. In his book, *Who is a Hindu*, Veer Savarkar promoted a radical view of Hindu school and political consciousness. He described a Hindu as a patriotic inhabitant of Bharatavarsha venturing beyond a religious identity. He regarded being Hindu as a cultural and political identity. He laid emphasis on social and community unity between Hindus, Sikhs, Buddhists, and Jains. It is unfortunate that some people regarded this as an implied criticism of minorities like Muslims and Christians. Modi too has been seen by some as anti-Muslim, but this is a huge misconception and an attempt by his political rivals to tarnish his image so that his popularity among the masses decreases and they get a foothold to grab the power again. The fact that he dealt them such a hard blow in 2014 Lok Sabha election that they are willing to use any and every method to take political revenge. Distorting Modi's Hindutva connection and creating rift between Modi and Muslims is one such attempt. What Modi admired in Savarkar was the qualities like patriotism, courage, love for reading, and free and frank speech.

Modi and Muslims

Even when Narendra Modi was Bharatiya Janata Party's prime ministerial candidate, he was aware of the woes of the Muslims and declared in one of his speeches, "We believe in economic development, while you [other parties] play the politics of votes, letting Muslims languish in poverty". He talked about inclusive development when he came to power. When he took office he knew that he'll be scrutinized at home and abroad for his ability to transcend religious divisions and, therefore, he showed that his promise of economic development extends to even minorities who didn't support him. An early test of how he'll manage tensions was to come from Hindu nationalist groups who may have interpreted his landslide win as a green light to fulfill their agenda, including a decade-long quest to build a temple at Ayodhya where a mosque was destroyed in 1992. As of now, the envisaged temple has not been built which bears testimony to the fact that Modi does not want to please Hindus at the cost of displeasing the Muslims. It is pertinent to mention here that Modi is not playing vote bank politics because the mandate of 2014 Lok Sabha election has amply proved that government can be formed without Muslim votes. In this election, BJP alone won 282 seats out of 427 contested. Adding its allies parties, it won 336 seats, while Congress won only 44 seats and 60 when its allies parties are added. BJP itself got the majority and did not need even its allies to from the government. According to a survey, only 1 in 10 Muslims voted for BJP. Thus, Muslim votes did not play much of a part in BJP's landslide victory.

Dr. Syed Zafar Mahmood, former OSD for Sachar Committee, President, Zakat Foundation of India, has this to say regarding Modi and his concern for the Muslims:

> During your conclusive remarks given toward the end of the debate on the President's address to the joint

session of Parliament, you acknowledged the national Muslim backwardness. You stated that you know Muslim families who for three generations have been repairing bicycles and wondered of the reasons for such a pathetic condition of the community. In order to bring about a positive change in the Muslim condition, you emphasized, "We will have to undertake focused activity and will have to initiate special purpose schemes. I do not consider such schemes as appeasement; rather I see these as an instrument of ameliorating the life of (Muslim) community". You explained that if in a human body one organ is disabled then nobody can consider that body as healthy. A body can be sturdy only if all its organs are equally agile; no part should remain comparatively weak. With this fundamental premise there is need to move forward, "We are under obligation to do so and we wish to work accordingly", you had concluded. Later, as a part of my usual, serialised writings addressed to the Muslim community, I counseled it that "As a seasoned community we need to take the PM's olive branch at its face value and give him reasonable opportunity to transform his initial promise into substantial praxis. We need to practically demonstrate the potential for harmonizing the relationship between faith and society and the creative interplay between unity and diversity. We need to examine in what manner the present moment offers an opportunity to inter-cultural understanding and social cohesion through new levels of partnership, dialogue and engagement. The present state of change and transformation mandates us to affirm mutual commitments towards living in a shared manner, for we are mindful of our scriptural injunction.

The community and its well-wishers, according to Dr. Mahmood, need not forthrightly reject the new Prime Minister's "white flag". In the electoral run up, he surely had one avatar as a prime ministerial aspirant when viewed from his utterances and omissions. Simultaneously, we should keep an eye on the overall ethos of the new government, as it develops, and the extent to which it allows the Sangh Parivar's hitherto theme lines to permeate its policies and programs.

Narendra Modi has brought a large number of schemes for the socio-economic development of the country. Schemes like Skill India, Make in India, Gram Uday to Bharat Uday, etc. are a few such schemes, and have been discussed at appropriate places in the book. Modi's scheme 'Sabka Saath, Sabka Vikas' (see Annexure) illustrates his guiding principle and underlies his aim of inclusive development. Narendra Modi says:

> Government has only one religion—India first.
>
> Government has one holy book—the Constitution.
>
> The Government must be immersed in only one Bhakti—Bharat Bhakti.
>
> The Government's only strength is Jan Shakti.
>
> Government's only ritual is the well-being of the 125 crore Indians.
>
> The only code of conduct of the Government should be 'Sabka Saath, Sabka Vikas'.

According to *The Diplomat*,[3] "When Prime Minister Narendra Modi won a resounding victory in the Indian general elections in 2014, leaders from around the world rushed to congratulate the new Prime Minister-elect of the world's biggest democracy. In the Persian Gulf, however, the reaction was cautious. Egypt and Qatar were initially the only two countries from that region to congratulate Modi on his win."

According to analysts, Modi's personal reputation among the public and polity alike in the Gulf has suffered because of the riots between Hindus and Muslims that took place in Gujarat while he was Chief Minister of the State in 2002.

However, Modi's meeting with Saudi Arabia's sixth king, late Abdullah bin Abdulaziz Al Saud on the sidelines of the G20 summit in Brisbane, Australia later in 2014 made clear that even if the members of the Gulf Cooperation Council (GCC) had reservations, India was too important to risk upsetting relations.[4] Besides development of political relations what prompted Modi's visit was the removal of apprehensions about Modi's governance that it will be discriminatory against the minorities. Modi's rule so far has not shown any favours and disfavours and there is commitment to develop all sections of society. That's why people in general are no longer vociferous about Modi's tilt towards Hindutva.

There is a call from Muslim quarters for Modi Government to show its commitment given on the floor of Parliament and undertake the fundamental long-term measures for Muslim upliftment in letter and spirit. There is a demand for implementing the recommendations of Justice Sachar Committee report, among other things.

We can conclude this issue with the words of Rajiv Pratap Rudy, a BJP general secretary, who said that the Congress party is to blame for the impression that the BJP is apathetic to minorities. Having said that, it's high time that in this new regime the Muslims should come into the national mainstream and should feel a part of India, which we believe they are.

Modi as Leader of Akhil Bharatiya Vidyarthi Parishad (ABVP)

Leadership qualities were evident in Modi even in his childhood. Therefore, Sangh Parivar established him as a leader of Akhil Bharatiya Vidyarthi Parishad (ABVP), the student wing of the RSS. He played an important role in Anti-Corruption Movement in 1974. During the period of Emergency (from 26 June 1975 until 1977), as pracharak in-charge of the ABVP, Modi was forced to go underground in Gujarat and frequently travelled in disguise to avoid arrest. He was involved in printing pamphlets opposing the government, sending them to Delhi and organising demonstrations. He became very popular among the students as their leader. During this period, he wrote a book in Gujarati, *Sangharsh Ma Gujarat*, describing events during the Emergency.

Modi as National Spokesman of BJP

Modi entered mainstream politics in 1987 by joining the BJP. Due to enthusiasm with which he took part in the activities of the party, he was elevated to the level of General Secretary of Gujarat unit within a year. Along with this he was given the responsibility of five states which honed his political and leadership skills. He travelled to various cities and preached the principles on which the party worked.

He had already acquired a reputation for being a highly efficient organizer, and took up the challenging task of energizing the party cadres in right earnest. The party started gaining political mileage and formed a coalition government at the Centre in April 1990. This partnership fell apart within a few months, but the BJP came to power with a two-thirds majority on its own in Gujarat in 1995. Since then, the BJP has been governing Gujarat.

Between 1988 and 1995, Narendra Modi was recognized as a master strategist who had successfully gained the necessary groundwork for making the Gujarat BJP the ruling party of the State. During this period, Modi was entrusted with the responsibility of organizing two crucial national events, the Somnath to Ayodhya Rath Yatra of L.K. Advani and a similar march from Kanyakumari (the southernmost part of India) to Kashmir in the north. The ascent of the BJP to power at New Delhi in 1998 has been attributed to these two highly successful events, substantially handled by Modi.

In 1995, he was appointed the National Secretary of the party and given the charge of five major states in India—a rare distinction for a young leader. In 1998, he was promoted as the General Secretary (Organization), a post he held until October 2001, when he was chosen to be the Chief Minister of Gujarat—one of the most prosperous and progressive states of India. During his stint at the national level, Narendra Modi was given the responsibility to oversee the affairs of several state level units, including the sensitive and crucial state of Jammu and Kashmir and the equally sensitive north-eastern states. He was responsible for revamping the party organization in several states. While working at the national level, Narendra Modi emerged as an important spokesman for the party and played a key role on several important occasions.

During this period, he travelled extensively across the world and interacted with eminent leaders of several countries. These experiences not only helped him develop a global perspective, but also intensified his passion to serve India and lead it towards the socio-economic supremacy in the comity of nations.

Hinduism in Gujarat

Gujarat is said to be a fertile ground for Hindutva. The key factor is its close proximity with Maharashtra which, as history tells us, has witnessed the initial days of Hindu fundamentalism upheaval after the foundation of RSS in 1925. RSS network immediately spread in Gujarat when Maratha Brahmins who had settled in Gujarat took up the roles of "shakha pramukh", and influenced local people to join RSS.

Another factor is that Gujarat remained deprived of any kind of major reform movement during the 18th and the 19th centuries, unlike most other Indian states. Therefore, Hinduism here is understood in its rigid form, different from the accommodating and compassionate perspective of Hinduism, and is marked by a dislike for non-Hindus.

Another, and perhaps the most important factor, that led to the spread of Hindutva in Gujarat is its location along the international borders and the seacoast, exposing the area to repeated Muslim invasions from the India's West. This has not happened in any other Indian state, at least to the degree experienced in Gujarat. History books are full of accounts how Muslim invaders, Mahmud Ghazni in particular, frequently attacked the area, destroyed the seaside Hindu temples and killed local people in large number. This not only sowed the seeds of hatred for Muslims but also made people united under a kind of Hinduism that gives little liberalism towards others. The anguish of destruction of Somnath temple has remained with the people of Gujarat for centuries. No wonder that L.K. Advani's Ram Rath Yatra, which created a tidal wave of Hindu nationalism in 1990, started from Somnath.[5]

These three factors have made the Sangh Parivar outfits, like RSS and VHP, keep the "flame of religious polarization burning in the state". These organizations have provided, so to speak, the agonized Hindus a true voice. Being a democratic socialist sovereign republic, as clearly mentioned in Indian Constitution, the country has given equality of law to all its citizens. But vote-bank politics has made our power-hungry politicians ignore some important facts, the most important being that the appeasement of one religious group at the cost of another, or at the cost of the fact that ours is by and large a Hindu state, may lead a division between people rather than unification. Whatever the claims of equality, it is a fact that in a state where some small religious minorities exist with a large religious majority, the former have to acquiesce in the latter. If that doesn't happen, there will be problems like communal riots. Ever since the creation of India as a secular state after Independence, the focus has been to make the society a melting pot of various communities and ethnicities. In this attempt, Hindutva, which is the base of our society, has not only been lost, but the word itself is being used even by the Hindus with apprehension so that it should not offend others.

There may be a sort of compulsion to make India a melting pot of a large number of religious beliefs and social systems, as we are, after all, people of one country, but that does not mean that we should lose sight of our individual bases and beliefs so long as it does not harm others. Keeping our group cultures and customs alive is also necessary for social development. In the past, many of our political leaders and the parties they belong to, have paid little attention to this important aspect of our society. The sole purpose has been to create a sizeable vote bank, rather than following what our Constitution says. It is pertinent to mention here that unnecessary appeasement of some groups and communities in order to capture their votes should not be considered as following the Constitution, but working for vested interest. Modi has been an exception. As an influential leader, he has not only kept regional cultures alive but also thought of developing all sections of society. In January 2003, in a rally at Mumbai he urged the people "not to be shy or apologetic about Hindutva". For him Hindutva is a way of life, which does not have hatred for people of other communities, but a faith in the development of Hindu ideologies without succumbing to a misled belief that we as Indians have no religious identity or that keeping a religious identity is harmful to India's social fabric.

Modi, working as a member of BJP and being close to Sangh over the years, keenly observed what the coalition led by Congress ruling at the Centre was doing. There was a constant appeasement of minority groups to secure votes and support for the representatives thereof. Included in this were populist measures like giving large subsidies which dented the economy, and pursuing a policy of reservations, and even adding to the quotas of reservations for lower and backward classes, often on faulty yardsticks and due to pressures from certain quarters.

Narendra Modi's political base is known for its belligerent version of Hinduism. It would be wrong to say that many BJP leaders denigrate Muslims, but this is also a fact that they don't have as strong affinities with the Muslims as with the Hindus, and in a situation where interests of both the communities clash, they will side with the latter. In a society divided with ethnicity, a better response can hardly be expected. It may be a relief for many that Modi's own philosophical underpinnings and cultural roots are far more inclusive, rather than divisive. In his remarks at Udvada in Gujarat in 2011 to a group of refugees whose ancestors originated from Persia, Modi made some assuring remarks, suggesting a sense of introspection about what had happened in Gujarat in the aftermath of Godhra incident in 2001.

Ever since BJP came to power in Gujarat in the mid-1990s, journalists and academics commonly referred to Gujarat as a 'laboratory' of Hindutva. But Modi, the former pracharak, was successful in projecting himself as an efficient pro-business leader, earning cheers from the Gujarati middle class and diaspora.

Modi's Rise to Power in Gujarat

Looking at how Modi was able to manoeuvre his position to power in Gujarat, a bit of background[6] is provided here.

Keshubhai Patel was the first BJP Chief Minister of Gujarat, in 1995, and was well entrenched in the state's politics. Modi is widely believed to have played a key role in helping to engineer his removal after eight months in office. The party was suffering due to differences between the RSS-Jan Sangh triumvirate of Keshubhai, Modi, and Shankersinh Vaghela. Vaghela subsequently revolted and left the party with 40-odd MLAs to launch his own outfit, which he later merged with the Gujarat Congress. Modi is said to have played a behind-the-scene role to ensure Vaghela's exit. In 2001, he dislodged Keshubhai from the Chief Minister's chair yet again (this time with clever machinations in New Delhi) and proceeded to replace him.

Modi may have brought socio-economic development in Gujarat, he was not free from the charge of eroding the Hindutva base of Sangh Parivar in the state. The veteran RSS leader Pravin Maniar said, "I brought Narendra Modi as Chief Minister at the insistence of the RSS top brass. But he worked to finish all Sangh organizations."

Keeping everything else aside, this clearly shows that Modi upheld the principles of secularism, and despite being called a partisan leader broke free from where regional and religious bodies wanted to confine him.

This was the reason why there were at least three serious attempts to unseat Modi as Gujarat Chief Minister, though each time he not only survived but emerged even stronger.

The Caravan, a journal of politics and culture, in one of its issues summed up the situation very adroitly as:

> To understand Modi's hold over Gujarat one has to return to October 2001 when he took charge of the state. The Ram temple issue had resulted in a groundswell of support for Hindutva, but the BJP was foundering because of its lack of good governance and an assured voter base. Ten years later, Modi has ensured more than a 49 percent vote share in two successive assembly elections, up from 27 percent in 1990, 42 percent in 1995 and 45 percent in 1998, besides an economy that is growing above the national average. Modi's detractors refuse to give him credit. Claiming that he worked within a more favourable set of conditions—a united party, a discredited and divided opposition, and an electorate inflamed by the post-Godhra landscape—they

maintain Modi has only slightly improved upon their performance.

In the 2012 assembly elections, Modi has declared his intention to win 151 of 182 seats—his aim is to surpass the record set by former Congress Chief Minister Madhavsinh Solanki, who took 140 seats, riding on a formula known as 'KHAM' (for Kshatriyas, Harijans, Adivasis and Muslims) in post-Emergency elections.

The important points to be noted in the situation then prevailing are: Firstly, the Ram temple was not built and what supported Modi in the elections was not Hindutva but his work. Secondly, Modi's claim of winning sizeable number of seats was built on getting votes not just from Hindus but from other classes, including Muslims.

Narendra Modi firmly believes in the unity of all sections and communities living in India. He has stated that the 'mantra' of unity should "constantly be a part of our thought, behaviour and expressions". "India is a diverse country, and this diversity is the pride of India.... Peace, harmony and unity...these are the key to development."

According to *The Hindu*, a particular aspect of Modi's persona seems to have confused many observers—his association with the RSS and affiliated bodies. One set of well-wishers has been cautioning him to guard against the Hindutva "fringe groups" that could challenge his good governance plank by opposing economic liberalization and stirring up social tension. A second group of well-wishers has been advising him that he must wholeheartedly embrace the Hindutva core and shun the Vajpayee model of maintaining a distance from them. Vajpayee cultivated his personality as a liberal who was resisting the Hindutva core. Both these suggestions assume a dichotomy between Modi and the Sangh Parivar.[7]

Modi has made it clear that he is interested in "pursuing the policies that Atal Bihari Vajpayee's NDA coalition followed during its five-year time in office. Modi has emphasized this in the past, noting that he appreciated Vajpayee's ability to project shakti (strength) and preserve shanti (peace)."[8]

It goes to the credit of Narendra Modi that he has been able to maintain a balance between his affinities and responsibilities as a Prime Minister and a leading political leader.

Notes

1. *Shakha* according to V.S. Apte's *Practical Sanskrit Dictionary* is a Hindu theological school that specializes in certain Vedic texts, or else the traditional texts followed by such school.
2. Arun Anand (2014), *Namo Vani*, Prabhat Prakashan.
3. *The Diplomat*: 13 March 2016.
4. zeenewsindia.com
5. Nirender Dev (2012), *Modi to Moditva*, Manas Publications, New Delhi.
6. Anosh Malekar, "The War Within: Keshubhai Patel Gathers Ranks to Take on Narendra Modi", 1 September 2012, http://www.caravanmagazine.in/perspectives/war-within#sthash.8jqzatse.dpuf
7. Varghese K. George, "A Pull Away from the Periphery", *The Hindu*, 21 August 2014.
8. Ankit Panda, "Modi: Hindutva Will Be An Asset in Foreign Affairs", *The Diplomat,* 24 April 2014.

ANNEXURE

Sabka Saath Sabka Vikas: Collective Efforts Inclusive Growth

> Government has only one religion—India first.
> Government has one holy book—the Constitution.
>
> The Government must be immersed in only one Bhakti-Bharat Bhakti.
> The Government's only strength is Jan Shakti.
> Government's only ritual is the well-being of the 125 crore Indians.
> The only code of conduct of the Government should be 'Sabka Saath, Sabka Vikas.'
>
> —Narendra Modi

Never before in the history of Independent India has a political leader given such a resounding and mature message of unity with inclusion.

Narendra Modi has come a long way from how the political discourse has been conducted in India. Politicians in India have very often used and thrived on vote banks by playing emotions of one against the other. While some leaders pit one religion against the other, others pit one caste against each other. Some political parties have also tried to ignite the people's sentiments against industrial development and encash it during the polls.

In such times, Narendra Modi's thoughts strike a refreshing contrast and provide a much needed alternate perspective on what unity really means. Narendra Modi has proven to be an apostle of unity and inclusivity, having demonstrated how his words could be put into action in Gujarat.

His actions while in office, his policies and his speeches have all reverberated with his message of unity and inclusivity. The most important thing that he has done is to break the myth that growth of a caste, community, religion, village, city or sector has to be at the cost of another. He has shown that development, upliftment and progress need not be a case of one against the other, but it can include everyone.

One of the landmark events happened when Narendra Modi went to Patna to address the Hunkar Rally in October 2013. Bombs were going off in the historic Gandhi Maidan just as he was about to speak. Any other leader would have either panicked or would have incited the crowd against the terror plot. No prepared speech would have been useful at that time. At such a time, Narendra Modi spoke from his heart and delivered a powerful message of peace and unity to both Hindus and Muslims that went to the crux of the principal challenge before our nation. He announced that Hindus and Muslims should together fight poverty instead of fighting among themselves. This is the only way forward for the nation.

At the heart of Narendra Modi's success lies his Panchamrut philosophy that drives it. This philosophy has a vision for the all-round development at the core of it. Panchamrut is the integration of five different streams which drives growth. This confluence of the panchshakti (five vital powers) of Knowledge, Water, Energy, Security and Human Resources, the five fundamental powers required to achieve holistic and sustainable growth have resulted in unprecedented growth and improvement in the quality of life in the state during his tenure as the Chief Minister of Gujarat. It is the amalgamation of mantra of 'Sabka Saath, Sabka Vikas' and Panchamrut philosophy that forms the corner stone of Narendra Modi's model of governance.

Narendra Modi's model of development has been unique in the sense that it has not created inequalities or conflicts between contrasting requirements. While his model embraced urbanisation as an opportunity rather than a threat, it made provisions to modernise and improve lives in urban areas. Similarly, while Gujarat has focused on industrial development and investments, agriculture and farmers have been given special attention too. While private entrepreneurs, big and small, have thrived in the business-friendly atmosphere, the public sector companies have achieved a miraculous turn around too. Gujarat's GDP growth increased significantly under Narendra Modi along with significant improvement in the social indicators. Technology has been given importance and at the same time great attention has been given to skill development.

Similarly, people from all castes, communities and religions including minorities, and underprivileged sections of the society have progressed, prospered in Gujarat under Narendra Modi.

This model is unique and worth emulating as it focuses on removing fault-lines of discrimination and prejudice. Once everyone is placed on an equal footing and given equal opportunities, it can only result in the creation of a truly equal and healthy society.

Chapter 3

Narendra Modi's Terms as Gujarat's Chief Minister, and the Gujarat Model of Development

Modi's political career started from Gujarat. In 1988, he was elected Organizing Secretary of the party's Gujarat unit, marking his entrance into electoral politics. He made rapid strides within the party when he helped to organize L.K. Advani's Ayodhya Rath Yatra in 1990 and Murli Manohar Joshi's Ekta Yatra (Journey for Unity) in 1991-92.

He made an electoral strategy which was considered central to BJP's victory in the 1995 state assembly elections. The same year he was elected BJP national secretary and transferred to New Delhi, where he assumed responsibility for party activities in Haryana and Himachal Pradesh. In 1996, Shankersinh Vaghela—one of the most prominent BJP leaders in Gujarat—defected to the INC following his defeat in the Lok Sabha elections.

Modi was on the selection committee for the 1998 assembly elections in Gujarat and he supported Keshubhai Patel over Vaghela to end factional division in the party. He was again credited with having played an important role in the BJP winning an overall majority in the 1998 elections, and was promoted to BJP General Secretary in May 1998. In 2001, he became the Chief Minister of Gujarat and served four terms until becoming India's Prime Minister. His economic policies were praised, though his administration was also criticized for failing to significantly improve the human development in the state, and for failing to prevent the 2002 Gujarat riots. The major events of his terms as the Chief Minister of Gujarat are described below.

First Term (2001-2002)

Narendra Modi's first stint as Chief Minister started in turbulent times in Gujarat as the allegations of corruption and poor governance were doing the rounds. When Shankarsingh Vaghela left BJP, Keshubhai Patel was made the Chief Minister of Gujarat. Modi became General Secretary of BJP in New Delhi. The natural disaster in the form of Bhuj earthquake[1] in 2001 and its poor handling made the party's national leaders to look for a new candidate as CM after the removal of Keshubhai Patel. In October 2001, Modi was made the Chief Minister of Gujarat despite his lack of experience in governance. Initially, BJP was not very keen on having him at the forefront and the party was contemplating the position of deputy CM for him, which he refused. In July 2007, he became the longest-serving Chief Minister in Gujarat's political history.

Godhra Incident, its Aftermath and its Impact

A terrible incident occurred in 2002 in Gujarat. On 27 February 2002, a train with several hundred passengers, including a large number of Hindu pilgrims returning from Ayodhya after a religious ceremony at the site of the demolished Babri Masjid, was burned near Godhra, in which about 60 people were killed. There were rumours that the fire was set by Muslim arsonists, due to which anti-Muslim violence spread throughout Gujarat. According to an estimate, death toll ranged from 900 to over 2,000, with several thousand injured. The Modi Government imposed a curfew in major cities, issued shoot-at-sight orders and called for the army to prevent the violence from escalating.[2] However, some human rights organizations, opposition parties and some media accused the Gujarat government of taking insufficient action against the rioters (to the point of condoning them).[3] Nirendra Dev, a senior journalist writes in his book, *Modi to Moditva*, "...one assessment was that during the initial hours of post-Godhra retaliation, Modi was not a direct accomplice to the violence; but he was rather caught almost clueless."[4]

A major effect of the incident was the polarization of Hindu voters which suited Modi well. Nirendra Dev, writes further, "Modi could be singled out and even now there are groups and individuals within BJP who are singling him out for the 2002 holocaust. But I have throughout given the Gujarat Chief Minister the benefit of doubt." Modi became popular in entire Gujarat. Even the OBCs and Dalits came close to the Sangh Parivar and the BJP. According to Dev, the absence of third political force of caste-based leadership (such as the one that exists in Uttar Pradesh headed by Mayawati or Mulayam Singh Yadav) was another factor that helped in attracting the OBC and Dalit Hindus towards BJP. In the assembly elections in Gujarat held in December 2012, BJP won 127 of the 182 seats and Modi was well entrenched as Chief Minister of Gujarat, which he continued right until he became India's Prime Minister.

In March 2008, the Supreme Court asked Gujarat Government to re-investigate nine cases from the 2002 riots establishing a Special Investigation Team (SIT).[5] In response to a petition from Zakia Jafri (widow of Ehsan Jafri, who was killed in the Gulbarg Society massacre), in April 2009 the court asked the SIT to investigate her allegation that Modi and another ministers were complicit in the killings. The SIT questioned Modi in March 2010 and in May, it presented to the court a report finding no evidence to substantiate the allegations. A subsequent protest petition was rejected by the Supreme Court in December 2013 accepting the SIT's finding that there was no evidence against the Chief Minister.

Second Term (2002-2007)

During Modi's second term as Chief Minister of Gujarat, attention was shifted from Hindutva to the economic development of the state. He took such decisions which curtailed the influence of organizations of the Sangh Parivar, like the Bharatiya Kisan Sangh (BKS) and the Vishva Hindu Parishad (VHP). Modi no longer consulted nor informed these organizations about his administrative decisions prior to their enactment, and even ordered to demolish 200 illegal temples in Gandhinagar, which further deepened his rift with the VHP.

Narendra Modi made important changes during the period 2002-07, which led to Gujarat being called an attractive investment destination. He started Financial and Technology Parks in the state. During the 2007 Vibrant Gujarat Summit, 363 MoUs for 454 projects were signed for ₹ 465310 Crore proposed investment, out of which real estate investment deals worth ₹ 6.6 trillion were signed.[6]

Modi focused on economic issues during the second term. Atal Bihari Vajpayee, then Prime Minister of India, asked Modi not to discriminate between citizens in the aftermath of the 2002 Gujarat violence. He pressed for Modi's resignation, and distanced himself from Modi. Vajpayee reached out to North Indian Muslims before the 2004 elections to the Lok Sabha. But BJP lost to the Congress. Vajpayee held that the violence in Gujarat had been one of the reasons for BJP's electoral defeat and acknowledged that not removing Modi immediately after the Gujarat violence was a mistake.[7]

Third Term (2007-2012)

In July 2007, Modi became the longest-serving Chief Minister of Gujarat and the BJP won 122 of 182 state-assembly seats in that year's election. Gujarat is a semi-arid state and the total geographical area of the state is 19,602,400 hectares, of which crops take up 10,630,700 hectares. According to Tushaar Shah, the state was "never known for agrarian dynamism". Modi took important steps to ensure that regular supply of water for irrigation—which is necessary for improving agriculture production—is made available in sufficient quantities. By the end of the year 2008, nearly five lakh structures had been constructed, of which, well over one lakh were check dams. Although most of these check dams remained empty during the pre-monsoon season, they helped in recharging the aquifers that lie beneath them. The result of Modi's efforts was that 60 of the 112 tehsils, which were found to have overexploited the groundwater table in 2004, had surprisingly regained their normal groundwater levels by 2010.[8] The groundwater level in many parts of Gujarat increased, as a result of which the fields could be irrigated with tube wells. The production of genetically modified agro-products, especially Bacillus thuringiensis (Bt) cotton, increased manifolds and the state became the largest producer of cotton in India. Gujarat's agricultural growth increased to 9.6 percent from 2001 to 2007. Gujarat recorded an agricultural growth rate of 10.97 percent, the highest of any state during 2001 to 2010.

The work of bringing electricity to the villages had been going on in Gujarat before Modi came to power but during his tenure electricity reached every village of the state. The state's power distribution system was transformed under Modi Government and it benefitted the farmers too. Gujarat expanded the Jyotigram Yojana scheme, in which the electric supply for agricultural needs was separately wired while there were separate distribution lines for domestic rural requirements. Agricultural electricity was rationed to fit the prioritized agriculture sector's scheduled irrigation demands, reducing its cost.

Under Narendra Modi, Gujarat became a state of dynamic development, economic growth and prosperity with the slogan, "Vibrant Gujarat".[9] He also facilitated the ease of doing business and ending bureaucratic logjam which made investment in Gujarat easy and rewarding. Gujarat also became the top-ranked Indian state in terms of "economic freedom", the index for which measures governance, growth, citizens' rights and labour and business regulation among the country's 20 largest states. However, the state still had to work on human development, poverty relief, nutrition, and education.

According to *Hindustan Times*, Gujarat outperformed India as a whole in improving several human-development indicators. School dropout rates declined from 20 percent in 2001 to two percent in 2011, and maternal mortality declined by 32 percent during the same period. In a review of the 1894 Land Acquisition Act, the Supreme Court of India identified Gujarat as one of the few states from which there were no complaints of forcible land acquisition.[10] Progress was made on the Gujarat International Finance Tec-City (GIFT) project, which is India's first International Financial Services Centre, located between

Ahmedabad and Gandhinagar, and has conductive multi-service SEZ and an exclusive domestic zone. A fully integrated city with a walk to work culture, it has the next-in-class Infrastructure, connectivity, people, technology and legal framework—emerging as a platform for businesses across the world. In its first phase, two skyscrapers were completed in 2012.

In July 2013, Nobel Laureate Amartya Sen expressed disapproval of Modi's governance record, saying that under his administration Gujarat's "record in education and healthcare is pretty bad".[11] However, according to economists Arvind Panagariya and Jagdish Bhagwati, Gujarat's social indicators have improved from a much lower baseline than that of other Indian states, and that Gujarat's performance in raising literacy rates has been superior to other states and the 'rapid' improvement of health indicators is evidence that "its progress has not been poor by any means."

Fourth Term (2012-2014)

In the 2012 Gujarat Legislative Assembly elections, Modi won from the Maninagar assembly constituency. The BJP won 115 of the 182 seats, continuing its majority during his tenure and allowing the party to form the government. After his election as Prime Minister, Modi resigned as Chief Minister and surrendered his MLA seat from Maninagar on 21 May 2014 after giving an emotional speech. Anandiben Patel was selected as his replacement.

In March 2012, Modi appeared on the cover of the Asian edition of the *Time* magazine, one of India's few politicians to have done so. His leadership was described as being strong and businesslike—one that could guide India towards honesty and efficiency.

Gujarat Model of Development

Gujarat model of development can be stated as the model which envisaged a balanced development of all the regions and communities of the state in all the parameters of socio-economic growth. This was a successful model and was praised by a large number of people in India and abroad as the state became richer, enjoyed faster GDP growth and a greater intensity of jobs and industry than India as a whole. Modi's reputation for clean government and economic competence made a record. When Indians voted for him in great numbers in May 2014 Lok Sabha elections, it was in large part because they wanted the country to be run as Gujarat was. The six key transformational initiatives that changed Gujarat under Modi, and that form the core of Gujarat Model of Development are briefly stated below.

1. Power Sector Reforms

Regular three phase electricity supply to all homes in Gujarat, including in villages was assured.

There was surplus electricity in Gujarat which was being given to states that were deficit in power supply to earn income. Alternative sources of power have been developed, especially solar power from the canal top solar panels. Gujarat has launched the Canal Solar Power Project to use the 19,000 km long network to Narmada canals across the state for setting up solar panels to generate electricity. Modi inaugurated a 1 MW pilot project on 24 April 2012; which will generate 1 MW of clean energy per year and also prevent evaporation of 9,000 kiloliters of water annually from the canal. It also eliminates the requirement to acquire vast tracts of land and limits evaporation of water from the 750 metres long canal, tackling two challenges simultaneously by providing energy and water security. The efficiency of electricity production has increased by 16 percent. Therefore, private companies that are in power business have acquired a good and stable financial health.

2. Agriculture and Water

There was development of check dams which recharged the aquifers. Water table in most parts of Gujarat has risen and there is better irrigation through pump sets. This also reduced state's dependence on the rain for agriculture. The state registered over 10% growth in agriculture during the first decade of the 21st century. The people's drinking water dependence changed to 85% on surface water from 75% on groundwater. The government took various steps to mitigate the effect of drought which occurred in some areas.

3. Infrastructure Build-up

The government ensured efficient delivery of public services, and model implementation of Bus Rapid Transit System (BRTS). Road transport was improved in a big way and today Gujarat has the best road network in the country. There was transition to next generation infrastructure, e.g. Wi-Fi and satellite spectrum.

4. Industry and Investments

Special industrial clusters were formed promoting investment in creating job opportunities. Pro-industry policies were made and implemented. Gujarat became the auto hub of India with brands like Nano, Maruti and Ford. More than 80 skill development centres were operationalized in the initial stage and there was plan to open more than 300 more such centres. Many investment summits were held to attract more investments promoting entrepreneurs and creating employment.

5. Healthcare

Childcare got a big boost in the state of Gujarat. There was 32% improvement in the reduction of malnutrition as against 9% improvement on all-India basis, the highest among all states. Maternal mortality rate went down from 172 to 125 during the period 2001-12. Infant mortality rate went down from 54 per 1000 live births to 39 during the period 2005-11. Institutional healthcare deliveries improved from 47% to 95%.

6. Women's Empowerment

Female literacy improved from 58% to 71% during the period 2001-11. Sex ratio improved for incremental births (0-6 year group). There was 100% enrollment of girls in the schools. School dropout rate reduced to low single digit.

Gujarat's development journey has received tremendous praise both across India and the world. Under Narendra Modi's leadership Gujarat was known for its development-oriented governance where the people were made active partners and stakeholders in the development journey. When Narendra Modi took over as the Chief Minister, Gujarat was reeling under the effects of a devastating earthquake. The drought, cyclone and floods on the preceding years too slowed the state's development journey.

Everyone thought the Gujarat would take years to recover from the damage, but Narendra Modi and his team proved everyone wrong by putting Gujarat on the path to recovery in a record time of less than three years. Besides, there was appreciable economic progress.

Gujarat's development journey is characterised as development oriented, inclusive and participative, because decisions were not taken behind closed doors by select individuals but by consulting all the stakeholders. Optimum use of technology was made to minimize corruption. This increased the pace of development in the state.

Development of Gujarat under Modi was not centered around any one sector. All the three sectors, namely agriculture, industries and services made an equal and active contribution towards the growth of Gujarat.

Under Narendra Modi, the farmers of Gujarat witnessed unprecedented prosperity. The annual Krishi Mahotsavs brought several services and opportunities at the doorstep of the farmers. The farmers received Soil Health Cards that gave them much needed guidance on enhancing their productivity. Special attention was also devoted to animal husbandry.

Industrial development scaled new heights in Gujarat from 2001 onwards. In 2003, the biennial Vibrant Gujarat Summits began that drew record investment to the state. At the same time, the land acquisition policy put in place by the government ensures that no injustice is done to the people where the industry is coming up.

Governance in Gujarat has reached the very last person in the queue. Due to the Garib Kalyan Melas, the fruits of development reach the intended beneficiaries without any middlemen. In 2008, the Gujarat Government launched the Vanbandhu Kalyan Yojana, a special package devoted to development of the tribal communities. Today the package is worth ₹ 40,000 crores and has brought smiles on the faces of several people across Gujarat.

A firm believer in youth-led development, Narendra Modi devoted a lot of efforts towards enhancing skill development among the youth. From building more ITIs, upgrading syllabus and infrastructure in the ITIs to integrating skill development programmes with technology, record number of steps have been taken for skill development among Gujarat's youth. In fact, Gujarat's Kaushalya Vardhan Kendra (KVK), the flagship scheme of the Directorate of Employment and Training to enhance skill development among the people, was awarded the Prime Minister's Award for Excellence in Public Administration for the year 2011-12 on 21st April 2013, which is commemorated as National Civil Services Day.

Modi's International Diplomacy as Chief Minister of Gujarat

As Chief Minister of Gujarat, Narendra Modi made serious efforts to attract foreign investment to Gujarat. He visited China, Singapore and Japan. He went to China in November 2006 to study the country's Special Economic Zones (SEZs) as some such SEZs were to be established in Gujarat. He again went to China in 2007 and 2011. A month after his 2011 visit, the Chinese Government released 13 Indian diamond traders charged with smuggling in Shenzhen, with Modi attributing their release to his diplomacy and statesmanship (*Mumbai Mirror*).

His relationship with many Western nations was troubled during his tenure as Chief Minister and there were misgivings about his role in the 2002 riots, resulting in travel bans to the UK, the US and the EU. According to *Times of India*, Modi was barred from entering the United States under a provision of the Immigration and Nationality Act banning violators of religious freedom, and according to *The Wall Street Journal*, he was the only person denied a US visa under this provision. The UK and the European Union refused to admit him because of what they saw as his role in the riots. However, as Modi rose to prominence in India, the UK and the EU lifted their bans in October 2012 and March 2013, respectively, and after his election as India's Prime Minister, he was invited to Washington.

In 2011, the Karachi Chamber of Commerce & Industry, impressed with development in Gujarat, invited Modi to visit Pakistan and address business leaders who asked him to consider a flight between Ahmedabad and Karachi because of the cultural and economic relationships between Gujarat and Sindh. Modi wanted to ease Pakistan's power crisis, particularly in Sindh, and suggested that the country could follow the examples of the "Gujarat model" set by Gujarat Solar Park and the Kalpasar Project.[12]

Modi visited Japan in 2012. According to Ryohei Kasai, research fellow at the Center for South Asian Studies at Gifu Women's University,

> There is a growing interest in Modi in Japan with much anticipation that he will reshape India by revitalising its economy and better governance. I believe Japan has an excellent relationship with him. Not only have successive Japanese ambassadors to India been regular guests in 'Vibrant Gujarat' investors' summit (organised biennially) but Japanese private companies also made a big amount of investment in the state.[13]

It has been recognized widely that as Chief Minister of Gujarat, Narendra Modi was instrumental in bringing socio-economic development at a fast pace in the state. All sections of society were benefited due to good policies and effective implementation thereof. The Gujarat Model of Development received praise from India and abroad. The people who have chosen him as India's Prime Minister are hoping that he will take India to fast development in all the key sectors. As of now the economy is doing better than before, but a lot needs to be done to reach the envisaged goals.

Notes

1. Bhuj is a city and a municipality in Kutch district in the state of Gujarat. The death toll in earthquake was 12,300. Bhuj, situated just 20 km away from the epicenter, was devastated. Considerable damage also occurred in Bhachau and Anjar with hundreds of villages flattened in

Taluka of Anjar, Bhuj, and Bhachau. Over a million structures were damaged or destroyed.

2. *The Hindu* (Chennai, India), 1 March 2002.
3. Somini Sengupta (28 April 2009), "Shadows of Violence Cling to Indian Politician", *The New York Times,* 28 April 2009.
4. Nirendra Dev (2012), *Modi to Moditva*, Manas Publications, New Delhi.
5. *Hindustan Times*, 26 December 2013.
6. Andy Marino (2014), *Narendra Modi: A Political Biography*, HarperCollins Publishers India.
7. Martha Craven Nussbaum, *The Clash Within: Democracy, Religious Violence, and India's Future*, Harvard University Press, pp. 50-51.
8. Uday Mahurkar, "A green rising", *India Today*, 4 June 2010.
9. Tommaso Bobbio (2012), "Making Gujarat Vibrant: Hindutva, development and the rise of subnationalism in India", *Third World Quarterly* 33 (4): 657-72.
10. *Hindustan Times*, 4 August 2011.
11. Amartya Sen, "I don't want Narendra Modi as my PM", *The Indian Express*, 22 July 2013.
12. *The News International,* 20 September 2012.
13. Roche, Elizabeth Roche, "Narendra Modi and the Art of Twiplomacy", *Live Mint,* 20 May 2014.

CHAPTER 4

Digital India Dynamics of Narendra Modi

Narendra Modi's vision of Digital India has larger aims to transform the country into a digitally-empowered society and knowledge economy. The programme is to be implemented in phases by 2018. Envisaged by the Department of Electronics and Information Technology (DeitY), the programme would bring in public accountability through mandated delivery of government's services electronically, providing a Unique ID and e-Pramaan based on authentic and standard based interoperable and integrated government applications and data basis. The source of funding for most of the e-governance projects at present is through budgetary provisions of the respective ministries or the departments in the Central or State Governments. Requirements of funds for individual project(s) for Digital India are being worked out by respective Nodal Ministries/Departments.

Vision areas of the digitalized India are the following:

(a) Infrastructure as utility to every citizen—high speed internet as a core utility to be made available in all gram panchayats; cradle to make digital identity unique, lifelong, online and authenticable; mobile phone and bank account would enable participation in digital and financial space at individual level; easy access to a common service centre within their locality; sharable private space on a public cloud, and safe and secure cyber space in the country.

(b) Governance and services on demand which encompass making services available in real-time from online and mobile platforms, would be integrated across departments or jurisdictions to provide easy and a single window access to all person. To ensure easy access, all citizens' entitlements are to be made available on the cloud. Government services are to be digitally transformed for improving Ease of Doing Business, in addition to making financial transactions above a threshold electronic and cashless, leveraging Global Information System (GIS) for decision support systems and development.

(c) The vision area focuses on citizens' digital empowerment by bringing about universal digital literacy. All government documents/certificates are to be made available on the cloud. For universal accessibility of digital services/resources in Indian languages, collaborative digital platforms are also to be made available for participative governance. Portability of individual entitlements will be looked after through the cloud.

Digital India programme will pull together many existing on-going schemes which are to be restructured and refocused for implementation in a synchronized manner as it weaves together a large number of ideas and thoughts into a single and comprehensive direction so that each of them is seen as part of the larger picture. The programme broadly aims to provide the much needed thrust to the nine pillars of growth areas, viz.

(i) Broadband highways,

(ii) Universal access to mobile connectivity,

(iii) Public internet access programme,

(iv) e-Governance—reforming government through technology,

(v) e-Kranti—electronic delivery of services,

(vi) Information for all,

(vii) Electronics manufacturing,

(viii) IT for jobs, and

(ix) Early harvest programmes.

The Necessity of Digitizing India

The idea of a Digital India drew initial doubts of its viability and success because the country has nearly a billion people without internet access, while 37 percent of all adult Indians are illiterate. Despite the nationwide mobile boom, poor network infrastructure means there is no significant difference between 2G and 3G speeds. A realistic digital nation would imply that its digital infrastructure must be supplemented by homegrown electronic manufacturing and institutionalized e-governance. Another very important component of Digital India, i.e., the National Optical Fibre Network (NOFN) project has remained behind schedule and is unlikely to be completed before December 2016. Government's plan for expanding network to one lakh gram panchayats (GPs) has been going on at a slow pace and, till now, just 20,000 GPs have been actually covered. The lack of specialized contractors and non-availability of Payload Loop Back (PLB) ducts at various sites strain deadlines further. Laying the optical fibre cables is not of much help either as more than 67 percent of NOFN points are found non-functional even during their pilot stage.[1]

Globally, many countries offer streamlined online processes and incentives to facilitate affordable housing. These include tax deductions, density bonuses, direct subsidies, land grants, land use changes, etc. Countries like Malaysia and Canada have revamped their administrative requirements through fee waivers and fast-tracking procedures. In the case of India, therefore, advanced technologies are need of the hour. A Digital India is a one where empowering technologies, in areas ranging from education, healthcare, e-governance to agribusiness, can add economic value of US$ 1 trillion per year by 2025 in addition to creating millions of well-paying productive jobs.

Other roadblocks in the way of countrywide digitalization in India can be connectivity and e-commerce. Mobile internet penetration in India hovers around 20-22 percent with around 371 million users, which is far below 50 percent of the 2025 target. Just 8 percent of all Small and Medium Enterprises (SMEs) have a significant web presence, while cloud-based e-governance initiatives remain paltry in number. The number of retail establishments accepting digital payments is limited to 0.6 million, 6 percent of the total, while one percent of all transactions are linked to a digital identity. Less than one percent of India's electricity grid is smart, while only five Indian cities have experimented with some smart type of transportation. Even GIS satellites, launched by ISRO, are trivially used by State Governments, offering just basic imaging of forests, groundwater, soil and mineral content. Hence, the last mile connectivity needs to be improved rapidly.

Instead of a centralised NOFN scheme, local initiatives as Andhra Pradesh's state-focused rollout, or Argentina's Community Telecommunication Cooperatives (CTCs) should be explored for faster rollout. The total cost of ownership needs to be reduced significantly through regulatory changes, tariff reductions and subsidies. A different approach based on the BSNL's mass deployment of Wi-Fi hotspots across the country could yield better results. The BSNL can be encouraged to deploy one Wi-Fi hotspot in every village which will create national impact.

Pushing for net zero imports in electronics in India would create the foundation for an electronics industry. Global mobile phone players like Foxconn are considering India as a sourcing destination, but are put off by labour troubles and inconsistent duty regimes. Even a booming e-commerce sector is beset with regulations. India currently permits 100 percent FDI in B2B e-commerce activities but not in B2C companies.

The government has experimented with various e-governance initiatives, most of which have failed to materialize, given poor cyber security, significant privacy and data protection risk. The e-governance initiative of Britain, called "Tell us Once" service, which allows citizens to inform public authorities about birth, death or significant life events just once, is an example here. Cities like San Francisco have taken this further (DataSF. org), allowing developers to build programs to display public transportation arrival and departure times, recycle zones and crime patterns.

Sweden established an e-Government Delegation to make public administration simple. Now, enterprises and entrepreneurs simply go to a website for business needs, while citizens use theme-based portals—healthcare, taxation, employment, social insurance, etc. All procurement and invoicing is conducted electronically restricting corruption opportunities.

India is ripe for a rapid diffusion of enabling technologies. The mobile internet could reach 900 million Indians by 2025. Combined with cloud-based services, a digital identity and secure digital payment schemes, such technologies can provide the foundation for the scale-up of remote healthcare, rapid advancements in agriculture and distance leaning. About 20 million SMEs could use cloud-based digital business tools instead of running them in-house at a higher cost. Over 100 million farmers could use real time market information, bolstering their marginal product and precision farming. Indeed, a digital India could create a nation of micro-entrepreneurs, operating from their kirana store or garage.

According to Ratan Tata, the promising start-ups in e-commerce and e-retail space are the ones that will change the face of Indian merchandising and marketing business. The ability to think out of the box has made the United States change its appearance from smoke-stacked companies to innovative companies that we see around us today such as Apple, Facebook, etc.

When Narendra Modi unveiled his government's Digital India programme on 1 July 2015, he knew that by any measure, it was a huge exercise. Even if the government manages to achieve 50 percent of what it has set out to do, it would change the lives of millions of Indians. If implemented earnestly, it has the potential to significantly reduce corruption in government offices, create a better environment for new start-ups and allow more people to access communication and information tools on the internet.

Many of the proposals that the government has put forward on this programme have existed on paper in some form or the other for the last several years. For example, the National

Optical Fibre Network (NOFN) project funded by Universal Service Obligation Fund, which would be implemented to provide broadband connectivity to over two lakh Gram Panchayats of India, has been going on since 2011, but so far none of these initiatives have resulted in anything concrete, and are stuck in bottlenecks. Given the complexity of many aspects of this programme, setting up of expensive infrastructure and interdepartmental cooperation within various ministries are required. Hence, a better solution to improve the digital infrastructure within the country should be found in right earnestness. Internet service providers are also more or less responsible for the sorry state of internet in India, to expand internet connectivity in the country.[2] It could have raised the minimum broadband speed from 512 kbps to 2 mbps to meet global standards, and could have cracked down on unfair trade practices like Fair use Policy. As Digital India is a grand vision, the country requires many policy changes and an intent to enforce the new norms.

India's top industrialists, including Cyrus Mistry, Anil Agarwal, Mukesh Ambani, Azim Premji, Pawan Munjal, Sunil Bharti Mittal, and Kumar Manglam Birla attended the much awaited Digital India launching programme in New Delhi. Anil Ambani joined through initiating special digital drive. India's top corporates then pledged around ₹ 4.5 lakh crore to the projects related to the ambitious initiative, which could generate employment for about 18 lakh people. Mukesh Ambani, Chairman of Reliance Industries, proposed to invest ₹ 2.5 lakh crore across different Digital India heads and also announced to set up of the 'Jio Digital India Start Up Fund' to encourage going entrepreneurs who are setting up businesses focused around the Digital India initiative. On the other hand, Kumar Mangalam Birla said to leverage Idea Cellular's network of 165 million subscribers across 350,000 towns and villages in India to provide mobile-based healthcare and education services as well as weather forecasting advisories and 'mandi' prices to over one million farmers. Anil Ambani, Chairman of Reliance Communications, pledged to invest ₹ 10,000 crore to fund transformational initiatives across the cloud, digital and telecom space. To further align the movement, Anil Agarwal, Chairman, Vedanta Group announced setting up of a fully integrated LCD panel fab in India over the next decade with an investment of ₹ 40,000 crore, which could be expected to generate employment for 50,000 people. His company, Sterlite Technologies has been part of India's digital empowerment journey over the past 20 years which successfully created a research-focused indigenous optic fibre facility in India, in addition to its key role in Rural Bharat Net, Smart City projects, establishing Indian Defence Communication network in Kashmir, and enabling e-education in municipal schools.

It would be a digital record when nearly 12 lakh soldiers will have their service records on their finger-tips as the Army has taken up a major initiative to go digital. To coincide with the National Digital India Week launched by Prime Minister, the Defence Ministry's launch of the Army Record Office Process Automation (ARPAN) software will maintain records of jawans and non-commissioned officers, which will be available to them in a secured network. In the inauguration ceremony of Digital India Week, Narendra Modi made a unique pitch, saying "'Design in India' is as important as 'Make in India' to move from e-governance to mobile governance, i.e. m-governance."

Digital India: The First Step Forward

The vision for Digital India is the first step forward to empower citizens with technology and focus on harnessing the power of technology to help India transform. Narendra Modi illustrated the dangers posed to cyber security by pointing out that "somebody with an education of 10th or 12th class, sitting thousands of miles away, can clean up your bank account with a click of mouse. Can India provide a shield to the world by providing innovative and credible solutions? Why should we not have such confidence? We should accept this challenge to ensure that entire humanity lives in peace." The benefits of this dream are not seen immediately with a growing economy and falling handset prices, but sadly the country's average internet speed was ranked 115th globally in the first quarter of 2015, among countries studied by services provider, Akamai Technologies. Another concern often expressed by many companies is that the country had just a little over 100 million broadband subscribers at the end of April 2015 out of a population of close to 1.3 billion, according to telecom regulator TRAI.

Interrelation of Modi's Skill India and Digital India

The Pradhan Mantri Kaushal Vikas Yojana (PMKVY)—another flagship scheme of the government which aims to enable a large number of Indian youth to take up industry-relevant skill training that will help them in securing a better livelihood is related to the digitalization which was launched on 15 July 2014. The date was strategically chosen as it coincides with "World Youth Skill Day". The National Skill Development Mission is to be run by a three-tier high powered committee, with PM in the chair. After Digital India, the main focus of the government is concentrated on skilled India with an ambitious target of imparting skills to 30 crore people, i.e. one out of every four Indians, by 2020.

The National Skill Development Mission would provide overall guidance to the National Skill Development Agency, the National Skill Development Corporation, and the Directorate of Training. Union Cabinet has already given its approval for an outlay of ₹ 1,500 crore for the PMKVY and also approved the introduction of common norms across all skill development schemes being implemented by various ministries and departments. The mission has decided to do away with multiplicity of norms on eligibility, duration and cost of training that had created a diffusive effect of the programmes for over 70 Skill Development Programmes, being implemented by the government presently.

The overall scheme would identify common norms and define the activities constituting skill development in the country, such as courses and their alignment with National Skills Qualification Framework, broad input standards for training programmes and the outcomes expected. For this purpose, Skill Development Management Systems (SDMS) would be put in place to verify and record details of all training centres, a certain quality of training locations and courses. Biometric system and video recording of the training process would also be put in place wherever feasible. All persons undergoing training would be required to provide feedback at the time of assessment, and this would become the key element of the evaluation framework to assess the effectiveness of the PMKVY scheme.

Mapping the Global Needs

Narendra Modi drew up a vision for mapping India's human resources to develop region-specific talents that would make India a hub for export of services to the world. According to him, India should assess its service capabilities in the global perspective. India has vast potential to meet the skilled manpower needs of the entire world. He therefore called for a careful mapping of global needs "as in the coming days, India is going to get younger, although it has made the transformation from a country worried about its brain drain to a country that thinks of brain-gain."

In a country as diverse as India "one-size-fits-all approach" may not be appropriate because people of different regions have different talents and the effort could be made to develop those specific skills. There is necessity to understand the needs of our trading partners and accordingly tailor our skills supply to meet their requirements and India could become a hub for global arbitration with changes in the legal system. The government has already introduced amendments to the Arbitration and Conciliation Act, 1996 to encourage international business community to settle commercial disputes in India. Success of the services sector becomes even more important for supporting the Make in India and Digital India initiatives.

Digitalizing Transport and Road Safety

As the UN had set a target of reducing the road accidents by 50 percent before 2020, the India Chapter of International Road Federation and the government decided to hasten the speed for building new roads, including express highways and widening, maintaining and repairing existing roads for which the need for a modern, digitalized asset management system has been emphasized. Road Asset Management System (RAMS) is being developed for all national highways, which is a modern system of management using Gagan and Bhuvan satellite systems to prepare a 360° mapping of road assets. This project is funded by the World Bank, and its outcome will assist in the accurate and scientific planning and finalising of road projects, maintenance of roads, executing road safety measures and development of the National Highways network in India. The software for RAMS is being developed using the international best practises has the functionality to interface with the indigenous Bhuvan satellite images. The data collected will be stored and managed through a web-based application which will be hosted in the public domain.

Knowledge Portal for Railways

Indian Railways have taken a big initiative by launching Indian Railways Knowledge Portal (www.kportal.indianrailways.gov.in) developed by the National Academy of Indian Railways (NAIR), Vadodara, which is in line with Modi's Digital India move. It will be a comprehensive platform for railways in particular as it tries to encompass as much knowledge as possible by linking websites, documents, etc. for dissemination of knowledge. The government believes that the training and learning environment of Indian Railways needs to be upgraded for the benefit of railway personnel. The knowledge about railway systems must not remain confined to a select few but must reach all enthusiasts, researchers, academicians and personnel to contribute ideas, solutions and schemes. Indian Railways have given topmost priority to safety in railway operations and ensured it in the most professional manner at all levels.

Digital India can transform the country, but not the way it is being implemented now.[3] The new government which has taken over in May 2014, has taken a number of initiatives out of which Digital India initiative stood out for its potential to transform governance, citizenship and entrepreneurship in India. This initiative has potential to leapfrog a nation and people into the technology age, creating unprecedented competitive advantages for India. It promises to transform utterly decrepit institutions of government and democracy, fulfilling the "minimum government, maximum governance" goal of Narendra Modi. A year and half on, the gap between vision and execution on the ground is wide and growing. It is therefore obvious that Digital India and connecting Indians to the internet needed serious work. It has taken about US$ 100 billion of investment over the last 21 years to get 900 million Indians behind a mobile phone, and in recent years about 200 million people have also been connected to the internet in India. An estimated US$ 80 billion is required to get 600 millions Indians connected to the internet.

Importance of Becoming Digital Indians

Focus on the rights of a billion Indians destined to become digital Indians is important because consumer rights in technology and telecom space have not been given due attention over the last decade. Telecom Regulatory Authority of India's (TRAI's) capacity needs to be strengthened to regulate a sector where disruptive practices are going on. Net neutrality is critical to the growth of Digital India, to investments, to supporting digital entrepreneurship and creating a smooth roadmap to future innovations around the Internet of Things and Industrial Internet. It is a defining issue having implications that millions of people will have their data and personal information in various government and private databases scattered around the country and overseas. While there is significant global interest amongst investors in Digital India, many government responses, including the policy of encryption, i.e. putting information into a form called a code that other people are unable to read, highlight the gap between the vision and its execution. To take the government and services to a billion Indians via the internet, TRAI, Department of Telecommunication (DoT) and DeitY also need to be transformed with the specialized capacity required to deal with technology policy making and regulation.

If India is empowered with this state-of-the-art technology, the PM's vision would also attract millions of others in need of jobs and services from outside the country, like African nations which have young population, with 65 percent of the population below 35 years of age. The UN estimates that by 2035, half of all Africans will live in cities. With improvements in economic governance and a rising middle class, there is huge potential in IT-enabled services. In this regard, there is an urgent need to facilitate collaboration between Indian and African start-ups. Additionally, if India establishes many more points of contact on the continent and goes beyond its traditional Anglophone friends to explore opportunities in Francophone countries such as Morocco, it can deliver new Indo-African synergy, as Africa today is looking for genuine growth partners.

The Government of India aims to achieve the following through Digital India initiative:

1. Infrastructure to provide high speed internet services to its citizens in all gram panchayats. Bank accounts will be given priority at individual level. People will be provided with safe and secure cyber space in the country.
2. Government services will be available online where citizens will be ensured prompt access to it and transactions will be made easy through electronic medium.
3. Digital empowerment of citizens is viewed as the most important factor of the Digital India initiative. It will provide universal digital literacy and make digital sources easily accessible. The services are also provided in Indian languages for active participation.

The government has undertaken several major projects under Digital India initiative, viz. manufacturing of electronics and provision of public access to internet; highways to have broadband services and easy access to mobile connectivity; e-governance and IT training for jobs; e-Kranti and global information as well as setting up of Wi-Fi facilities in all universities across the country. The government is focusing on zero imports of electronics. In order to achieve this, the government aims to put up smart energy meters, micro ATMs, mobile, consumer and medical electronics. The government aims to provide internet services to 2.5 lakh villages, which comprises of one in every panchayat by March 2017 and 1.5 lakh post offices in the next two years. These post offices will become multi-service centres for the people.

All these 2.5 lakh gram panchayats will be connected by national optic fibre network. Broadband for the rural region will be laid by December 2016, and for all urban regions it will mandate communication infrastructure in new urban development and buildings. By March 2017, the government aims to provide nationwide information infrastructure. Steps are afoot to ensure that by 2018 all villages are covered through mobile connectivity. The aim is also to increase network penetration and cover gaps in all 44,000 villages. Processing and delivery of services through e-governance are to be improved with Unique Identification Authority of India (UIDAI), payment gateway, electronic data interchange (EDI) and mobile platforms. School certificates, voter ID cards, etc. will be provided online as well as faster examination of data are also aimed.

As far as IT training for jobs is concerned, it has been aimed to train around one crore students from small towns and villages for IT sector by 2020. Under this programme, setting up of BPO sectors in North Eastern States is also covered. e-Kranti aims to deliver electronic services to people, dealing with health, education, farmers and farming, justice, security and financial inclusion. MyGov.in is a website lauched by the government for a two-way communication between citizens and the government by which people can send in their suggestions and comments on various issues raised by the government. Social media platforms have been engaged for governance by hosting data online. Email will be made the primary mode of communication and Aadhar Enabled Biometric Attendance System will be deployed in all Central Government offices where recording of attendance will be made online.

Global investors like Sundar Pichai, Satya Nadella, Elon Musk, and others have supported Digital India initiative. Microsoft CEO, Satya Nadella intends to become India's partner in this programme. He said that his company will set up low cost broadband technology services to five lakh villages across the country. The CEO of Google, Sundar Pichai also hoped that

India will play a big role in driving technology forward in future improving the lives of the people. Modi Government wants technology to speed up development as much of India is yet to be built.

Global evidence suggests that simply providing computers or cheap broadband will not automatically lead to greater usage. What is most cost-effective in one place, may not be the same at another place. The main driver of the programme—the National Informatics Centre is itself not fully capable. According to a 2012 report, 25 percent of attempts to book ticket on the railway site end in failures. Another survey indicates that one-fifth of those who have a smartphone do not think it is reliable for transactions.

Employment and Livelihood through Digitalization

India's young age structure offers a potential demographic dividend for growth, but it will be realized if the extent and quality of education and skill development among new entrants to the workforce are greatly enhanced. One of the most remarkable things brought out by the 66th round of National Sample Survey Organization (NSSO) survey on Employment (2009-10) is that the number of young people in education is fast rising and therefore the workforce has increased dramatically, causing a drop in the labour participation rate.

Liberalization has driven more and more people from the organized sector to the unorganized sector. Former member of Planning Commission, Dr. S.R. Hashim emphasized the need for promoting informal sector which employs a very large proportion of casual workers and self-employed persons in the total labour force.[4] Dr. Hashim's two very useful suggestions in this context include creating an environment in which informal economic activity does not appear to be illegal, undesirable, or unproductive, but is looked upon as a useful productive and respectable activity. For this, the legal and regulatory hurdles need to be removed. Secondly, several hurdles arise from locational earmarking of activity in the urban sector. The need of the hour is to take care of the 92 percent of the labour force engaged in the unorganized sector.

Information Technology undoubtedly has opened large avenues for educated youth in the country. In its one segment, i.e. computers—both hardware and software—computer engineers and system analysts are having a million jobs at present. The IT sector provided 2.2 million jobs to computer professionals and other related personnel and has great potential of generating more employment, but a disturbing aspect of the present situation is that IT education is very costly, and IT-related jobs are the preserve of the better-off sections of the society. To enable the poor to acquire IT education, the government requires to make provision in the form of subsidies or charge differential fees. Computer education should also be expanded to rural areas so that the capabilities of the rural people are developed to acquire better quality jobs in the IT sector.

Digital India, according to Prime Minister Narendra Modi, is an enterprise for the transformation of India in a way unmatched in human history. In it, he sees technology as a means to empower and as a tool that bridges the distance between hope and opportunity. Sameer Kochhar[5] wrote,

> The intensity in Modi's words, whenever he enunciates his Digital India dream, reflects the deep-rooted conviction that technology can bring governance closer to the people and enhance transparency and efficiency. His belief is technology, when it was applied to practice, had produced results. Technology and e-Governance embedded in it had been the driving forces in Modi's governance successes in Gujarat much before he became the Prime Minister of India.

As envisioned by the Prime Minister, Digital India, is a very vital initiative to prepare India for a knowledge future and make technology the key enabler of change. Justice, good governance, development, opportunity creation, equal participation in the economy and democracy would be the equal winners of this programme when implemented earnestly. With the Digital India campaign in full swing, he expected farmers to get a major benefit from it, as the programme is all set to connect over 550 farmer markets in the country, in addition to a national agricultural market which is expected to be established online, where the farmers would be able to get a fair price for their produce. According to Modi, the need for this market has emerged as it has been noticed that there is a vast difference between the prices farmers pay in the farmer markets and many a times their produces sell for much lower than a fair rate.

While India warmed up gradually to the adoption of technology as compared to the developed world, increasing globalization and the use of technology to improve the lives of the poor is the driving force. Hence, the general consensus of 2016 budget was on strong rural focus and the IT sector is no exception. Use of the unique identification number as the base platform to connect farmers to e-market portals and a new rural digital literacy scheme were the highlights of the budget.

With US$ 304.3 million for ICT projects across e-learning, e-panchayat and land record modernization, three main sectors, viz. rural, skill and job creation, and Ease of Doing Business, the budgetary, provisions are reflected as under:

Rural Sector—Unified Agricultural Marketing ePlatform to provide a common e-market platform for wholesale markets; Pashudhan Sanjivani, Nakul Swasthya Patra, E-pashudhan Haat, and National Genomic Centre for indigenous breeds; Digital Literacy Mission scheme for rural India to cover around 6 crore additional household within the next three years, and National Land Record Modernisation Programme worth US$ 22.2 million.

Skill and Job Creation—Digital Depository for school leaving certificates, college degrees, academic awards and mark-sheets to be set up; interlink state employment exchanges with the National Career Service Platform, and Entrepreneurship Education and Training through open online courses.

Ease of Doing Business—Introduction of direct benefit transfer (DBT) of fertilizer subsidy to farmers on pilot basis; targeted delivery of financial and other subsidies; Benefits and Services Bill to use Aadhaar; Automation facilities in 300,000 fair-price shops by March 2017; Director-General of Supplies and Disposal (DGS&D) to establish a technology-driven platform to facilitate procurement of goods and services by various ministries/agencies, expansion in the scope of e-assessments in seven mega cities; e-sahyog to be expanded for small tax payers, and financial data management centre to facilitate integrated data aggregation and analysis in the financial sector.

In some key announcements made by Finance Minister Arun Jaitley, custom and excise duty in the IT sector has been removed. Under the digital literacy, six crore families are to be covered in three years. More and more use of mobile equipment, accessories and other smartphone components will promote domestic manufacturing. New innovations like Li-Fi (Light Fidelity) which is said to be gaining acceptance in the industry can be examined as suggested by Harald Haas, a world renowned expert in wireless communications and holding the Chair of Mobile Communications at the Edinburgh University. Haas is convincing the world including India that Li-Fi (Light Fidelity)-enabled LED light bulb can also transmit data at a speed that is much higher than Wi-Fi (wireless fidelity).

Digital India's focus areas and its big challenges are now most talked about in seminars and conferences also as its focus areas are vast. Following are the projects and products that have been launched or are ready for deployment as part of the initiative, like digital locker system to minimize usage of physical documents and enable their e-sharing via registered repositories; MyGov.in as an online platform to engage citizens in governance through a "Discuss, Do and Disseminate" approach; Swachh Bharat Mission Mobile app to achieve the goals set by this mission; e-Sign framework to allow citizens to digitally sign documents online using Aadhaar; e-Hospital system for important healthcare services such as online registration, fee payment, fixing doctors' appointments, online diagnostics and checking blood availability online; National Scholarship Portal for beneficiaries from submission of application to verification, sanction and disbursal; Digitize India Platform for large-scale digitization of records in the country to facilitate efficient delivery of services to the citizens; Bharat Net programme as a high-speed digital highway to connect all 2,50,000 gram panchayats—the world's largest rural broadband project using optical fibre; BSNL's Next Generation Network to replace 30-

year old telephone exchanges to manage all types of services like voice, data, multimedia and other types of communication services; BSNL's large-scale deployment of Wi-Fi hotspots throughout the country; broadband highways as one of the pillars of Digital India to address the connectivity issue while enabling and providing technologies to facilitate delivery of services to citizens; outsourcing policy to create such centres in different northeastern states and in smaller towns across the country; Electronics Development Fund to promote innovation, research and product development to create a resource pool within the country, as also a self-sustaining eco-system of venture funds; National Centre for Flexible Electronics to promote research and innovation in the emerging area of flexible electronics; and Centre of Excellence on Internet on Things (IoT) as a joint initiative of the government agencies and private institutions such as Nasscom.

Narendra Modi in his address at the Digital India event had spoken at length on technological advancements and its impact on people and the nation as a whole. The following are the key takeaways from his speech at Digital India event in Silicon Valley:

- Facebook, Twitter and Instagram are the new neighbourhoods of our new world.
- If Facebook were a country, it would be the third most populous one and the most connected.
- Google today has made teachers less awe-inspiring and grandparents more idle.
- Twitter has turned everyone into a reporter.
- The traffic lights that need to work the best are on Cisco routers.
- The status that now matters is not whether you are awake or asleep, but whether you are online or offline.
- The most fundamental debate for our youth is the choice between Android, iOS and Windows.
- In India, a mother in a distant hill village has a better chance to save her new born infant. A child in a remote village has better access to education.

- The pace at which people are taking to digital technology defies our stereotypes of age, education, language and income.
- There may be still some who see digital economy as the tool of the rich, educated and the privileged. But ask the taxi driver or the corner vendor in India what he has gained from his cell phone, and the debate gets settled.
- I see technology as a means to empower and as a tool that bridges the distance between hope and opportunity. Social media is reducing social barriers. It connects people on the strength of human values, not identities.
- Technology is forcing governments to deal with massive volume of data and generate responses, not in 24 hours but in 24 minutes.
- We want to free our 1.25 billion citizens from the burden of excessive paper documents in every office. We want paperless transactions. We will set up a digital locker for every citizen to store personal documents that can be shared across departments.
- We must bridge the digital divide and promote digital literacy in the same way that we seek to ensure general literacy. We must ensure that technology is accessible, affordable, and adds value.
- We want our 1.25 billion citizens to be digitally connected. We already have broadband usage across India go up by 63 percent last year.
- We have launched an aggressive expansion of the National Optical Fibre Network that will take broadband to our 600,000 villages. We will connect all schools and colleges with broadband. Building I-ways are as important as highways.
- We want to ensure that free Wi-Fi is not only there in airport lounges, but also on our railway platforms. Teaming up with Google, we will cover 500 railway stations in a short time.

Information and Communication Revolution in India

Although IT is of recent origin, it is spreading fast in India. It emerged as an industry which through the use of computers and other supporting equipment helps in the spread of knowledge. With the rapid advancement in various information delivery systems such as radio, TV, telephone, newspapers, Fax and of course computers and computer networks, it broadly refers to the entire range of media and devices that are used to transmit and process information for use by people to perform various types of functions. IT has pervaded a wide range of industries, viz. manufacturing, education, entertainment, defence, trade and communications, among others. It can be segregated into four main components—(i) software products and engineering services, (ii) IT services, (iii) IT-enabled services, and (iv) hardware. The services of the industry are spanned over various segments covering software development, software services, software products, consulting services, BPO services, e-commerce and web services, engineering services off shoring and animation and gaming. Banking, Financial Services and Insurance (BFSI) is an industry which is highly dependent on IT-sector.

According to Mr. Low (2000), the activities of generating, processing, transmitting, disseminating, storing, achieving and retrieving information constitute the information industry, and the raw material that matters is intellectual. He states:

> The knowledge economy implies shift in the geographical centre from raw material and capital equipment to information and knowledge, especially in education and research centres and man-made brain industries. According to him, the influence of information technology is so strong that there is no sphere of human life in which it is not able to make a niche for itself. The knowledge economy depicts the automation of labour-intensive manufacturing and service activities, as well as growth in new service industries such as health care, distance learning, software production and multimedia entertainment.

Slowdown Signals

Low investment and capital expenditure by India Inc. has emerged as a cause of concern amidst declining revenue growth and low capacity utilization for companies. As a result, job creation in the corporate world has also taken a big hit. While infrastructure companies witnessed the biggest dip in employment numbers, the IT and pharma sectors provided the silver lining with increased staff strength. According to *The Indian Express* report by Sandeep Singh dated 23rd Dec. 2015, a look at the group of 230 leading companies listed on the Bombay Stock Exchange (BSE 500), with an aggregate market cap of over ₹ 55 lakh crore, shows that for the first time in at least four years they witnessed a decline in their aggregate employee strength as it fell by 14,000 in the year ended March 2015. While 105 out of 230 companies reduced their headcount by an aggregate of 84,688 during the year, 114 companies within the list increased their staff strength by 69,910. For the remaining 11 companies, the numbers remained constant.

Table 4.1: India Inc: Comparison of Employees Strength

(Number of Employees)

	Mar 2014	Mar 2015	Change
Biggest Falls			
Larsen & Toubro	54,579	44,081	- 10498
Vardhman Textiles	26,000	17,393	- 8607
Reliance Communications	14,169	9111	- 5058
McLeod Russel India	80,000	75,000	- 5000
Simplex Infrastructures Ltd.	8115	3195	- 4920
Biggest Additions			
Tata Consultancy Services	3,00,464	3,19,656	19,192
Apollo Hospitals Enterprise	35,878	40,065	4,187
Jubilant Foodworks Ltd.	24,969	27,122	2,153
Page Industries Ltd.	16,566	18,717	2151
Aurobindo Pharma Ltd.	9,500	11,500	2,000
Total for 230 cos.	2,156,136	2,141,358	14,778

All figures are number of employees for companies on standalone basis. Sun Pharma and Kotak Mahindra Bank too witnessed rise in employees strength but since it is on account of mergers, it has been kept out of the analysis.

Source: CMIE Prowess.

The biggest drop in the number of employees during the year was witnessed by companies in manufacturing, construction and infrastructure, and capital goods, whereas IT and pharma companies saw net addition to their employee strength. Banking and finance sector has seen a positive trend. A group of 33 banks—24 PSBs and nine private for whom data were available, shows that these banks have added an aggregate of 24,896 employees during the year. While Canara Bank and Bank of Maharashtra added a net of 5,190 and 4,617 employees respectively, HDFC Bank added 8,121 employees. The State Bank of India saw a drop by 9,571 from 2.22 lakh in March 2014 to 2.13 lakh in March 2015. ICICI Bank also witnessed a decline in employees strength by 4,369.

Job creation is emerging as a major concern in the formal sector. Chief Economic Advisor (CEA) to the Indian Government Arvind Subramanian says that there was job growth but mostly in the informal sector: "In India, we have a lot of employment growth but it is not registered and it is not high wage and high productivity...."

The internet gender gap is widening the global development gap and it needs to be bridged, says the chief operating officer of Facebook, Sheryl Sandberg.[6] The internet opens up a world of knowledge from digital books and Wikipedia to online courses. Research shows that when women have access to reading apps, they use them significantly more than men. Becoming connected also opens up economic opportunities. In a survey of large developing countries, nearly half of the women who were connected had applied for a job on the internet, and nearly a third had earned extra income online. On the South African site, Smart Business, which helps entrepreneurs, women make up 28 percent of the users and ask more than 60 percent of the questions. Armed with information, they grow economies. In India, the online store Pelli Poola Jada was started three years ago by three women and now they have employed 200 workers.

Empowering women economically is good for everyone. Improving their access to income and technology further improves child welfare and nutrition. Research shows that countries with more equality in employment and education have lower child mortality and faster economic growth. The Internet gives women voice and allows their voices to be heard. In Congo, the Hero Women have set up their own internet café to tell their stories, and they successfully petitioned for the appointment of a US special envoy to the war-torn region. In Kenya, women have set up 'Her Voice' to fight gender-based violence by advocating for legal reform and working with victim support groups. In Brazil, women have created 'I Will Not Shut Up', an app that maps assaults on women so that community leaders can be held accountable.

Internet helps women to get educated, start businesses, build communities, and assert their rights, but access to this vital resource is still restricted and sharply divided by gender. Globally, four billion people lack internet access, most of them women. In the developing world, nearly 25 percent fewer women than men are connected; in sub-Saharan Africa, it is 45 percent. This internet gender gap is widening the global development gap. The United Nations is committed to providing internet access for all by 2020. NGOs, governments and businesses are working together to get there—including tech firms like Google, whose Loon and Titan Aerospace projects aim to reach remote communities; Space X, which is planning a network of satellites to provide access; and Facebook, whose internet.org initiative uses the Free Basics app and website to connect people in 30 countries. Free Basics makes basic internet services—including news, search and health information—available for free. It is open to all developers, so anyone can create content for it.

Maya is an app that answers anonymous questions about everything from health to legal protection, and so is Baby Center, which 3.4 million families have used to learn about parenting. In just one month, in India, people on Free Basics accessed healthcare information one million times. In rural Colombo, people are using a Free Basics Service called 1DOC3 to speak to doctors. Free Basics is not the full internet—there is no sustainable economic model that can deliver that to everyone for free—but it is a bridge to the full internet. More than 50 percent of people who start with Free Basics pay for the full internet after 30 days—and in countries where Free Basics has been launched, the rate of new-user internet adoption is twice as fast. In a connected world where all people can find a way to a better future for themselves and their children, by working together to connect women, it is possible to make better future a reality.

Digital India and Make in India have been two of the major programmes launched by Prime Minister Narendra Modi. A number of initiatives have been taken under Digital India in the field of IT to empower people to access services relating to health, education, labour and employment, and commerce, among others. Digital India Week was launched on 1 July 2015 to impart knowledge to people about how they can empower themselves through this programme.

Digital India is comprised of a number of initiatives, each of which is targeted to prepare India for becoming a knowledge economy and for bringing good governance to citizens through synchronized and co-ordinated engagement of the entire government. The programme is being coordinated by the Department of Electronics and Information Technology (DeitY) in collaboration with various Central Ministries/Departments as well as State Governments. All the existing and ongoing e-governance initiatives are being revamped to align them with the principles of Digital India.

The Digital India programme aims at inclusive growth in areas of electronic services, products, manufacturing and job opportunities, etc. Its vision is centred on three key areas—Digital Infrastructure as a Utility to Every Citizen; Governance & Services on Demand; and Digital Empowerment of Citizens. The programme aims to provide Broadband Highways, Universal Access to Mobile Connectivity, Public Internet Access Programme, E-Governance which inter alia includes Reforming Government through Technology, e-Kranti—Electronic Delivery of Services, Information for All, Electronics Manufacturing with a target of net zero imports, IT for Jobs and Early Harvest Programmes. A number of projects/products like the following have already been launched:

- Digital Locker System which aims to minimize the usage of physical documents and enable sharing of e-documents across agencies.
- MyGov.in which has been implemented as a platform for citizen's engagement in governance, through a "Discuss", "Do" and "Disseminate" approach.
- eSign framework which would allow citizens to digitally sign a document online using Aadhaar authentication.
- Online Registration System (ORS) which has been introduced under the eHospital application, and would provide important services like online registration, payment of fees and appointment, online diagnostic reports, enquiring availability of blood online, etc.
- National Scholarships Portal which is a one-stop solution for end-to-end scholarship process—right from submission of student application, verification, sanction and disbursal—to end beneficiary for all the scholarships provided by the Government of India.

The estimated impact of Digital India by 2019 would be the provision of broadband connectivity in all panchayats, Wi-Fi in schools and universities and Public Wi-Fi hotspots. The programme will generate sizeable number of jobs in IT, Telecom and Electronics, both directly and indirectly. Success of this programme will make India digitally empowered and a leader in usage of IT in delivery of services related to different domains like health, education, agriculture, banking, etc.

During PM Narendra Modi's visit to America in September 2015, leaders from Silicon Valley, San Jose, and California expressed their support for Digital India. Mark Zuckerberg, CEO of Facebook changed his profile picture in support of Digital India and started a chain on Facebook and promised to work on Wi-Fi hotspots in rural area of India. Google committed to provide broadband connectivity on 500 railway stations in India. Microsoft agreed to provide broadband connectivity to five hundred thousand villages in India and make India its cloud hub through Indian data centres. Qualcomm announced an investment of US$ 150 million in Indian startups.[7] Oracle plans to invest in 20 states and will work on payments and Smart city initiatives.[8] However, cyber experts expressed their concern over internet.org and viewed the Prime Minister's bonhomie with Zuckerberg as the government's indirect approval of the controversial initiative. Later Prime Minister office clarified that net neutrality will be maintained at all costs and vetoed the Basic Internet plans.

According to *The Statesmen*, the government and the Telecom Regulatory Authority of India (TRAI) are blending towards the view that there is a need for a public law bringing out "dos and don'ts" to ensure net neutrality. According to, Zafar Rais, CEO, MindShift Interactive,

> At present, there are no legal provisions for either the government or the regulator to enforce non-discriminatory access to the Internet.... Net neutrality is extremely important for small business owners, start-ups and entrepreneurs, who can simply launch their businesses online, advertise the products and sell them openly, without any discrimination. It is essential for innovation and creating job opportunities. Big companies like Google, Twitter and several others are born out of net neutrality. With increasing internet penetration in India and given that we are becoming a breeding ground for start-ups and entrepreneurs, the lack of net neutrality should worry us greatly. Besides, it is very important for freedom of speech, so that one can voice his option without the fear of being blocked or banned.[9]

If the government implements this programme as enthusiastically as it is launching it and is able to muster support of the big companies, the programme will bring India to the forefront of highly digital nations. In taking support from abroad it has to be ensured that our own businesses do not suffer in any way, but are the beneficiaries for further development of the nation in the fields covered under the programme.

It goes to PM Modi's credit that he has envisioned this programme which is likely to change the life of millions in India.

Notes

1. Varun Gandhi, "On why Digital India is actually a good thing." *Daily O*, 16 July 2015.
2. Tech Talk: Digital India is too complex an idea by Javed Anwer, Mail Online India, *Mail Today*, 4 July 2015.
3. Rajeev Chandrasekhar, Rajya Sabha M.P. and a technocrat. *Times of India,* New Delhi. 26 October 2015.
4. S.R. Hashim, "Employment and Unemployment in a Society in Transition". *Indian Journal of Labour Economics* (Vol. 43, No. 1, 2000.
5. Sameer Kochhar, Chairman SKOCH Group in "Modi's Odyssey: Digital India, Developed India". *The Indian Express.* 14 December 2015.
6. Sheryl Sandberg, "Empowering women economically is good for everyone", *The Indian Express*, 10 December 2015.
7. K. Thomas, "Modi effect: Silicon Valley giants commit to Digital India." *The Hindu*, 27 September 2015.
8. "Digital India to propel economy to its best era: Oracle", Moneycontrol.com. 8 October 2015.
9. Saket Suman, "Digital India at the expense of net neutrality?" *The Statesman*, 8 October 2015.

ANNEXURE–I

Press Information Bureau
Government of India
Cabinet

20-August-2014 20:57 IST

Digital India—A Programme to Transform India into Digital Empowered Society and Knowledge Economy

The Cabinet today at the meeting chaired by the Prime Minister, Shri Narendra Modi gave its approval for Digital India—a programme to transform India into digital empowered society and knowledge economy. This is a follow-up to the key decisions taken on the design of the programme during the meeting of the Prime Minister on Digital India Programme on August 7, 2014, and to sensitize all ministries to this vast programme touching every corner of the government. This programme has been envisaged by Department of Electronics and Information Technology (DeitY).

The vision of Digital India aims to transform the country into a digitally empowered society and knowledge economy. The programme will be implemented in phases from the current year till 2018. The Digital India is transformational in nature and would ensure that government services are available to citizens electronically. It would also bring in public accountability through mandated delivery of government's services electronically, a Unique ID and e-Pramaan based on authentic and standard-based inter-operable and integrated government applications and data basis.

The source of funding for most of the e-governance projects at present is through budgetary provisions of respective Ministries/Departments in the Central or State Governments. Requirements of funds for individual project(s) for Digital India will be worked out by respective Nodal Ministries/ Departments.

The vision areas of Digital India are as under:

I. Infrastructure as Utility to Every Citizen:

(i) High speed internet as a core utility shall be made available in all gram panchayats.

(ii) Cradle to grave digital identity—unique, lifelong, online and authenticable.

(iii) Mobile phone and bank account would enable participation in digital and financial space at individual level.

(iv) Easy access to a Common Service Centre within their locality.

(v) Shareable private space on a public Cloud.

(vi) Safe and secure cyberspace in the country.

II. Governance and Services on Demand:

(i) Seamlessly integrated across departments or jurisdictions to provide easy and a single window access to all persons.

(ii) Government services available in real time from online and mobile platforms.

(iii) All citizen entitlements to be available on the Cloud to ensure easy access.

(iv) Government services digitally transformed for improving Ease of Doing Business.

(v) Making financial transactions above a threshold, electronic and cashless.

(vi) Leveraging GIS for decision support systems and development.

III. Digital Empowerment of Citizens:

(i) Universal digital literacy.

(ii) All digital resources universally accessible.

(iii) All government documents/certificates to be available on the Cloud.

(iv) Availability of digital resources/services in Indian languages.

(v) Collaborative digital platforms for participative governance.

(vi) Portability of all entitlements for individuals through the Cloud.

Scope of Digital India

The overall scope of this programme is:

(i) to prepare India for a knowledge future.

(ii) on being transformative that is to realize IT (Indian Talent) + IT (Information Technology) = IT (India Tomorrow)

(iii) making technology central to enabling change.

(iv) on being an Umbrella Programme—covering many departments.

- The programme weaves together a large number of ideas and thoughts into a single, comprehensive vision, so that each of them is seen as part of a larger goal. Each individual element stands on its own, but is also part of the larger picture.
- The weaving together makes the Mission transformative in totality.

(v) The Digital India Programme will pull together many existing schemes which would be restructured and re-focused and implemented in a synchronized manner. The common branding of the programmes as Digital India, highlights their transformative impact.

Digital India aims to provide the much needed thrust to the nine pillars of growth areas, namely

(i) Broadband Highways,

(ii) Universal Access to Mobile Connectivity,

(iii) Public Internet Access Programme,

(iv) e-Governance: Reforming Government through Technology,

(v) e-Kranti—Electronic Delivery of Services,

(vi) Information for All,

(vii) Electronics Manufacturing,

(viii) IT for Jobs, and

(ix) Early Harvest Programmes.

all foreign investments can only function after authorization from the MHA. Under the new system, serious offences like money laundering and clearly stated threats to national security will be the reasons for denying security clearances. It will be more transparent and even more liberal so as to do away with subjective reasoning, often relied upon by officials to deny clearance.

In fact, "starting a business in a day" tops the government's agenda and the MHA's security clearance is part of a blueprint for allowing business to be hassle-free, and removing several obstacles in doing business in India. The reforms that are being deliberated target improving India's position in the 'Ease of Doing Business' Index according to which India is ranked at 134 among the 189 countries. Now the aim is to bring it in the top 50 list by introducing radical measures planned by the Department of Industrial Policy and Promotion which is functioning under the Ministry of Commerce. India's ranking in the case of doing business is below its neighbouring countries such as China (96), Nepal (105), Pakistan (110) and Bangladesh (135). As in Canada and New Zealand, the reforms are being targeted in India to reduce the time taken from 27 days to one day for starting a business.

Since the launch of Make in India campaign in September 2014, FDI into the country has witnessed a 48 percent jump in the seven-month period between October 2014 and April 2015, and a 31 percent increase, valued at US$ 9.50 billion, between April and June 2015. Renewed relationships with other countries have helped the initiative attract a lot of interest from foreign investors. India has received US$ 19.78 billion of FDI in 2014-15 from a dozen countries visited by Narendra Modi. Among the countries he visited, Japan has committed to invest US$ 35 billion in five years, South Korea US$ 10 billion, China US$ 20 billion in five years France US$ 2 billion, and UAE has assured to pump in money for India's US$ 75 billion infrastructure fund.

At the domestic front, the government's decision to insist that the Indian Air Force (IAF) inducts a large number of Light Combat Aircraft (LCA) fighters is a kind of renewed thrust that was needed to push the Make in India project. It has rejected the

IAF's demand for 44 more Rafale aircraft in addition to the deal for 36 announced by the government earlier. Instead, the IAF was told that the kind of numbers it wanted could only be met by inducting the LCA. As per India's security requirements, the government wants to encourage manufacture of lighter fighter planes like the home-grown Tejas of which about 120 are to be inducted for the use of IAF. The government is making an overall strategy assessment and then pinning down the kind of capabilities needed by India's armed forces.

The first and foremost step that the current incumbent government took in shaping the skills landscape was the creation of a separate Ministry of Skill Development and Entrepreneur ship which in the last one year has invested heavily on restructuring and re-energising the skill ecosystem in the country. It has made some significant efforts in ensuring coordination and convergence across all initiatives and schemes that were active in the skill ecosystem.

MSDE took its mandate as the nodal agency for skill training, a step forward by translating its policy framework into a coherent programme of action, to deliver results on the ground. Its programme interventions are guided by the principles of "Speed, Scale and Quality".

The newly-constituted Ministry of Skill Development and Entrepreneurship has a mammoth task to realize the government's dream. Given the fact that 65 percent of the population is below the age of 35 and a majority of them are not properly skilled, one can estimate the challenges ahead. Only two percent workforce in the country is skilled and about 1.2 crore youths enter the market every year. At the time of launching the scheme by Narendra Modi, it appeared a distant dream for many people because the target for skilling will be aligned to demand from other flagship programmes, including Make in India, Digital India, National Solar Mission, Clean Ganga, and Swachh Bharat Abhiyan.

The government had set a target of 10 lakh skilling in 2014. National Skill Development Corporation (NSDC) has trained only about 3.50 lakh people and the target of about six lakh people remained as on 2015. India's position is beyond comparison if we look at the skilled workforce in a few select countries. Only 10 percent of the total workforce in the country receive any kind of skill training—2% with formal training and 8% with informal training, and further more, 80 percent of the entrants do not get the opportunity for skill development. This is in sharp contrast to countries like South Korea, which has 96 percent of its population trained in vocational skills, in Japan it is 80 percent, in Germany 75 percent, and 70 percent in Britain. Though the new ministry has been constituted, it vitally needs wider coordination from other ministries to achieve the set objectives of this idealistic initiative.

International Acceptance for Make in India

Modi-led NDA Government's manifesto itself had stated that it will build a strong, self-reliant and self-confident India and regain its rightful place in the comity of nations. Massive efforts were planned to leverage all resources and people to play a greater role on the international level too. Modi's vision, thus, redefines India's interests in technological and economic development. During 2014-15, he visited 17 countries to strengthen India's relations with international community. Some of the visits were to attend routine meetings, of which India has been a member. He went to Australia for a G-20 meeting, to Brazil for a BRICS meeting, to Nepal for SAARC meeting, and to the U.S. for the UN General Assembly meeting. He also went to Myanmar for a meeting of ASEAN, of which India is not a member. His other visits were state visits for which India has been an official invitee. International acceptance for Make in India vis-à-vis select countries is summarized below.

U.S.

India and U.S. made a new beginning with the visit of Narendra Modi, after becoming the Prime Minister of India. Both the nations issued a joint vision statement promising that their strategic partnership would work to combat terror threats, respond to humanitarian disasters, prevent the spread of weapons of mass destruction, and to mitigate the impact of climate change. India-U.S. strategic ties are a joint endeavour for peace, and security cooperation between the two will make the world secure, said the vision called "Chalein Saath Saath: Forward Together We Go." Both the sides agreed to support an "open and inclusive rules-based global order, in which India assumes greater multilateral responsibility, including in a reformed United Nations Security Council." Skill development, joint research and collaboration in space and health, besides cooperation at international for a such as the WTO were the other areas where both sides promised to collaborate. "We have a vision that the U.S. and India will have a transformative relationship as trusted partners in the 21st century. Our partnership will be a model for the rest of the world," the statement added. Fast track diplomacy and smart development objective took Modi to the U.S. where he attended a huge reception hosted by the Indian diaspora. He addressed UNGA on 27 September 2014 expressing his concerns over the relevance of a 20th century setup in 21st century and the need to evaluate UN's performance in the past 70 years.

The main purpose of his U.S. visit was to attract investments for India and part of his attempt to brainstorm for getting ideas in promoting his vision of exclusive development. During his deliberations with President Obama, Modi reiterated his Make in India plan, his development vision and how he felt the U.S. could help out in this vision.

Recognising the important role that India and U.S. play in promoting peace, prosperity, stability and security in the Asia-Pacific and India Ocean Region, and noting that India's 'Act East Policy' and the United States' rebalance to Asia provide opportunities for India, the U.S. and other Asia-Pacific countries to work closely to strengthen regional ties, a joint strategic vision was announced to guide their engagement in the region. The two countries signed an implementing agreement between the National Aeronautics and Space Administration (NASA) and Indian Space Research Organisation (ISRO) to conduct the joint NASA-ISRO Synthetic Aperture Radar (NISAR) mission. They convened a defence policy group and its subgroups to pursue stranger and expanded bilateral defence cooperation. They had made a breakthrough on issues relating to the implementation of the Bali Ministerial Decisions regarding public stockholding for food security purposes, the WTO Trade Facilitation Agreement, and post Bali work. They have convened a Joint Commission Meeting on Science and Technology Cooperation to review, exchange views, and advance cooperation in diverse areas of science and technology and foster engagement in techno-entrepreneurship and innovation partnership for mutual benefit. The India-U.S. Higher Education Dialogue has strengthened the bilateral cooperation in the field of higher education by strengthening partnerships between Indian and U.S. universities and community colleges, improving student and scholar mobility, and promoting faculty collaboration. Indian Renewable Energy Development Agency Ltd. and the Export-Import Bank of the U.S. have signed a MoU, which would make available upto $1 billion in financing to facilitate expanded cooperation and enhance U.S. private sector investment in Indian clean energy projects. The High Technology Cooperation Group has been convened to shape a cooperative agenda on high technology goods, including export control-related trade in homeland security technologies, high technology manufacturing equipment including machine tools, defence trade, and fostering collaboration in biotechnology, pharmaceuticals, medical devices, and health-related information technology.

There MoUs have been signed between the State Governments of Andhra Pradesh, Uttar Pradesh, and Rajasthan and the U.S. Trade and Development Agency to develop Vishakhapatnam, Allahabad, and Ajmer as Smart Cities. The Trade Policy Forum has been convened at the ministerial level where India and U.S. Agreed to work towards resolving commercial impediments in both markets, to help realize the potential of bilateral trade in goods and services, and to promote investment and manufacturing. A framework on investment initiative has been signed to jointly cooperate on facilitating capital market development conductive to financing investment, creating an environment that encourages investment in various sectors in India; and working to overcome any obstacles to such investment. The Information and Communications Technology (ICT) Working Group has been convened for signing of the Joint Declaration of Intent to advance implementation of the

Digital India programme and further bilateral commercial ICT cooperation. Both the countries have signed on the Statement of Cooperation for Supervisory Cooperation and Exchange of Supervisory Information between the Reserve Bank of India and Federal Deposit Insurance Corporation (FDIC), Federal Reserve System, and Office of the Comptroller of Currency (OCC). A MoU has been signed between the United States for International Development (USAID) and the Ministry of Urban Development to enable USAID to share expertise, best practices, innovation and technologies in support of India's efforts to strengthen water, sanitation and hygine (WASH) in urban areas. A MoU between the U.S. Department of Treasury and India's Ministry of Finance has been signed to enhance cooperation to combat money laundering and the financing of terrorism. A Joint Declaration of Intent between USAID and the Ministry of Human Resource Development has been signed for technical support to the Indian Institutes of Technology (IITs), starting with IIT Gandhinagar, to strengthen research and entrepreneurship capabilities. The U.S.-India defense relationship has been finalized which will guide and expand the bilateral defence and strategic partnership over the next ten years. An agreement for bilateral engagement on the Defence Technology and Trade Initiative (DTTI) has been signed to pursue co-production and co-development of four pathfinder projects, form a working group to explore aircraft carrier technology sharing and design, and explore possible cooperation on development of jet engine technology.

Obama reiterated his support for Modi's vision to transform India, and recognized that India's focus on its development priorities presented substantial opportunities for forging stronger India-U.S. economic ties and greater people-to-people contacts. The two leaders pledged to translate their commitment of "Chalein Saath Saath: Forward Together We Go" into action through "Sanjha Prayaas; Sab ka Vikaas: Shared Effort; Progress for All." They committed to explore areas of collaboration in skill development ranging from establishing quality assurance systems for skilling certification standards, setting up of skill development centres, nurturing and promoting social entrepreneurship and strengthening the innovation and entrepreneurship ecosystem. They agreed to collaborate in the implementation of India's ambitious Digital India programme and expand commercial cooperation, including by encouraging investment engagement in the Information and Communication Technology (ICT) sector. They also pledged to collaborate through India's Global Initiative of Academic Networks (GIAN), to facilitate short-term teaching and research programmes by upto 1000 visiting U.S. academics in Indian universities. They also reaffirmed the importance of on-going efforts to strengthen women's participation in science, technology, engineering, and math through networking and mentoring programmes. They agreed to further promote cooperative and commercial relations between India and the United States in the field of space. They noted the on-going interactions between their space agencies, including towards realizing a dual frequency radar imaging satellite for Earth Sciences, and exploring possibilities for cooperation in studying Mars.

India and U.S. reaffirmed their commitment to the Global Health Security Agenda (GHSA) and announced specific actions at home and abroad to prevent the spread of infectious diseases, including a CDC-Ministry of Health Ebola and GHSA preparedness training, expansion of the India Epidemic Intelligence Service, and development of a road map to achieve the objectives of the GHSA within three years.

Both the countries acknowledged the bilateral military ties as the foundation of the defense relationship and encouraged their respective militaries to pursue additional opportunities for engagement through exercises, military personnel exchanges, and defense dialogues. The two countries also acknowledged the need for the two-way defence engagement to include technology cooperation and collaboration, coproduction and codevelopment. Obama welcomed. Modi's initiatives to liberalize the Foreign Direct Investment Policy regime in the defence sector and agreed to cooperate on India's efforts to establish a defence industrial base in India, including through initiatives like 'Make in India'.

Under the 'Make in India' initiative, the U.S. has proposed joint development and production of futuristic military helicopters as well as infantry combat vehicles in the first such big-ticket programmes under the DTTI with India. India has already shown interest in the U.S. offer for participation in its "future vertical-lift (FVL) aircraft" programme, which includes development of five different helicopters or "capability sets" overt he next 15 years at a cost of around $ 8 billion. The U.S. has also suggested that the future infantry combat vehicle (FICV) project can be a trilateral venture with the inclusion of Israel. With the U.S. now officially designating India as a "major defence partner" at par with its closest allies to facilitate the transfer of advanced technology, the two new projects are quite ambitious in scope. The U.S. also pushing F/A-18 or F-16 fighter production line under 'Make in India' policy. India has also inked $3.1 billion deal for 22 Apache attack and 15 Chinook heavy-lift helicopters from the U.S., which are slated for delivery in 2019-20.

Japan

Modi chose Japan as his first destination for bilateral visit outside the Indian subcontinent, during 30 August to 3 September 2014, indicating the Government's intention to make ties with Japan the heart of India's Look East Policy. Japan is of paramount importance for India to realize its Make in India dream and also for peace, stability and prosperity of India in particular and Asia at large. He visited Japan twice, in 2007 and 2012, as Chief Minister of Gujarat and has been successful in attracting Japanese companies to his home state of Gujarat. Japanese PM Shinzo Abe was invited as the Chief Guest at the Republic Day celebrations on 26 January 2015.

Over 1,000 Japanese companies have set up base in India, making Japan the fourth largest investor in India which include Sony, Toyota, Hitachi and Mitsubishi. In the last 12 years, Japanese companies have invested US$ 12.66 billion in India which accounts for seven percent of total FDI inflow into India. During Modi's visit, the two countries upgraded the relationship to a 'Special Strategic and Global Partnership'. Both sides also agreed to establish the 'India-Japan Investment Promotion Partnership.' Japanese PM Abe pledged to realize public and private investments worth JPY 3.5 trillion and doubling of the number of Japanese companies in India over the next five years. The investments are for financing projects in the areas of infrastructure, connectivity, transport systems, smart cities, rejuvenation of Ganga and other rivers, manufacturing, clean energy, skill development, water security, food processing, agro industry, agricultural cold chain, and rural development. A 'Japan-India Make in India Special Finance Facility' of JPY 1.3 trillion was also established.

Japan also pledged Overseas Development Assistance (ODA) loan of 50 billion yen to India Infrastructure Finance Company Ltd. (IIFCL) for PPP infrastructure projects in India. Japanese PM urged Modi to introduce Shinkansen high speed railway system for Ahmedabad-Mumbai route for which Japan agreed to provide financial, technical and operational support. The two Prime Ministers welcomed the progress in the on-going flagship projects of India-Japan economic partnership, such as the Western Dedicated Freight Corridor (DFC), Delhi-Mumbai Industrial Corridor (DMIC), Chennai-Bengaluru Industrial Corridor (CBIC) and committed to accelerate their implementation.

Joint statement on India and Japan Vision 2025 states that the two Prime Ministers, Modi and Abe, resolved to transform the India-Japan Special Strategic and Global Partnership, a key relationship with the largest potential for growth, into a deep, broad-based and action-oriented partnership, which results a broad convergence of their long-term political, economic and strategic goals. They committed to realise a peaceful, open, equitable, stable and rule-based order in the Indo-Pacific region and beyond. For it they underlined the need for closer coordination and effective communication, bilaterally and with partners, to address existing and emerging challenges in spheres of security, stability and sustainable development. Recognising the importance of people to people exchanges and cultural ties, they resolved to boost opportunities for study, tourism, youth exchanges and educational collaboration to deepen broad-based and diversified engagement between the two peoples.

Seeking the synergy between India's "Act East" policy and Japan's "Partnership for Quality Infrastructure," the two prime ministers decided to develop and strengthen reliable, sustainable and resilient infrastructures that augment connectivity within India and between India and other countries in the region. They pledged to advance industrial networks and regional value chains with open, fair and transparent business environment in the region.

Prime Minister Abe commended Modi's strong initiatives such as Make in India, Digital India, Skill India, Clean India, and Smart City; and expressed his intention to support India's efforts by sharing its advanced skills and technologies and through active mobilisation of Japanese public and private sector involvement, including Overseas Development Assistance (ODA). Modi welcomed the "Japan-India Make-in-India Special Finance Facility" up to 1.5 trillion Yen by Nippon Export and Investment Insurance (NEXI) and Japan Bank for International Cooperation (JBIC), which aims to promote direct investment of Japanese companies and trade from Japan to India, to support their business activities with counterparts in India, including development of necessary infrastructure, and to help Materialise Make-in-India policy of the Government of India. Japanese PM Abe also expressed Japan's intention to provide ODA loans for the improvement of road network connectivity in north eastern states of India, the peripheral ring road surrounding Bengaluru, and the horticulture irrigation in Jharkhand.

The two PMs reaffirmed the intention to develop "Japan Industrial Townships" (JITs), with investment incentive for companies that would not be lower than under the prevailing policy framework such as Special Economic Zone (SEZ), and National Investment and Manufacturing Zone (NIMZ). Moreover, both sides will work toward evolving special packages for attracting Japanese investment in the Japanese Industrial Townships in India. The Japanese side also expressed the intention of establishing a new mechanism, "Japan-India IoT Investment Initiative", to promote investment in Internet of Things (IoT) related area from India to Japan.

The two PMs recognised the importance of close collaboration in the electricity and energy sector through such measures as use of high-efficiency and environmentally friendly coal-fired power generation technology, and Clean Coal Technology (CCT) including Integrated Gasification Fuel Cell (IGFC) once developed, and renewable energy and promotion of energy efficiency.

India and Japan expressed satisfaction to the continuous strengthening of their institutionalised Science and Technology cooperation. They shared their intention to raise the level of their ambition through the establishment of joint research laboratories; enhanced exchanges between young scientists and those under "Japan-Asia Youth Exchange Programme in Science"; the establishment of joint research centres in India in the field of ICT; stem cell research collaboration; and the joint fellowship programme for young researchers.

Japanese PM Abe welcomed India's intensified engagement with export control regimes. The two PMs affirmed their commitment to work together for India to become a full member in the four international export control regimes—Nuclear Suppliers Group, Missile Technology Control Regime, Wassenaar Arrangement and Australia Group, with the aim of strengthening the international non-proliferation efforts.

The two PMs welcomed the launch of cooperation in the field of healthcare. They appreciated the growing cooperation in the field of women empowerment. Abe briefed Modi on his efforts to create a 'society in which all women shine'; and Modi stressed the need to recognise the power of women and their important role in nation-building and the development journey of the country.

Australia

Narendra Modi became the first Indian Prime Minister to embark on a bilateral visit to Australia after 28 years, from 16 to 18 November 2014, following the G-20 Summit. He held wide-ranging talks with Australian Prime Minister Tony Abbott, addressed a joint sitting of both houses of the Parliament (the first time an Indian prime minister has done so) and met the President of the Senate, the Speaker of the House of Representatives and the Leader of the Opposition in Canberra.

He also visited Brisbane, Sydney and Melbourne and took the opportunity to meet various political leaders, academics, business people and sportspersons; and addressed members of the Australian Indian community. Australia comes under India's extended neighbourhood. Touching upon the Make in India initiative, Modi said that India considers Australia as a vital partner in its quest for progress and prosperity and invited Australia to be a major partner in India's inclusive development in every sector—agriculture, food processing, mining, infrastructure, manufacturing, finance, technology, and energy.

The two PMs Modi and Abbott recognised that the partnership has tremendous room for growth and agreed to unlock the vast potential of the economic relationship, especially in priority areas such as resources, education, skills, agriculture, infrastructure, investments, financial services and health. They directed that an equitable, balanced, mutually beneficial and high quality Comprehensive Economic Cooperation Agreement be brought to an early conclusion to realise the potential of commercial relations. They agreed to expedite approvals for key mining investment projects and cooperate on clean coal technologies and welcomed the intention to explore opportunities for partnership between Australian institutions and the Indian School of Mines in Dhanbad. They also agreed on a new Framework for Security Cooperation to guide closer bilateral collaboration across the security spectrum, including in defence, counter-terrorism, cyber policy, disarmament and non-proliferation and maritime security. They have welcomed the signing of a Social Security Agreement, which will enhance two-way mobility and lower business costs.

Australia participated in Make in India Week in Mumbai with a large delegation of government and business leaders representing a wide range of Australian ingenuity in multiple sectors. Australia's engagement in Make in India Week was an important step in converting business opportunities into outcomes for the two nations. According to Chris Elstoft, Acting High Commissioner, "Each of the sectors from Australian business taking part in the event will be crucial to India achieving its Make in India dream." As Prime Minister Modi suggested when he visited Australia, in every area of national priority for India, he sees Australia as a natural partner: "this delegation embodies that seamless fit between Indian priorities and Australian capability." The sectors represented included energy, resources and water, industrial design, infrastructure investment, pharmaceutical research, agribusiness, metals recycling for manufacturing inputs, etc. Hosting a Country Session, Australia showcased its expertise across a number of sectors and highlighted its engagement in India by large corporations to small companies.

Two of Australia's biggest resource companies—Rio Tinto and Woodside, and industrial design expert Mark Watson have shown interest in Smart Cities. It was mutually agreed that India would hold a Make in India show in Australia and Australia would hold a Business Week in India.

France

France was first destination of Prime Minister Modi's state visit of three European countries which commenced in April 2015. France is an important country enjoying growing cooperation with India in strategic sectors, especially in defence, space, civil nuclear energy, and security as well as expanding trade and investment ties, cooperation in science and technology, among other sectors.

Francois Hollande, President of France appreciated Modi's initiative for the development of smart cities as a key area to foster sustainable development solutions and showed his country's willingness to be a partner in it. He said France was ready to implement its best technological solution and share its experience in the field of integrated sustainable cities, particularly in urban planning, urban grids, water and sanitation, sustainable mobility, and digital technologies. Cooperation in the field of transport included a study by National Society of French Railways (SNCF) on upgradation of the Delhi-Chandigarh line to run 200 kmph and for redevelopment of Ambala and Ludhiana railway stations.

Current global trends and rapid socio-economic changes in India are creating a range of new opportunities for France and India to work together; particularly for Make in India initiative for which considerable potential for expansion, startup and skilling for India was noted. The French President welcomed the initiative aimed at transforming India and acknowledged that it presented significant opportunities for French business and industry. It was also noted with satisfaction that a number of new and ongoing projects of French companies were in line with the Make in India policy. France appreciated Modi's initiative to receive delegations of French CEOs in infrastructure and defence sectors to encourage them further in this direction.

Defence manufacturing in the key to Make in India programme and, for instance, French company, DCNS, is reportedly in negotiations with the Indian companies for collaboration in manufacturing in India. France has shown interest in intensification of cooperation in collaboration in defence technologies and research and development, apart from defence cooperation.

France has also shown its major emphasis on the Make in India programme and is ready to assist India's ambitious programme in the manufacturing sector. In the Business meeting with industry leaders, both and PMs Modi and Hollande advocated the economic needs and opportunities of 'Make in India' programme. France and India have also launched the CEO forum. In the Joint Statement, both the PMs appreciated the first meeting of the CEO forum, which was held in a short time frame of nine months. As part of 'Make in India' initiative, an agreement was signed between Airbus Group and Mahindra to Manufacture helicopters.

France is already supporting India's efforts to secure its energy supply and develop its sources of renewable energy, including solar power. India welcomed the target set by French companies aimed at developing 8 to 10 GW of solar energy in India by 2020-22. France also extended its support for other renewable sources such as wind, biomass, and hydropower in addition to confirming the target of AFD (Agence Francaise de

Development) credit line of one billion euros over the next three years for sustainable infrastructure and urban development in India. Welcoming the decision of Government of India to support the organization of a Regional Hindi Conference, for the first time in Paris in view of the growing interest in Hindi in that country, France expressed a mutual interest in boosting the number and quality of student exchanges and signed an MoU for knowledge partnership and cooperation in the area of qualification registers between National Skill Development Agency (NSDA) under the Ministry of Skill Development and Entrepreneurship of India and Commission Nationale de la Certification Professionnelle (CNCP) of France. Another MoU was signed between the Department of Biotechnology under the Indian Ministry of Science and Technology, and the Centre National de la Recherche Scientifique (CNRS) and the Universite Pierre et Marie Curie (UPMC) to collaborate towards the establishment of a National Institute of Marine Biology and Biotechnology in India.

Prime Minister Modi in his April 2015 tour to France paid a visit to the Airbus facility at Toulouse where he promoted Make in India campaign and urged the aerospace giant to cultivate manufacturing opportunities in India, and consequently Airbus committed to increase its outsourcing from India from current level of US$ 400 million to US$ 2 billion by 2020.

China

The MoUs signed by India and China span a wide range of industries including renewable energy, power infrastructure, steel, small and medium industries, among others and are a reflection of the strong interest of Chinese companies to invest in India and contribute towards Make in India initiative. They will also facilitate cooperation between Indian and Chinese companies in the film and entertainment industry. Establishment of a new Consulate General at Chengdu and in Chennai, by India and China, respectively would facilitate enhanced trade and economic engagement, people-to-people exchanges and tourism.

Bilateral cooperation in the field of vocational education and skill development will strengthen technical cooperation and help share best practices and knowledge, and will work towards capacity development and delivery of vocational education in India, including the setting up of vocational training institutes in India. Setting up of Skill Development and Entrepreneurship Institute in India will help develop curriculum in trade and industry. Cooperation in railway will get further boost in India with cooperation in speed-raising of existing routes (Chennai-Bengaluru-Mysore) and cooperation in high-speed rail (Delhi-Nagpur or Delhi-Chennai route). Cooperations in railway station redevelopment, heavy-haul training and establishment of Railway University constitute the Action Plan between the National Railway Administration of the people's Republic of China and the Ministry of Railways of the Republic of India on Enhancing Cooperation in the Railway Sector (2015-2016).

Education Exchange Programme between India and China will encourage government departments and the educational institutions of the two countries to enhance the contacts and cooperation in the field of education, and provide scholarships to students from the two countries in each other's educational institutions. Cooperation in the fields of mining and mineral sector will establish a basis for the mutually beneficial exchange of information concerning progress on geoscience, investigation and management of geohazards, mineral exploration, etc. It also envisages encouraging mining investment and mining sideline products, service and technology exchange between India and China. The themes selected for space cooperation include cooperation on remote-sensing missions, space-based meteorology, lunar and deep-space exploration, piggy-back launching, satellite navigation, components, education and training.

Agreement on tourism between India and China attains a special significance in view of the Year 2015 and 2016 being designated as Visit India Year and Visit China Year, respectively. It aims at enhancing bilateral cooperation in tourism sector through cooperation between hotels and tour operators, capacity-building in tourism sector, investment in tourism and hospitality sectors and exchange of visits of tour operators, media and opinion-makers. The India-China Think-Tanks Forum will bring together scholars of both the countries to deliberate on contemporary issues of regional and international significance. It will enhance exchanges in the fields of area studies, security, economics, strategic thought, and demographics.

The MoUs also seek furthering cooperation and understanding on strategic macroeconomic and policy issues and establishment of a basis for exchange of research information, visits, joint workshop and joint research, providing a framework for collaboration for research in earthquake sciences, earthquake engineering and geosciences, exchange of scientific resources, personnel and technical knowledge, cooperation in the fields of trade and investment, agriculture, skill development, smart cities, urban planning, clean energy, etc. Two significant MoUs include establishment of a Center for Gandhian and Indian Studies focusing on Gandhian thought and practice, Indian politics, economy, language, religion and culture, Buddhism and ancient India-China contacts, promoting academic exchanges and teaching of Indian languages. Establishment of a Yoga College at Yunnan Minzu University (YMU) in Kunming will promote yoga education, therapy and research. Under this MoU, Indian Council for Cultural Research (ICCR) will assist in planning, training, promotion and coordination, while YMU will provide physical infrastructure and other facilities for a Yoga College in Yunnan.

Prime Minister Narendra Modi's visit to China from 14-16 May 2015 saw a record of 24 agreements signed by both the countries in key sectors, including railways and education worth over US$ 10 billion. Included in it were protocol for setting up Consulates-General at Chengdu and Chennai besides an MoU on consultative mechanism for cooperation in trade negotiations, cooperation in vocational education, skill development and setting up of Mahatma Gandhi institute on skill development at Ahmedabad in India, and an action plan between the Indian Railways and China National Railways for enhancing cooperation in the railway sector.

Other very important agreements signed in Beijing by Narendra Modi and his Chinese counterpart Keqiang included cooperation in the fields of mining and minerals, space cooperation outline, safety regulations on importing Indian rapeseed meal, broadcasting agreement between Chinese state-run CCTV and Doordarshan, cooperation in the field of tourism, MoU on establishing India-China Think-Tank Forum, MoU between NITI Aayog and China's Development Research Centre, cooperation in earthquake science and engineering, in ocean sciences, climate change and cryosphere, geosciences, and cooperation between India's Foreign Ministry and Central Committee of Communist Party of China.

For the first time India and China signed agreements on cooperation between states and municipalities, establishment of India-China State Leaders Forum, establishment of sister states Sichuan and Karnataka, sister cities Chennai and Chongqing; Hyderabad and Gingdao; Aurangabad and Dunhuang, and MoUs between ICCR and Fudan University for establishment of Centre for Gandhian Studies, and for the establishment of yoga college in Kunming.

On the economic front, India and China signed 12 different agreements worth a total value of US$ 20 billion Chinese investment in India over five years in a bid to boost economic ties and address India's concerns over trade deficit. India looks at possible investors for its infrastructure sector, which needs around US$ 1 trillion. According to India-China Business Forum, China has a foreign reserve of around US$ 4 trillion. During his visit to China, Modi tried to communicate India's needs and opportunities for Chinese investments. He also raised the issue of imbalance in India-China bilateral trade which has reached around US$ 48 billion that needs to be corrected. India, being an eager partner in the Asia Infrastructure Investment Bank (AIIB), looks forward to benefitting from Chinese initiative.

People's Republic of Korea and Mongolia

In his Korea visit on May 18 and 19, 2015, Modi and President Park Geun-hye of the Republic of Korea agreed to upgrade the bilateral relationship to a 'Special Strategic Partnership' and resolved to add new substance, speed and content in the partnership in a wide range of areas including foreign affairs, defence, trade and investment, science and technology, culture and people-to-people exchanges and regional cooperation to take the bilateral relations to a qualitatively higher level. India sees Korea as an indispensable partner in its "Act East" strategy. The Ministry of Strategy and Finance and the Export-Import Bank of Korea expressed their intention to provide US$ 10 billion for infrastructure, comprising Economic Development Cooperation Fund (US$ 1 billion) and export credits (US$ 9 billion) for India's priority sectors, including smart cities, railways, power generation and transmission, etc. Cooperation in the steel sector and shipbuilding, including the construction of Indian vessels such as LNG carriers, Korean Industrial Park in Rajasthan, etc. has been vital for Make in India initiative.

Indian PM, Narendra Modi, paid a state visit to Mongolia from 16 to 18 May 2015. The two Prime Ministers, Modi and Chimediin Saikhanbileg, Prime Minister of Mongolia, underscored the significance of the visit in the backdrop of 60th anniversary of diplomatic relations between Mongolia and India. It is the first ever visit by an Indian Prime Minister marking the dawn of a new era in Mongolia-India relations. Both the countries have been cooperating with each other in the area of cyber security domain. Mongolian PM expressed his appreciation to India's support to set up a cyber security centre in Mongolia. He agreed to encourage Indian companies to explore more opportunities in Mongolia's mining sector through joint ventures and investment. He also appreciated India's gesture of providing Bhabhatron-II tele-therapy unit and a radiotherapy simulator, designed, developed and manufactured in India to the National Cancer Centre of Mongolia.

The two Prime Ministers noted with satisfaction the decision to set up a joint school in Ulaanbaatar, and welcomed the selection of a project management consultant for the utilization of US$ 20 million line of credit to expand the Atal Bihari Vajpayee Centre for Excellence in Information Technology and Communication in Ulaanbaatar to include an Outsourcing Centre. Development of new and renewable energy technologies, viz. solar energy and wind energy, and exchange of trainees, students, faculty and experts between India and Mongolia will enhance skills and improve the training programme.

Cooperation in the minerals sector was also sought including coal, copper, rare earths and uranium. Earlier in March 2013, the fourth meeting of the India-Mongolia Joint Committee on Cooperation was held in New Delhi to take stock of the situation and expand the overall relationship. India continued to provide its development assistance to Mongolia.

Canada

Narendra Modi undertook a historical visit to Canada during 14-16 April 2016. It was the first visit by an Indian Prime Minister to Canada in 42 years. The visit was worked by "New Vigour, New Steps." Modi commended Canadian PM Stephen Harper for his leadership in renewing the momentum of the bilateral relationship through his visits to India in 2009 and 2012. Both the leaders recognized that bilateral business and commercial linkages constitute key drivers of wide-ranging partnership. PM Harper appreciated his Indian counterpart, Modi for his forward looking vision of energizing the Indian economy and welcomed the policy measures and specific initiatives taken by him to improve the ease of doing business in India.

Both the leaders noted that specific initiatives launched by Modi such as Make in India, Affordable Housing for all by 2022 and smart cities offered significant collaborative commercial opportunities for Indian and Canadian businesses and industry. They also noted that Canada's prioritization of India in its Global Markets Action Plan aligned well with bilateral objectives and they reaffirmed the need to elevate bilateral trade and investment linkages to their full potential by pursuing specific measures to diversify trade and enhance investment cooperation to increase the two-way flow of goods and services. Both the PMs expressed support for bilateral partnerships for urban transformation and smart city development which would leverage Canadian expertise in a number of relevant fields, including public private partnerships, intelligent transportation systems, civil engineering and urban planning, water and wastewater management, pre-cast and wood construction, energy technology and efficiency and affordable housing along with cooperation in rail transportation (dealing with technical cooperation) and the establishment of a Joint Working Group to bring together key industry and government stakeholders to advance opportunities for cooperation in civil aviation.

The two Prime Ministers also took positive note of the useful discussions in the Economic and Financial Sector Policy Dialogue held on 13 February 2015 in New Delhi and agreed to encourage a collaborative programme to leverage their industries' respective strengths in the field of pressurised heavy water reactor technology for mutual benefit, as well as for the benefit of global nuclear energy needs. The setting up of the Indian Nuclear Insurance Pool with potential participation of foreign companies and Global Initiative of Academic Networks (GIAN) of India to enable Canadian researchers to cooperate in learning, research and teaching in select Indian educational institutions were worked out. They took particular note of the partnership between the India-Canada Centre for Innovative Multidisciplinary Partnerships to Accelerate Community Transformation and Sustainability (IC-IMPACTS) and the National Mission for Clean Ganga to find innovative technological solutions to clean the River Ganga, the "Water for Health" collaboration, and the Safe and Sustainable Infrastructure and Integrated Water-Management initiatives.

For Joint industrial R&D projects through International Science and Technology Partnership Program, an annual contribution of CAD $1 million by both the countries was endorsed. Canada welcomed India's offer to be a partner country in the 2017 Technology Summit to be hosted by India. Both the PMs welcomed an investment of CAD $2.5 million in five health innovations in India by Grand Challenges Canada and India's Department of Biotechnology. India and Canada have also agreed to accelerate on-going efforts towards elimination of Visceral Leishmaniasis in India by jointly supporting an existing Grand Challenges Canada project.

Germany

Indian PM, Narendra Modi and the Federal Chancellor of Germany exchanged views on upgrading and further strengthening strategic partnership. Modi was on a visit to Germany on 12 April 2015. Common objective of his visit was to encourage greater synergies between German and Indian engineering, experience in sustainable development, innovation and skills, and the new opportunities available in India and through Make in India, Clean India, Digital India and other initiatives towards achieving economic growth and sustainable development. For this, India's participation as Partner Country at Hannover Messe 2015 proved encouraging to foster stronger ties between business and industry on both sides in order to support India's Make in India initiative. Manufacturing, skill development and urban development need a positive investment climate. The discussions in Germany have established a robust road map for expanding multi-faceted and mutually beneficial ties between India and Germany. As many as 350 companies across several sectors from India and 120 CEOs participated at the Hannover fair.

Qatar

The Emir of the State of Qatar, Sheikh Tamim bin Hamad Al Thani paid a state visit to India from 24-25 March 2015. Qatar expressed keen interest in India's Make in India programme. The MoUs signed include enhanced business opportunities for Indian IT industry in Qatar which has embarked on an ambitious programme for overall development as part of their Qatar 2030 vision and has also created a dedicated Ministry for ICT for capacity building. It has also expressed desire for cooperation with Indian Meteorological Department in the field of atmospheric and ocean sciences.

Brazil

India termed Brazil as its key global partner. During his 13-15 July 2014 visit to Brazil, PM Modi thanked Brazilian President, Fortaleza for successful conclusion of the BRICS summit and agreed on a number of initiatives that included expansion and diversification of trade and investment flow, boosting agriculture and dairy science, conventional and renewable energy, space research and application, defence, cyber security and environment conservation. Drawing a parallel between the theme of the Summit, Modi remarked that inclusive growth is a challenge for a country like India.

Russia

Narendra Modi paid an official visit to the Russian Federation on 23-24 December 2015 for the bilateral Annual Summit. Prime Minister Modi and the President of Russian Federation Vladimir Putin reaffirmed the unique character of Russia-India relations, based on time-tested and deep mutual trust and friendship between the two nations. They noted with satisfaction the continued support among the people of both countries to further strengthen and expand the bilateral relationship. They emphasized the remarkable convergence in their foreign policy priorities and underlined the significance of their special and privileged strategic partnership for their respective countries both bilaterally and in addressing regional and global issues in the days ahead. A number of important agreements in diverse fields of bilateral cooperation, including several commercial agreements between Russian and Indian companies, were signed during the visit. Both the leaders welcomed the outcomes of the twenty first meeting of the Russian-Indian Intergovernmental Commission (IGC) on Trade, Economic, Scientific, Technological and Cultural Cooperation held in Moscow on 20th October 2015, as well as decisions of various working groups of the commission, particularly on trade and economic cooperation, modernization and industrial cooperation. They reiterated their assessment that the "Make in India" initiative provides a new and durable framework for engagement by Russian corporate entities in the fast growing Indian economy as well as noted the efforts made by the Indian Government to improve ease of doing business.

Both the leaders agreed to actively work towards localization of manufacturing in India under the aegis of 'Make in India' and in tandem with the serial construction of nuclear power plants.

In this context, they welcomed the finalization of Programme of Action for localization between RosAtom of Russia and the Department of Atomic Energy of India. They noted mutual interest in developing cooperation in joint implementation of electric power projects, including hydro, thermal and solar power plants, as well as supply of Russia's electric power equipment to India.

As an important measure to boost the effectiveness of cooperation among Russian-Indian research centers, both the leaders called for the creation of an Russian-Indian data base of scientific and educational institutions and joint projects proposed by those institutions, as well as the development and maintenance of a catalogue of initiatives through which the Russian-Indian cooperation in science and technology is implemented. Tomsk State University of Russia and the Indian Institute of Technology in Mumbai were nominated as coordinators of these initiatives as a "Russia-India Resource Centre". Both the leaders took note of achievements in the field of joint design, development and production of high-technology military equipment. They reaffirmed their intention to expand the scope of such cooperation and to avail of the opportunities provided by the Make in India initiative in the defence sector and directed the concerned agencies to finalize such projects between relevant entities and enterprises of the two countries at the earliest.

Invest India Vehicle

Modi has always been a person of trade and investment, who organized events like Vibrant Gujarat and invited businessmen from all over the world. As PM, he wanted to follow up his success in Gujarat on a larger national scale. It is for this reason that trade and investments has been a major area of his discussion when dealing with foreign countries like China, Japan and U.S. to make Make in India campaign successful. In this effort, Japan alone brought in an investment worth US$ 35 billion and promised further to give financial, operational and technical help, even in introducing bullet trains in India. Modi was also able to woo the American businessmen and returned to

India with a promised investment of US$ 41 billion by American companies in India.

In order to give a fillip to investment promotion and hand-holding services to foreign investors, particularly the small and medium enterprises and investors in a structured manner, India has launched "Invest India" vehicle for providing inputs on all aspects of doing business in India. Invest India is the official Investment Promotion and Facilitation Agency of the Government of India, mandated to facilitate investments into India. It is the first point of reference for potential investors. A team of domain and functional experts provides sector- and state-specific inputs, and hand-holding support to investors through the entire investment cycle, from pre-investment decision-making to after-care. It assists with location identification; expediting regulatory approvals; facilitating meetings with relevant government and corporate officials; and also provides aftercare services that include initiating remedial action on problems faced by investors. All facilitation and hand-holding support to investors under the "Make in India" programme is being provided by Invest India which is promoted by the Department of Industrial Policy and Promotion (DIPP), Ministry of Commerce and Industry (Government of India), the State Governments of India and the Federation of Indian Chambers of Commerce and Industry.

India is a credible investment destination due to its nearly two decades of economic liberalization, coupled with robust domestic demand, a growing middle class, a young population and a high return on investment. A growing India offers opportunity across sectors, notably infrastructure, pharma, automobiles, education, and many more, in an investor-friendly environment. The steady improvement in India's relative position in the global economy is reflected in New Delhi's growing influence in international institutions (G-8, G-20) and negotiating free trade areas (with ASEAN, EU). Another achievement is the improved efficiency in the economy and adoption of international 'best practices' in the production of a range of goods and services, which bring India amongst the top ten investment destinations since 2007-08, attracting US$ 195 billion in FDI and US$ 97 billion in FII over the past 5 years. Thus, the purpose of Invest India vehicle is to utilize the potentials of Indian economy to attract foreign investment in India and provide a homely atmosphere to investors. It is the investment made by Indian companies in Latin America not in India which is the purpose of Invest India initiative.

Make in India Mobilization

India has become one of the most attractive destinations for investment in the manufacturing sector. The government has received investment proposals of over 1,10,000 crore (US$ 16.56 billion) during 2014 itself from various companies. The government has taken several steps since the start of the campaign. In a bid to push the 'Make in India' initiative to the global level, Modi pitched India as manufacturing destination at the World International Fair in Germany's Hannover in 2015. He showcased India as a business friendly destination to attract foreign businesses to invest and manufacture in the country.

To make India a business friendly destination, the Government of India has taken several initiatives to promote a healthy environment for the growth of manufacturing sector in the country. Following are some of the notable initiatives taken by the Government of India:

- NITI Aayog has advocated a financial package to support manufacturing sectors with large-scale employment generation opportunities, such as electrical and electronics engineering, footwear and light manufacturing segments, which also have export potential.
- The Ministry of Labour and Employment has relaxed compliance measures for MSMEs by exempting them from inspections related to key labour laws in order to encourage entrepreneurs to help promote manufacturing in India.
- To give a big boost to local manufacturing, government has introduced the new 'Made in India Green Channel', which will reduce the time taken for

cargo clearance at ports from about a week to a few hours without any upfront payment of duties.

- The Ministry of Heavy industries and Public Enterprise has created a start-up centre and a technology fund for the capital goods sector to provide technical business and financial resources and services to start-ups in the field of manufacturing and services.
- A new Defence Procurement Policy (DPP) has been planned under which priority is given to the indigenously made defence products and 25 percent share of defence production is open to private firms.
- NITI Aayog has released a blueprint for various technological interventions which need to be incorporated by the Indian manufacturers with a view to have a sustainable edge over competing neighbours like Bangladesh and Vietnam over the long-term.
- The Technology Acquisition and Development Fund (TADF) under the National Manufacturing Policy (NMP) has been launched to facilitate acquisition of Clean, Green, and Energy Efficient Technologies, by MSMEs.
- Indian envoys in over 160 countries have been asked to focus on economic diplomacy to help government attract investment and transform the 'Make in India' campaign a success to boost growth of the country.
- Government of India has planned to invest US$ 10 billion in two semiconductor plants in order to facilitate electronics manufacturing in the country.
- To promote small-scale businesses in India, the Government will make available loans to entrepreneurs under Pradhan Mantri MUDRA Yojana (PMMY). The three products available under the PMMY include, Shishu—covering loans up to ₹ 50,000 (US$ 735); Kishor—covering loans between ₹ 50,000 (US$ 735) to ₹ 50,00,000 (US$ 7340); and Tarun—covering loans between ₹ 5,00,000 (US$ 7340) and ₹ 10,00,000 (US$ 14700).

The Government has an ambitions plan to locally manufacture as many as 181 products which will help infrastructure sectors such as power, oil and gas, and automobile manufacturing that require large capital expenditure and revive the ₹ 185000 crore (US$ 27.42 billion) Indian capital goods business.

Defence and aerospace are being increasingly looked upon as among the most promising segments to push indigenous manufacturing. The government has placed defence orders worth ₹ 2 lakh crore under buy and Make in India category to boost local manufacturing, giving flexibility to domestic industry. According to Department of Industrial Policy and Promotion (DIPP), over the next seven years there is expected spending of US$ 130 billion on defence forces and additional US$ 110 billion on homeland security which has been a type of opportunity for domestic manufacturers and also for foreign investors.

As per a report by India Electronics and Semiconductor Association in partnership with Roland Berger, Indian aerospace and defence market is the seventh largest globally with strong demand emanating across the triad of user services. At a sub-system level, the total opportunity for electronics sector that emerges in user service segment is about US$ 58 billion over the next 12-15 years, considering platform requirements for the user services.

The Indian automobile industry is one of the largest in the world and accounts for over 7.1% of India's GDP and contributes to nearly 22% of the country's manufacturing GDP. India is also currently the 6th largest market in the world for automobiles and is expected to become the world's third-biggest car market by the year 2020. Now, 100 percent FDI is allowed in this sector through the automatic approval route which means that foreign investors do not require the prior authorization of the Government of India. The impact of this decision is that the industry has attracted FDI worth US$ 15.065 billion during the period April 2000 to March 2016. Thus, India has emerged as one of the key global players, both as a consumer and a producer, in the automobile industry. It has witnessed tremendous growth, especially in the last few years and has become a base for global manufacturers. Volkswagen, Nissan, Renault, General Motors, Ford, Honda, Suzuki, Hyundai, Daimler, BMW, Skoda, Audi are all present in India and are manufacturing and assembling locally. Mercedes-Benz recently decided to make the entry level GLA-class Sport Utility vehicle (SUV) in India. Japanese two-wheeler manufacturer Honda Motorcycle and Scooter (HMSI) opened its 4th and world's largest scooter plant in Gujarat while Chrysler has planned to invest US$ 513.5 million in Maharashtra to manufacture Jeep Grad Cherokee model. The Automotive Mission Plan 2016-26 (AMP2026) lays out the government's collective vision on how the automotive sector should grow regarding size, contribution to national development technological maturity, global competitiveness and institutional structure. It aims to make India among the top three automotive industries in the world and increase exports exponentially to reach 35-40% of overall output. It intends to increase its contribution to the GDP to over 12%, generating 65 million more jobs as well as increasing the size of US$ 300 billion by 2026. Volkswagen (VW) looks at the possibility of a full-fledged development centre in India near the factory so that it can work together in production planning. The company's centre in India undertakes specialized work for India with localization and concepts, and it is expected to showcase the Indian compact Sedan[2] possibly at the Auto Expo. Even Skoda India is playing a major role in the facelift of travel. According to the sources, Skoda is looking at two-three launches by next year.

BMW and Mercedes Benz too have intensified their localization efforts to be part of Make in India initiative that would reduce the waiting period and accelerate the servicing process of their cars as they had to previously depend on their plants overseas for supply. Mercedes Benz has doubled its India assembly capacity to 20,000 units annually thereby making India one of the first markets to make the GLA entry SUV outside Germany. The company which has seen a 40 percent growth in sales in 2015, has been expanding its local assembly capacity. India is one of the focus markets for Mercedes Benz globally.

Suzuki Motor Corp. too is planning to make automobiles for Africa, the company's next big bet, as well as for India at its upcoming factory at Hansalpur in Gujarat.

Japan's US$ 15 Billion Loan for India's Bullet Train

Japan has offered to finance India's first bullet train, estimated to cost US$ 15 billion at an interest rate of less than one percent, stealing a march on China, which is bidding for other projects on the world's fourth largest network of India. Japan was earlier chosen to assess the feasibility of building the 505-km corridor linking Mumbai with Ahmedabad. It concluded that it would be technically and financially viable. The project to build and supply the route will be put out to tender, but offering finance makes Japan the clear frontrunner. China won the contract to assess the feasibility of a high speed train between Delhi and Mumbai, a 1,200-km route, estimated to cost twice as much. Japan's decision to give virtually free finance for Narendra Modi's pet programme, Make in India, is part of its broader push back against China's involvement in infrastructure development in South Asia over the past several years.

The country's first bullet train between Mumbai and Ahmedabad is expected to pass through a 21-km long undersea tunnel. While the better part of the 505-km corridor will be on an elevated track, there will be a stretch after Thane creek towards Virar which will be underwater. The ambitious project is likely to cost around ₹ 97,636 crore, with a 81 percent of the funds to come from Japan as a soft loan for 50 years at 0.1% annual interest with 15 years' moratorium.[3]

The Joint Committee formed under NITI Aayog Vice-Chairman, Arvind Panagariya for timely completion of the project will visit Japan to ensure its quick execution. The railways has formed a special purpose vehicle, National High Speed Rail Corporation Ltd. (NHSRCL) for the project.

Make in India Week

Prime Minister Narendra Modi inaugurated Make in India Week in Mumbai on 13 February 2016 in the august presence of Kjell Stefan Lofven, Sweden's Prime Minister; Juha Sipila,

PM of Finland; Piotr Glinski, First Deputy PM of Poland, and distinguished dignitaries from many other countries; Governor and CM of Maharashtra, and Nirmala Sitharaman, MoS for Commerce and Industry. Modi said in his inaugural address: "We launched the Make in India campaign to create employment and self-employment opportunities for our youth. We are working aggressively towards making India a global manufacturing hub. We want the share of manufacturing in our GDP to go up to 25 percent in the near future."

The government was aware that under the pressure of Make in India campaign its machinery will be required to make a number of corrections on the policy front, including a commitment to make India an easy place to do business and offer a base for manufacturing, design, research and development. Modi said, "The eventful week is an opportunity to take stock of how we have performed and what could be the road ahead. It will showcase different aspects of the progress that we have made. This is the biggest multi-sectoral event and exhibition ever held in India."

Global firms marked their presence prominently in this week-long event. The general sentiment about the Indian economy so far has been that in the BRICS countries, Brazil is a mess, Russia has collapsed, South Africa still struggling, and China seems to be melting down. There is no other major economy that is growing at 7.3 percent. For India to become more attractive, the consistency in the government's message is that India is open and transparent for business needs. However, if examined critically, the country remains far behind its goals. Modi Government's efforts are likely to put India on the right track.

Since the launch of Make in India initiative, the Government of India has taken several reform initiatives to create an enabling environment that has provided a push to manufacturing, design, innovation and entrepreneurship. With a growth rate of 7.5%, India has emerged as the fastest growing economy globally and it remains an oasis in the midst of a subdued economic landscape. Several innovative initiatives of Government of India such as "Digital India", "100 Smart Cities", and "Skill

India" have given further impetus to India's growth. The Make in India initiative aims to make India an integral part of the global supply chain. Key focus sectors such as defence, railways construction, insurance, pension funds and medical devices have all been rapidly opened up for FDI. The Government of India has also taken up a series of measures to radically improve its 'Easy of Doing Business' ranking. With an objective to make the regulatory environment easy and simple for business to flourish, the Government has effectively used technology to converge and integrate different departments. 14 services are integrated within the 'eBiz portal', which will function as a single window portal for obtaining clearances from various government agencies.

Over 2,500 international and 8,000 domestic companies are claimed to have participated in the week-long multi-sectoral event, apart from foreign government delegations from 68 countries, and business teams from 72 nations. As many as 17 Indian states participated in the expo and there were over 50 seminars. The theme of the Make in India Week was innovation, design and sustainability, and Make in India initiative has already created a strong impact with the tangible results as under:

1. India is now first amongst the world's fastest growing economies. (*Source*: IMF)
2. India is first amongst the world's topmost greenfield FDI destinations, January-June 2015. (*Source*: *Financial Times*)
3. India is first amongst the 100 countries in the growth, innovation and leadership index. (*Source*: Frost & Sullivan)
4. India is first amongst the world's fasted growing economies in both 2016-17. (*Source*: WESP Report 2016, United Nations)
5. India is the first choice for technological MNCs to set up R&D centres outside their home countries. (*Source*: Zinnow Management Consulting Report)
6. India is the seventh most valued nation brand in the world. (*Source*: Brand Finance)

7. India is first amongst the world's most attractive investment destinations. (*Source*: Ernst & Young-2015, India Attractiveness Survey)
8. India is now first amongst 110 investment destinations polled globally. (*Source*: Foreign Policy Magazine, *Baseline Profitability Index*, 2015)
9. India is amongst the top ten investment destinations. (*Source*: World Investment Report 2015, UNCTAD)
10. India's ranking jumped 12 places on the Ease of Doing Business 2016 List. (*Source*: World Bank)
11. India moved 16 places on the Global Competitiveness Index 2015-16. (*Source*: World Economic Forum)
12. India has recorded 35% growth in FDI Equity Inflows. (*Source*: Department of Industrial Policy & Research)

In order to keep the momentum going, the Government of India has organized the landmark event, the Make in India Week, the theme of which had been "innovation, design and sustainability". Many other events were planned around the theme like an exhibition of India's most innovative products and manufacturing processes; state investment seminars in Maharashtra, Andhra Pradesh, Jharkhand, Gujarat, Madhya Pradesh, Chhattisgarh, Haryana and Odisha—the states which had confirmed their participation; sector seminars around the key focus sectors of the Make in India initiative; CNN Asia Business Forum to discuss and debate ideas which will shape Asia's economic and social future; panel discussion on innovation, entrepreneurship, intelligent manufacturing and awards on innovation; an urban planning session and an exhibition on the best practices for building cities by adopting technology at the Make in India centre; industry and academia interaction featuring manufacturing success stories, start-ups, an exhibition on innovation by IIT Bombay as well as a competition on urban design problems; an exhibition on India's maritime manufacturing capabilities; a day-long session on global design and innovation for global brand-building, and a forum on rethinking contemporary design practices to create empowerment through design.

In fact, that event was part of the government's push to create jobs by increasing the share of manufacturing in the GDP to 25 percent over the next decade, from 16-17 percent now. India needs funds to build industries which in turn need infrastructure, which is in itself in short supply and requires more finance. The event happened at a time when the Supreme Court wanted to know about the pile-up of bad loans in India's banking system which is not in a position to lend much unless its balance sheets are cleared. State-controlled banks are neck-deep in losses after making provisions to cushion bad loans, which total around ₹ 443,000 crore, most of it from the corporate sector, which is hardly in a position to take up massive investments. It would leave FDI as the best bet, but that cannot come in big doses unless other issues are resolved, especially for doing business. A bankruptcy law to enable smoother shut-down of companies is yet to be passed. The government is said to be wooing oil-rich Gulf countries to participate in the ₹ 40,000 crore National Investment and Infrastructure Fund.

Make in India: A Great Dawn

'Make in India' is one of the most ambitious programmes of Modi, launched on 25th September, 2014, with a objective of increasing the contribution of manufacturing output to 25 percent of GDP from 16 percent currently over the next ten years, there by creating a 100 million jobs and improving skill efficiency; via increasing foreign direct investment (FDI), and removing or relating foreign equity caps in several areas.

Over the last 20 years, Indian manufacturing has by and large grown at the same pace as the overall economy. The sector accounted for 15 percent GDP in 1993 which remains about the same even today. Whereas several Rapidly Developing Economies (RDEs) have increased their manufacturing share to above 20 percent of their GDP, in particular Thailand (34 percent in 2012), China (32 percent), Malaysia (24 percent), Indonesia (24 percent), and the Philippines (31 percent).[4] India suffers from some critical drawbacks like lack of an enabling infrastructure, poor perception in terms of ease of doing business, and a lack of proven ability to compete at a global scale. The National Manufacturing Policy (NMP) set out plans for the sector to reach 25 percent of GDP and create 100 million additional jobs by 2022. The policy is expected to focus on—

(a) improving the business environment and facilitating easy technology acquisition and development;

(b) providing access to capital for SMEs; and

(c) enhancing the private sector's role in skill development.

According to NMP, every job created in the manufacturing sector creates two-three additional jobs in related activities.

Industrial production growth has high correlation with FDI inflows. The effect of FDI on economic development ranges from productivity increase to enabling greater technology transfer. The investment made by the foreign persons under 'Make in India' scheme would be one from of FDI. Under Make in India initiative, Government of India will facilitate foreign investors to manufacture in India by making easy business laws and streamlining taxation policies. It is presumed that successful 'Make in India' will transform India into a global manufacturing bub, give push to exports and improve the productivity of both capital and labour inputs.

New policies were framed under 'Made in India' initiative to facilitate the expansion of Micro, Small and Medium Enterprises (MSME) and increase the focus on innovation. It includes the launch of ₹ 10,000 crores venture capital fund dedicated to MSMEs. Modi has made strategic visits overseas to drive increased investment (including a visit to Japan, where the Japanese Government has committed to investments in India of US$ 35 billion, and to the US where a VS-India business body has committed to a US$ 42 billion investment in India over the next two to three years). Another key area of progress for India would be the development of its SMEs to achieve and manage scale effectively. The government has also set up the National Skills Development Council (NSDC) to encourage private participation/management of industrial training institutes (IIIs). Among its objectives, NSDC seeks to contribute significantly (about 30 percent) to the overall target of skilling/upskilling 500 million people in India by 2022.

To achieve the objective of National Manufacturing Policy, the Government has proposed to develop National Investment and Manufacturing Zones (NIMZs), which will be integrated industrial townships, with world class infrastructure built on minimum size of 5000 hectares. To improve the business environment in the country, these NIMZs will enjoy single window clearance and a liberal exit policy. The policy also provides incentives for units in NIMZs such as exemptions from capital gains tax, and incentives for green manufacturing and technology acquisitions.

Thus, Make in India initiative seeks to facilitate job creation, foster innovation, enhance skill development and protect intellectual property. The logo of Make in India, a lion made of gear wheels, itself reflects the integral role of manufacturing in government's vision and national development. The initiative is built on following four pillars:

(a) New Processes—Several reforms are to be introduced to create possibilities for getting FDI and foster business partnerships. Some initiatives have already been undertaken to alleviate the business environment from outdated policies and regulations. The reforms are aligned with parameters of World Bank's 'Ease of Doing Business' index to improve India's ranking on it.

(b) New Infrastructure—To create a business friendly infrastructure, the government intends to develop industrial corridors and build smart cities with state-of-the-art technology and high-speed communication. Innovation and research activities are supported by a fast-paced registration system and improved infrastructure for Intellectual Property Rights (IPR) registrations. Along with development of infrastructure, the training for the skilled workforce for the sectors is also being taken care of.

(c) New Sector—25 sectors have been identified to promote with the detailed information being shared through an interactive web-portal.

(d) New Mindset—Make in India initiative intends to change the government's position as a regulator, by bringing a paradigm shift in the way government interacts with various industries. Government wants to focus on acting as a partner in the economic development of the country alongside the corporate sector.

A key phrase 'zero defect zero effect' is associated with the Make in India initiative. In the words of Prime Minister Modi, "Let us think about making our product which has 'zero defect' and 'zero effect' so that the manufacturing does not have an adverse effect on our environment". Thus, sustainable development in the country can be made possible by imposing high-quality manufacturing standards while minimising environmental and ecological impact. While introducing his vision of 'Make in India' to the public, Prime Minister Modi said, "Sell anywhere, but make in India."

Notes

1. Puja Mehra, 'Make in India' Pitch from September 25. *The Hindu*. 21 September 2014.
2. A car with four doors and a boot/trunk (i.e. space at the back for carrying things) which is separated from the part where the driver and passengers sit.
3. *The Times of India*. 21 April 2016.
4. "Make in India: Turning Vision into Reality", CII, 13th Manufacturing Summit, 2014.

CHAPTER 6

Startup India: New Opportunities for Business

On 15th August 2015, from the Red Fort, Prime Minister Narendra Modi announced a new campaign 'Start-up India: Stand up India' to promote bank financing for start-ups and offer incentives to boost entrepreneurship and job creation Startup India as a flagship initiative of the Government of India, intended to build a strong eco-system for nurturing innovation and startups in the country. It serves as a platform for facilitation of startup recognition, access to information related to incubators, mentors, Angel Funds, Venture Funds, etc. Since various Ministries of the Government of India are associated with Startup India initiative, to bring uniformity in the identified enterprises, an entity will be considered as a startup if it fulfils the following basic conditions:

(a) An entity will be a startup to five years from the date of its incorporation/registration.

(b) The turnover of the entity for any of the financial years should not exceed ₹ 25 crore.

(c) The entity should be involved in innovation, development, deployment or commercialization of new products, processes or services driven by technology or intellectual property.

Here it should be noted that any such entity formed by splitting up or reconstruction of a business already in existence will not be considered a 'startup'. It should also be noted that in order to obtain tax benefits a startup so identified under the above condition will be required to obtain a certificate of an eligible business from the Inter-Ministerial Board of Certification consisting of

(a) Joint Secretary, Department of Industrial Policy and Promotion;

(b) Representative of Department of Science and Technology; and

(c) Representative of Department of Biotechnology.

An entity will be considered as a 'startup' only if it aims to develop and commercialize

(a) a new product or service or process;

(b) a significantly improved existing product or service or process, that will create or add value for customers or workflow.

An entity will not be considered as a 'startup' only for the mere act of developing

(a) products, services, or processes which do not have potential for commercialization;

(b) undifferentiated products, services, or processes; and

(c) products, services, or processes with no or limited incremental value for customers or workflow.

The process of recognition as a 'startup' will be through mobile app or portal of the Department of Industrial Policy and Promotion (DIPP).

In order to meet the objectives of the 'Startup India' initiative, an Action Plan was formulated that addresses all aspects of the Startup ecosystem. With this Action Plan, the aim of the government is to accelerate spreading of the Startup initiative

(a) from digital or technology sector to a wide array of sectors including agriculture, manufacturing, social sector, healthcare, education, etc.; and

(b) from existing tier 1 cities to tier 2 and tier 3 cities including semi-urban and rural areas.

The areas covered by the Action Plan are

(a) simplification and Handholding
(b) Funding Support and Incentives
(c) Industry-Academia Partnership and Incubation.

The focus of the initiative is on restricting the role of the states in policy domain, get rid of license raj and remove hindrances like the ones found in land permissions, foreign investment proposal, and environmental clearances. Prime Minister Narendra Modi unveiled the action plan for startups in the country on 16th January 2016. He announced a self-certification scheme in respect of nine labour and environment laws and said there will be no inspection during the first three years of launch of the venture. Addressing the first conference of startup entrepreneurs, Modi announced an action plan to boost such ventures which are seen as key to employment generation and wealth creation.[1]

The main features of the Startup India initiative are enumerated below. They are also known as 19-point action plan.

(i) Compliance Regime based on Self-Certification—Its objective is to reduce the regulatory burden on Startups thereby allowing them to focus on their core business and keep compliance cost low. The self-certification is applied to regulatory formalities requiring compliance with various labour and environment laws. Startups are allowed to self-certify compliance with 9 labour and environment laws, such as the building and other constructions Workers' Act, the Inter-State Migrant Workmen Act, the Payment of Gratuity Act, the Provident Funds and Miscellaneous Provisions Act, the Water Act, the Air (Prevention and control of Pollution)Act, etc. In case of the labour laws, no inspections will be conducted for a period of 3 years and in case of environment laws, Startups which full under the 'white category' would be able to self-certify compliance and only random checks would be carried out in such cases.

(ii) Startup India Hub—Its objective is to create a single point of contact for the entire Startup ecosystem and enable knowledge exchange and access to funding. It will be a key stakeholder in the vibrant ecosystem and will

- work in a hub and collaborate with central and state governments, Indian and Foreign VCs, angel networks, banks, incubators, legal partners, etc.;
- assist startup through their lifecycle with specific focus on important aspects like obtaining financing, feasibility testing, business structuring advisory, enhancement of marketing skills, etc; and
- organise mentorship programs in collaboration with government, organisations, incubation centers, educational institutions, etc.

(iii) Rolling-out of Mobile App and Portal—Its objective is to serve as the single platform for Startups for interacting with Government and Regulatory Institutions for all business need and information exchange among various stakeholders. The Startup Mobile App will provide on-the-go accessibility for

- registering Startups with relevant agencies of the Government.
- tracking the status of the registration application and anytime downloading of the registration certificate.
- filing for compliances and obtaining information on various clearances/approvals/registrations required.
- collaborating with various Startup ecosystem partners.
- applying for various schemes being undertaken under the Startup India Action Plan.

(iv) Legal Support and Fast-tracking Patent Examination at Lower Costs—Its objective is to promote awareness and adoption of IPRs by Startups and facilitate them in protecting and commercializing the IPRs by providing access to high quality Intellectual Property services and resources, including fast-track examination of patent applications and rebate in fees.

(v) Relaxed Norms of Public Procurement for Startups—Its objective is to provide an equal platform to Startups (in the manufacturing sector) vis-a-vis the experienced companies in public procurement. In the manufacturing sector, Startups are exempted from the criteria of "prior experience/turnover" without any relaxation in the quality standards or technical parameters.

(vi) Faster Exit for Startups—Its objective is to make it easier for Startups to wind up operations. Startups with simple debt structures or those meeting such criteria as may be specified may be would up within a period of 90 days from making of an application for winding up on a fast track basis.

(vii) Providing Funding Support through a Fund of Funds with a corpus of ₹ 10,000 crore—Its objective is to provide funding support for development and growth of innovation driven enterprises. In order to provide funding support to Startups, a fund has been set up with an initial corpus of ₹ 2500 crore and a total corpus of ₹ 10,000 crore over a period of 4 years. The fund is in the nature of 'Fund of Funds', which means that it will not invest directly into Startups, but shall participate in the capital of SEBI registered Venture Funds. Key features of the Fund of Funds are:

- It is managed by a Board with private professionals drawn from industry bodies, academia, and successful Startups.
- It has Life Insurance Corporation (LIC) as a co-investor.
- It will contribute to a maximum of 50 percent of the stated daughter fund size.
- It will ensure support to a broad mix of sectors such as manufacturing, agriculture, health, education, etc.

(viii) Credit Guarantee Fund for Startups—Its objective is to catalyse enterpreneurship by providing credit to innovators across all sections of society. Debt funding to Startups is perceived as high risk area and to encourage Banks and other lenders to provide Venture Debts to Startups, credit guarantee mechanism through National Credit Guarantee Trust Company (NCGTC)/SIDBI is being envisaged with a budgetory corpus of ₹ 500 crore per year for the next four years.

(ix) Tax Exemption on Capital Gains—Its objective is to promote investments into Startups by mobilizing the capital gains arising from sale of capital assets. With this objective, tax exemption will be given to persons who have capital gains during the year, if they have invested such capital gains in the Fund of Funds recognised by the Government.

(x) Tax Exemption to Startups for 3 years—Its objective is to promote the growth of Startups and address working capital requirements. To stimulate the development of Startups and provide them a competitive platform, it is imperative that the profits of Startup initiatives are exempted from income-tax for a period of 3 years. This fiscal exemption will facilitate growth of business and meet the working capital requirements during the initial years of operations.

(xi) Tax Exemption on Investments above Fair Market Value—Its objective is to encourage seed-capital investment in Startups.

(xii) Organising Startup Fests for Showcasing Innovation and Providing a Collaboration platform—Its objective is to galvanize the Startup ecosystem and to provide national and international visibility to the Startup ecosystem in India. Startup fests would provide a platform to Startups in India to showcase their ideas and work with a larger audience comprising of potential investors, mentors, and fellow Startups. In this direction, Government proposes to

- hold one fest at the national level annually to enable all the stakeholders of Startup ecosystem to come together on one platform.

- hold one fest at the international level annually in an international city known for its Startup ecosystem.

(xiii) Launch of Atal Innovation Mission (AIM) with Self-Employment and Talent Utilization (SETU) Program—Its objective is to serve as a platform for promotion of world-class Innovation Hubs, Grand Challenges, Startup businesses and other self-employment activities, particularly in technology driven areas. The Atal Innovation Mission (AIM) has two core functions?

- Entrepreneurship promotion through Self-Employment and Talent Utilization (SETU), wherein innovators would be supported and mentioned to become successful entrepreneurs.
- Innovation promotion to provide a platform where innovative ideas are generated.

The main components proposed to be undertaken as part of the mission include entrepreneurship and innovation promotions. Entrepreneurship promotion involves

- establishment of sector specific incubators including in PPP mode.
- establishment of 500 Tinkering debts.
- pre-incubation training to potential entrepreneurs in various technology areas in collaboration with various academic institutions having expertise in the field.
- strengthening of incubation facilities in existing incubators and mentoring of Startups.
- seed funding to potentially successful and high growth Startups.

Innovation promotion involves

- institution of Innovation Awards, 3 per state/UT, and 3 National level awards.
- providing support to State Innovation Councils for awareness creation and organizing state level workshops/conferences.

- launch of Grand Innovation Challenge Awards for finding ultra-low cost solutions to India's pressing and intractable problems.

(xiv) Harnessing Private Sector Expertise for Incubator Setup—Its objective is to ensure professional management of Government funded incubators. Government will encourage setting up of:

- 35 new incubators in existing institutions. Funding support of 40% will be provided by Central Government for establishment of new incubators for which 40% funding by the respective State Government and 20% funding by the private sector has been committed. The private sector will manage and operate the incubator.
- 35 new private sector incubators. A grant of 50% will be provided by Central Government for incubators established by private sector in existing institutions and the incubator will be managed and operated by the private sector.

(xv) Building Innovation Centres at National Institutes—Its objective is to propel successful innovation through augmentation of incubation and R&D efforts. In order to augment the incubation and R&D efforts in the country, the Government will set up/scale up 31 centres of innovation and entrepreneurship at national institutes, including

- setting-up 13 Startup centres—annual funding support of ₹ 50 lakhs will be provided for three years for encouraging student driven Startups from the host institute.
- setting-up/scaling-up 18 Technology Business Incubators (TBIs) at NITs/IITs/IIMs, etc. as per funding model of DST with MHRD providing smooth approvals for TBI to have separate society and built-up space.

(xvi) Setting up of 7 new Research Parks Modeled on the Research Park Setup at IIT Madras—Its objective is to propel successful innovation through incubation and joint R&D efforts between academia and industry. The Government will set up 7 new Research Parks in premier institutes—IIT Delhi, IIT Kharagpur, IIT Kanpur, IIT Guwahati, IIT Hyderabad, IIT Gandhinagar, and IISc Bangalore—with an initial investment of ₹100 crore each. The guiding principles behind these Research Parks include:

- creating a collaborative environment between academia and industry through joint research projects and consulting assignments.
- creating a self-sustaining and technologically fertile environment.
- encouraging and enabling R&D activities and Startups that are aligned to potential needs of the industry.
- providing world class infrastructure for R&D activities and incubation.
- enabling development of high quality personnel and motivating professional growth for researchers.

(xvii) Promoting Startups in the Biotechnology Sector— Its objective is to foster and facilitate bio-entrepreneurship. The Department of Biotechnology will be implementing the following measures along with its public sector undertaking Biotechnology Research Assistance Council (BIRAC).

(a) Bio-incubators, Seed Fund and Equity Funding:

- 5 new Bio-clusters, 50 new Bio-incubators, 150 Technology transfer offices, and 20 Bio-connect offices are being set up in research institutes and universities across the country.
- Biotech Equity Fund in partnership with National and Global Equity Funds will provide financial assistance to young Biotech Startups.

(b) Encouraging and leverage global partnerships:

- Bengaluru-Baston Biotech Gateway to India has been formed which will be used to share ideas and mentor the entrepreneurs especially in the areas of Genomics, Computational Biology, Drug Discovery and new vaccines.

- Amplification of Bio-entrepreneurship through BIRAC Regional Entrepreneurship Centres (BREC). Department of Biotechnology is to setup 5 Regional centres or Mini-BIRACs in the next 5 years.

(xviii) Launching of Innovation Focused Programs for Students—Its objective is to foster a culture of innovation in the field of Science and Technology amongst students. The following measures are being taken to promote research and innovation among young students.

- Innovation core program are being initiated to target school kids with an outreach to 10 lakh innovations from 5 lakh schools.
- A grand challenge program, National Initiative for Developing and Harnessing Innovations (NIDHI), is being instituted through innovation and Entrepreneurship Development Centres (IEDCs) to support and award ₹ 10 lakhs to 20 student innovations from IEDCs.
- Uchhattar Avishkar Yojana, a joint MHRD-DST scheme, has been started, which has allotted 250 crore per annum towards fostering "very high quality" research amongst IIT students.

(xix) Annual Incubator Grand Challenge—Its objective is to support creation of successful world class incubators in India. An "Incubator Grand Challenge" exercise is to be carried out for identification of these incubators. The exercise entails:

- open invitation of applications from incubators.
- screening and evaluation based on pre-defined Key Performance Indicators (KPIs).

The Ministry of Human Resource Development and the Department of Science and Technology have agreed to partner in an initiative to set up over 75 startup support hubs in the

National Institutes of Technology (NITs), the Indian Institutes of Information Technology (IIITs), the Indian Institutes of Science Education and Research (IISERs) and National Institutes of Pharmaceutical Education and Research (NIPERs).[2]

Under the scheme, the Reserve Bank of India committed to take steps to help improve the 'ease of doing business' in the country and contribute to an ecosystem that is conducive for the growth of start-up businesses.[3]

The government measures include tax waiver for three years, ending inspector raj and a mega fund to help boost the startup ecosystem. The 19-point action plan comes with the promise that the government will play the role of a facilitator and not burden entrepreneurs with complicated compliance requirements.

Investments in Startup India

Startup India initiative was launched on 16th January 2016 by the Finance Minister Arun Jaitley. The event was attended by around 40 top CEOs and startup founders and investors from Silicon Valley as special guests including Masayoshi Son (CEO of SoftBank), Kunal Bahl (founder of Snapdeal), Bhavish Aggarwal (founder of Ola), Vijay Shekhar Sharma (founder of Paytm), Travis Kalanick (founder of Uber), Adam Nuemann (CEO of WeWork), Sachin Bansal (founder of Flipkart), and others.

SoftBank, headquartered in Japan, has invested US$ 2 billion into Indian startups. The Japanese firm had pledged the total investments at US$ 10 billion. Google declared to launch a startup, based on the highest votes in which the top three startups will be allowed to join the next Google Launchpad Week, and the final winner could win an amount of US$ 100,000 in Google cloud credits.[4] Oracle CEO Safra Catz, on 12 February 2016, announced three major investments that support the country's global digital leadership. It is investing over US$ 400 million in Bengaluru, 9 incubation centers throughout India, and an initiative to train more than half a million students each year to develop computer science skills. To contribute to India's "Startup India" and "Make in India" initiatives, Oracle is opening nine incubation centers throughout the country to support entrepreneurship and development of innovative startups by providing software, tools, and training to new software and technology companies utilizing Java and the Oracle platform. These centres will be located in Bengaluru, Chennai, Gurgaon, Hyderabad, Mumbai, Noida, Pune, Trivandrum, and Vijayawada. The list of ten top funded startups is given in Table 6.1.

What industry expects from Startup India initiative is worth noting: "I expect 10,000 entrepreneurs to be born on Saturday (16 January) itself. Kudos to PM Modi for having the vision to think of this event. I haven't seen anything like this before," said Kunal Bahl, co-founder and CEO, Snapdeal. "We expect greater focus on...registering and starting up a company and a simplified tax regime," according to Albinder Dhindsa, co-founder and CEO, Grofers. Avnish Bajaj, founder and M.D., Matrix Partners India, noted: "[We are] hoping for something concrete which brings taxation on private company investments on par with publicly listed equities." Ashish Goel, founder CEO, Urban Ladder emphasized, "Clarity of listing norms, faster clearances and inclusive growth will encourage entrepreneurs to build innovative businesses. There is a need for a seasoned entrepreneur to chair the government's Entrepreneurial Cell to have a better perspective of the challenges faced and resolve issues faster. If India wants to leapfrog and build product startups, there is a need for high quality design standardization to instil basic design principles for world class product design."

Table 6.1: Ten Top Funded Startups (2014-16: in USD)

1.	Flipkart	3.2 bn
2.	Snapdeal	1.76 bn
3.	Ola Cabs	1.23 bn
4.	Paytm	740 million
5.	Quikr	346 million
6.	Big Basket	246 million
7.	OYO	230 million
8.	Zomato	223 million
9.	InMobi	220 million
10.	Car Trade	188 million

Source: Officechai, 8 December 2016.

Narendra Modi hinted at the launch of Startup India that government will get out of the way: "Please tell us what not to do." One reason India became an important IT centre was that there were few domestic laws governing this field. The break from license raj in 1991 was only partial, that needs to be completed now. The World Bank's ease of doing business report shows that the number of days it takes to start a business in India has come down from 127 to 29 during the last decade, but it is still very high as compared to 5-6 days in the US.

The policy recognizes the potential that startups can play in the coming years after a recent spurt which saw the numbers in the technology space jumping over nine times from 501 entities in 2010 to over 4,500 in 2015. The increase has come with the rise of Flipkart, Snapdeal, Ola Cabs and Paytm, which have become household names attracting huge investor interest. Currently, Indian entrepreneurs depend on overseas investors for over 90 percent of the funding, which has been a major area of concern. The Modi Government has sought to address this partly through a ₹ 10,000 crore fund and a ₹ 200 crore credit guarantee fund. The corpus was seen to be small, and the steps announced were just the beginning.

The startup founders view that the action plan for new ventures will have a significant impact on driving enthusiasm among aspiring entrepreneurs to start their business without worrying too much about regulation and taxation. Startups could emerge as an alternative growth engine when the global economy poses challenges. The government is pursuing a policy where more freedom is being given to companies. It is evident from fewer businessmen visiting the Finance Ministry or the pile of files in Foreign Investment Promotion Board which thankfully is now coming down as more files are being cleared. Another significant difference of what makes Startup a landmark event, according to Jaitley, is a final break or the ultimate break that one has with the conventional license raj of India. The government and RBI would ensure that the ability of banks to lend more is enhanced. Besides Startup India, the government will launch 'Standup India' under which bank branches will lend to SC/ST and women entrepreneurs. Each bank branch—public or private—would adopt an SC/ST entrepreneur and a woman. So they will adopt two such entrepreneurs and fund them to set up establishment. Modi said, "There are ways to close doors to new ideas. We want to open them. We are lacking in intellectual property (IP), but we have a lot of youth property (YP). We have to bring them on a single plane. Failures shouldn't stop you forever. One who runs away from water cannot learn to swim. We have a million problems but at the same time we have over a billion minds."

Top industry giants have been expressing their views on the new scheme including slogans plastered all over Vigyan Bhawan, grabbing attention like "Way to New India", "Seed Today, Tree Tomorrow", "Creating Creators", and "We Unobstacle". Vijay Sharma, founder of Paytm, remarked, "Three-year tax holiday is a big relief. I did not expect this much from government but this was huge; 110 out of 100 to Modi Government." Albinder Dhindsa, founder of Grofers, commented, "Government spoke about the right things including ending license raj, etc. This sets the right tone.... It looks very promising for emerging businesses." Nidhi Agarwal, founder of Kaaryah, stated. "The event will give more courage to the thousands who have been sitting on the fence to start up and make a difference." Similarly, Naveen Tewari, founder of InMobi, said, "Localized capitalists are better at understanding local solutions. Foreign investors might not understand that, which is why local investors are important."

An array of initiatives for startups announced by Modi are "good to have" for promoting an entrepreneurial ecosystem, but not really 'necessary to have'. Startups can survive and thrive even otherwise. The first budget presented by Finance Minister Arun Jaitley on 10 July 2014 proposed to set up a ₹ 10,000 crore fund "to act as a catalyst to attract private capital by way of providing equity, quasi-equity, soft loans and other risk capital for startup companies." More than a year later, on 19 August 2015, he launched the "India Aspiration Fund" (IAF), essentially a fund of funds to invest in venture capital firms for meeting the equity needs of micro, small and medium (MSM) startups. The government set aside ₹ 2,000 crore for the IAF. Small Industries Development Bank of India (SIDBI), which is managing the fund, has given the job of screening proposals from Venture Capital firms to an independent six-member committee comprising experts such as Kiran Karnik, T.V. Mohandas Pai, Saurabh Srivastava and R. Vaidyanathan of IIM Bengaluru. The committee has held 3-4 meetings over the last couple of months and committed about ₹ 1,000 crore to various funds. What is commendable about the investment process is that there is no interference by the political class or the bureaucracy, and the funds available for investment are five times the government contribution. Express editors interpret[5] that startup announcement is essentially a reiteration or a repackaging of the 2014-15 budget proposals. The amount of ₹ 10,000 crore will come over four years, with annual tranches of ₹ 2,500 crore. Narendra Modi, however, introduced a twist in the eligibility criteria of investee companies—funding support will be available for development and growth of innovation-driven entrepreneurs. Unless there are clearly laid down criteria that define innovation, sanction and disbursement carries an element of discretion or subjectivity.

To put the size of the fund of funds in perspective, ₹ 2,500 crore (US$ 375 million) a year is just about 2-3 percent of the total Venture Capital funding Indian entrepreneurs attract. In 2015, total investments by Private Equity and Venture Capital firms stood as US$ 16.87 billion, according to Venture Intelligence, a firm that tracks the industry. As far as eligibility is concerned, the Department of Industrial Policy and Promotion definition of a startup runs into a page and a half (over 500 words). To take advantage of the government schemes, the startup cannot be more than five years old, and cannot have a turnover of over ₹ 25 crore. It must aim to develop and commercialize a new product, service or process, or significantly improvise an existing product, service or process. To be eligible for tax benefits, the innovative nature of the business must be validated by an inter-ministerial board set up by the DIPP. Ironically, many startups, including the likes of Flipkart, Grofers and InMobi, have domiciled themselves outside the country. Besides the Silicon Valley in the US, two other countries that have taken the lead are Israel and Singapore. This has a lot to do with a liberal tax regime, ease of doing business, and a significantly reduced regulatory burden. T.V. Mohandas Pai and Sharad Sharma of iSpirit have blogged that 54 percent of all new-age startups in 2014 were domiciled overseas. This is expected to have increased to 75 percent in 2015. Not only startups, even Private Equity and Venture Capital funds structure themselves in a complicated manner to base themselves in Mauritius or other countries, where they do not have to pay tax on capital gains when they exit a startup. It is not surprising then that foreign Private Equity funds invested US$ 9.4 billion in 2015, thrice the investment by India-dedicated Private Equities (US$ 3.05 billion).

Khadi to be the Most Ecofriendly Fabric

The Modi Government is all set to make khadi a "zero effect, zero defect" global product. It has decided to harness solar energy to power "charkhas" (spinning wheels) across the country to enable handspun khadi to become the zero-carbon footprint green fabric of India. The Ministry of Micro, Small and Medium Enterprises (MSME)—a branch of the Government of India—has received the PM's go-ahead for the project and the field trial of the solar wheels has already begun on a pilot basis in the Khanwa village of Nawada district in Bihar. The vision of this initiative is multi-pronged: ideological, economic, and social—creating 80 lakh jobs by this initiative in 2016-17, in addition to boosting production by 20 times, involving least drudgery.

The vision is to add technology to spinning wheels as per the foresight of Gandhiji who wanted the application of science to the spinning wheel; only it should not replace humans. While harnessing solar power for spinning would not involve the use of electricity, it would also drastically reduce water consumption. For making a metre of mill fabric, 55 litres of water is needed, while for making a metre of khadi fabric, only three litres of water is required. These new-age charkhas have been named Nano Spinning Mills. The need of the hour is decentralized production, which is able to create more jobs and make khadi competitive in terms of reducing the cost of yarn and production.

In the next phase of implementation, the ministry would extend the solar charkha scheme to all the villages in India that are covered under Adarsh Gram Yojana. Even at the experimental stage, the technology has yielded ₹ 6,000 to ₹ 9,000 a month for every household involved in the exercise. The ministry plans to introduce 1,000 such spinning wheels in all villages. With just 400 spinning wheels now, the Khanwa village in Bihar is earning around ₹ 15 crore a month, with 10000 such wheels, the income of the villagers will go up to ₹ 30 crore.

The solar spinning wheels would also generate employment. Estimates say 10 persons are engaged in every solar spinning wheel; thus in the village alone, 10000 jobs would be created. Given the number of parliamentary constituencies and the villages under the Adarsh Gram Yojana, about 70-80 lakh jobs can be created.

Chinese Investments in India

A real estate group owned by China's richest man, Wang Jianlin has reached an understanding with the Haryana Government for setting up an industrial park, likely to come up on 3,000 acres of land and projected to have a total investment value of US$ 10 billion. This will be the biggest Chinese investment project in India so far; till date it is between US$ 2-3 billion, according to official figures. The understanding was announced after Wang met with Haryana Chief Minister Manohar Lal Khattar during latter's visit to Beijing. The Wanda Industrial Park would likely to come up near Kharkhoda along the Kundli-Manesar-Palwal (KMP) expressway. Under the plan, the Wanda group will develop an industrial park as well as an entertainment theme park, and it would also bring in Chinese investors in tourism and real estate to develop the park.

Dalian Wanda Group is aggressively spending on projects and acquisitions ranging from entertainment to financial services in a bid to diversify away from its core business. The conglomerate, which posted US$ 44 billion in revenue in 2015, wants more than a third of its revenue to come from abroad by 2020. ZTE Corporation is also to develop smart cities in Haryana. China Fortune Land Development Company (P) Ltd.

is to develop large industrial parks, either in Madina (Rohtak), or Bidhal Lath Gohana (Sonipat) over an area of more than 300 acres, and Inspur Group plans to invest US$ 100 million in IDC, CDN and cable-box manufacturing plant. All these projects will provide lots of opportunities in India.

Chinese Internet giants have promised to pour funds into digital startups, turning drought into a deluge. For years, Chinese investment in India remained a trickle—just US$ 1.2 billion between 2000 and September 2015, which was only 0.47 percent of India's total FDI inflow. While China became India's largest trading partner in 2008, investment flow from the country remained low. But now things have changed significantly. Wanda, China's largest commercial real estate developer, announced investment worth US$ 10 billion in Haryana; SAIC Motor, China's largest carmaker, proposed to buy GM's Gujarat facility. About 100 small and medium Chinese enterprises have promised investments worth US$ 1 billion. In the startup space, Chinese companies are no more restricted to proposals, but have been making aggressive and widespread investments. The year 2016 began with Chinese online travel company, Ctrip picking up a strategic stake in Makemytrip and Baidu unveiling discussions with multiple Indian Internet startups for investments. This comes in the backdrop of Alibaba's high-profile investments in Snapdeal and Paytm last year. Another Chinese internet giant, Tencent Holdings, started investing when it took a wager on Bengaluru-based healthcare startup Practo last year.

"Chinese internet companies have recognized the big potential in India's digital startups where there are similarities in learning curves and experiences", Frank Hancock, Managing Director, Barclays said. He explained that the broader FDI investments have pivoted towards the East with Japan competing with the US and UK among the top three sources of capital. "In that context, the incremental Chinese private investments are important from a signaling perspective", Hancock added. India's internet and e-commerce journey bears close similarity with that of China, with a lag of 8-10 years. "The presence of such investors on the boards of investee companies enables access to insightful market advice and winning business models", said

Anup Vikal, CFO, Snapdeal which has attracted investments from Alibaba, Taiwan's Foxconn and Japanese telecom and internet giant SoftBank.

Between 1 January 2015 and 22 January 2016, investors from Asia chose 48 Indian startups to provide financial backing. The 22 companies from countries including Japan, China, South Korea, Taiwan, Singapore and Malaysia participated in funding rounds worth US$ 3.4 billion in this period. Chinese companies Alibaba, Tencent-Ctrip, Didi Kuaidi, Hillhouse Capital, and Tybourne (Hong Kong) were significant investors. Most of China's cash reserves are said to be invested in dollar and euro denominated assets, though the country has started taking risk exposures in other geographies as well. While Chinese investor interest in Indian internet startups has gathered momentum, it is yet to translate into other sectors which China has eyed for some years now. So far, the US internet companies have had a hold on the Indian market. However, about a year ago, the Chinese internet conglomerates started to stitch things together in India with strategic bets. Their approach is very long-term which bodes well for Indian startups which were dependent on very few deep-pocketed funds for writing the larger cheques.

Hancock of Barclays said he would expect Chinese investors to overtake their US counterparts. Outside the digital economy, Japan has clearly signaled its intent for aggressive investments in infrastructure as it wants India to be a geopolitical counterweight to China. They, however, are counting on Chinese investments into Indian healthcare and real estate segments. Wanda's fresh proposal of investment of US$ 10 billion in India (Haryana) follows earlier announced joint ventures with Anil Ambani's Reliance Group to develop integrated townships in Navi Mumbai and Hyderabad. As China joins Japan, Taiwan and South Korea to pump FDI into India, much depends on how its private businesses muscle up in the face of a slump after an extended economic miracle.

China-type Ecozones

India is drawing up plans to build mega coastal economic zones, hoping to replicate China's success with such enclaves to boost exports and command a global presence in the leading markets in several sectors, particularly electronics and textiles. Discussions are on to prepare a plan to build these zones in states such as Gujarat, Maharashtra, Tamil Nadu and Andhra Pradesh. These zones will be like special economic zones (SEZs) and will be located along the coast. So far, the emphasis has been on serving the domestic market but with these zones Indian products can be shipped to global markets.

The plan is to push the Make in India initiative along with job creation, to build cities around these zones. In the 1960s, India first conceived of export processing zones (EPZs), along the coastal cities such as Kandla, Mumbai and Chennai, with Noida being the sole inland zone. In the first decade of the new century, the country started developing special economic zones (SEZs). So far, the emphasis has been on serving the domestic market, but with these zones, Indian products can be shipped to overseas markets. Concessions will be provided to help build these zones. The current incentives for the electronics sector can be applied to units in these enclaves.

The coastal zones are expected to be a step forward, although it is still unclear if the government is willing to walk the extra mile by easing labour laws and offering other concessions. It is expected to complement the government's initiative on port development and also help build cities around these new zones. If China has been able to capture global markets, why can't India? Certainly, India can emerge as a large player in the electronics and electrical segments and reduce its dependence on imports. Similarly, India can hope to regain prominence in some of the markets in textiles, where other small countries have made large inroads. The plan comes at a time when there is concern about the trajectory of the country's exports and there is an effort to cast the net wider for Made in India goods.

Startup and Women Entrepreneurs

There has been a sharp increase in the number of startups owned by women entrepreneurs in the last two years as the "ecosystem has started to accept them", according to leading women business leaders. Shaili Chopra, founder, SheThePeople.

TV, said the number of women participating in the startup ecosystem is growing rapidly. There has been 50 percent jump in women participating in the startup ecosystem in the last two years. According to Pranshu Patni, co-founder of educational app company Culture Alley, things have changed dramatically over the years and nowadays people look at her as just another co-founder of the app giant and not merely as a woman. Similarly, Nidhi Agarwal, founder of women's clothes and accessories brand Kaaryah, said that woman-owned businesses have a very large space to catch up. Women are often asked questions about their marriage plans when they approach investors. This needs to be changed.

Anisha Singh, founder, Mydala, expressed the view that she has seen a change in the environment for women entrepreneurs from 2009, when she started. In 2009, there were few women in businesses and she had to challenge the investors' imagination as she started raising funds. She added that women-led businesses don't have adequate funding and they face several challenges, but the environment is changing and people are more aware now. Although a lot more women entrepreneurs have come forward, things need to change faster.

Women entrepreneurs are breaking gender shackles in the startup nation drive. Anisha Singh was two months pregnant when she started Mydala.com, a website that offers deals online. The deals business was on the rise in India around 2009; as many as 70 odd companies had started to offer everything on discount—food in restaurants, gym membership and salon services, dancing lessons, body art, adventure sports, etc. But after two years the deals business came down. Some, such as Snapdeal, pivoted to become online marketplace. However, Anisha Singh was the only woman in the deals business—all the other companies had been founded by men. Fast forward six years, her company, Mydala has been profitable, enabling ₹ 4,000 crore of retail.

According to Sreedhar Prasad, partner, e-commerce and startups at KPMG, 15 to 17 percent of entrepreneurs in e-commerce are women, instead of just 2-3 percent a few years ago. Anisha Singh was one of the early birds in this business.

Sabina Chopra quit her job with Japan Airways to start ticketing website yatra.com in 2005. Then she was the only woman in the trade. India had only 21 million internet users (250 million in 2015). She would get excited when the site sold 100 tickets. Today it does 25,000 a day. Radhika Aggarwal, co-founder of Shopclues, who looks after branding, marketing, acquisitions, sales, hiring and product mix, made her venture a billion-dollar company.

Nidhi Agarwal's startup, Kaaryah, promises clothes for every female body type. "We studied 1,500 body types across the country and incubated our own stitching units. We make clothes suitable to almost every body type," she said. Suchi Mukherjee's Limeroad is into social commerce, and is changing the way people dress, allowing people to create their own style. Not just clothes, they can be curator of an entire scrapbook, or look with all kinds of accessories like shoes and jewellery, using products from 2,000 vendors featured on Limeroad. Upasana Taku, co-founder of mobile wallet company MobiKwik, with her spouse and co-founder Bipin Preet Singh built up the company, and ensured that the work would not get affected. Her company is the country's second largest mobile wallet company.

Even the world of glamour is not untouched by the e-commerce phenomenon. While Deepika Padukone launched her fashion line on Myntra, Priya Sachdev has become a serial entrepreneur. Her company, RockNShop, has partnered many designers and tailors to develop premium clothing. Many of her suppliers are women, who sell on various e-commerce sites. Aarti Goel was a housewife before she started selling on e-commerce marketplaces. She started with a single product and is now shipping 10,000 orders a day. She has made her own identity.

In the last two years, the number of women among sellers on the online marketplaces has grown five-fold to 35 percent, selling mostly apparel, art and craft and boutique items. The value of Indian e-commerce now stands at US$ 15-16 billion, and 10 percent of that is with companies having women owners or founders, up from 2 percent five years ago. According to

Harvard Business Review, 10 percent of all startups in India are set up by women, 30 to 35 percent are into e-commerce and related businesses; 17 percent of e-commerce startups have women founders.

Standup India for Boosting Entrepreneurship

Prime Minister Narendra Modi, on 5th April 2016, launched the 'Standup India' initiative aimed at boosting entrepreneurship among women, SC & ST communities and it has a strong motive behind as to make India as a developed nation by 2022.

The standup India aims to turn women into job-creators from job-seekers and will benefit at least 2.5 lakh borrowers with main focus on women entrepreneurs and those from SC/ST backgrounds. Under the scheme, the loans will be provided at the lowest possible rates so that the target beneficiaries can get maximum assistance. The scheme intends to facilitate at least two such projects per bank branch, on an average of one for each category of entrepreneurship.

Existing women entrepreneurs will be asked to provide their assistance and expertise to the new aspirants. Women would be provided with proper training on entrepreneurship and shall be informed about the challenges in starting business. They shall also be taught about respective sectors they are interested in. The overall intent is to reach out to these underserved sectors of the population by facilitating bank loans repayable up to seven years and between ₹ 10 lakh to ₹ 1 crore for enterprises in the non-farm sector set up by such SC, ST and women borrowers. The enterprise may be in manufacturing, services or the trading sector. In case of non-individual enterprises at least 51% of the shareholding and controlling stake should be held by either an SC/ST or woman entrepreneur. The tax benefit will also be provided for a certain period. In startup India, the tax benefit is for three years, and it can be five years for women entrepreneurs in the Standup India scheme. The loan under the scheme would be secured and backed by a credit guarantee through a credit guarantee scheme for which the Department of Financial Services would be the settler and National Credit Guarantee Trustee Company Ltd. (NCGTC) would be the operating agency.

Male members from SC/ST can also get assistance under the scheme on the name of their wives. But the women members will have to actively participate in the business as well besides getting training.

Key features of Standup India initiative are:

Loan Amount—The loan amount can be between ₹ 10 lakh to ₹ 1 crore, including both long-term and working capital loan.

Nature of the Loan—Standup India is a composite loan program under which the borrower can apply for either term loan or working capital or for both.

Types of Businesses Eligible—(a) The loan is for first time entrepreneurs, i.e., the project for which loan is being taken should be first venture of the entrepreneur. (b) It can be a sole proprietorship, a partnership firm, private or public limited company. 51% of the stakes must be held by SC/ST/ woman.

Interest on Loan—The interest rate will include the following elements:

(a) Base rate or MCLR (Marginal cost of fund based leading rate).

(b) Tenor premium, longer period loan has higher interest rate.

(c) Spread of 3% towards banks operational cost. The rate of interest would be lowest applicable rate of the bank for that category (rating category) not to exceed (MCLR+3%+tenor premium).

Security—Security would depend on the banks discretion, there are two options:

(a) Collateral security offered by the entrepreneur.

(b) Guarantee from credit guarantee fund set up under Standup India scheme.

Repayment—The loan can be repaid in 7 years with a moratorium period of 1.5 years.

Margin Money—25% of the project cost, part of it can be met through other Central Government and State Government schemes. However, entrepreneur must bring in 10% of the project cost as his/her contribution.

Ease of Applying—The application for the loan can be forwarded through:

(a) online registration,
(b) the branch of any scheduled band, and
(c) the lead district manager of the chosen bank.

Standup for Smart City

Pradhan Mantri Smart City Yojana is a project that has been suggested by Narendra Modi under which the Indian cities will be developed in such a way so that they can match the standards of the Modern cities in the global platform. The scheme aims at developing the cities into a modern and sustainable living place with all the amenities of modern infrastructure, education, healthcare, public transport, Wi-Fi connectivity, 24 × 7 electricity, water supply, proper waste disposal, and other opportunities. The purpose of Smart City Yojana is not just to build multi-storied buildings but to develop a city in which people have easier lifestyle and have to put lesser effort to avail basic facilities along with having sanitation and other services at bay. The project would ensure that cities and towns of India are made better in all the spheres. It would bring in smart solutions within the targeted cities and towns so that the day to day lives of citizens living in these cities is convenient and efficient at the same time. Within a span of 20 years, a total of 100 cities and towns would be covered and built on international standards. The major metros of the country are already at some par, therefore, in the first phase the project would target the B grade towns and cities and bring them up in terms of infrastructure and facilitaties.

The approach of the Smart City Yojana is to promote cities that provide core infrastructure and give a decent quality of life to its citizens, a clean and sustainable environment and application of 'Smart Solutions'. The focus is on sustainable and inclusive development and the idea is to look at compact areas, create a replicable model which will act like a light house to other aspiring cities. Thus, the purpose of the Smart City Yojana is to drive economic growth and improve the quality of life of people by enabling local area development and harnessing technology, especially technology that leads to smart outcomes. Area-based development will transform existing areas; including slums, into better planned ones, thereby improving liveability of the whole city. New areas will be developed around cities in order to accommodate the expanding population in urban areas. Application of Smart Solutions will enable cities to use technology, information and data to improve infrastructure and services. Comprehensive development in this way will improve quality of life, create employment, and enhance incomes for all, especially the poor and the disadvantaged, leading to inclusive cities.

By the government's definition, a smart city is "not a destination but a series of small steps in that direction". The list of 20 smart cities and towns shortlisted by the Centre, though, appears to be a decisive step in this direction, considering that these cities have already furnished plans to cumulatively mobilize resources to the tune of ₹ 50,802 crore over the next five years under the public-private-partnership route and invest these funds for rolling out "smart" interventions across an area spanning 26,735 acres through a mix of redevelopment and greenfield development. These include an integrated urban planning effort with a sharper focus on infrastructure, land use planning, transport, design and architecture.

Uttar Pradesh and many other states fall short in smart city test as they have missed to make the required cut. Odisha's capital Bhubaneswar tops the list of 20 cities as part of the first batch of the smart city initiative that will attract investment of over ₹ 50,000 crore to leap into a modern and dynamic landscape. It was for the first time in the country and even in the world that investments in the urban sector were being made on competition-based selection of cities. Pune, Jaipur, Surat, Kochi, Ahmedabad, Jabalpur, Visakhapatnam, Solapur, Devangere, Indore, Coimbatore, Kakinada, Belgaum, Udaipur, Guwahati, Chennai, Ludhiana and Bhopal are the other cities selected in the first batch. Three cities of Madhya Pradesh, two each from

Andhra Pradesh, Karnataka, Tamil Nadu, Gujarat, Maharashtra, and Rajasthan, and one each from the remaining five states made it to the winning list. The Urban Development Ministry said 23 states and UTs that have missed the first chance will be given an opportunity to participate in a fast-track competition. Each top ranking city from these left-out states can upgrade their smart city proposals and submit them for inclusion in the mission. Investment of ₹ 50,802 crore has been proposed for the development of these cities over five years with public-private-partnership as a major vehicle of resource mobilization. New Delhi is one of India's 20 smart cities to be developed under the Centre's flagship scheme.

The core infrastructure elements in a smart city would include adequate water supply; assured electricity supply; sanitation, including solid waste management; efficient urban mobility and public transport; affordable housing, especially for the poor; robust IT connectivity and digitalization; good governance, especially e-Governance and citizen participation; sustainable environment; safety and security of citizens, particularly women, children and the elderly; and health and education.

The urbanization level in India is still at just around 31 percent as compared to China's 54 percent, Brazil's 90 percent and well over 80 percent in most developed economies. Modi Government's policy thrust on upgrading urban infrastructure could see the list of 20 smart cities being expanded to 100 urban centres and the upgradation of basic infrastructure—under the Atal Mission for Rejuvenation and Urban Transformation (AMRUT)—across 500 cities with outlays of ₹ 48,000 crore and ₹ 50,000 crore, respectively.[6]

The availability of affordable housing and large enough public transportation networks are necessary for the growth of big cities like state capitals and large metropolitan areas. States need to prioritize the long-term development of these cities and areas, with the centre stepping in wherever they overlap across states.

The Core Infrastructure Elements in a Smart City

The following are the core elements in a smart city:[7]

(i) Promotion of mixed land use in area-based developments with planning for 'unplanned areas' containing a range of compatible activities and land uses close to one another in order to make land use more efficient. The states will allow some flexibility in land use and building bye-laws to adapt to change.

(ii) Expansion of housing opportunities for all.

(iii) Reduction in congestion, air pollution and resource depletion, boost to local economy, and promotion of interactions and ensuring security. Ensuring that the roads are created or refurbished not only for vehicles and public transport, but also for pedestrians and cyclists. Necessary administrative services will be offered within walking/cycling distance.

(iv) Preservation and development of open spaces—parks, playgrounds, and recreational spaces in order to enhance the quality of life of citizens, reduce the urban heat effects in areas and promote eco-balance.

(v) Promotion of a variety of transport options—Transit Oriented Development (TOD), public transport and last mile para-transport connectivity.

(vi) Increasing reliance on online services to bring about accountability and transparency, especially using mobiles to reduce cost of services and provision of services without having to go to municipal offices; formation of e-groups to listen to people and obtain feedback and use of online monitoring of programs and activities with the aid of cyber tour of worksites.

(vii) Giving an identity to the city based on its main economic activities like local cuisine, healthcare, education, culture, sports goods, furniture, hosiery, textile, dairy, etc.

(viii) Application of Smart Solutions to infrastructure and services in area-based development in order to make them better, which will include making areas less vulnerable to disasters, using fewer resources, and providing cheaper services.

Startup India has the objective of promoting bank financing for start-up ventures to boost entrepreneurship and encourage start-ups with jobs creation. It aims to restrict the role of States in policy domain and to get rid of license raj and other hindrances, particularly in land permissions, foreign investment proposal and environmental clearances, among other things. The programme has been organized by Department of Industrial Policy and Promotion (DIPP). The government has already launched iMADE, an app development platform which set for itself the target of producing 1,000,000 apps and Pradhan Mantri MUDRA Yojana (PMMY), the Micro Units Development and Refinance Agency (MUDRA) Bank—a new institution set up for development and refinancing activities relating to micro units with a refinance fund of ₹ 200 billion. Under the scheme, three categories of interventions has been named which includes:

- Shishu—loan up to ₹ 50,000.
- Kishore—loan ranging from ₹ 50,000 to ₹ 5 lakh.
- Tarun—loan above ₹ 5 lakh and below ₹ 10 lakh.

These three categories will signify the growth, development and funding needs of the beneficiaries as well as it will assure the loan amount to be allotted by MUDRA Bank.

The Ministry of Human Resource Development and the Department of Science and Technology have agreed to partner in an initiative to set up over 75 startup support hubs in the National Institutes of Technology (NITs), the Indian Institutes of Information Technology (IIITs), the Indian Institutes of Science Education and Research (IISERs), and National Institutes of Pharmaceutical Education and Research (NIPERs).[8]

The Reserve Bank of India has also entrusted upon itself the task of taking suitable steps to help improve the "ease of doing business" in the country and contribute to create an environment that is conducive for the growth of start-up businesses.

Southern States like Karnataka, Kerala, Andhra Pradesh and Telangana have shown better results than others in terms of their policy implementation for supporting startups. They have focused on improving infrastructure, especially in the Tier-II cities. Bengaluru, a metro city of Karnataka, known as the Silicon Valley of India has implemented the startup policies in letter and spirit. Kerala brought a startup policy, "Kerala IT Mission", which focuses on fetching ₹ 50 billion in investments for the State's startup ecosystem. It also made India's first telecom incubator Startup village in 2012.[9]

Telangana has launched the largest incubation centre in India, known as "T-Hub". Andhra Pradesh has allocated a 17,000 sq.ft. Technological Research and Innovation Park as a Research and Development Laboratory. It has also created a fund called "Initial Innovation Fund" of ₹ 100 crore for entrepreneurs.[10] The Government of Madhya Pradesh has collaborated with the Small Industries Development Bank of India (SIDBI) to create a fund of ₹ 200 crore. Rajasthan has also launched "Start-up Oasis" scheme.

Some stakeholders of the Indian startup ecosystem have raised concerns about the fact that the top 200 startups in India have re-domiciled their headquarters outside the country, primarily to the US and Singapore, in a bid to enjoy more freedom in doing business. In light of this, a think-tank initiative Product Nation has identified 34-key issues that need to be resolved immediately to stop the exodus. The list includes issues ranging from company incorporation to fund raising, operations, taxation, exits, closure, payments, and intellectual property.[11]

Startup India gives wide opportunities to start a new business in India. During the last two and a half decades, the Indian IT Industry grew from US$ 50 million to US$150 billion. The IT revolution has been brought about by the country's first generation in circumstances that were not favourable at home or abroad. And now when the circumstances are much better, it is time that India's young generation comes forward, and venturing into entrepreneurship, brings a similar revolution in other sectors as well.

Notes

1. India Today.in
2. "Startup India: This is the beginning of big bang startup boom in India, says Softbank CEO." *The Hindu*. 16 January 2016.

3. "RBI to create enabling framework for growth of start-ups". *The Hindu*. 2 Feb. 2016.
4. *The Financial Express*. 16 January 2016.
5. P. Vaidyanathan Iyer. "In Fact: Start-up sops are good. Are they essential?" *The Indian Express*. 19 January 2016.
6. http://indianexpress.com/article/india/india-news-india/smart-city-mission-selection-done-its-time-for-execution/
7. smartcities.gov.in
8. *The Hindu*. 16 January 2016.
9. "Startup Mission to ink pact for innovation zone." *The Hindu*. 3 January 2016.
10. "PM Modi to launch 'Startup India' campaign today". *Business Standard*. 16 Jan. 2016.
11. http://forbesindia.com/article/startup-india-2016/startup-india-is-workinprogress/41945/1#ixzz4BiZ7sNu6

CHAPTER 7

Skill India Programme: Way to Enhance Employability and Generate More Employment

On the occasion of the first-ever World Youth Skills Day, Prime Minister Narendra Modi launched Skill India programme on 15 July 2015 with an objective to create opportunities, space and scope for the development of the talents of the Indian youth and to develop more of those sectors which have already been put under skill development for the last so many years and also to identify new sectors for skill development. He also unveiled the Skill India logo with the tagline—'Kaushal Bharat, Kushal Bharat' (Skilled India, Successful India), suggesting that Kaushal Bharat (Skilling Indians) will result in a happy, healthy, prosperous and strong nation (Kushal Bharat). The Skill India programme is a multi-skill programme which aims at providing training and skill development to over 40 crore youth of our country by 2022, covering each and every village and city. Of these, at least 110 million workers are required in over 25 select sectors such as textiles, automobiles, construction, banking and retail. The programme includes various initiatives of the government such as National Skill Development Mission, National Policy for Skill Development and Entrepreneurship, 2015, Pradhan Mantri Kaushal Vikas Yojana (PMKVY), and the Skill Loan Scheme.

The Ministry of Skill Development and Entrepreneurship will be responsible for the co-ordination of all skill development efforts across the country, removal of disconnect between demand and supply of skilled manpower, building of vocational and technical training framework, upgradation of skills, building of new skills and innovative thinking for existing jobs as well as for jobs that are to be created. The Ministry aims to skill people on a large scale with speed and high standards in order to achieve its vision of a 'Skilled India'.

The Ministry is aided in these initiatives by its functional arms—National Skill Development Agency (NSDA), National Skill Development Corporation (NSDC), National Skill Development Fund (NSDF) and 33 Sector Skill Councils (SSCs) as well as 187 training partners registered with NSDC. The Ministry also intends to work with the existing network of skill development centres, universities and other alliances in the field. Further, collaborations with relevant Central Ministries, State Governments, international organizations, industry and NGOs have been initiated for multi-level engagement and more impactful implementation of skill development efforts.[1]

Features of Skill India

The important features of the programme are listed below:

(i) The emphasis will be to skill the youths in such a way that their employability increases and entrepreneurship in general is improved.

(ii) Training, support and guidance shall be provided for all occupations, including those of traditional type, such as carpenters, welders, tailors, weavers, and blacksmiths.

(iii) There will be more emphasis on new areas like real estate, construction, textile, tourism, banking, and jewellery designing.

(iv) The training programmes would be of high standard so that the youths match international standards in manufacturing goods and providing services.

(v) There is also a plan to create a hallmark called 'Rural India Skill', so as to standardise and certify the training process.

(vi) Tailor-made, need-based progammes would be initiated for specific age groups which can be like language and communication skills, life and positive thinking skills, personality development skills, management skills, behavioural skills, including job and employability skills.

(vii) The course methodology of 'Skill India' would be innovative, which would include games, group discussions, brainstorming sessions, practical experiences, case studies, etc.

UK has entered into a partnership with India under Skill India. Virtual partnerships will be initiated at the school level to enable young people of either country to experience the school system of the other country and develop an understanding of the culture, traditions and social and family systems. A commitment to achieve mutual recognition of UK and Indian qualifications was also made.[2]

Skill India—Different from the Previous Skill Development Policies

Skill development is not new in India. Previous governments also laid emphasis on development of skills as a national priority. But this time, the approach is new and magnitude is higher. Earlier, the emphasis was on traditional jobs. Now, all kinds of jobs have been brought within the ambit of the scheme. Earlier, the responsibility was divided among various ministries. But now these ministries have been clubbed together. The principal ministry is the Ministry of Skill Development and Entrepreneurship (MSDE), which will coordinate with other ministries and organisations.

The idea of the programme is to raise confidence, improve productivity and give direction through proper skill development. Skill development will enable the youths to get blue-collar jobs. Development of skills, at a young age is very essential to channelize the youths for proper job opportunities. There is also necessity for a balanced growth in all the sectors and all jobs should be given equal importance. Every job aspirant would be given training in soft skills to lead a proper and decent life. Skill development would also reach the rural and remote areas. Corporate educational institutions, non-government organizations, government, academic institutions, and society would help in the development of skills of the youths so that the desired results are achieved in the shortest time possible.[3]

According to Prime Minister Narendra Modi, Skill India won't be just a programme but a movement. Under this programme, youths who are jobless, college and school dropouts, along with the educated ones, from rural and urban areas—all will be given value addition. The new Ministry will be the certifying agency. Certificates will be issued to those who complete a particular skill or programme, and this certificate has to be recognized by all public and private agencies and entities, including overseas organizations. Skill India is a programme for the entire nation.[4]

The National Skill Development Agency (NSDA) was created with the mandate to coordinate and harmonise skill development activities and it is part of the Ministry of Skill Development and Entrepreneurship (MSDE). As per the Gazette Notification, the functions of NSDA will be the following:

(a) Take all possible steps to meet skilling targets as envisaged in the 12th Five-Year Plan and beyond.

(b) Coordinate and harmonize the approach to skill development among various Central Ministries/ Department, State Governments, the NSDC and the private sector.

(c) Anchor and operationalize the National Skill Qualification Framework (NSQF) to ensure that quality and standards meet sector specific requirements.

(d) Be the nodal agency for State Skill Development Missions.

(e) Raise extra-budgetary resources for skill development from various sources such as international agencies, including multilateral agencies and the private sector.

(f) Evaluate existing skill development schemes with a view to assessing their efficacy and suggest corrective action to make them more effective.

(g) Create and maintain a national database related to skill development, including development of a dynamic Labour Market Information System (LMIS).

(h) Take affirmative action for advocacy.

(i) Ensure that the skilling needs of the disadvantaged and marginalized groups like SCs, STs, OBCs, minorities, women, and differently-abled persons are taken care of.

(j) Discharge any other function as may be assigned by the Government of India.

Besides anchoring and implementation, the National Skills Qualifications Framework (NSQF), some of the other actions taken by the NSDA are:

(a) Rationalization of the Skill Development Schemes of the Government of India.

(b) Creation of an integrated Labour Market Information System, which would bring in operational efficiencies, transparency, and would be available to all, and would help reduce considerably the situation of one individual being benefitted under different schemes.

(c) Engagement with States—Through technical assistance programmes with the Asian Development Bank (ADB), European Union (EU) and Department for International Development of the Government of UK, NSDA is helping the State Skill Development Missions of eleven states build their respective capacities.

(d) Skills Innovation Initiative—The NSDA invites innovative ideas, concepts and practices on skill development; and the selected innovative practices will be facilitated and propagated for wider application.

PM Modi said that the government would work to promote both apprenticeship and entrepreneurship. It is important for

India, according to him, to be able to predict future possibilities, and to "prepare for them today itself". Job seekers, job providers, students and policy-makers need to think alike. Linking aspirations to skill training, the PM said that if the 20th century saw India's foremost technical institutes—the Indian Institutes of Technology—make a name for themselves globally, the 21st century requires that India's ITIs (Industrial Training Institutes) acquire global recognition for producing quality-skilled manpower. He said that India's less privileged sections want to live with respect and that the acquisition of skills will give them energy and confidence.

Skill Development, Productivity and Employment Potential

Productivity which explains an input-output relationship is a crucial factor whose benefits can be distributed in a number of different ways such as better wages and working conditions to workforce, increased profits and dividend to shareholders, environmental protection, and increase in revenue to governments. This also helps both the enterprises and the the country to remain competitive in the domestic and global markets. The increase in productivity can be attributed to new technology, new machines, better management practices, investment in plant and equipment and technology, occupation safety improvement in the skill level of workers, macroeconomic policies, labour market conditions, business environment, and public investment in infrastructure and education.

The workplace training plays an important role in productivity enhancement, but in the developing economies the huge informal economy poses a challenge which could be addressed by developing clusters or a lead firm taking the initiative which would help in achieving economies of scale in the skills development, competencies development within and between firms, and availability of lead firm facilities. The government can facilitate linkages among various companies and stimulate adoption of technologies and skill upgradation programmes. The lack of access to education and training or the low quality or relevance of training keeps the vulnerable and marginalized sections in the vicious circle of low skills, low employment and low productivity. The National Skill Policy initiated by Narendra Modi in its present manifestation provides a framework to offer enough opportunities to various target groups to realize their potential for productive work and contribute more in economic and social development of the country.

However, different approaches need to be adopted (which may overlap as groups are not mutually exclusive) such as improving agricultural marketing extension, investing in rural infrastructure, making available quality education, on-the-job and targeted training for the disabled, and identifying the requirement of migrant workers. The question is how one links the skill development to future challenges so as to address the demand of the growing Indian economy. The National Skill Development policy provides for integration of skill development into the national development policies such as developing infrastructure, reducing poverty and decent work agenda. Thus, the skill strategy of the government focuses on strategy of skill development aiming at addressing the skill needs of the self-employed as well as the casual employed. According to Economic Survey 2013-14, India can increase its long-term trend growth by unleashing the entrepreneurial spirit of millions across the country by strengthening the economic freedom of the people. Therefore, the National Policy on Skill Development and Entrepreneurship 2015 emphasises on entrepreneurship development as the pathway for creating more wage employment and in turn growth of the economy. The policy has identified following policy strategy for promoting entrepreneurship:

(a) Educate and equip potential and early stage entrepreneurs across India.
(b) Connect entrepreneurs to peers, mentors and incubators.
(c) Support entrepreneurs through Entrepreneurship Hubs (E-Hubs).
(d) Catalyse a culture shift to encourage entrepreneurship.
(e) Encourage entrepreneurship among the under-represented groups.

(f) Promote entrepreneurship amongst women.

(g) Improve ease of doing business.

(h) Improve access to finance.

(i) Foster social entrepreneurship and grassroots innovations.

Skill development of the self-employed is essential to make the transition from own account workers to employers or entrepreneurs. The success of the various programmes of Modi Government, such as Make in India, Digital India, Smart City, Namami Gange, Swachh Bharat depends on the success of the Skill India Mission in skilling and reskilling 460 million workforce by 2022. The skill development programmes to promote entrepreneurship are also important, namely:

(a) Self-Employment and Talent Utilization (SETU) Scheme—It is a techno-financial, incubation, and facilitation programme to support all aspects of startup businesses, and other self-employment activities, particularly in technology-driven areas.

(b) Atal Innovation Mission (AIM)—It is an innovation promotion platform involving academics, entrepreneurs, and researchers drawing upon national and international experiences to foster a culture of innovation, R&D in India.

(c) Startup India—It is to promote bank financing for startups and offer incentives to boost entrepreneurship and job creation in the country.

Countries that have succeeded in linking skill development to gains in productivity, employment and development have targeted skill development policy towards the following three main objectivities:

(i) Matching supply to current demand for skills,

(ii) Helping workers and enterprises adjust to change, and

(iii) Building and sustaining competencies for future labour market needs.

The first objective is about the relevance and quality of training. It is also about equality of opportunity in access to education, training, employment services and employment, in order that the demand for training from all sectors of society is met. The second objective is about easing the movement of workers and enterprises from declining or low-productivity activities and sectors into expanding and higher productivity activities and sectors. Learning new skills, upgrading existing ones and lifelong learning can help workers to maintain their employability and enterprises to adopt and remain competitive. And the third objective calls for a long-term perspective, anticipating the skills that will be needed in the future and engendering a virtuous circle in which more and better education and training fuels innovation, investment, technological change, economic diversification and competitiveness, and thus job growth.

To achieve the above stated objectives convergence across policies is essential. Skill development and employment policy should be inter-linked. The full value of one policy can be realised only if it supports the objectives of the other policy. For investments in skill development to yield maximum benefit to workers, enterprises and for the economy, the country's capacity for coordination is most important in the following three areas.

(a) Connecting basis education to technical training, technical training to labour market entry, and labour market entry to workplace and lifelong learning.
(b) Ensuring continuous communication between employers and training providers so that training meets the needs and aspirations of workers and enterprises.
(c) Integrating skill development policies with other policy areas—not only labour market and social protection policies, but also industrial, investment, trade and technology policies, and regional or local development policies.

On the education front, the National Skill Qualification Framework has been introduced to facilitate the smooth transition from general education to vocational education and vice versa at all levels. Under the National Skill Development Mission, the skill training of the heterogeneous labour force consisting of youth, women, school dropouts, disabled, minorities, tribal groups is mandated.

Demographic Dividend—A Unique Opportunity

As compared to other countries—developed and the developing—India has a unique opportunity for another 20-25 years, which is called the demographic advantage. If the country is able to skill its people with the requisite life skills, job skills or entrepreneurial skills in the years to come, the demographic advantage can be converted into demographic dividend wherein those entering labour market or are already in the labour market contribute productively to economic growth both within and outside the country. The demographic dividend is essentially due to two factors—declining birth rates and improvement in life expectancy. The declining birth rate changes the age distribution and makes for a smaller proportion of population in the dependent ages and for relatively larger share in the productive labour force. The result is low dependency ratio which can provide comparative cost advantage and competitiveness to the economy. The demographic dividend accounts for India having world's youngest workforce with a median age way below that of China and Organisation for Economic Cooperation and Development (OECD) countries. Alongside this window of opportunity for India, the global economy is expected to witness a skilled manpower shortage to the extent of around 56 million by 2020. Thus, the demographic dividend in India needs to be exploited not only to expand the production possibility frontier but also to meet the skilled manpower requirements of India and abroad.

To reap the benefits of demographic dividend, government had favoured the creation of a comprehensive National Skill Development Mission. As a result, a "Coordinated Action on Skill Development" with three-tier institutional structure consisting of PM's National Council, National Skill Development Coordination Board (NSDCB), and National

Skill Development Corporation (NSDC) was created in early 2008. Whereas, PM's National Council on Skill Development has spelt out policy advice, and direction in the form of "Core Principles" and has given a vision to create 500 million skilled people by 2022 through skill systems, NSDCB has taken upon itself the task of coordinating the skill development efforts of a large numbers of Central Ministries or Departments and States. The NSDC has taken the task of preparing comprehensive action plans and activities which would promote Public-Private-Partnership (PPP) models of financing skill development. The three-tier structure has laid the institutional foundations for a more proactive role of public (Centre plus States) and private and third sector interactions and interfaces for harnessing the benefits of demographic dividend. It has also been able to focus on skill development through the creation of a coordinating mechanism. It has also made the issue of skill development as an important agenda for the Governments at Centre as well as States. It has also articulated the importance of State Governments in the delivery of skill development.

In 2004-05, the total employment in the country was estimated at 459.1 million out of which 56.8 percent of workforce were self-employed, 28.9 percent casual labour, and 14.3 percent were regular wage earners. About 8 percent of the total workforce is employed in the organised sector, while the remaining 92 percent are in the non-formal sector. Therefore, employment needs to be generated in all sectors, namely primary, secondary, and territory. The quality of employment in organised sector is generally high though the scope of additional employment generation in this sector is rather limited. Significant employment generation is taking place in tertiary sector, particularly, in services industries. Self-employment and small business continue to play a vital role in this regard. Therefore, it is necessary to promote main employment generation activities like agriculture; labour intensive manufacturing sector such as food processing, leather products, textiles; services sectors such as trade, restaurants and hotels, tourism, construction and information technology; and small and medium enterprises.

According to a survey, the total number of young working-age (15-24 years) people who continued their study in educational institutions doubled from about 30 million in 2004-05 to over 60 million in 2009-10. The survey also shows that during this period, the overall labour force expanded by only 11.7 million, because of the much larger retention of youth in education, and also because of lower labour force participation among working-age women. However, over the same period, 18 million job opportunities were created on current daily status basis. Thus, in absolute terms, unemployment rate which had increased from 6.06 percent in 1993-94 to 7.31 percent in 1999-2000 and further to 8.28 percent in 2004-05, came down to 6.60 in 2009-10. According to *The Hindu*, unemployment was 9.6 percent in 2011, based on official census data. On an average basis, unemployment rate for the period 1983 to 2013 was 7.3 percent. Though the percentage come down in 2014 to around 5 percent, the number of unemployed persons increased due to increase in population.

Promotion of skill development is considered vital by Modi Government as renewed technologies are overtaking the earlier ones at a very fast rate. The short life cycle of modern technology necessitates re-training of the existing employees and skill development of new entrants to the labour force. For this purpose, it is essential that new institutions be established to meet the growing needs of the market. These institutions, set up by the government, should be totally free from bureaucratic control so that they redesign the training programmes and make people employable in their respective fields. Universities should also reorient their courses to meet the needs of market and promote university industry partnership in designing new courses.

India Skills Report

The India Skills Report is a joint initiative of CII, PeopleStrong, Wheebox and Linkedin. The report presents not only the employability factor of the youth from across the country from different educational background but also the needs and expectations of the employers. It is the scientific tool that can help address the skill gaps in labour market and facilitate better employment opportunities for the youth, thereby increasing India's industrial productivity.

Today, India is its own initiative, an initiative to rebuilt, reinvent and reenergize. The golden 'growth' era in the demographic dividend context is no longer a progression of thoughts but a reality that reflects youthful India's firm strides towards overall economic development. The focus towards both job generation and skill development, is leading the nation to greener demographic dividend pastures.

In the era of Knowledge based economy, skilled and employment ready manpower is utmost important. There are various initiatives undertaken by the government, such as Skill India to hone skilled power, career centres to connect the dots in the employment zone; Make in India to create entrepreneurial capabilities and generate more employment facilities.

Creating a platform for the supply and demand side of talent to come together and bridge the demand with the expectations was the reason why India Skills Report was launched in the year 2013 which was based on Wheebox Employability Skill Test (WEST). Today, the test maps 29 states and 7 union territories in India, and it is conducted to identify the skill gap that exists in the industry today by deploying a scientific approach across 320 domain areas. The basic objective of the test is to bring reliable and authentic assessment to various aspects of education, training and employment. With each year as the focus on skills and jobs increased, the reach of the report was increased as well. In the third edition of the report (2016), with an increase of about 73% in the supply side, the test was able to reach out to over 520000 students across domains. Reach for corporate survey also increased by 20% and over 150 employers spread across 12 industry sectors were surveyed.

Based on researches that say that knowledge, skill, aptitude and behavioural components make the recipe of success in a jab, WEST-2016 assessed about 5.2 lakh candidates across 29 states and 7 union territories on various parameters—numerical and logical ability, communication skills, and domain knowledge. In addition to the parameters used there were three behavioural parameters introduced—Learning Agility, Adaptability, Interpersonal Skills as now a days they form an important assessing parameter for corporates. All the candidates were evaluated on all these sections and a combined score of the three sections was used to come up with the final score. All those who scored more than 60% in the overall score were considered employable.

Out of about 520000 candidates who appeared for the test across domains 38.12% were found employable. Though this number is an improvement from the number of past two years—37.22% (2015) and 33.95% (2014), but it clearly shows the need for the initiatives taken up by government towards skill development. However, these initiatives need to be immediate and impactful, if the gap between the supply and the demand side is to be diminished. As per this year's data candidates from Tier 2 cities were found to be more employable (over 50% candidates assessed were found employable) than Tier 1 cities (employability was 30%). As the government is pushing to establish business at the level of pin codes, it is important that the talent supply is available in these cities.

Moving to domain specific employability ratios, B.Tech. grades had the highest percentage of employability. Out of all the test takers from various domains, the ones with the lowest percentage of employable candidates are B.A., B.Com., ITI, and Polytechnic. It is imperative that special focus should be given to these domains—may be to the course curriculum or include more internship or apprenticeship programmes which can help in making the candidates job ready. Apart from the domain knowledge, there are other skills which are of high importance to employers for hiring a candidate. They include communication skills, computer skills, numerical and logical ability and few behavioural traits like learning agility, adaptability and interpersonal skills. With these skills added to the technical skills candidates will reach the potential where employer will be more than happy to absorb them in his organization.

From the result of the test, it can be seen that maximum numbers of employable resources are present in the age group of

18-21 years. Out of total number of candidates in the age group of 18-21 years who appeared for the test about 37% scored more than 60% and hence were part of the employable pool. For age group 22-25 years this number was 31.59% and for age group 26-29 years this number was 21.88%. Thus, it can be seen that the employability in younger age is a bit higher than the age group 26-29 years. A deeper dive in the candidates belonging to this age group revealed that most of the candidates belonging to this age group are those studying part time (open schools, weakened classes, etc.). So, it is clear that merely working on the mainstream candidates (who are attending regular classes) might not be enough. The stakeholders should try to increase the employability of the open school, and part time candidates too. This might be one of the steps that can help in bringing more "employable" candidates to organised job sector. The scores of the test were also studied on the basis of gender. The corporates are increasingly trying to maintain the gender diversity in their organizations by hiring more female candidates. As per the data, the employability of female candidates is higher than the male candidates. Employability of female candidates was assessed to be 39.95%, while that of male candidates was assessed to be 36.01%. Both these numbers show a slight improvement from previous year, where 37.88% females and 34.26% male candidates were found employable. The numbers have shown improvement from previous year, but it clearly shows that focused efforts are needed to improve employability of female candidates. For it, several new initiatives have been introduced, such as "Beti Bachao, Beti Padhao" launched at the centre and various initiatives at the state level.

India is passing through an exciting phase of growth and development. An encouraging GDP growth rate, increased FDI, Government's ambitious initiatives 'Make in India', 'Smart City', 'Digital India' will help to leapfrog India on the growth trajectory. The most important resource required to fuel this growth is Human Capital, which India is blessed with, in abundance. However, more than 93% of our workforce is unorganised. It is estimated that only 4.69% of the total workforce in India has undergone formal skill training as compared to more than 50% across the developed countries in the world. To add to this conundrum, with the average age of Indian becoming 29 years by 2020, it is estimated that our labour force will increase by 32% due to this demographic shift. The Government is well aware of this problem and skill development is considered as a national priority with a dedicated Ministry of Skill Development and Entrepreneurship (MSDE) being created. The Ministry is responsible for co-ordination of all skill development efforts across the country, matching of demand and supply of skilled manpower, building the vocational and technical training framework, skill upgradation, building of new skills and innovative thinking for jobs. The National Skill Development Mission launched by Prime Minister Modi will provide a strong institutional framework at the Centre and States for implementation of skilling activities in the country. National Skill Development Corporation (NSDC), one of its Kind Public Private Partnership, was created in 2008 with the following pillars:

(a) Create—catalyse creation of large, quality vocational training institutions.

(b) Fund—reduce risk by providing patient capital, including grants and equity.

(c) Enable—creation and sustainability of support systems required for skill development.

In order to increase the out reach of skills and to make it aspirational NSDC has been working closely with schools, universities and state government for implementation of vocational courses aligned with general education. It has also launched an advocacy campaign called "Hunar Hai to Kadar Hai" (With Skills comes Respect) to generate awareness about skill development programmes and to break the social stigma towards blue-collar jobs among youth. The efforts of NSDC to build an ecosystem around the demand and supply side of skills through interventions of advocacy, capacity creation, standards and quality assurance, and an evidence base through research has given the government a robust foundation to realize the untapped potential of youth in India.

Pradhan Mantri Kaushal Vikas Yojana (PMKVY)

The Prime Minister launched the Pradhan Mantri Kaushal Vikas Yojana (PMKVY), a flagship skill training scheme that aims to incentivize skill training by providing financial rewards to candidates who successfully complete approved skill training programmes. It is an outcome-based skill training scheme of the newly created Ministry of Skill Development & Entrepreneurship (MSDE). This is a skill certification and reward scheme having an objective of enabling and mobilizing a large number of Indian youths to take up outcome-based skill training so that they become employable and earn their livelihood. The monetary reward under the scheme would be provided to trainees who are successfully trained, assessed, and certified in skill courses run by affiliated training providers. This scheme will provide monetary incentives for successful completion of market driven skill training and certification to approximately 24 lakh youths in a span of one year from the date of implementation of the scheme. Key components of the scheme are:

(a) Short Term Training—It will be imparted at PMKVY Training Centres (TCs) which is expected to benefit candidates of Indian nationality who are either school/college dropouts or unemployed. Apart from providing training according to the National Skills Qualification Framework (NSQF), TCs shall also impart training in Soft Skills, Entrepreneurship, Financial and Digital Literacy. Duration of the training will be according to the job, ranging between 150 and 300 hours. Upon successful completion of training, candidates shall be provided placement assistance by Training Partners (TPs). Under this scheme, the entire training and assessment fees are paid by the Government.

(b) Recognition of Prior Learning—Individuals with prior learning experience or skill shall be assessed and certified under the Recognition of Prior Learning (RPL) component of the scheme. The aim of RPL is to align the competencies of the unregulated workforce of the country to the NSQF. Project Implementing Agencies (PIAs), such as Sector Skill Councils (SSCs) or any other agencies designated by MSDE/NSDC, shall be incentivized to implement RPL projects in any of the three Project Types—RPL Camps, RPL at Employers Premises, and RPL Centres.

(c) Special Projects—This component of PMKVY envisages the creation of a platform that will facilitate trainings in special areas and/or premises of Government bodies, Corporates or Industry bodies, and trainings in special job roles not defined under the available Qualification Packs (QPs) or National Occupational Standards (NOSs). Special projects are projects that require some deviation from the terms and conditions of Short Term Training under PMKVY for any stakeholders who can be either Government Institutions of Central and State Government(s)/ Autonomous Body/Statutory Body or any other equivalent body or corporates who are interested to provide training to candidates.

(d) Kaushal and Rozgar Mela—For the success of PMKVY, social and community mobilisation is extremely critical. Active participation of the community ensures transparency and accountability, and helps in leveraging the cumulative knowledge of the community for better functioning. PMKVY also assigns special importance to the involvement of the target beneficiaries through a defined mobilisation process. Training Partners (TPs) shall conduct Kaushal and Rozgar Melas every six months with press/media coverage. They are also required to participate actively in National Career Service Melas and on-ground activities.

(e) Placement Guidelines—PMKVY envisages to link the aptitude, aspiration, and knowledge of the skilled workforce it creates with employment opportunities and demands in the market. Every effort thereby needs to be made by the PMKVY TCs to provide placement opportunities to candidates, trained, and certified under the scheme. TPs shall also provide support to entrepreneurship development.

(f) Monitoring Guidelines—For ensuring high standards of quality maintained by PMKVY TCs, NSDC and empaneled Inspection Agencies shall use various methodologies, such as self-audit reporting, call validations, surprise visits, and monitoring through the Skills Development Management System (SDMS).

The objective of PMKVY is to encourage and promote skill development for the youth throughout the country by aligning itself with the common norms guidelines. The scheme also needs to be aligned to complement all other Missions of the Government, such as Make in India, Digital India, Swachh Bharat, and Smart Cities.

The key features of the PMKVY are mentioned below:

(i) Training will be done against standards (National Occupational Standards—NOS and Qualification Packs—QPs for specific job roles) formulated by industry-driven bodies, namely the Sector Skills Councils (SSCs). Third party assessments for skill training will be done based on national (and often) global standards.

(ii) There will be transparent funding of skill training without any intermediaries. Monetary rewards will be directly transferred to the trainee's bank account. This will ensure financial inclusion with a provision of unique multi-wallet facility linked to debit card and accidental insurance. Aadhaar number will be used for unique identification of each candidate.

(iii) Based on assessment of skill demand and the Skill Gap Studies, target for skill training would be allocated to training providers by job-role and by district/city to the extent possible, by NSDC in consultation with the SSCs, States/UTs and the Central Ministries/Departments. The Steering Committee of PMKVY will oversee these functions.

(iv) Target for skill training would be aligned to the demand from the Central Government's other flagship programmes, like Swachh Bharat, Make in India, Digital India, and National Solar Mission, among others.

(v) Skill training under the PMKVY would target dropout students after class 10 and class 12 and these numbers will be taken into consideration while deciding state/district wise targets. There will be special focus on youth in regions affected by left-wing extremists and from North Eastern States and J&K.

(vi) The trainees who have prior experience, skills and competencies will also be given monetary rewards for undergoing assessments. This will enable the inclusion of workers working in the informal sector. This will also facilitate the process of skill upgradation and re-skilling of the existing workforce.

(vii) Monetary reward for various job roles within a sector would be arrived at after taking into account factors such as cost of training, willingness of trainees for pay and other relevant factors. Training in manufacturing, construction and plumbing sectors will be given higher incentives.

(viii) Government-affiliated training centres and other training partners will be approved by the SSCs on the basis of guidelines issued by NSDC. Each training partner would be responsible for its entire franchisee network and the infrastructure of training centres.

(ix) Awareness building and mobilization activities have been planned to be carried out with the involvement of local State and district governments as well as involve Members of Parliament in the activities to ensure greater outreach and ownership. A camp-based approach by organizing Kaushal Melas to disseminate information about various skill training options, outline possible career paths and income generation potential once the training is imparted would be held in every district. Efforts will be made to ensure that the coverage of the scheme is across all the 543 constituencies in India. Skill Yatras through bus journeys have been planned to take awareness to the hinterlands and include live demonstration of skills in the buses. Non-governmental and community-based organizations have also been involved in this activity to ensure widest possible reach and create an environment for skilling in the country.

(x) Support for improved curricula, better technology enabled pedagogy and upgrading the capacity of instructors would be given for improving the overall ecosystem for high quality skill training in the country. All skill training would include soft skill training, personal grooming, behavioural change for cleanliness, and good work ethics as a part of the training curricula.

(xi) SSCs will verify and record details of all training centres on the Skill Development Management System (SDMS), and ascertain quality of training locations and courses through certified assessors during the time of assessments. SSCs will also be responsible for certifying the training curriculum and for ensuring that it is aligned to QPs of job roles. In addition, SSCs will be tasked with certifying all trainers for the scheme.

(xii) A mentorship programme will be put in place to support trainees who have successfully completed the training programme and are in the process of looking for employment opportunities. Training providers will identify mentors who will support and guide trainees in the post-training phase, and also provide career guidance and counselling for trainees who have completed training and will also help connect them to employment opportunities.

(xiii) Trainee feedback based on validated standard format obtained at the time of assessment will become the key element of the evaluation framework to assess the effectiveness and scaling up of the scheme in future.

(xiv) There would be a proper grievance redressal mechanism. Online Citizens Portal would be set up to disseminate information about PMKVY. This would also serve as a platform for the redressal of grievances. The portal would also include a complete database of all available courses and training centres under the scheme.

Over the next year, PMKVY aims to skill 2.4 million youths across India. For the first time, the skills of young people who lack formal certification, such as workers in India's vast unorganized sector, will be recognized. Through an initiative known as Recognition of Prior Learning (RPL), a million youths will be assessed and certified for the skills that they already possess.

Skill Loan Scheme

The Skill Loan Scheme was launched by the Prime Minister Narendra Modi on 15th July 2015 with a view to support youth who wish to go through skill training programmes in the country. It has replaced earlier Indian Banks Association (IBA) Model Loan Scheme for Vocational Education and Training. The Scheme guidelines and applications forms have been simplified with a view to reduce paper work and ensure sanction and prompt disbursement of skill loans. Such a skill loan would be particularly useful for youth who undergo medium to long-term training programmes for which grant/reward support that is generally available is insufficient. The eligibility criteria and the main features of the scheme are as follows.

(a) Eligibility Criteria—Any Indian National who has secured admission in a course run by Industrial Training Institutes (ITIs), Polytechnics or in a school recognised by Central or State education Boards or in a college affiliated to recognised university, training partners affiliated to National Skill Development Corporation (NSDC)/Sector Skill Councils, State Skill Mission, State Skill Corporation, preferably leading to a certificate/diploma/degree issued by such organization as per National Skill Qualification Framework (NSQF) is eligible for the loan.

(b) Quantum of Loan—Loans may be given from ₹ 5000 to ₹ 150,000 depending on the NSQF level and classification on the basis of Service or Manufacturing courses at an approximate estimate of ₹ 5000 to ₹ 10,000 per month. The estimated per month fees, based on sector and NSQF level, cover tuition fees, examination fees, etc.

(c) Rate of Interest—1.50% above Base Rate, presently 11.45% p.a. (floating) or at such other rate or rates stipulated by the bank from time to time. Penal interest 2% will be levied on the overdue amount for the overdue period if any. During moratorium period, interest will be charged at applicable simple rate, and will be compounded after that.

(d) Moratorium—For courses of duration upto 1 year, moratorium period will be 6 months from the completion of the course. And for courses of duration above 1 year, moratorium period will be 12 months from the completion of the course.

(e) Repayment—Loan upto ₹ 50,000—upto 3 years.

Loan between ₹ 50,000 to ₹ 1 lakh—upto 5 years.

Loan above ₹ 1 lakh—upto 7 years.

However, the banks will have flexibility to choose the structure of repayment—flat Equated Monthly Instalments (EMI), tube payments or moratorium period as deemed fit for various sectors and student categories. In case a student is not able to complete the course because of accident/death/disability, the bank can seek a pro-rata reimbursement the unfinished portion of the course amount from the training institute. This will reduce the loan burden on the student.

(f) Margin—The banks may charge a nominal margin money as down-payment from the student to keep the student serious about the course. However, the down-payment and the amount paid is interest during the course together should not exceed 10% of the total course amount.

(g) Processing Charges and Security—No processing fee will be charged by banks for skilling loan. Also, no collateral for such loan will be taken. Banks can apply to the National Credit Guarantee Trust Company Ltd. (NCGTC) for credit guarantee against defaults and NCGTC will provide such guarantee at nominal guarantee fee which will not exceed 0.5% of the amount outstanding. Such credit guarantee cover will be for a maximum of 75% of the outstanding loan amount, including interest (if any). In cases of North Eastern (NE) region and Left Wing Extremism (LWE) affected areas, the percentage may be increased on the discretion of NCGTC. It will depend on banks whether to pass on levy of guarantee fee to the borrower or not.

(h) Insurance—It will be optional at the requirement of the borrower.

(i) Bank Mitra—Bank Mitra will work as a bridge between bank, training institute and trainee/loan aspirants. A bank employee or its bona fide agency representative will meet the student to explain the loan details.

Deen Dayal Upadhyaya Grameen Kaushalya Yojana

The Ministry of Rural Development announced the Deen Dayal Upadhyaya Grameen Kaushalya Yojana (DDU-GKY) on 25th September 2014, with vision—Transform rural poor youth into an economically independent and globally relevant workforce. DDU-GKY is a part of the National Rural Livelihood Mission (NRLM), tasked with the dual objectives of adding diversity to the incomes of rural poor families and cater to the career aspirations of rural youth. It is uniquely focused on rural youth between the ages of 15 and 35 years from poor families. As a part of the Skill India Campaign, it plays an instrumental role in supporting the social and economic programmes of the government, such as Make in India, Digital India, Smart Cities, Startup India, and Standup India Campaigns. Its unique implementation structure involves partners, who are by nature, committed to changing lives and are experts in their areas, and form a part of the Skilling Ecosystem integrated by DDU-GKY. Partners are supported through investment, capacity building, strategies for retention, linkages to international placement and technology support for training purposes.

Following are some of the key features of DDU-GKY.

(a) Multi-partner Approach—DDU-GKY engages the support of multiple partners to ensure success and maximise on the investment made in time and resources. In order to energies and build mass support as well as create awareness amongst the rural youth, DDU-GKY projects are market linked and implemented in PPP mode. The involvement and partnership between civil society organizations, educational institutions, apex skill partners and regulating organizations, the Government and private organizations, ensures that DDU-GKY can leverage on the strengths of all and achieve transformative change.

(b) Curriculum Framing—National Council on Vocational Training (NCVT) or Sector Skills Councils (SSCs) gives curriculum framing and assessment support to DDU-GKY. Industry partnerships allow access to new technology and on the job training. There are dedicated training hours for soft skills, spoken English, and basic computers, in residential as well as non-residential well equipped campuses, with adequate technology as per industry standards.

(c) Focus on Sustainability—Industry interactions have emphasised the need for training in soft skills, team work, etc., as more important than domain skills, which they learn on the job. To ensure that candidates can perform in their work areas as well as assimilate into the organisation and society, DDU-GKY has mandated a minimum of 160 hours of training in soft skills, functional English and computer literacy. A finishing module, known as Work Readiness training, will be provided to ensure that trained candidates hit the ground running wherever they join. Benefits to candidates would be in the form of free training, free uniform, free course material, free lodging and boarding in case of residential programmes, reimbursements of expenses in non-residential programmes, post placement salary top-ups every month for 2-6 months depending on location of placement and placement for at least 70% of all trained with a maximum salary of ₹ 6000 per month (at cost to company).

(d) Quality Assurance Framework—Introducing predictability in government process by defining minimum service level benchmarks and standards, controls and audits, defaults and remedial actions to reduce Inspector Raj in an all pervasive quality assurance framework comprising of the Guidelines and Standard Operating Procedures. Also, transparency and accountability is fostered through the end-to-end implementation of Public Financial Management System (PFMS) as the channel for fund disbursals and audits. This permits DDU-GKY to invest in capacity building of the private sector, front-loading 25% of the training costs so that PIAs are not constrained to invest in quality training centres.

(e) Employing Technology in Implementation—DDU-GKY through its training partners has employed the following.

- A geo-tagged time stamped biometric attendance record—It serves a dual purpose of being a monitoring tool, and also makes candidates familiar with modern technology.
- Provision of a tabled PC per candidate at the training centre. This enables candidates to learn at their own comfort.

- Presence of computer labs and e-learning at training centers, to ensure that all candidates have access to a wider curricula and adequate learning opportunities.

In order to ensure complete social and regional inclusion the following special initiatives have been launched.

- Himayat—A special scheme for the youth of Jammu and Kashmir.
- Roshni—A special initiative for the rural youth of poor families in 27 Left-Wing Extremist (LWE) districts across 9 states.
- Northeast Region—10% of DDU-GKY programme funds are reserved for projects in North-East, wherein the centre contributes 90% of training costs to ensure opportunities for rural youth from North-East.

DDU-GKY is present in 21 states and UTs across 568 districts, impacting youth from over 6215 blocks. It currently has over 690 projects being implemented by over 300 partners, in more than 330 trades from 82 industry sectors.

Deen Dayal Upadhyaya Antyodaya Yojana

The Ministry of Housing and Urban Poverty Alleviation (HUPA) announced an overarching scheme for uplift of urban poor through enhancement of livelihood opportunities through skill development and other means on 25th September 2014. The scheme has been named as Deen Dayal Upadhyaya Antyodaya Yojana (DAY). Under the earlier urban poverty alleviation programmes, only 790 cities and towns were covered. But, under the current scheme, the government has decided to extend the poverty alleviation measures to all the 4,041 statutory cities and towns, there by covering almost the entire urban population of the country. Under this scheme, focus will be on:

- Imparting skills with an expenditure of ₹ 15,000—₹ 18,000 on each urban poor.
- Promotion of self-employment through setting up individual micro-enterprises and group enterprises with interest subsidy for individual projects costing

₹ 2 lakhs and ₹ 10 lakhs for group enterprises. The interest rate will be 7% per annum.

- Training urban poor to meet the huge demand from urban citizens by imparting market oriented skills through City Livelihood Centres. Each centre would be given a capital grant of ₹ 10 lakhs.
- Enabling urban poor form Self-Help Groups (SHGs) for meeting financial and social needs with a support of ₹ 10,000 to each group which would in turn be helped with bank linkages.
- Development of vendor markets besides promotion of skills of vendors.
- Construction of permanent shelters for urban homeless and provision of other essential services.

The Ministry for Housing and Urban Poverty Alleviation has a tie-up with National Skill Development Corporation (NSDC) under which,

(i) NSDC will give training to the poor according to market needs, via its training centres.

(ii) NSDC will also help in the identification of beneficiaries besides certification of training programmes through Sector Skill Councils (SSCs), which are industry led bodies that define standards and syllabi for different training programmes in given industrial sectors.

(iii) NSDC will identify beneficiaries and design their training programme with the help of SSCs.

Thus, MoHUPA-NSDC tie-up will help in speedy and result oriented implementation of Deen Dayal Antyodaya Yojana.

The above two schemes are together now called Deen Dayal Antyodaya Yojana: Skill Training for Urban and Rural Poors. The above schemes are a welcome step. The poor people have less opportunities to bring a perceptible change in their lives. Although they have access to primary education, thanks to the free education policies of the successive governments, they do not have the means to get college education or join an after-school technical course which increases the chance of getting employed. Under the above Antyodaya scheme, they will now acquire the much-needed skills and have more chances of getting employed. This will also help in poverty alleviation.

However, the Antyodaya scheme is not sufficient for the number of people we have in our country. We need similar schemes for all categories of people, be it BPL or general. Skill development schemes that focus on infrastructure development in rural India are the need of the hour. It could be a great initiative if government schools can add vocational training along with other subjects across the nation. Apart from these, new schemes should be floated to use school infrastructure in post-school hours for training and skill development. There should be special incentive schemes under Make in India policy for industries to set up their units in rural locales utilizing local resources.[5]

Skill India is an excellent initiative by Prime Minister Narendra Modi. India is one of the few counties whose working age population is very high. Providing skills to people will equip them to find suitable jobs and contribute to fast development of the country. As government officials also agree, apart from mere fund allocations from the private sector, proper handholding from private sector is what will boost the new phase of skilling. Since most companies prefer to hire candidates who already possess the right skill sets required for particular roles, there should be more channels to propagate in-demand skills aligned with employability. Experiential learning courses, i.e., a mix of classroom and practical training, can help increase retention of students. Presently, only a few institutions offer such courses in India.[6]

So far the responses to the scheme have been good. Oracle is going to invest over $400 million in Bengaluru, opening 9 incubation centers, and training half a million students each year during its expansion phase to support India's Make in India initiative. The incubation centres will house substantial software and technology capabilities, tools, and training to help launch new technology startups built utilizing Java and the Oracle platform. It will increase diversity and create opportunities for women in technology starts with investing in STEM and computer science education for girls. According to Live Mint, Oracle announced on 12 February 2016 that it will build a new 2.8 million sq. ft. campus in Bengaluru which will be the company's largest outside of its iconic headquarters in Redwood Shores, California. Expected to be the epicenter of its operations throughout India, more than 11,000 employees from diverse fields, including engineering, sales and marketing, global support, finance and consulting, will converge at the high-tech site. Oracle Academy will launch an initiative to train more than half a million students each year to develop computer science skills by expanding its partnerships to 2,700 institutions in India from 1,700 at present. According to the *Economic Times*, as of 15 February 2016, the "Indian Leather Development Programme" trained 51,216 youths in a span of 100 days and it plans to train 1,44,000 young persons annually. Four new branches of "Footwear Design & Development Institute"—at Hyderabad, Patna, Banur (Punjab) and Ankleshwar (Gujarat)—are being set up to improve training infrastructure. The industry is experiencing acute skill shortage and most of the people trained are being absorbed by the industry.[7]

It is pertinent to mention here that skill development is not the responsibility of governments, corporates and training institutes alone. The students pursuing various types of courses also need to recognize the changing scenario of employment. For India to become a truly skilled nation, better training and learning opportunities need to be created with the approach to holistic development. If the Skill India scheme is implemented as per envisaged plans and targets, India will soon be among the developed and prosperous nations of the world.

Notes

1. skilldevelopment.gov.in
2. "Daily News and Analysis", ANI. 13 November 2015.
3. http://www.mapsofindia.com/my-india/society/skill-india-a-new-programme-to-be-launched-in-march-2015
4. http://blog.iasscore.in/mains_special/national-skill-development-mission/

5. Ajay Chhangani. "Skill development in rural India: A roadmap to efficient utilisation of human resources." News18. 23 June 2015.

6. http://blog.iasscore.in/mains_special/national-skill-development-mission/

7. *The Economic Times*. 15 February 2016.

CHAPTER 8

The Schemes and Initiatives Brought by Modi

The Central Government headed by Prime Minister Narendra Modi has become quite famous for launching a number of schemes throughout the country in a short span of time. The schemes cover a range of initiatives the government tends to bring for fast socio-economic development of the nation. No wonder, President Pranab Mukherjee has lauded Modi's "dynamism" and "out of box" thinking. The major schemes brought by PM Modi include Digital India, Make in India, Startup India, and Pradhan Mantri Kaushal Vikas Yojana (PMKVY), which have been taken up in exclusive chapters and discussed in detail. The main features of other schemes and programmes are given below.

1. Pradhan Mantri Jan Dhan Yojana (PMJDY)

Pradhan Mantri Jan Dhan Yojana (PMJDY) the biggest financial inclusion initiative in the world was announced by PM Narendra Modi on 15th August 2014 and Mega launch was done by him on 28th August 2014 across the country. Simultaneous launch functions were held in State Capitals and Districts through 79 Mega Camps in the presence of Union Ministers, State Chief Ministers, MPs/MLAs and other dignitaries. More than 70000 account opening camps were held all over the country.

PMJDY is a national mission for financial inclusion to ensure access to financial services, such as banking savings and deposit accounts, remittance, credit, insurance, pension in an affordable manner to the excluded sections, i.e., weaker sections and low income groups. Under this scheme, a zero balance saving account can be opened in any public or private sector bank branch or Business Correspondent (Bank Mitra) outlet with minimum documentation. However, if the account-holder wishes to get cheque book, he will have to fulfill minimum balance criteria.

Some of special benefits to account holder under PMJDY scheme are:

(a) Interest on deposit.

(b) Accidental insurance cover of ₹ 1 lakh.

(c) No minimum balance required.

(d) Life cover of ₹ 30,000 payable on death of the beneficiary, subject to fulfillment of the eligibility condition.

(e) Easy transfer of money across India.

(f) Beneficiaries of Government schemes will get direct benefit transfer in these accounts.

(g) After satisfactory operation of the account for 6 months, an overdraft facility will be permitted. Overdraft facility upto ₹ 5000 is available in only one account per household, preferably lady of the household.

(h) Access of pension and insurance products.

(i) The claim under Personal Accidental Insurance under PMJDY will be payable if the RuPay card holder has performed minimum one successful financial or non-financial customer induced transaction of any Bank Branch, Bank Mitra, ATM, PoS, E-com, etc. channel both intra and inter-bank, i.e., on-us (bank customer/RuPay card holder transacting at some bank channels) and off-us (bank customer/RuPay card holder transacting at other bank channels) within 90 days prior to date of accident including accident date will be included as eligible transactions under the RuPay Insurance Program.

On the inauguration day, ₹ 1.5 crore (15 million) bank accounts were opened under this scheme.[1] The number of accounts opened under the scheme reached 219 million (including 57 million zero balance accounts) by 18 May 2016. The amount of deposits rose to ₹ 380.47 billion (US$ 5.7 billion) by April 2016. As many as 19 lakh householders had availed the overdraft facility of ₹ 2.56 billion (US$ 38 million) by May 2016. Uttar Pradesh and West Bengal have got 29% of the total deposits under the scheme, whereas Kerala and Goa became the first states in the country to provide one basic bank account to every household.

The scheme has been started with a target to provide 'universal access to banking facilities' starting with "Basic Saving Bank Account" with an overdraft facility of ₹ 5,000 subject to satisfactory operation in the account for six months and RuPay debit card with inbuilt accident insurance cover of ₹ 1 lakh, and providing social security schemes, i.e., Pradhan Mantri Suraksha Bima Yojana, Pradhan Mantri Jeevan Jyoti Bima Yojana and Atal Pension Yojana.

Guinness World Records recognised the achievements made under PMJDY for opening 18,096,130 accounts by Banks in a week (from 23 to 29 August, 2014) as a part of financial inclusion campaign. A dedicated website for PMJDY was launched an 27 October 2014, which consists of information on administrative structure with contact details of Central/State/District level mission directors/nodal officers monitoring implementation of PMJDY, information of latest events and latest circulars issued under the scheme. More than ₹ 4273 crore have been routed through these accounts till June 2015 towards payment of wages under MNREGA. Also the subsidy of more than ₹ 17446 crore has been transferred through these accounts from November 2014 to 31st July 2015.

2. Swachh Bharat Abhiyan

The Swachh Bharat Abhiyan (Mission) is a massive mass movement that seeks to create a clean India. To accelerate the efforts to achieve universal sanitation coverage and to put focus on sanitation, the PM Narendra Modi launched the

Swachh Bharat Mission (SBM) on 2nd October 2014, the 145th birth anniversary of Mahatma Gandhi. The program will be implemented by the Ministry of Urban Development in urban areas and Ministry of Drinking Water and Sanitation in rural areas. The aim is to achieve Swachh Bharat by 2019, as a fitting tribute to the 150th Birth Anniversary of Mahatma Gandhi, which in rural areas means improving the levels of cleanliness in rural areas through Solid and Liquid Waste Management activities and making Gram Panchayats Open Defecation Free (ODF), clean and sanitised.

The main objectives of SBM are:

(a) Bring about an improvement in the general quality of life by promoting cleanliness, hygiene, and eliminating open defecation.

(b) Accelerate sanitation coverage to achieve the vision of Swachh Bharat by 2nd October 2019.

(c) Motivate Communities and Panchayati Raj Institutions to adopt sustainable sanitation practices and facilities through awareness creation and health education.

(d) Encourage cost effective and appropriate technologies for ecologically safe and sustainable sanitation.

(e) Develop wherever required, community managed sanitation systems focusing on scientific Solid and Liquid Waste Management systems for overall cleanliness in the urban and rural areas.

(f) To effect behavioral change regarding healthy sanitation practices.

(g) To generate awareness about sanitation and its linkage with public health.

(h) To create an enabling environment for private sector participation in Capex (capital expenditure) and Opex (operation and maintenance).

All the statutory towns and villages will be covered under the mission. Comprehensive Sanitation Planning includes city level sanitation plans, state sanitation concept, state sanitation strategy, behavioural change strategy, enabling environment for private sector participation, and capacity building.

The State Governments shall pursue the following:

(a) All manual scavengers in urban areas will be identified, insanitary toilets linked to their employment shall be upgraded to sanitary toilets, and that the manual scavengers shall be adequately rehabilitated.

(b) In their efforts to streamline and formalize SWM systems it will be the endeavor of ULBs that the informal sector workers in waste management (rag pickers) shall be given priority to upgrade their work conditions and shall be enumerated and integrated into the formal system of SWM in cities.

(c) All temporary accommodation for migrants and the homeless in urban areas shall have adequate provision for toilets either on the premises or linked to a public or community toilet.

(d) Mandating that construction labour in urban areas have access to temporary toilets at all sites in urban areas, buildings, parks and roads where construction/ maintenance work is taking place or where construction labour is temporarily housed.

(e) Priority shall be accorded pro-actively to cover households with vulnerable sections such as pensioners, girl children, pregnant and lactating mothers.

The estimated cost of implementation of SBM (Urban) based on unit and per capita costs for its various components is ₹ 62009 crore. The Government of India share as per approved funding pattern amounts to ₹ 14623 crore. In addition, a minimum additional amount equivalent to 25% of Government funding, amounting to ₹ 4874 crore shall be contributed by the States as State/ULB share. The balance funds is proposed to be generated through various other sources of fund which are, but not limited to:

- Private Sector Participation
- Additional Resources from State Government/ULB

- Beneficiary Share
- User Charges
- Land Leveraging
- Innovative Revenue Streams
- Swachh Bharat Kosh
- Corporate Social Responsibility
- Market Borrowing
- External Assistance

Without a proper city sanitation plan and resulting state sanitation strategy, as indicated in National Urban Sanitation Policy, Comprehensive Planning cannot be achieved to attain the objectives of Swachh Bharat Mission. However, both the activities require time and wide consultation at various levels including citizen engagements. In order to give a quick start to the Swachh Bharat Mission, it is, therefore proposed that all states may submit a brief concept note on state sanitation strategy in order to claim their first installment for individual household toilets, (Information Education and Communication) IEC and capacity building as well as the revolving fund for other components.

The corporate or PSUs may take up the issues of sanitation through IEC, HRD or through direct targeted interventions such as:

- By establishing demonstration fields/rural sanitation parks for exposure of various technology options available under SBM to the rural populace.
- By organising exhibitions or sanitation melas.
- By providing necessary exposure to the children in schools about proper sanitation and hygiene.
- By providing additional incentive to rural households in form of suitable sanitary materials or by creating sanitation facilities for the rural populace through appropriate local organisations.
- By providing sanitary complexes in market or other public places/around work places or alike.

- By providing assistance in effective Solid and Liquid Waste Management (SLWM) technology and resources.
- By providing trained manpower for maintenance of sanitation facilities and/or SLWM establishments.
- By propagating the programme through mass media and gram panchayat level interventions.
- By adopting habitations/villages/gram panchayats to make them ODF (open defecation free).

Effective monitoring of the programme is essential. Monitoring of outcomes will be the prime focus to be measured in terms of toilet usage as reflected in creation of ODF communities. Monitoring of outputs will also be done for administrative purposes in terms of monitoring of expenditure and assets created. The monitoring framework would be able to identify:

- Whether adequate IEC/IPC/Triggering activities have been carried out for behaviour change;
- Whether toilets have been constructed as reported;
- Whether constructed toilets are being used; and
- Whether ODF communities/GPs have been created.

The monitoring framework proposed will essentially be of the two types—annual monitoring survey and concurrent monitoring. The Swachh Bharat Mission at the national level, state level, and district level will have dedicated specialised monitoring units constituting experts in the district which shall be responsible for monitoring the mission activities which shall include field level monitoring. Monitoring reports will be prepared by the unit every quarter. The monitoring would be at GP/Cluster/Block and district levels.

Response, Funding and Performance

As of May 2015, 14 companies including Tata Consultancy Services, Mahindra Group and Rotary International had pledged to construct 3,195 new toilets. As many as 71 Public Sector Undertakings in India supported the construction of 86,781 new toilets as on that month. The programme has also received funding and technical support from the World Bank and from corporations as part of their corporate social responsibility initiatives as well as from State Governments under the Sarva Shiksha Abhiyan and Rashtriya Madhyamik Shiksha Abhiyan schemes.

The programme is expected to cost over ₹ 620 billion (US$ 9.2 billion). The government provides an incentive of ₹ 12,000 (US$ 180) for each toilet constructed by a BPL family. Total fund mobilized under Swachh Bharat Kosh (SBK) as on 31 January 2016 stood at ₹ 3.69 billion (US$ 55 million). An amount of ₹ 90 billion (US$ 1.3 billion) was allocated for the mission in 2016 Union Budget of India.

Government and the World Bank signed a US$ 1.5 billion loan agreement on 30 March 2016 for the Swachh Bharat Mission to support India's universal sanitation initiative. The World Bank will also provide a parallel US$ 25 million technical assistance to build the capacity of select states in implementing community-led behavioural change programmes targeting social norms to help ensure widespread usage of toilets by rural households.[2]

Between April 2014 and January 2015, 31.83 lakh toilets were built. Karnataka led all states in construction of toilets under the programme. As of August 2015, 80 lakh toilets have been constructed under the programme. As of 18 March 2016, 10 districts in India were ODF (Open Defecation Free).

3. Prime Minister's Employment Generation Programme (PMEGP)

This is a new credit linked subsidy programme introduced by merging the two schemes that were in operation till 31 March 2008, namely Prime Minister's Rojgar Yojana (PMRY) and Rural Employment Generation Programme (REGP), having the aim of generating employment opportunities through establishment of micro enterprises in rural as well as urban areas.

Main Features

The man features of the scheme are mentioned below:

(i) It is a central sector scheme administered by the Ministry of Micro, Small and Medium Enterprises.

(ii) At the national level, the scheme will be implemented by Khadi and Village Industries Commission (KVIC)—a statutory organization under the administrative control of the Ministry of MSME as the single nodal agency. At the state level, it will be implemented through State KVIC Directorates, State Khadi and Village Industries Boards (KVIBs), District Industries Centres (DICs), and banks.

(iii) The government subsidy under the scheme will be routed by KVIC through the identified banks for eventual distribution to the beneficiaries/entrepreneurs in their bank accounts.

(iv) The implementing agencies, namely KVIC, KVIBs and DICs will associate reputed Non-Government Organization (NGOs)/reputed autonomous institutions/Self-Help Groups (SHGs)/National Small Industries Corporation (NSIC)/Udyami Mitras empanelled under Rajiv Gandhi Udyami Mitra Yojana (RGUMY), Panchayati Raj Institutions and other relevant bodies in the implementation of the scheme, especially in the area of identification of beneficiaries, of area specific viable projects, and providing training in entrepreneurship development.

Objectives

The objectives of the scheme are as under:

(i) To generate continuous and sustainable employment opportunities in rural and urban areas of the country through setting up of new self-employment ventures/projects/micro enterprises.

(ii) To provide continuous and sustainable employment to a large number of traditional and prospective artisans, rural and urban unemployed youth in the country, so as to help arrest migration of rural youth to urban areas.

(iii) To bring together widely dispersed traditional artisans/rural and urban unemployed youth and give them self-employment opportunities to the extent possible, at their place.

(iv) To increase the wage earning capacity of artisans and contribute to increase in the growth rate of rural and urban employment.

Eligibility

The eligibility criteria for beneficiaries are mentioned below:

(i) The programme provides assistance to new projects that have been sanctioned specifically under the PMEGP. To start with, the applicant needs to be of 18 years of age or more to be eligible to receive assistance under the programme. There is no upper limit of income as far as granting the assistance is concerned.

(ii) For setting up of project costing above ₹ 10 lakh in the manufacturing sector and above ₹ 5 lakh in the business or service sector, the beneficiaries should possess at least VIII standard pass educational qualification.

(iii) Self Help Groups can receive assistance under the programme. This is also applicable to BPL families provided that they should not be the beneficiary of any other similar programme.

(iv) Any institution registered under Societies Registration Act, 1860 is eligible for assistance under PMEGP.

(v) The programme is also open to charitable trusts and production-based cooperative societies. However, if an existing unit is already a beneficiary of the REGP, PMRY, or any similar programme of the Indian or State Government, it will not be eligible for PMEGP.

The following industries will not be eligible under PMEGP for setting up of micro enterprises/projects/units.

(i) Any industry or business that deals with meat (slaughtered), beedi, pan, cigar, cigarette, liquor, tobacco or toddy.

(ii) Any industry that is in the business of pashmina wool or similar products that need hand weaving and hand spinning as these are already being benefited by the Khadi Programme and enjoy sales rebates.

(iii) Any industry or business that is related to tea, coffee, rubber, sericulture, horticulture, floriculture and animal husbandry.

(iv) Rural transport, but with the exceptions of cycle rickshaws, auto rickshaws in Andaman and Nicobar Islands, and house boats, tourist boats, and shikaras in Jammu and Kashmir.

(v) Any industry that is related to items that may cause environmental pollution, like polythene carry bags of less than 20 microns thickness and carry bags or containers made of recycled plastic for storing, carrying, dispensing or packaging of food stuff and any other item which causes environmental problems.

Modalities of the Operation of the PMEGP

Under PMEGP, project proposals will be invited from potential beneficiaries at district level through press, advertisement, radio and other multi-media by KVIC, KVIBs and DICs at periodical intervals depending on the target allotted to that particular district. The scheme will also be advertised or publicised through the Panchayati Raj Institutions which will also assist in identification of beneficiaries.

Sponsoring of project by any agency is not mandatory. The beneficiary can directly approach Banks or Financial Institutions along with his project proposal or it can be sponsored by KVIC, KVIBs, DIC, Panchayat Karyalayas, etc. However, the applications received directly by the Banks shall be referred to the task force for its consideration. The task force will consist of District Magistrate or Deputy Commissioner or Collector (as chairman), Lead Bank Manager (as member), Representative of KVIC or KVIB (as member), Representative of NYKS or SC or Corporation (as special invite), Representative of MSME-DI, ITI or Polytechnic (as special invitee), Representatives from

Panchayats (three members, to be nominated by Chairman/ District Magistrate/Deputy/Commissioner/Collector by rotation), and General Manager, DIC or State Director of KVIC (as member Convenor).

The task force will scrutinize the applications and based on the experience, technical qualification, skill viability of the project, etc., it will short list the applications and call for an interview of the applicants separately for rural and urban areas to assess their knowledge about the proposed project, aptitude, interest, skill and entrepreneurship abilities, market available, sincerity to repay and make the proposed project success. The selected candidates will be provided project formulation guidance and orientation by KVIC, KVIBs and DICs who will also assist and guide them in project formulation and submission to the concerned Bank in the area. KVIC will identify the Nodal Banks at State level in consultation with State Governments and will forward the list to all the implementing agencies.

The release of funds to the implementing agencies will be in the following manner.

(a) Government will provide funds under PMEGP to the nodal implementing agencies, i.e., KVIC, which will in turn place the margin money (subsidy funds) with the implementing Banks at the State level in their respective accounts in accordance with the targets allocated to each implementing agency.

(b) DICs, in close coordination with implementing Banks, will ensure that at least 50% of the total margin money (subsidy) allocated to them will be utilised in setting up of projects in rural areas.

(c) KVIC will ensure that it will reserve and allocate at least 25% of the total allocation under Forward and Backward linkages, under the scheme to DICs of different participating States appropriately taking into account the demand and extent of implementation. This money will be released to DICs, only after obtaining an undertaking from the State Government that the funds already provided under the erstwhile

PMRY Scheme's Training and Pre-motivational Campaigns have been fully utilised by the DICs.

(d) Banks will take their own credit decision on the basis of viability of each project. No collateral security will be insisted upon by Banks in line with the guidelines of RBI for projects involving loan upto ₹ 5 lakh in respect of the projects cleared by the task force. However, they will appraise projects both technically and economically after ensuring that each project fulfills inter alia the criteria of industry, per capita investment, own contribution, rural areas, and negative list. It is essential that the applications cleared by the district task force also fulfill these requirements at that stage itself so as to avoid delays in approval of loans in Banks.

(e) First installment of the loan will be released to the beneficiary only after completion of Entrepreneurship Development Programme (EDP) training of at least two weeks specially designed for the purpose, which will be organised by KVIC/KVIBs/DICs or the institutions recognised by or under the administrative control of Ministry of MSME or at any other training centre of repute. Those who have already undergone training from the recognised institutions need not undergo further EDP training.

(f) After the successful completion of EDP training arranged by the KVIC/KVIBs/State DICs, the beneficiary will deposit with the bank, the owner's contribution. Thereafter, the bank will release first installment of the Bank Finance to the beneficiary. Projects sanctioned will be declared ineligible for Margin Money (subsidy) assistance of the EDP training is not completed.

(g) Though the margin money (subsidy) will be released by the designated Nodal Branch of the Bank, KVIC/ State DIC is the final authority to either accept the project/claim or reject, based on the parameters of the scheme.

(h) Once the margin money is released in favour of the loanee, it will be kept in the Term Deposit Receipt of three years at branch level in the name of the beneficiary or institution. No interest will be paid on the TDR and no interest will be charged on loan to the corresponding amount of TDR.

(i) Since subsidy is to be provided in the form of grant, it will be credited to the Borrowers loan account after three years from the date of first disbursement to the borrower/institution, by the Bank.

(j) Margin money (subsidy) will be 'one time assistance', from the Government. For any enhancement of credit limit or for expansion/modernization of the project, margin money (subsidy) assistance is not available. Margin money (subsidy) assistance is available only for new projects sanctioned specifically under the PMEGP. Existing units are not eligible under the scheme. Also, projects financed jointly, i.e., financed from two different sources (Banks or Financial institutions), are not eligible for margin money (subsidy) assistance.

4. Beti Bachao Beti Padhao Yojana

The Census data for 2011 shows a significant declining trend in the Child Sex Ratio (CSR) with an all time low of 918 girls for every 1000 boys between age group of 0-6 years in 2011 from 976 in 1961. The decline in CSR has been unabated since 1961. It is an alarming indicator for women disempowerment and reflects both pre birth discrimination manifested through gender biased sex selection, and post birth discrimination against girls. The trend is widespread across the country and has expanded to rural as well as tribal areas.

After observing various campaign drives from the past government, the Modi Government is heading strong towards the new initiative to bring in more awareness among the citizens to save and educate their girl child. Focusing upon the overall development of natives and nation, the Prime Minister Narendra Modi has come up with the new campaign named as

"Beti Bachao, Beti Padhao" with the aim to make the nation more strong with the strength of its women. In this initiative, the most highlighting factor is to make the nation aware of the current scenario of girl children present in India and the status of their education which may not only empower them of they continue their studies, but also be helpful in making them firm to tackle the difficulties of life which after being educated will be solved to some extent as per the eligibility they can outstand comparatively brighter and can take up the responsibility of family while spreading the wisdom and knowledge.

The overall aim of the "Beti Bachao, Beti Padhao (BBBP)" initiative is to "Celebrate the Gril Child and Enable her Education."

The objectives of the scheme are to:

(i) prevent gender-biased sex selective elimination;
(ii) ensure survival and protection of the girl child; and
(iii) ensure education of the girl child.

The BBBP initiative has two major components:

(a) Mass Communication Campaign on BBBP—It aims at ensuring girls are born, nurtured, and educated without discrimination to become empowered citizens of the country. It interlinks National, State and District level interventions with community level action in 100 districts, bringing together different stakeholders for accelerated impact.

(b) Multi-Sectoral Interventions in 100 Gender Critical Districts Covering all States/UTs—Coordinated and convergent efforts are undertaken in close coordination with Ministry of Health and Family Welfare and Ministry of Human Resource Development to ensure survival, protection, and education of the girl child. The District Collectors/Deputy Commissioners lead and coordinate actions of all departments for implementation of BBBP at the District level. Multi-sectoral interventions includes:

(i) Ministry of Women and Child Development—It promotes registration of pregnancies in first trimester in Anganwadi Centres (AWCs); undertakes training of stakeholders; helps in community mobilization and sensitization; involves gender champions; and rewards and recognises institutions and frontline workers.

(ii) Ministry of Health and Family Welfare—It monitors implementation of Pre-Conception and Pre-Natal Diagnostic Techniques (PCPNDT) Act, 1994; increases institutional deliveries by registration of births, strengthening PNDT Cells, and setting up monitoring committees.

(iii) Ministry of Human Resource Development—It takes into consideration universal enrolment of girls, decreased drop-out rate, girl child friendly standards in schools, strict implementation of Right to Education, and construction of functional toilets for girls.

A 2012 UNICEF report has ranked India 41st among 195 countries in sex ratio. It is unfortunate that in India, sex-selective abortions or female foeticides have led to a sharp drop in the ratio of girls born as compared to boy infants in some states in India. Ultrasound technology has made it possible for pregnant women and their families to know the gender of a foetus early in pregnancy. Discrimination against girl infants has combined with the technology to bring about a rise in abortions of foetuses identified as female during ultrasonic testing. Sex ratio (0-6 years) in Punjab is 846, in Rajasthan 888, in Gujarat 890, Uttarakhand 890, Maharashtra 894, UP 902 and in Himachal 909.

The situation calls for saving the girl child. The female literacy rate at 65.46% is much lower than the male literacy rate of 82.14%. The situation calls for educating the girl child. Thus, the scheme is according to the need of hour and will serve the twin objective of improving sex ratio as well as improving female literacy rate in our country.

The BBBP scheme is being implemented through a national campaign and is a joint initiative of Ministry of Women and Child Development, Ministry of Health and Family Welfare, and Ministry of Human Resource Development. Speaking on the occasion of International Day of the Girl Child, Prime Minister Modi called for the eradication of female foeticide and invited suggestions from the citizens of India on "Beti Bachao, Beti Padhao" on the MyGov.in portal.

Strategies

The strategies for the scheme include the following:

(i) Implementation of a sustained Social Mobilization and Communication Campaign to create equal value for the girl child and promote her education.

(ii) Placement of the issue of decline in child sex ratio in public discourse, improvement of which would be an indicator for good governance.

(iii) Focus on Gender Critical Districts and Cities low on CSR for intensive and integrated action.

(iv) Mobilization and training of Panchayati Raj Institutions in villages and Urban Local Bodies in towns and cities, and grass-roots level workers as catalysts for social change, in partnership with local community/women's/youth groups.

(v) Making sure that service delivery structures, schemes and programmes are sufficiently responsive to issues of gender and children's rights.

(vi) Enabling inter-sectoral and inter-institutional convergence at district, block, grass-roots levels, etc.

The Beti Bachao campaign is supported by numerous medical organizations in India, including the Indian Medical Association.[3]

Sukanya Samriddhi Yojna

Sukanya Samriddhi Yojna (SSY) is a small deposit scheme of the Government of India for girl child launched as a part of the Beti Bachao Beti Padhao campaign, which would fetch a higher interest rate than regular saving bank account and provide tax rebate. Under SSY, Sukanya Samriddhi Account (SSA) (literally Girl Child Prosperity Account) would be opened, which is a Government of India-backed saving scheme targeted at the parents of girl children. It encourages parents to build a fund for the future education and marriage expenses for their female child.[4]

The scheme was launched by Prime Minister Narendra Modi on 22 January 2015 as a part of the Beti Bachao, Beti Padhao campaign. The scheme currently provides an interest rate of 8.6% (for FY 2016-17) and tax benefits. The account can be opened at any Indian Post Office or branch of authorised commercial banks.

The account can be opened anytime between the birth of a girl child and the time she attains 10 years of age by the guardian. Only one account can be opened per child. Parents can open a maximum of two accounts for each of their children (exception allowed for twins and triplets). The account can be transferred to another branch of Post Office or bank anywhere in India. A minimum of ₹ 1,000 must be deposited in the account annually. The maximum deposit limit is ₹ 1,50,000 in a financial year. If the minimum deposit is not made in a year, a fine of ₹ 50 will be levied. Deposits in the account can be made till the completion of 15 years, from the date of the opening of the account, for example, for a 6-year old girl child, deposits have to continue till the child turns 21. An irregular account where the minimum amount has not been deposited may be regularised on payment of a penalty of ₹ 50 per year, along with the minimum specified subscription for the years of default. If the penalty is not paid, the entire deposit, including those made before the date of default, will receive interest a post office savings bank account rate. If excess interest has been paid, it will be reversed. The girl can operate her account after she reaches the age of 10. The account allows 50% withdrawal at the age of 18 for higher education purposes. The account reaches maturity when the child attains the age of 21. If the account is not closed, then it will not continue to earn interest at the prevailing rate. If the girl is over 18 and married, normal closure is allowed.

At the time of launch, only the deposits in the account were eligible for tax deduction under Section 80C of the Income Tax Act, which was ₹ 1,50,000 in 2015-16. However, Finance

Minister Arun Jaitley announced, during the 2015 Union Budget, tax exemption on the interest from the account and on withdrawal from the fund after maturity, making the tax benefits similar to those of the Public Provident Fund. These changes were applied retrospectively from 1 April 2015. These benefits will be reassessed annually.

The number of accounts opened up to October 2015 under Sukanya Samriddhi Yojna across the country was over 76 lakh. Thus, more than 76 lakh girl children got ₹ 28.38 billion (US$ 420 million) deposited in their name.

5. Atal Pension Yojana (APY)

It is a government-backed pension scheme targeted at the unorganized sector. Originally mentioned in the 2015 Budget speech by Finance Minister Arun Jaitley in February 2015, the scheme was formally launched by Prime Minister Narendra Modi on 9 May in Kolkata. As of May 2015, only 11% of India's population had the benefit of any kind of pension scheme. APY aims to increase this number and will provide a defined pension, depending on the contribution, and its period. It is primarily for all citizens in the unorganised sector, who join the National Pension System (NPS) administered by the Pension Fund Regulatory and Development Authority (PFRDA).

Under APY, for every contribution made to the pension fund, the Central Government would also co-contribute 50% of the total contribution or ₹ 1,000 (US$ 15) per annum, whichever is lower, to each eligible subscriber account, for a period of five years, i.e., from Financial Year 2015-16 to 2019-20, who join the NPS between the period 1st June, 2015 and 31st December 2015 and who are not members of any statutory social security scheme and who are not income tax payers. However, the scheme will continue after this date but Government co-contribution will not be available. The minimum age of joining APY is 18 years and maximum age is 40 years. The age of exit and start of pension would be 60 years. Therefore, minimum period of contribution by the subscriber under APY would be 20 years or more.

For the identification of beneficiaries, spouse and nominees, Aadhar would be the primary Know Your Customer (KYC) document to avoid pension rights and entitlement related disputes in the long-term. The subscribers are required to opt for a monthly pension between ₹ 1000-5000, at the age of 60 years, depending on their contributions, which itself would be based on the age of joining the APY, and ensure payment of monthly contribution regularly. The subscribers can opt to decrease or increase pension amount during the course of accumulation phase, according to the available monthly pension amounts. However, the switching option shall be provided once in a year during the month of April.

This scheme will be linked to the bank accounts opened under the Pradhan Mantri Jan Dhan Yojana scheme and the contributions will be deducted automatically from the subscriber's account. Most of these accounts had zero balance initially. The government aims to reduce the number of such zero balance accounts by using this and related schemes.[5]

The government has also given an option to the spouse of the subscriber to continue contributing to the Atal Pension Yojana account of the subscriber, for the remaining vesting period. As per amendment in the scheme, the contribution can continue till the original subscriber would have attained the age of 60 years instead of present provision of handing-over lump-sum amount to spouse on the premature death (death before 60 years of age) of the subscriber. After the death of both the subscriber and the spouse, the nominee of the subscriber will be entitled to receive the pension wealth, as accumulated till age of 60 years of the subscriber.

Performance under the Scheme

Government has enrolled over 12.50 lakh subscribers under Atal Pension Yojana (APY) within six months of its launch. As on 8 October 2015, NPS (₹ 1,00,163 crore) and Atal Pension Yojana (₹ 112 crore) together have more than one crore subscribers with total assets under management (AUM) of ₹ 1,00,275 crore, as stated by the Finance Ministry.

6. Atal Mission for Rejuvenation and Urban Transformation (AMRUT)

The focus of Modi Government is on infrastructure creation that has a direct link to provision of better services to people, such as, providing basic services, e.g., water-supply, sewerage, urban transport, etc., to households and build amenities in cities which will improve the quality of life for all, especially the poor and the disadvantaged. To achieve these goals, Prime Minister Narendra Modi launched three major urban development initiatives—Atal Mission for Rejuvenation and Urban Transformation (AMRUT), Smart Cities Mission, and Housing for All (Urban) on 25 June 2015 at Vigyan Bhawan in New Delhi. The PM said these urban development schemes were not prepared by the Government alone, but involved perhaps all biggest consultation exercise ever taken by the Union Government, involving all stakeholders and examining global best practices.

The purpose of Atal Mission for Rejuvenation and Urban Transformation (AMRUT) is to

(a) ensure that every household has access to a tap with assured supply of water and a sewerage connection;

(b) increase the amenity value of cities by developing greenery and well maintained open spaces; and

(c) reduce pollution by switching to public transport or constructing facilities for non-motorised transport (e.g., walking and cycling).

All the above-mentioned outcomes are valued by citizens, and indicators and standards have been prescribed by the Ministry of Urban Development (MoUD) in the form of Service Level Benchmarks (SLBs). All the benchmarks will be targeted following a step-by-step process after achieving the benchmark of universal coverage. The thrust areas of AMRUT are:

(a) Water supply, sewerage facilities and septage management;

(b) Storm water drains to reduce flooding;

(c) Pedestrain, non-motorised and public transport facilities, parking spaces; and

(d) Enhancing amenity value of cities by creating and upgrading green spaces, parks and recreation centers, especially for children.

The AMRUT will cover five hundred cities of the following categories, which will be notified at the appropriate time.

(a) All cities and towns with a population of over one lakh with notified municipalities, including cantonment boards, such as, civilian areas.

(b) All capital cities and towns of States/UTs, not covered in (a).

(c) All cities and towns classified as Heritage Cities by MoUD under the HRIDAY Scheme.

(d) Thirteen cities and towns on the stem of the main rivers with a population above 75,000 and less than 1 lakh.

(e) Ten cities from hill states, islands, and tourist destinations; not more than one from each State.

The AMRUT will required a huge amount of funds. As estimate of the funds required over a 20 year period, at 2009-10 prices, was made by the High Powered Expert Committee (HPEC) during 2011. The Committee estimated that ₹ 39.2 lakh crore was required for creation of urban infrastructure, including ₹ 17.3 lakh crore for urban roads and ₹ 8 lakh crore for services, such as water supply, sewerage, solid waste management, and storm water drains. Moreover, the required for Operation and Maintenance (O & M) was separately estimated to be ₹ 19.9 lakh crore. The total outlay for AMRUT is ₹ 50,000 crore for five years from FY 2015-16 to FY 2019-20 and the Mission will be operated as a Centrally Sponsored Scheme. The AMRUT may be continued thereafter in the light of an evaluation done by the MoUD and incorporating learnings in the Mission. The Mission funds will consist of the following four parts.

(a) Project Fund—80 percent of the annual budgetary allocation.

(b) Incentive for Reforms—10 percent of the annual budgetary allocation.

(c) State Funds for Administrative and Office Expenses—8 percent of the annual budgetary allocation.

(d) MoUD Funds for Administrative and Office Expenses—2 percent of the annual budgetary allocation.

Service Level Improvement Plans (SLIPs)—The primary purpose of AMRUT is to cover all households with water supply and sewerage, including septage. For this the Service Level Improvement Plan (SLIP), has to be prepared by each Urban Local Bodies (ULB).

The following are strategic steps for preparing SLIP by ULB.

(a) Assessment of the service level gap

(b) Bridging the gap

(c) Examining the alternatives

(d) Estimating the cost

(e) Prioritizing the zones to be taken up in the first, second, third, fourth and fifth year of the Mission.

(f) Out-of-box thinking—there should be a 'decisive break with the past' during the preparation of the SLIP by the ULB.

(g) Conditionalities—in the AMRUT no projects would be included which do not have land available and no project work order would be issued of all clearances from all the departments have not been received by that time.

(h) Resilience—incorporation of resilience and securing projects against disasters would be done at the stage of preparation of the SLIP itself and at the project development stage where disaster-secure engineering and structural norms would be included in the design.

(i) Financing—different sources of finance have to be identified. At the ULB level the contribution from internal sources (e.g., taxes, fees, others), external sources (e.g., transfers from states, project fund from Central/State Governments, others) and possibilities of debt, bonds, and other have to be assessed.

(j) Reforms—implementation of reforms is an important objective of the SLIP. The ULB has to prepare a roadmap for reforms which will be consolidated by the State Mission Director and included as part of the SAAP.

State Annual Action Plan (SAAP)

The SAAP is basically a State level service improvement plan indicating the year-wise improvements in water-supply and sewerage connections to households. The basic building block for the SAAP is the SLIP prepared by the ULB. At the State level, the SLIPs of all Mission cities will be aggregated into the SAAP. The States will decide on the inter-ULB allocation based on gap analysis and financial strength of ULBs and choose those ULBs in the first year that have higher gaps in provision of water supply and sewerage. The prioritization of ULBs for funding will be alone after consultation with local MPs, Mayors and Commissioners of the concerned ULBs. Based on prioritization by the States and resources available, the States will sent the SAAP up to three times the Central Assistance allocated to the State during 2015-16 and the outstanding Central Assistance of the previous year plus the annual allocation of the year in the subsequent years. As a result, different ULBs within a State may become entitled to different funding patterns, but the share of the center will be fixed. The maximum share of funding will be born by the Central Government. The States/ULBs have to plan for the remaining resource generation at the time of preparation of the SAAP. However, the State contribution to the SAAP will not be less than 20 percent of the total project cost. During the process of developing the SAAP, the States/UTs should explore the possibility of using Public Private Partnerships (PPP), which should be the preferred execution model. The PPP should include appropriate Service Level Agreements (SLAs) with strong citizen feedback built into it. This will lead to the People Public Private Partnership (PPPP) model.

The SAAP will be approved by the MoUD once a year according to the schedule given by the Apex Committee. The Apex Committee may revise the SAAP, approve with conditions or return it for rectification of gaps. The AMRUT will provide project funds to ULBs through the States.

Implementation

In the first phase, 89 cities in Andhra Pradesh, Gujarat and Rajasthan were allocated funds. The Apex Committee of AMRUT, did a huge allocation of funds under the State Annual Action Plans (SAAPs) for these states for the year 2015-16. At each city level, a City Mission Management Unit (CMMU) is proposed to be set up which will assist the Urban Local Body (ULB) in terms of staff and technology. The scheme has invited participation of big companies. In the later stage, the rest of the cities out of 500 will be finalized and implemented in the next phase.

7. Pradhan Mantri Awas Yojana (PMAY)

Prime Minister Narendra Modi has envisioned housing for all by 2022 when the nation completes 75 years of its Independence. To achieve this objective, the government has launched a comprehensive mission, "Housing for All by 2022". This much-awaited scheme was launched by the Prime Minister on 17 June 2015 as Pradhan Mantri Awas Yojana.

The scheme seeks to address the housing requirement of urban poor, including slum dwellers through following programmes:

(i) Rehabilitation of slum dwellers with participation of private developers using land as a resource.

(ii) Promotion of affordable housing for weaker sections by means of credit linked subsidy.

(iii) Affordable housing in partnership with public and private sectors.

(iv) Subsidy for beneficiary-led individual house construction.

In the spirit of cooperative federalism, the mission provides flexibility to the states for choosing the best options amongst four verticals of mission to meet the demand of housing in their states. The process of project formulation and approval in accordance with the mission guidelines has been left to the states so that projects can be formulated, approved, and implemented faster. A Technology Sub-Mission under the mission has been set up to facilitate the adoption of modern, innovative, and green technologies and building material for faster and quality construction of houses. Technology Sub-Mission also facilitates preparation and adoption of layout designs and build plans suitable for various geo-climatic zones. It will also assist states/ cities in deploying disaster resistant and environment-friendly technologies.[6]

A beneficiary family will consist of husband, wife and unmarried children. To be eligible under the scheme, the family should not own a *pucca* house, either in his/her name, or in the name of any member of his/her family in any part of India.

Implementation

The scheme will be implemented as Centrally Sponsored Scheme (CSS) except for the component of credit linked subsidy which will be implemented as a Central Sector Scheme. The scheme with all its component has become effective from 17 June 2015 and will be implemented upto 31 March 2022.

All 4041 statutory towns as per Census 2011 with focus on 500 Class I cities would be covered in three phases as follows:

Phase I (April 2015 - March 2017) to cover 100 cities selected from States/UTs as per their willingness.

Phase II (April 2017 - March 2019) to cover additional 200 cities.

Phase III (April 2019 - March 2022) to cover all other remaining cities.

The Ministry of Housing and Urban Poverty Alleviation may include more cities in earlier phases in case there is a resource backed demand from States/UTs.

The scheme will support construction of houses upto 30 square meter carpet area with basic civic infrastructure and the minimum size of houses constructed under the scheme under each component should conform to the standards provided in

National Building Code (NBC). The houses under the scheme would be designed and constructed to meet the requirements of structural safety against earthquake, flood, cyclone, landslide, etc. conforming to the NBC and other relevant Bureau of Indian Standards (BIS) codes.

8. Deendayal Upadhyaya Gram Jyoti Yojana (DDUGJY)

Deendayal Upadhyaya Gram Jyoti Yojana (DDUGJY) was launched by Prime Minister Narendra Modi on 25th July 2015. It is one of the flagship programmes of the Ministry of Power to facilitate 24 × 7 supply of power to rural households and adequate power to agricultural consumers. The earlier scheme for rural electrification, viz., Rajiv Gandhi Grameen Vidyutikaran Yojana (RGGVY) has been subsumed in the DDGJY as its rural electrification component. The major components of the scheme are:

(a) Separation of agriculture and non-agriculture feeders—It will facilitate judicious rostering of supply to agricultural and non-agricultural consumers in the rural areas.

(b) Strengthening and augmentation of sub-transmission and distribution infrastructure in rural areas, including metering at distribution transformers, feeders, and consumers end.

(c) Rural electrification, as per Cabinet Committee on Economic Affairs (CCEA) approval dated 1st August 2013 for completion of the targets laid down under RGGVY for 12th and 13th Plans by subsuming RGGVY in DDUGJY and carrying forward the approved outlay for RGGVY to DDUGJY.

The scheme has an outlay of ₹ 760 billion (US$ 11 billion) for implementation of the projects under which Government of India shall provide grant of ₹ 630 billion (US$ 9.4 billion).

The main objectives of the scheme are given below:

(i) Providing electrification to all villages;

(ii) Bring about feeder separation to ensure sufficient power to farmers and regular supply to other consumers;

(iii) Improvement of sub-transmission and distribution network to improve the quality and reliability of the supply; and

(iv) Complete metering to reduce the losses.

The perceived benefits from the scheme are as under:

(i) All villages and households shall be electrified.

(ii) With regular electricity supply, there will timely agricultural operations and activities and increase in agriculture yield.

(iii) Business of small and household enterprises shall grow creating new avenues for employment.

(iv) There will be improvement in health, education, and banking and other services.

(v) There will be improvement in accessibility to TV, radio, telephone, internet and mobile, etc.

(vi) There will be betterment in social security due to regular availability of electricity.

(vii) The scheme will enhance accessibility of electricity to schools, panchayats, hospitals, and police stations, etc.

(viii) Rural areas shall get increased opportunities for comprehensive development.

DDUGJY is an excellent initiative started by Modi Government. As we all know, the rural agricultural and non-agriculture consumers in India are generally serviced through the local distribution network. Many rural areas of the country get insufficient and erratic electricity supply, consequently the distribution utilities are forced to resort to load shedding, thus affecting the power supply to both agriculture and non-agriculture consumers. Moreover, due to changing consumer base, and improving living standards, the demanding for electricity is increasing every year, for which augmentation of rural infrastructure needs to be regularly undertaken. Investment in the distribution network is low due to bad financial health of the distribution companies. Therefore, in order to augment the reliability and quality of supply distribution network needs to be strengthened. DDUGJY is likely to address all these issues.

9. Pradhan Mantri Suraksha Bima Yojana (PMSBY)

It is a government-backed accident insurance scheme, which offers a one year accidental death and disability cover; and can be renewed annually. It was originally mentioned in the 2015 Budget speech by Finance Minister Arun Jaitley in February 2015, and was formally launched by Prime Minister Narendra Modi on 9 May 2015 in Kolkata. As of May 2015, only 20% of India's population has any kind of insurance, this scheme aims to increase the number.[7]

The main features of the scheme are as under:

(i) People between 18 and 70 years of age with bank accounts will be eligible for the scheme.

(ii) The annual premium is ₹ 12 per annum for each member, excluding service tax. The amount would be deducted from the policy holder's saving bank account with an auto-debit facility, in the month of June every year.

(iii) In case of accidental death or full disability, the nominee will get ₹ 2 lakh (US$ 3,000) and in case of partial permanent disability ₹ 1 lakh (US$ 1,500).

(iv) This scheme will be linked to the bank accounts opened under the Pradhan Mantri Jan Dhan Yojana scheme. Most of these accounts had zero balance initially. The government aims to reduce the number of such zero balance accounts by using this and other related schemes.

(v) If the individual has a multiple saving account, he/she would be eligible to get just one insurance scheme attached to just one saving account.

In following cases, the cover will be terminated and no benefit will be payable to the subscribers.

(i) On attaining the age of 70 years or the age nearest birthday;

(ii) At the time of renewal in subsequent years, due to insufficiency of balance to keep the insurance in force, the account gets closed;

(iii) In case a subscriber is covered by more than one policy under the scheme and premiums are paid by the subscriber intentionally, the insurance cover will be restricted to only one scheme only and the premiums shall be liable to be forfeited.

The scheme has been criticized for focusing on the poorer sections and ignoring lower and upper middle classes. Some people and political parties have stated that serving such large number of people would increase the burden and workload of public sector. But, the scheme is important from the social security point of view. It focuses on the poorer sections who have much greater need of such security than others. It is a noble scheme that aims to bring the uninsured into the mainstream insurance services. As on 2 Feb. 2016, as many as 124 million Indians have already enrolled for this scheme. If the scheme succeeds, at least those living below poverty line in far flung areas would have a sigh of relief in case of event of accidents in their life.

10. Pradhan Mantri Jeevan Jyoti Bima Yojana (PMJJBY)

On 9th May 2015, Prime Minister Narendra Modi launched three schemes, namely Jeevan Jyoti Bima Yojana, Pradhan Mantri Suraksha Bima Yojana and Atal Pension Yojana. These schemes have been launched for the welfare of the needy people. The Jeevan Jyoti Bima Yojana is a helpful insurance scheme that will provide benefit of ₹ 2 lakh, which will be payable to the family of the member in case of his death due to any reason.

The main features of the scheme are:

(a) The annual premium will be ₹ 330, that means less than ₹ 1 per day and ₹ 27.5 per month.

(b) The payment of premium will be debited from the bank account of the individual in single installment.

(c) The scheme has the risk coverage of ₹ 2 lakh in case of death for any reason.

(d) The scheme will be offered by Life Insurance Corporation and all other life insurers who are willing to join the scheme and tie-up with banks for this purpose.

(e) The policy will be renewable each year.

(f) The contribution of government towards this scheme is to be decided separately every year. It is to be noted that the contribution amount to be paid by the government will come from the unclaimed money that has been lying idle in various public welfare funds.

Any person who is in the age group of 18 to 50 years and has a saving bank account in any of the participating bank is eligible for the scheme. The applicant joining the scheme must provide a self-certification of good health in the consent cum declaration form as on the date of enrollment or earlier. The insurance cover will be for the one year period stretching from 1st June to 31st May for which option to join/pay be auto-debit from the designated savings bank account on the prescribed forms will be required to be given by 31st May of every year. Delayed enrollment with payment of full annual premium for prospective cover may be possible with submission of a self-certificate of good health.

The termination of assurance under PMJJBY—In any of the following mentioned aspects, the advantages and assertions that fall under the PMJJBY would be right away concluded and no cash amount will be offered to the nominee or the subscriber.

(a) The assurance can be concluded in case the concerned person attains the 55 years of age.

(b) The declarations and advantages can be concluded in case the saving account of the subscriber gets shut.

(c) The insurance cover will be concluded if a person owns multiple saving accounts linked to the scheme and also in the situation of he/she holds multiple Bima policies on those accounts.

11. Pradhan Mantri Fasal Bima Yojana (PMFBY)

Prime Minister Narendra Modi launched a new crop damage insurance scheme on 13 January 2016, replacing the existing two schemes National Agricultural Insurance Scheme (NAIS) as well as Modified NAIS. The new crop insurance scheme, named as Pradhan Mantri Fasal Bima Yojana (PMFBY), will be implemented in every state of India with association with the respective State Governments and it will be administered under the Ministry of Agriculture and Farmers' Welfare, Government of India. The primary objectives of PMFBY are:

(a) To provide insurance coverage and financial support to the farmers in the event of failure of any of the notified crop as a result of natural calamities, pests, and diseases.

(b) To stabilise the income of farmers to ensure their continuance in farming.

(c) To encourage farmers to adopt innovative and modern agricultural practices.

(d) To ensure flow of credit to the agriculture sector.

The PMFBY covers Kharif, Rabi crops as well as annual commercial and horticultural crops. For kharif crops, the premium charged would be up to 2 percent of the sum insured. For Rabi crops, the premium would be up to 1.5 percent of the sum assured. For annual commercial and horticultural crops, premium would be 5 percent. The remaining share of premium will be brone equally by the central and respective state governments. Some of the innovative features of the scheme are:

(a) The scheme will be implemented on an 'Area Approach Basis'. For major crops, the Unit of Insurance will ordinarily be village or village panchayat level and for minor crops may be at a higher level depending upon the requirement.

(b) All farmers growing notified crops in a notified area during the season who have insurable interest in the crop are eligible for the scheme.

(c) The enrollment under the PMFBY, subject to possession of insurable interest on the cultivation of the notified crop in the notified area, will be compulsory for following categories of farmers.

  (i) Farmers in the notified area who possess a Crop Loan Account/KCC account, called as Loanee Farmers, to whom credit limit is sanctioned/ renewed for the notified crop during the crop season.

  (ii) Such other farmers whom the Government may decide to include from time to time.

(d) There will be one insurance company for the whole state. The Ministry of Agriculture and Farmers' Welfare designated/empanelled Agriculture Insurance Company of India (AIC) and some private insurance companies shall be roped to implement the scheme.

(e) Following risks leading to crop loss are to be covered under the scheme.

  (i) Yield Losses (standing crops, on notified area basis)—Comprehensive risk insurance is provided to cover yield losses due to non-preventable risks, such as Natural Fire and Lightning; Storm, Hailstorm, Cyclone; Flood, Inundation and Landslide; Drought and Dry Spells; Pests/ Diseases; etc.

  (ii) Prevented Sowing (on notified area basis)—In cases where majority of the insured farmers of a notified area, having intent to sow/plant and incurred expenditure for the purpose, are prevented from sowing/planting the insured crop due to adverse weather conditions, shall be eligible for indemnity claims up to a maximum of 25 percent of the sum-insured.

(iii) Post-Harvest Losses (individual farm basis)—Coverage is available up to a maximum period of 14 days from harvesting for those crops which are kept in "cut and spread" condition to dry in the field after harvesting, against specific perils of cyclone/cyclonic rains, unseasonal rains throughout the country.

(iv) Localised Calamities (individual farm basis)—Loss or damage resulting from occurrence of identified localised risks, i.e., hailstorm, landslide, and inundation affecting isolated farms in the notified area.

(f) In case of Loanee farmers under compulsory component, the Sum Insured would be equal to Scale of Finance for that crop as fixed by District Level Technical Committee (DLTC) which may extend up to the value of the threshold yield of the insured crop at the option of insured farmer. Where value of the threshold yield is lower than the Scale of Finance, higher amount will be the Sum Insured.

Multiplying the National Threshold Yield with the Minimum Support Price (MSP) of the current year arrives at the value of sum insured. Wherever current year's MSP is not available, MSP of previous year will be adopted.

(g) PMFBY is exempted from Service Tax liability of all the services involved in the implementation of the scheme.

(h) The scheme proposes mandatory use of remote sensing, smart phones and drones for quick estimation of crop loss. This will speed up the claim process.

(i) The settlement of claims will be fastened for the full sum assured. About 25% of the likely claim will be settled directly on farmers account. There will not be a cap on the premium and reduction of the sum insured.

The PMFBY is different from earlier schemes on the account of following:

(a) It is open to all farmers but not mandatory to anyone. It is optional for loanee as well as non-loanee farmers.

(b) It has lowest premium. The earlier premium rates were between 2.5 percent and 3.5 percent for kharif crops and 1.5 percent for rabi crops, but the coverage was capped, meaning farmers could, at best, recover a fraction of their losses. In the new scheme, the farmers' premium has been kept at a maximum of 2 percent for food grains and up to 5 percent for annual commercial horticulture crops. For rabi crops, it is 1.5 percent. The balance premium will be paid by the government to provide full insured amount to the farmers. Since, there is no upper cap on government subsidy, even if the balance premium is 90 percent, the government will bear it.

(c) This scheme provides full coverage of insurance. While NAIS had full coverage, it was copped in the modified-NAIS scheme.

(d) It also covers the localised risks such as hailstorm, landslide, inundation, etc. Earlier schemes did not cover inundation.

(e) It provides post harvest coverage. The NAIS did not cover while the modified NAIS covered only coastal regions.

Thus, the new crop insurance scheme has the potential to deal with the vagaries of nature on Indian farming.

12. Kisan Vikas Patra (KVP)

It is a saving certificate scheme which was first launched on Ist April 1988 by India Post. The scheme provided facility of unlimited investment by way of purchase of certificates from post offices in various denominations. The maturity period of the scheme when launched was 5-1/2 years and the money invested doubled on maturity. The scheme was very popular among the investors and the percentage share of gross collections secured in

KVP was in the range of 9 percent to 29 percent against the total collections received under all National Savings Schemes in the country. Gross collections under the scheme in the year 2010-11 were ₹ 21631.16 crores which was 9 percent of the total gross collections during the year. In the year of its closure, the scheme secured gross collections of ₹ 7575.95 crores (April 2011 to November 2011). It was successful for some time, but after the Shayamla Committee Report to the government that KVP could be misused, the scheme was closed in 2011. However, in a bid to encourage the habit of small savings among citizens, the Modi Government has relaunched this scheme in 2014.

The main features of the scheme are as under:

(i) KVP can be purchased by an adult in his own name, or on behalf of a minor, two adults jointly, and by a trust.

(ii) KVP certificates are available in the denominations of ₹ 1000, ₹ 5000, ₹ 10000 and ₹ 50000. The minimum amount that can be invested is ₹ 1000. However, there is no upper limit on the purchase of KVPs.

(iii) KVP does not offer any income tax benefits to the investor. However, withdrawals are exempted from Tax Deduction at Source (TDS) upon maturity.

(iv) KVP can be purchased from any post office. It will also soon be made available to the public through designated branches of nationalised banks.

(v) KVP can be transferred from one person to another and from one post office to another, multiple times.

(vi) The facility of nomination is available.

(vii) KVP can also be pledged as security to avail loans from the banks and in other case where security is required to be deposited.

(viii) The among invested in KVP matures in 112 months and the rate of interest is 7.7 percent annually. The investment made in KVP will double in 112 months.

(ix) KVP can be encashed after the lock-in period of 2 years and 6 months and thereafter in any block of six months on pre-determined maturity value.

Reintroduction of KVP is a good step not only in the direction of providing safe and secure investment avenues to the small investors but will also help in augmenting the savings rate in the country. The scheme will also safeguard small investors from fraudulent schemes. With a maturity period of 112 months, the collections under the scheme will be available with the Government for a fairly long period to be utilised in financing developmental plans of the Centre and State Governments, and will also help in enhancing domestic household financial savings in the country.

13. Saansad Adarsh Gram Yojana (SAANJHI)

Launched by the Prime Minister Narendra Modi on the birth anniversary of Jayaprakash Narayan, on 11 October 2014, this rural development programme focuses on the development in the villages, including social development, cultural development, and spread motivation among the people on social mobilization of the village community. It is a demand driven scheme, inspired by society, and based on people's participation. The main objectives of the scheme include: (i) the development of model villages, called Adarsh Grams, through the implementation of existing schemes, and certain new initiatives to be designed for the local context, which may vary from village to village; and (ii) creation of models of local development which can be replicated in other villages.

Inspired by the principles and value of Mahatma Gandhi, the scheme places equal stress on nurturing values of national pride, patriotism, community spirit, self-confidence and on developing infrastructure. The SAANJHI will keep the soul of rural India alive while providing its people with quality access to basic amenities and opportunities to enable them to shape their own destiny. It is unique and transformative as it has a holistic approach towards development. It envisages integrated development of the selected village across multiple areas such as agriculture, health, education, sanitation, environment, livelihoods, etc. Far beyond mere infrastructure development, SAANJHI aims at instilling certain values, such as people's participation, antyodaya, gender equality, dignity of women, social justice, spirit of community service, cleanliness, eco-friendliness, maintaining ecological balance, peace and harmony, mutual cooperation, self-reliance, local self-government, transparency and accountability in public life, etc. in the villages and their people so that they get transformed into models for others.

Under this scheme, gram panchayat is the basic unit for development. It should have a population of 3000-5000 in plain areas and 1000-3000 in hilly, tribal, and difficult areas. In districts where this unit size is not available, gram panchayats approximating the desirable population size may be chosen. The MP will identify one gram panchayat to be taken up immediately, and two others to be taken up a little later. Lok Sabha MP has to choose a gram panchayat from within his/her constituency and Rajya Sabha MP a gram panchayat from the rural areas of a district of his/her choice in the State from which he/she is elected. Nominated MPs may choose a gram panchayat from the rural area of any district in the country. In the case of urban constituencies where there are no gram panchayats, the MP will identify a gram panchayat from a nearby rural constituency. Primarily, the goal is to develop three Adarsh Grams by March 2019, of which one would be achieved by 2016. Thereafter, five such Adarsh Grams, one per year, will be selected and developed by 2024.

The MPs will engaged with the community, facilitate the Village Development Plan and mobilise the necessary resources. The Development Plan will place a special emphasis on enabling every poor household to come out of poverty. Prior to the plan formulation, there will be a systematic environment creation and social mobilisation, which will be led and guided by the MPs. The planning process in each village will be a participatory exercise coordinated by the District Collector. The MPs will also directly support activities at village level like health camps, organising grievance redressal camps, community mobilisation, etc. They will give a direction to holistic development and our ingenuous villagers will pave their own path through their hard work and entrepreneurial skills. Following are some of the crucial features of the SAANJHI.

(a) It gives focus to community participation. Social mobilization of village community can trigger a chain of other development activities in the village.

(b) Strengthening of local democracy through strong and transparent gram panchayats and active gram sabhas and facilitating good governance.

(c) Women participation in the decision-making process will be encouraged. The scheme envisages holding Mahila Sabhas and Bal Sabhas to discuss women and children specific issues and concerns.

(d) It will also ensure universal access to education facilities, adult literacy, e-literacy, and pay attention to providing infrastructure in schools like toilets, libraries, and supporting smart schools.

(e) It will promote among young generation a sense of confidence and values such as respect for women, martyrs and elders, good hygiene, respect for the environment, good heading habits, etc.

(f) It will ensure quality health care for the people of the village. The outcomes will include 100 percent immunization, 100 percent institutional delivery, reduced IMR, MMR, reduction in malnutrition among children, etc.

(g) To create vibrant and harmonious society within the village activities, like honouring village elders, folk art festivals, having a village song, etc. will be promoted.

(h) Adoption and adaptation of technology and introduction of innovations are critical to this programme. This will include use of space application and remote sensing for planning, mobile based technology for monitoring, agriculture technology for increasing productivity, etc.

(i) Ministry of Rural Development is the nodal Ministry coordinating and monitoring the scheme closely to ensure its efficient implementation. In order to operationalize the strategies the central sector and centrally sponsored schemes along with the state schemes will be implemented in a convergent and integrated manner to generate maximum synergy.

(j) To make the Adarsh Grams replicable and sustainable models, four kinds of awards have been decided to be given—(i) Best Practices, (ii) Best Charge Officers, (iii) Best District Collectors, and (iv) Best Adarsh Grams.

Funding for the Scheme

No new funds have been allocated to SAANJHI scheme. The funds needed will be raised through the following:

(i) Funds from existing schemes, such as the Indira Awas Yojana, Pradhan Mantri Gram Sadak Yojana, Mahatma Gandhi National Rural Employment Guarantee Scheme, and Backward Regions Grant Fund, etc.

(ii) The Member of Parliament Local Area Development Scheme (MPLADS),

(iii) The gram panchayat's own revenue,

(iv) Central and State Finance Commission Grants, and

(v) Corporate Social Responsibility funds.

Strategies to Implement the Scheme

Some strategies have been planned to convert the identified village into an Adarsh Gram through the specified activities, which include the following:

(i) There will be entry point activities to energise and mobilize the community towards positive common action.

(ii) The exercise for participatory planning to identify the needs of the people will be done in an integrated manner.

(iii) The government will endeavour to converging resources from Central Sector and Centrally Sponsored Schemes and also other State Schemes to the extent possible.

(iv) The existing infrastructure will be repaired and renovated to the extent possible.

Gram Panchayats and peoples' institutions within them will be strengthened; and transparency and accountability will be promoted.

(v) At the national level, the member of parliament will: (i) identify and select the Adarsh Gram, (ii) facilitate the planning process, and (iii) mobilize additional resources to the extent possible, and monitor the progress periodically and take the lead in sorting out issues and problems.

(vi) Two committees, headed by the Minister of Rural Development, and Secretary of Rural Development, respectively will: (i) monitor the process of identification and planning, (ii) review the implementation of the scheme, (iii) identify bottlenecks and problems in the scheme, (iv) issue operational guidelines, and (v) indicate specific resource support which each ministry will provide to build capacity across states.

(vii) At the state level a committee head by Chief Secretary will: (i) supplement central guidelines for the scheme, (ii) review Village Development Plans, (iii) review implementation, (iv) outline monitoring mechanisms supplementary to the web-based monitoring system, and (v) design a grievance redressal mechanism for the scheme.

(viii) At the district level, the collector will: (i) conduct the baseline survey, (ii) facilitate the preparation of the Village Development Plan, (iii) converge relevant schemes, (iv) ensure grievance redressal, and (v) review monthly progress of the scheme.

(ix) At village level, gram panchayat and functionaries of the scheme at various levels will: (i) implement the scheme, (ii) identify common needs of the village, (iii) leverage resources from various programmes, and (iv) ensure participation in the scheme.

The scheme will make the adopted villages the model village taking care of education, health, and housing facilities. Other villages that have not been adopted can also take and implement the development programmes on their own. A Mid-term evaluation of performance would be conducted through a competent independent agency. A post-project assessment of performance and outcome would be undertaken.

14. National Heritage City Development and Augmentation Yojana (HRIDAY)

Launched on 21 January 2015, with a focus on holistic development of heritage cities, this scheme aims at bringing together urban planning, economic growth and heritage conservation in an inclusive manner to preserve and revitalise soul of the heritage city to reflect the city's unique character by encouraging aesthetically appealing, accessible, informative and secured environment. The objective is to undertake strategic and planned development of heritage cities aiming at improvement in overall quality of life with specific focus on sanitation, security, tourism, heritage revitalization and livelihoods retaining the city's cultural identity. The initiatives shall include development of water supply, sanitation, drainage, waste management, approach roads, footpaths, street lights, tourist conveniences, electricity wiring, landscaping and such citizen services.

The scheme shall support development of core heritage infrastructure projects including revitalization of linked urban infrastructure for heritage assets such as monuments, ghats, temples, etc. along with reviving certain intangible assets like couture and customs. These initiatives shall include development of sanitation facilities, roads, public transportation and parking, citizen services, information kiosks, among other such things.

With a duration of 4 years (completing in November, 2018) and a total outlay of ₹ 500 crore (US$ 74 million), the scheme is set to be implemented in 12 identified cities, namely Ajmer, Amaravati, Amritsar, Badami, Dwarka, Gaya, Kanchipuram, Mathura, Puri, Varanasi, Velankanni and Warangal.[8]

Objectives of the Scheme

As per the Ministry of Urban Development, the objectives of the scheme are as under:

(i) Planning, development and implementation of heritage-sensitive infrastructure; service delivery and infrastructure provisioning in the core areas of the historic cities.

(ii) Preserve and revitalize heritage wherein tourists can connect directly with city's unique character.

(iii) Develop and document a heritage asset inventory of cities making natural, cultural, living and built heritage the basis for urban planning, growth, service provision, and delivery.

(iv) Implement and enhance basic services delivery with focus on sanitation services such as public conveniences, toilets, water taps, street lights, with use of latest technologies in improving tourist facilities.

(v) Enhance local capacity for inclusive heritage-based industry.

(vi) Creating effective linkages between tourism and cultural facilities and also the conservation of natural and built heritage.

(vii) Urban heritage adaptive rehabilitation and maintenance, including appropriate technologies for historic buildings retrofitting.

(viii) Establishing and managing effective public private partnership for adaptive urban rehabilitation.

(ix) Development and promotion to core tangible economic activities to enhance avenues of livelihoods amongst stakeholders. This would also include necessary skill development amongst them including making public spaces accessible and developing cultural spaces.

(x) Making cities informative with use of modern ICT tools and making cities secure with modern surveillance and security apparatus.

India is endowed with different cultures, religions, traditions, arts, handicrafts, architectural styles, music and literature. Efforts made to conserve historic and cultural resources in Indian cities have mostly been carried out in isolation from the immediate aspirations of the local communities. The main urban development issues such as local economy, urban planning, livelihoods, service delivery and infrastructure provision have often been neglected. Basic amenities like toilets, signages, street lights are missing at many such cities. Managing these heritage cities is a big challenge. The development of a heritage city is not just about development and conservation of a few monuments, but development of the entire city, its planning, its basic services, quality of life of its communities, its economy and livelihoods, cleanliness, security, reinvigoration of its soul and an explicit manifestation of its character. HRIDAY will inculcate a planned approach to tap the unlimited potential underlying tourism and heritage sector of these cities, further giving a boost to the traditional and national economy. This will also enable smooth dovetailing of modern concept of economic development through locally available knowledge, resources, and skills.[9]

The scheme would be implemented in a mission mode. Each city has been granted a specific amount of fund, based on its population and size. The funding is as follows.[10]

Table 8.1: Funds allotted for cities under HRIDAY

S.No.	City	Funds (₹ Crore)
1.	Ajmer	40.04
2.	Amaravati	22.26
3.	Amritsar	69.31
4.	Badami	22.26
5.	Dwarka	22.26
6.	Gaya	40.04
7.	Kanchipuram	23.04
8.	Mathura	40.04
9.	Puri	22.54
10.	Varanasi	89.31
11.	Velankanni	22.26
12.	Warangal	40.54

HRIDAY is a central sector scheme, where 100 percent funding will be provided by Government of India. For each of the 12 cities, agencies with significant expertise in the field of heritage have been selected to act as the HRIDAY City Anchor. The primary objective of HRIDAY City Anchors is to handhold the cities in successful implementation of the scheme.

15. Pradhan Mantri Krishi Sinchayee Yojana (PMKSY)

Agriculture is the mainstay of Indian economy. India's large population and high rate of growth of population means a huge demand for food and hence the need of growing more and more of it with each passing year. Since irrigation is the most important part of farming, the yield depends on the availability of irrigation facilities, especially keeping in view the fact that monsoons are irregular. Most of the crop failures are caused by lack of rainfall and inadequate irrigation. Food and retail inflation are natural corollaries to the situation and this hurts the economy. In 2014-15, food grain production in the country dropped by about 5.3 percent.

According to current estimates, out of the 142 million hectares of agricultural land in India, only about 45 percent has any arrangement for artificial irrigation. The remaining agricultural land depends on rainfall for its water needs. A delay in rainfall or a failure leads to poor yield.

In an attempt to improve agricultural productivity, the Modi Government has come up with a new scheme, the Pradhan Mantri Krishi Sinchayee Yojana (PMKSY), which has been approved by the cabinet committee on Economic Affairs chaired by PM in its meeting held on 1st July, 2015.

The PMKSY has been formulated with the vision of extending the coverage of irrigation (Har Khet ko Pani) and improving water use efficiency (More crop per drop) in a focused manner with end to end solution on source creation, distribution, management, field application, and extension activities. Its major objective is to achieve convergence of investments in irrigation at the field level, expand cultivable area under assured irrigation, improve on-farm water use efficiency to reduce wastage of water, enhance the adoption of precision-irrigation and other water saving technologies, enhance recharge of aquifers and introduce sustainable water conservation practices by exploring the feasibility of reusing treated municipal waste water for peri-urban agriculture and attract greater private investment in precision irrigation system.

The PMKSY has been formulated amalgamating ongoing schemes, viz. Accelerated Irrigation Benefit Programme (AIBP) of the Ministry of Water Resources, River Development and Ganga Rejuvenation (MOWR, RD&RG), Integrated Watershed Management Programme (IWMP) of Department of Land Resources (DoLR) and the On Farm Water Management (OFWM) of Department of Agriculture and Cooperation (DAC).

It will be implemented by Ministries of Agriculture, Water Resources and Rural Development. Ministry of Rural Development will mainly undertake rain water conservation, construction of farm pond, water harvesting structures, small check dams and contour bunding, etc. MoWR, RD&GR will undertake various measures for creation of assured irrigation source, construction of diversion canals, field channels, water diversion or lift irrigation, including development of water distribution systems. Ministry of Agriculture will promote efficient water conveyance and precision water application devices like drips, sprinklers, pivots, rain-guns in the farm, construction of micro-irrigation structures to supplement source creation activities, extension activities for promotion of scientific moisture conservation and agronomic measures.

Under PMKSY, a 'decentralised state level planning and projectised execution' structure will be adopted that will allow states to draw up their own irrigation development plans based on District Irrigation Plan (DIP) and State Irrigation Plan (SIP). PMKSY will be operative as convergence platform for all water sector activities including drinking water and sanitation, MGNREGA, application of science and technology, etc. through comprehensive plan. State Level Sanctioning Committee (SLSC) has been intrusted with the authority to oversee the implementation of PMKSY and sanction projects.

PMKSY will be supervised and monitored by an Inter-Ministerial National Steering Committee (NSC), which will be constituted under the chairmanship of PM with Union Ministers from the concerned Ministries. A National Executive Committee (NEC) will be constituted under the Chairmanship of Vice-chairman, NITI Aayog to oversee programme implementation, allocation of resources, inter ministerial coordination, monitoring and performance assessment, addressing administrative issues, etc.

Components of PMKSY

There are four components of PMKSY.

(a) AIBP by MoWR, RD and GR—It will focus on faster completion of ongoing major and medium irrigation including National Projects.

(b) PMKSY (Har Khet Ko Pani) by MoWR, RD and GR—It will take care of following activities.

  (i) Creation of new water sources through Minor Irrigation (both surface and ground water).

  (ii) Repair, restoration and renovation of water bodies; strengthening carrying capacity of traditional water sources, construction of rain water harvesting structures.

  (iii) Command area development, strengthening and creation of distribution network from source to the farm.

  (iv) Improvement in water management and distribution system for water bodies to take advantage of the available source which is not tapped to its fullest capacity.

  (v) Diversion of water from source of different location where it is plenty to nearby water scarce areas, lift irrigation from water bodies/rivers at lower elevation to supplement requirements beyond IWMP and MGNREGA irrespective of irrigation command.

  (vi) Creation and rejuvenation of traditional water storage systems.

(c) PMKSY (watershed) by Department of Land Resources, MoRD—It will take care of following activities.

(i) Create water harvesting structures such as check dams, nala bund, farm ponds, tanks, etc.

(ii) Capacity building, entry point activities, ridge area treatment, drainage line treatment, soil and moisture conservation, nursery raising, afforestation, horticulture, pasture development, livelihood activities for the asset-less persons and production system and micro enterprises for small and marginal farmers.

(iii) Effective rainfall management like field bunding, contour bunding/trenching, staggered trenching, land levelling, mulching, etc.

(d) PMKSY (per drop more crop) by Department of Agriculture and cooperation, MoA—It will take care of following activities.

(i) Programme management, preparation of State/ District Irrigation Plan, approval of annual action plan, monitoring, etc.

(ii) Promoting efficient water conveyance and precision water application devices like drips, sprinklers, pivots, rain-guns in the farm.

(iii) Topping up of input cost particularly under civil construction beyond permissible limit under MGNREGA for activities like living inlet, outlet, silt traps, distribution system, etc.

(iv) Construction of micro irrigation structures to supplement source creation activities including tube wells and dug wells, which are not supported under PMKSY (WR), PMKSY (watershed) and MGNREGA.

(v) Construction of secondary storage structures at tail end of canal system to store water when available in abundance or from perennial sources like streams for use during dry periods through effective on-farm water management.

(vi) Providing water lifting devices like diesel/electric/ solar pumpsets including water carriage pipes.

(vii) Extension activities for promotion of scientific moisture conservation and agronomic measures including cropping alignment to maximise use of available water including rainfall and minimise irrigation requirement.

(viii) Capacity building, training for encouraging potential use of water source through technological, agronomic and management practices including community irrigation.

(ix) Carrying out awareness campaign on water saving technologies, practices, programmes, etc.; organisation of workshops, conferences, publication of booklets, pamphlets, success stories, documentary, advertisements, etc.

(x) Improved and innovative distribution system like pipe and box outlet system with controlled outlet and other activities of enhancing water use efficiency.

Allocation of Funds

PMKSY has been approved for implementation across the country with an outlay of ₹ 50,000 crore in five years. For 2015-16, an outlay of ₹ 5300 crore has been made which includes ₹ 1800 crore for Department of Agriculture and cooperation (DAC); ₹ 1500 crore for Department of Land Resources (DoLR); and ₹ 2000 crore for Ministry of Water Resources (MoWR) of which ₹ 1000 crore for Accelerated Irrigation Benefit Programme (AIBP) and ₹ 1000 crores for Pradhan Mantri Krishi Sinchayee Yojana (PMKSY).

16. Paramparagat Krishi Vikas Yojana (PKVY)

It is an initiative launched by Narendra Modi Government in 2015 to support and promote organic farming in the country and thereby improving soil health. This will encourage farmers to adopt eco-friendly concept of cultivation and reduce their dependence on fertilizers and agricultural chemicals to improve yields. According to the scheme, farmers will be encouraged to form groups or clusters and take to organic farming methods over large areas in the country. Each cluster or group must have 50 farmers willing to take up organic farming under the PKVY and possess a total area of at least 50 acres. Each farmer enrolling in the scheme will be provided ₹ 20,000 per acre by the government, spread over three years, which they can utilize for obtaining organic seeds, harvesting of the crops, and transporting the produce to the local markets.

Targets and Objectives

The scheme has the following targets and objectives:

(i) Form 10,000 clusters over the next three years and bring about five lakh acres of agricultural area under organic farming.

(ii) Cover the certification costs and promote organic farming through the use of traditional resources.

(iii) Link organic food with modern marketing tools and local markets.

(iv) There will be special focus on north eastern states of India. Efforts shall be stepped up to connect the organic produce in these parts with both domestic and export markets.

(v) A sum of ₹ 412 crore has been allocated by the government to implement the Paramparagat Krishi Vikas Yojana in the financial year 2016-17.

Importance of the Scheme

According to the Deptt. of Agriculture and Cooperation, the growth of organic agriculture in India has three dimensions. First category of organic farmers are those which are situated in no-input or low-input use zones. For them organic agriculture is a way of life and they are doing it under compulsion in the absence of resources needed for conventional high input intensive agriculture. Second category of farmers are those who have recently adopted the organic farming in the wake of ill-effects of conventional agriculture such as reduced soil fertility, food toxicity or increasing cost and diminishing returns. The third category is comprised of farmers and enterprises who/which have systematically adopted the commercial organic agriculture to capture emerging market opportunities and premium prices. By March 2010, India brought more than 4.48 million hectare area under organic certification process. Out of this, cultivated area accounts for 1.08 million hectare, while the remaining 3.4 million hectare is wild forest harvest collection area.[11]

According to a 2013 study conducted by the International Federation of Organic Agricultural Movements (IFOAM), there are about two million farmers across the globe who practice organic farming methods and roughly 80 percent of these farmers are in India. Thus, organic farming has become increasingly important in India given the rising number of concerns that the use of chemical fertilizers and pesticides is growing up. Promotion of organic-farming techniques leaves India best poised to cash in on the immense export potential of these foods. The PKVY is thus an important initiative brought by the Modi Government.

17. Soil Health Card Scheme (SHCS)

National Mission for Sustainable Agriculture (NMSA) will be implemented with the objectives to make agriculture more productive, sustainable and climate resilient; to conserve natural resources; to adopt comprehensive soil health management practices; to optimize utilization of water resources; etc. Soil Health Management (SHM) is one of the most important interventions under NMSA. SHM aims at promoting Integrated Nutrient Management (INM) through judicious use of chemical fertilizers including secondary and micro nutrients in conjunction with organic manures and bio-fertilizers for improving soil health and its productivity; strengthening of soil and fertilizer testing facilities to provide soil test based recommendations to farmers for improving soil fertility; ensuring quality control requirements of fertilizers, bio-fertilizers and organic fertilizers under Fertilizer Control Order, 1985; upgradation of skill and knowledge of soil testing laboratory staff, extension staff and farmers through training and demonstrations; promoting organic farming practices, etc.

SHCS is a scheme launched by the Modi Government in February 2015, under which it was planned to issue 'Soil Card' to farmers which will carry crop-wise recommendations of nutrients and fertilizers required for the individual farms to help farmers to improve productivity through judicious use of inputs. All soil samples are to be tested in various soil testing laboratories across the country. Thereafter, soil scientists and experts will analyze the strengths and weaknesses of the soil and suggest measures to deal with the deficiencies found in it. The result and suggestion will be displayed in the soil health cards. Under the scheme, the government plans to issue these cards to 14 crore farmers. The scheme also aims to promote soil test-based and balanced use of fertilizers to enable farmers realize higher yields at lower cost.

An amount of ₹ 568 crore was allocated by the government for the scheme. In the 2016 Union budget of India, ₹ 100 crore has been allocated to states for making soil health cards and set up labs.

Benefits to the Farmers

The SHCS has the following benefits for the farmers:

(i) The farmers will get a well-monitored report of the soil of their fields for the cultivation of crops.

(ii) There will be regular monitoring of the soil so that the deficiencies developed after the crops can be detected.

(iii) The farmers will be guided by experts to come up with solutions to improve the quality of the soil.

(iv) Regular monitoring will also help the farmers to get a long-term soil health record.

(v) The study and evaluation of the results of different soils will help us develop useful management practices which will be of great help for agriculture in India.

(vi) The Soil Health Cards (SHCs) will become very helpful and effective when filled out regularly by the same person over a period of time and will tell the farmer which crop consumes which nutrients more than others.

(vii) The card will help the farmers access the different types of soil and their ability to support crop production despite limitations.

(viii) The soil card will give the farmers an idea about the crop-wise recommendations of nutrients and fertilizers required in each type of soil. This will help in increasing the crop yield.

It has been seen that the per hectare yield of various crops in India is much lower than that in other countries. The major reason for this is that our soil lacks necessary strength in terms of nutrients to give high yield. The Soil Health Cards will tell the farmers about which crop is suitable to their fields so that they may grow it and get a higher yield. If they want a particular crop, they will know which nutrients they need to add to their fields. This will reduce the gap between the yields in our country and that in developed countries.

As of February 2016, the State Governments have distributed 1.12 crore SHCs to farmers and were expected to provide another two crore by the end of March 2016. The government plans to distribute 14 crore SHCs by 2017. For the year 2016-17, ₹ 100 crore has been allocated to states for making SHCs and set up labs.

Soil Health Card Web Portal

In order to make SHCS more successful, the Government of India, along with the Agriculture Department of India, has launched a soil health card agriculture portal. Under this, the farmers need to register at the web portal www.soilhealth.dac.gov.in along with the details of the soil samples and test lab reports. Once registered, the farmer can keep a track of the following in the portal: (i) Test results by soil testing labs; (ii) Fertilizer and nutrients recommendations; (iii) Soil Health Card generation; and (iv) MIS module for monitoring progress.

The objective behind the launch of the web portal is to create a single national database on soil health which can be used in the future for research and planning, both by farmers and soil experts.

18. One Rank One Pension (OROP) Scheme

The current pension system takes into consideration, the last drawn pay while deciding one's pension amount. However, the One Rank One Pension term suggests that armed force personnel holding the same rank and same length of service must be given same pension, regardless the last drawn pay. The Modi Government announced the OROP scheme on 6th September 2015 accepting the old demand of the retired armed personnel. OROP, in simple terms, implies that a uniform pension be paid to the armed forces personnel retiring in the same rank with the same length of service, regardless of their date of retirement. Future enhancements in the rates of pension would be automatically passed on to the past pensioners. This will bridge the gap between the rate of pension of current and past pensioners at periodic intervals. Under the OROP scheme, the government would revise the pension every five years, which will bridge the gap between rate of pension of current pensioners and past pensioners.

Features of the Scheme

The salient features of OROP are enumerated below:

(i) The benefit will be given with effect from Ist July 2014.

(ii) Arrears will be paid in four half-yearly instalments. However, all widows, including war widows, will be paid arrears in one instalment.

(iii) To begin with, OROP would be fixed on the basis of calendar year 2013.

(iv) Pension will be re-fixed for all pensioners retiring in the same rank and with the same length of service as the average of minimum and maximum pension in 2013. Those drawing pensions above the average will be protected.

(v) Personnel who voluntarily retire will not be covered under the scheme.

(vi) In future, pension would be re-fixed every five years.

Modi Government has also committed to examine the interests of retirees of different periods and different ranks. It will also address the issues of three wings of armed forces—Army, Air Force, and Navy. The estimated cost to implement OROP will be between ₹ 8,000 crore and 10,000 crore at present, and will increase further in future.

A one-member judicial committee headed by Justice L. Narasimha Reddy, former Chief Justice of Patna High Court, was constituted to give its report in six months. Since the six-month tenure of the one-man judicial commission ended on June 15, it was given an extension of six months. According to the Ex-Defence Minister, Manohar Parrikar, "four deviations in the implementation order" on OROP will be addressed, and that the recommendations of Seventh Pay Commission would be applicable to all ex-servicemen above and beyond the award of OROP.

In 1973, two years after the 1971 Bangladesh war, the Indira Gandhi-led Congress (I) Government, terminated One Rank One Pension which had been the basis for deciding pension of Indian Armed Forces personnel and was in vogue for 26 years since independence, through an ex-parte administrative order. In 1986, the sense of unease and distrust prompted by the Third Central Pay Commission (CPC) was exacerbated by the Rajiv Gandhi-led Congress (I) Government's decision to implement Rank Pay, which reduced basic pay of captain, majors, colonels, and brigadiers, and their equivalent in the air-force, and the navy, relative to basic pay scales of civilian and police officers. The decision to reduce the basic pay of these ranks, implemented without consulting the armed forces, created radically asymmetries between police-military ranks.

In 2008, after decades of failed attempts to get the government to address armed forces' grievances, often voiced by veterans under the banner of OROP, the protest movement gained wide support following decision by the PM Manmohan Singh-led UPA Government to controversially sanction a career path for all civil servants and Indian Police Service (IPS) officers that ensured all retire with OROP at the highest pay grade called the apex pay grade and created hundreds of new posts of Secretaries, Special Secretaries, Director General of Police (DGP) at the apex grade pay level; upgraded scores of police posts to DG-apex grade pay level, to ensure that all police officers retire at the highest pension scale and rewarded all civil services, including the IPS with Non-Functional Upgradation (NFU) to ensure all, irrespective of job title or responsibility, retire at the pay and pension of Armed Forces Lt Generals and equivalents.

These decisions downgraded and depressed armed forces' pay grades, allowances, pension, ranks, etc. as well as created asymmetries between armed forces and police-civil pay grades and pension outcomes. Armed forces veterans, often voiced armed forces' grievances and started a campaign in the latter half of 2008, wherein there were nationwide public protests, which included hunger strikes.

In 2011, the UPA Government appointed a parliamentary committee which found merit in the veterans demands for OROP. In May 2014, the UPA Government was replaced by the National Democratic Alliance (NDA) Government led by Bharatiya Janata Party (BJP), which had included implementation of OROP in its election manifesto. But, after it assumed office, it continued to make pledges and promises, but did not implement OROP. The BJP ambivalence provoked nationwide protests by the veterans, starting 15 June 2015. After five months of nationwide protests by veterans, the BJP Government decided to implement OROP. The implementation ended many controversies and protest by retired armed personnel.

19. Modi and Khadi Promotion

In 2012, when Narendra Modi was serving his third term as Chief Minister of Gujarat, he made an appeal to the people of the State to buy khadi and promote khadi culture. He asked people to buy khadi in large quantity, individually and in group, for self and for family, as a campaign during the Gandhi Jayanti Week as it will help the poor dependents on the khadi cottage industry earn their livelihood. He recalled how Mahatma

Gandhi had propagated the concept of khadi as a philosophy to economically empower lakhs of poor people in India.

After becoming India's Prime Minister, Narendra Modi called on the nation to embrace Mahatma Gandhi's legacy—khadi—and said that the fabric signified the culture of India. "Khadi has the power to provide employment to crores of people. It has now become a symbol and a centre of interest of the nation's youth," he said in his first 'Mann Ki Baat' address in 2016.[12] "Sardar Patel said India's independence is in khadi, India's civilization represents khadi, farmers' welfare is in khadi," he added.

Lauding the people associated with khadi, he said that the fabric was quickly gaining attention among the youth and was carving a niche for itself in the world of fashion. PM Modi added that the railways ministry, police, navy, Uttarakhand postal service and other government offices had taken up initiatives to promote khadi. "Due to the efforts of many government organizations in the field of khadi, around 18 lakh people can be granted employment," Modi said.

The Friday dressing may have a new meaning for government employees—wearing khadi to work, as the government is considering a plea from the Khadi & Village Industries Commission (KVIC) to appeal to the employees to wear clothes made from the hand-spun fabric at least once a week as part of a plan to boost khadi production and benefit small weavers across the country.

"We are discussing this with the government and will make an appeal. Employees can wear it to work on just one day," said KVIC chairman V.K. Saxena. Although the exercise would be voluntary, but the idea is to increase sales. If everyone buys just one khadi garment, there will be huge rise in sales. The central government currently has around 35 lakh employees, excluding the railways and defence personnel. KVIC is entering into tie ups with companies such as Fabindia and Raymond to retail high-end khadi at their outlets.

Promotion of khadi is yet another very good initiative taken by the Modi Government. According to Micro and Small Enterprises Minister, Kalraj Mishra, khadi production in the country will cross ₹ 1,300 crore in 2016-17 and create 19.5 lakh jobs. He said that village industries production is expected to cross ₹ 45,000 crore during 2016-17, creating employment for more than 163 lakh persons. The MSME Minister said that 2016-17 will be the development year for the sector with more allocation and increased job creation.[13]

20. Modi's Yoga Mission

Yoga is a physical, mental, and/or spiritual practice attributed mostly to India. Prime Minister Narendra Modi in his UN address suggested the date of June 21 to be the International Day of Yoga, as it is the longest day of the year in the Northern Hemisphere and shares special significance in many parts of the world. The idea of an International Day of Yoga was first proposed by Narendra Modi during his speech at the United Nations General Assembly (UNGA) on 27 September 2014. He said:

> Yoga is an invaluable gift of India's ancient tradition. It embodies unity of mind and body; thought and action; restraint and fulfilment; harmony between man and nature; a holistic approach to health and well-being. It is not about exercise but to discover the sense of oneness with yourself, the world and the nature. By changing our lifestyle and creating consciousness, it can help in the well-being. Let us work towards adopting an International Yoga Day.

After getting the United Nations to declare 21 June as International Yoga Day in 2015, Prime Minister Narendra Modi's Government is continuing with its push to promote this part-spiritual and part-physical exercise form. Narendra Modi also announced two annual awards—one will be for excellent contribution in the field of yoga internationally and the other for excellent contribution to yoga in the country. These awards will be called International Yoga Award and National Yoga Award, respectively.

Spending on Yoga

Ministerial spending on yoga, siddha and naturopathy increased by almost 2.5 times between FY15 and FY16, the highest proportionate increase among the four medicinal forms (the other three are Ayurveda, Homeopathy and Unani systems) under the ministry of AYUSH.[14] However, in absolute terms, yoga still has the lowest spending.

The Ministry of Human Resource Development announced that yoga courses would be started in at least six central universities and the number would be increased to 20 within a year. Running full-fledged departments in 20 central universities would entail a greater annual cost than the ₹ 20 crore increase for yoga under the Ministry of AYUSH in the 2016 budget. If the governments in States follow similar policies in State universities, the government funding other than through non-AYUSH ministry could see a further jump. Yoga is more popular among the relatively better-off and well-educated sections of the population, which is likely to be less dependent on government initiatives to provide facilities. Given these facts, the government's strategy for promoting yoga seems to be right.

Narendra Modi has appealed to the nation to focus on mitigating the effect of diseases like diabetes through yoga. It remains to be seen how many Indians can follow the strict discipline and perseverance required to reap such benefits of yoga.

It is because of Prime Minister Narendra Modi's initiatives that yoga has got a high level of international recognition. While highlighting the importance of Yoga, the AYUSH Minister Mr. Naik said, "It is not only a health practice, but also a means to unite the people due to its inherent connection with the mind."

Following the adoption of the UN Resolution, several leaders of spiritual movement in India voiced their support for Modi's initiative. Founder of Isha Foundation, Sadhguru, stated that "this could be a kind of a foundation stone to make scientific approach to the inner well-being of the human being, a worldwide thing. It's a tremendous step for the world." Founder of Art of Living, Ravi Shankar lauded the efforts of Modi, stating that "It is very difficult for any philosophy, religion or culture to survive without state patronage. Yoga has existed so far almost like an orphan. Now, official recognition by the UN would further spread the benefit of yoga to the entire world."

In his address, PM Modi advocated for popularization of the practice across the world and desired for more yoga teachers to be produced from India. Given below are ten quotes[15] made by PM Modi as part of his address:

(i) We did not have health insurance in olden times. But, yoga is a practice which gives health 'assurance' with zero spending.

(ii) Yoga is not about what one will get, it is about what one can give up.

(iii) Yoga is also turning into a profession and is providing employment to many.

(iv) There are countries around the world which have 24-hours dedicated TV channels for yoga.

(v) Eminent gynecologists suggest pregnant women to practice yoga as it helps them stay healthy.

(vi) We are disconnected from ourselves in today's times. Therefore, yoga helps us in reconnecting with ourselves.

(vii) I announce two awards for Yoga Day celebrations next year. One award is for those who are doing good work in the field of yoga on international level and other for national level.

(viii) Let yoga be popularised across the world. Let yoga teachers be produced from India.

(ix) Yoga is not just about getting rid of diseases (ailments) but it is a guarantee of wellness.

(x) The way mobile phone has become a part of life, you can make yoga a part of your life too.

Modi's promotion of yoga is an appreciable act of maintaining and improving the health of the people of India. Those who get connected with yoga also improve their eating habits. This will also have economic benefits as healthy people are more energetic and productive. With the opening of yoga centres in almost every city, a large number of people have got employment. As yoga and meditation keep the mind calm and composed, there will be social benefits too, like reduction in crime rate.

Conclusion

It can be seen that after becoming India's Prime Minister, Narendra Modi has brought a number of schemes for the benefit of people, society, and the country at large. Some schemes aim to help particular sections, while others are more open and can prove beneficial to anyone who fulfils the eligibility criteria. For example, Prime Minister's Employment Generation Programme (PMEGP) aims to generate continuous and sustainable employment opportunities in rural and urban areas of the country; and to provide continuous and sustainable employment to a large number of traditional and prospective artisans, rural and urban unemployed youth in the country by setting up micro enterprises. Beti Bachao, Beti Padhao is Modi Government's scheme that aims to generate awareness and improve the efficiency of welfare services meant for women.

Atal Pension Yojana (APY) is a government-backed pension scheme targeted at the unorganized sector. As of May 2015, only 11% of India's population had the benefit of any kind of pension scheme. APY aims to increase this number. Through Pradhan Mantri Awas Yojana (PMAY), Prime Minister Narendra Modi has envisioned housing for all by 2022 when the nation completes 75 years of its Independence.

Pradhan Mantri Suraksha Bima Yojana (PMSBY) is a government-backed accident insurance scheme for people between 18 and 70 years of age with bank accounts, while Pradhan Mantri Jeevan Jyoti Bima Yojana (PMJJBY) is a government-backed life insurance scheme available to people between 18 and 50 years of age with bank accounts.

Pradhan Mantri Fasal Bima Yojana (PMFBY) envisages a uniform premium of only 2 percent to be paid by farmers for Kharif crops, and 1.5 percent for Rabi crops. The premium for annual commercial and horticultural crops will be 5 percent. Pradhan Mantri Krishi Sinchayee Yojana (PMKSY) aims to attract investments in irrigation system at field level; develop and expand cultivable land in the country; enhance ranch water use in order to minimize wastage of water; and enhance crop per drop by implementing water-saving technologies and precision irrigation. Under Soil Health Card Scheme (SHCS) it has been planned to issue soil cards to farmers which will carry crop-wise recommendations of nutrients and fertilizers required for the individual farms to help farmers improve productivity through judicious use of inputs.

Saansad Adarsh Gram Yojana (SAANJHI) focuses on the development in the villages, including social development, cultural development, and spread motivation among the people on social mobilization of the village community. National Heritage City Development and Augmentation Yojana (HRIDAY) aims at bringing together urban planning, economic growth, and heritage conservation in an inclusive manner to preserve the heritage character of each heritage city.

Thus, there is some scheme or the other for all sections of society, for villagers as well as for city-dwellers, for the young and for the old, for farmers and for people engaged in other occupations. Narendra Modi has so far proved to be the most active Prime Minister of India so far. He has a broad vision as is evident from the plethora of initiatives taken by him. All of his schemes have been suitably funded with adequate provisions in the budget. There is proper implementation policy in each scheme with related ministry/ministries being actively involved to see that everything goes on smoothly. There has been good response from the people too in every scheme. For example, in Jan Dhan Yojana, which was launched on 15 August 2014, millions of accounts have been opened (219 million, including 57 million zero balance accounts by 18 May 2016). The amount of deposits was ₹ 380.47 billion by April 2016, and as many as 19 lakh householders have availed the overdraft facility of ₹ 2.56 billion (US$ 38 million) by May 2016. At Modi's call to promote khadi, many institutions and their employees have committed to adopt it. The Indian Institute of Technology-Bombay has chosen khadi *angavastrams*, a Hindu traditional white piece of cloth or stole, for the convocation ceremony of its graduating batch. Earlier Gujarat Technological University made khadi compulsory for its convocation.

The schemes and initiatives brought by Narendra Modi are likely to benefit millions of Indians. If these schemes are implemented in letter and spirit and the problems faced, if any, are solved with timely action, India will progress by leaps and bounds by the end of the current decade.

Notes

1. *The Economic Times*. 28 August 2014.
2. *The Economic Times*. 30 March 2016.
3. Indian Medical Association, *Journal of the Indian Medical Association* (Indian Medical Association) 105 (7-12): 711. 2007.
4. *The Financial Express*. 30 March 2015.
5. "Jan Suraksha schemes to help eliminate Jan Dhan's zero balance accounts." *Business Standard*. 8 May 2015.
6. http://www.mhupa.gov.in/User_Panel/UserView.aspx?TypeID=1493
7. "Jan Suraksha schemes to help eliminate Jan Dhan's zero balance accounts," *Business Standard*, 8 May 2015.
8. *The Times of India*. 1 Dec. 2014.
9. HRIDAY official website.
10. Press Information Bureau, Govt. of India Official Website.
11. A.K. Yadav (Director National Centre of Organic Farming, Ghaziabad). *Organic Agriculture (Concept, Scenario, Principals and Practices)*.
12. 'Mann Ki Baat' is an Indian radio programme hosted by Prime Minister Narendra Modi in which he addresses the people of the nation on radio, DD National and DD News.
13. Business Standard, 8 March 2016.
14. The Department of Ayurveda, Yoga and Naturopathy, Unani, Siddha and Homoeopathy, abbreviated as AYUSH, is a governmental body in India purposed with developing education and research in ayurveda (Indian traditional medicine), yoga, naturopathy, unani, siddha, and homoeopathy, and other alternative medicine systems.
15. Indianexpress.com

CHAPTER 9

Narendra Modi's Foreign Visits: Agreements, Benefits and Strategies

After becoming India's Prime Minister in June 2014, Narendra Modi has visited a number of countries in Asia, Europe, America, Africa, and Australia, holding meetings with state heads, discussing issues of importance for both the countries, the region, and the world at large. Under the prime ministership of Narendra Modi, India signed several agreements with other countries breaking new grounds for India's economic development through increased flow of Foreign Direct Investment (FDI) into India. Modi also requested each host country to participate in India's flagship schemes like Make in India, Skill India, and others, and make them successful. He urged the nations to cooperate with each other in fighting terrorism, ensure clean environment, develop clean sources of energy, make judicious use of available resources, and share use of technology for fast development. He stressed the need for enhancing friendship among the nations. Modi also attended important international meetings, plenaries, and held discussions on the sidelines of summit meetings like that of BRICS nations.

High Level Diplomacy

Modi's foreign visits are highly important for developing international diplomacy. Building a personal rapport with the leaders through personal connect with leaders has been an important element of Modi's diplomacy since coming to office in

June 2014. He has been actively involved in official discussions with high-level political and military leaders and in focusing on cease-fires, peace talks and treaties, and singed a number of agreements with the countries he visited relating to various plans for mutual development. His is a style of multi-track diplomacy which means that many initiatives are simultaneously going on helping the two countries to achieve their mutual goals.

When the Head of a State visits another country, it is the highest track diplomacy and sends out a message that the country is important to them. By visiting a number of countries, Narendra Modi has shown that India holds them important and is willing to build bigger and better partnerships with them for development and on issues of mutual or global concern. With mutual dialogues and making of joint statements, Narendra Modi has spread the message of cooperation, as also a warning to other nations like China and Pakistan that India has full support of other nations and they should think twice before taking any action that is against India. This is a high level of diplomacy that Modi has been able to build, the like of which was never reached by any earlier Indian Prime Minister.

Modi has visited even to remote countries like Mongolia, island nations like Seychelles and Mauritius, and to major powers like the US, China, France, Germany and UK. He also visited countries like Canada, UAE, UK, Turkey and other countries where no Indian Prime Minister visited for decades. At home also, Modi received many world leaders starting with a big-bang diplomacy by inviting US President Barack Obama as the chief guest at the Republic Day celebrations in January, 2015; Japanese Prime Minister Shinzo Able's extraordinary visit to new Delhi in December, 2015; Chinese President Xi Jinping's visit in September, 2014; Russian President Vladimir Putin's visit in December, 2014; Emir of Qatar Tamim bin Hamad Al Thani's visit in March 2015; German Chancellor Angela Markel's visit in October 2015; French President Francois Hollande's visit in January 2016; Crown Prince of UAE Mohammed bin Zayed Al Nahyan's visit in February 2016; South African President Jacob Zuma's visit in October 2016; U.K. Prime Minister Theresa May's visit in November 2016; and Israeli President Reuven

Rivlin's visit to New Delhi in November 2016. These visits have very large strategic and economic content for India to achieve concrete economic, diplomatic, and strategic goals.

Modi has received high priority from the world leaders at the UNGA, BRICS Summit in Ufa, ASEAN-India and East Asia Summit in Kuala Lumpur, G-20 Summit in Turkey, and Climate Summit in Paris. All these have helped energise India's foreign policy to raise its profile on the world stage. Modi not only managed to reset India's foreign policy but also transformed its discourse. In fact, India rarely made rapid turns in its foreign policy and never fluctuated with the change in Governments. But Modi subtly changed the widely perceived notion of India being a reluctant power in its exercise of realpolitik. Now, India has taken a dramatic shift away from the ideological fantasies of 'non-alignment' policy to pursuing a more practical self-interest driven approach in world affairs. This well-thought-out change aims to project India as a 'rising power' rather than a 'balancing power' in the matrix of global power politics.

Modi has used the best possible tools of state craft for pursuing multiple relationships simultaneously with confidence, energy and style remarkably different from previous leaders. His methodology includes changing India's global narrative, i.e., drawing attention to India's global narrative, i.e., drawing attention to India's sacrifices in WWI, its contribution to UN peacekeeping operations, and forcefully reiterating India's right for a permanent seat in the UN Security Council. To make diplomacy more robust, Modi Government created new metaphors—whether it is Act East policy or projecting India as a 'first responder' in humanitarian assistance and post-disaster operations in Yemen and Nepal.

Political and Economic Cooperation

Ever since Narendra Modi became the Prime Minister of India in May 2014, he has given special importance to international relations of India and has focused to improve political, economic, and strategic relations of India globally, especially with the nations which are important from the point of trade, economy, and defence. His 'neighbourhood first policy' has become pragmatic and even muscular in 2015, thus breaking the traditional notion of India being unable to resolve problems with smaller neighbours. He visited first the neighboring nations like Bhutan, Bangladesh, Nepal and Sri Lanka which are strategically very important for India's defence and security. This has also resulted in significant improvement in India's relationship and understanding with these countries. For example, the land boundary agreement with Bangladesh has been a historic milestone achievement for Modi. Ties with Dhaka have now entered a new phase, with collaboration on issues from economy to tackling terrorism. Improving relationship with Sri Lanka was very important from the point of view of increasing influence of China in our neighborhood. Similarly, the Bhutan and Bangladesh visits too have been very productive in terms of various treaties with these countries for cooperation in development of various energy and infrastructure projects in these countries, which may benefit mutually.[1]

Thus, the main objective of Modi's foreign policy is economic development, i.e., skillfully linking diplomacy and national development for leveraging international financial and technological support to speed up his 'Make in India' campaign. The imperatives of his domestic reforms agenda to promote business, trade tourists, national security, employment, etc. are craftily embedded into diplomacy. Playing on India's ethereal values-based soft power is Modi's another diplomatic craftsmanship. He understood that no country can match India's benign and non-threatening image, which he thought could be advantaged into hard strategic and economic gains. He has fine-turned India's soft power to suit the present times, for example by getting a global tag for International Yoga Day. He tried to revive India's own lost Buddhist heritage for geopolitical and economic interests. As he learnt to grapple with the challenges of international diplomacy, Modi understood that Buddhism occupies critical space in the Asian balance of culture, economics, and politics. Aside from the market factor of Buddhism, Modi has grasped the threat of China taking over the foremost role over Buddhism in Asia and, therefore, he has been trying hard to reconnect India with every Asian Buddhist institutions, including the Chinese ones built by Xuanzang and Faxian.

On the economic front, Modi has inked big deals—from nuclear deals to mammoth infrastructure investment accords—with key countries. On the diplomatic front, Modi has stabilised India's relations with major economies, and the core of his diplomacy included strengthening ties with the US that had drifted away from the track under the previous Government. The framework for the US-India defence relationship is being-renewed and envisaging collaboration in defence, intelligence, maritime security, cyber security, and space exploration among others. India and US have signed an agreement under Defence Technology and Trade Initiative (DTTI) which includes developing militarily useful technologies in 17 new areas, such as manufacturing fighter aircraft, unmanned aerial vehicles, and aircraft carriers.

India is also seeking Chinese investments in its major infrastructure projects, therefore, it cannot afford to have sides, neither in India-China relations nor in India-US relations. Modi's foreign policy is, therefore, neither pro-US nor anti-China, but to make best use of US-China competition in the economic, military, and geopolitical realms. His visits to France and Germany were aimed at getting support for improving India's digital infrastructure, healthcare and clean environment, upgrade information and services and plan for building Smart Cities in the country. He has succeeded in attracting European investors in India's manufacturing sector to translate his 'Make in India' initiative into success. His visit to the UK is certain to bring mutual economic, military and diplomatic gains for both sides.

Modi has also ensured that India is not left on the sidelines of the dynamics occurring in East Asia. He followed the Act East policy more robustly when he attended two important summits—the ASEAN-India and East Asia Summits. He also visited Malaysia as the "core" of India's Act East policy to discuss the threat of terrorism, and in Singapore, he focused on building private sector interest in the 'Make in India' initiative besides strengthening the defence and security cooperation. The relationship with other countries like Vietnam and the Philippines has improved as Modi has become more outspoken on maritime and territorial disputes, particularly in South China Sea. Modi has unveiled India's Africa policy by gathering 54 African countries to the third India-Africa Forum Summit. He used no declarative words or the third world solidarity rhetoric, instead he focused on the partnership of pragmatism and potential as well as to confront global challenges together. It helps to cultivate Africa, whose nations court India as a responsible global leader, offer India economic opportunities and finally their support is critical for India to secure a permanent seat in the Security Council. While Modi has largely pursued a US-centric approach, he has also not given up on the multi-polarity of maintaining closer coordination between India, China, and Russia. He participated in the BRICS meeting in Ufa and joined the Shanghai Cooperation Organisation along with Pakistan to change the balance of forces in the Eurasian region.

India and Japan have set a concrete action plan and signed major deals on military weapon and technology transfer to India, building high-speed trains, upgrading India's infrastructure and on the peaceful use of nuclear energy. The memorandum on civil nuclear energy cooperation, an agreement for commerce and clean energy symbolised a new level of strategic partnership between India and Japan. The agreements on transfer of defence equipment and technology and on protection of classified military information and the Japanese decision to join as a formal partner in Malabar naval exercises are high paints in the security relationship. To boost the 'Make in India' initiative, Japan will import cars manufactured by the Japanese in India. Japan has also created $11-12 billion fund to promote Make in India.

India and Russia have signed agreements on transferring technology in aerospace sectors, defence sector, i.e., manufacturing Kamov-226K helicopters, spare parts for Sukhoi jets to contribute to the Make in India initiative.

Foreign Direct Investment

Apart from being a critical driver of economic growth, foeign direct investment (FDI) is a major source of non-debt financial resource for the economic development of India. The Indian government's favourable policy regime and robust business environment have ensured that foreign capital keeps flowing into the country. The government has taken many initiatives in recent years such as relaxing FDI norms across sectors such as defence, PSU oil refineries, telecom, power exchanges, and stock exchanges, among others.

According to Department of Industrial Policy and Promotion (DIPP), the total FDI India received during April-September 2016 rose 30 percent year-on-year to US$ 21.6 billion, indicating that government's effort to improve ease of doing business and relaxation in FDI norms is yielding results. The data indicates that the services sector attracted the highest FDI equity inflow of US$ 5.29 billion, followed by telecommunications—US$ 2.79 billion, and trading—US$ 1.48 billion. The total FDI equity inflows for the month of September 2016 touched US$5.15 billion. During April-September 2016, India received the maximum FDI equity inflows from Mauritius (US$ 5.85 billion), followed by Singapore (US$ 4.68 billion), Japan (US$ 2.79 billion), and USA (US$ 1.44 billion). Impact investments in India is expected to grow at a compound annual growth rate (CAGR) of 20-24 percent to touch US$ 6-8 billion by 2025, from US$ 1 billion in 2015.

According to United Nations conference on Trade and Development (UNCTAD) World Investment Report 2016, India acquired 10th slot in the top 10 countries attracting highest FDI inflows globally in 2015. The report also mentioned that among the investment promotion agencies, India has moved up by one rank to become the sixth most preferred investment destination.

All these increases in FDI inflows and overall trade in goods are credited to Modi's foreign visits. As a result of these visits, the FDI inflows have witnessed a 40 percent increase in 2015 (up to December) over the corresponding period in 2014. Moreover, India's overall trade in goods with these countries has risen by 2.3 percent from 2013-14 to 2014-15.

The foreign visits undertaken by Modi have been instrumental in creating a positive momentum and boosting the bilateral relations between India and respective countries. The visits have also resulted in signing of several trade pacts, establishing framework for enhanced security, border defence, and space cooperation, promoting cooperation flagship campaigns like Digital India, Make in India, Clean India and Skill Development. These visits also facilitated meetings of CEO Forums and several B2B meetings to enhance business opportunities and investments.

The major countries visited by Prime Minister Narendra Modi, the agreements signed by him and the respective state head are discussed below:

1. Japan

Modi has cordial relations with Japan ever since his days of being Gujarat's Chief Minister. Needless to say, his visit to Japan in September 2014 was a thumping success. Japan has committed to invest huge amount to help India in building its smart cities.

Prime Minister Narendra Modi's five-day visit to Japan (from 30 August to 3 September 2014) was very successful with Japan pledging financial support for building infrastructure in India. Sticking to his "Make in India" slogan, Modi gave an open invitation to Japanese companies to consider India as a competitive low-cost manufacturing hub. Modi's visit was instrumental in strengthening the relationship between the two countries. Ten takeaways from his visit are mentioned below:[2]

(i) PM Modi emphasized that India can provide low-cost manufacturing hubs to Japan. Addressing Japan's Nikkei Exchange, Modi said that India offers the three essential 'Ds' for businessmen to thrive, namely Democracy, Demography and Demand. He said that his government has eased off a lot of regulations.

(ii) Japan committed to fund bullet train in India. Modi's dream project got a big push after Japan expressed readiness to provide financial, technical and operational support to introduce bullet trains in India. The first high-speed train is expected to run between Ahmedabad and Mumbai at an estimated cost of around ₹ 60,000-70,000 crore.

(iii) Taking a unique decision, PM Modi announced that a special management team would be set up directly under the Prime Minister's Office to facilitate investment proposals from Japan. The decision to include two nominees of Japan in the special management team is unprecedented and such a system of having nominees of the foreign government will happen for the first time. The two nominees selected by Japan would also be part of the decision-making team which evaluates business proposal.

(iv) The two countries signed a defence pact for regional stability. Japan decided to double FDI in India, upgrading and strengthening their defence cooperation as they asked officials to launch consultations to promote military equipment collaboration and accelerate discussions on modalities for the sale of Japanese US-2 amphibian aircraft.

(v) In spite of last-minute negotiations, the two sides could not narrow down differences over Tokyo's insistence for a tougher safeguard regime and "no nuclear test" clause in the bilateral agreement. Japan wanted India to guarantee not to conduct nuclear tests and more stringent inspections of its nuclear facilities to ensure that spent fuel is not diverted to make bombs.

(vi) The two countries also decided to have joint objectives in space and cyber security reforms. They felt the need to realize the mutual potential. The decisions they took were aimed to enhance their understanding of nuclear energy for civilian use.

(vii) There were also new developments in partnership, with removal of Japanese sanctions, and restrictions on some Indian companies, so that MoUs could be signed in defence cooperation.

(viii) There was a decision to open up collaboration in youth exchange, language training, cultural exchange, research and development.

(ix) There were five other agreements to collaborate on healthcare, clean and renewable energy, women's development, development of roads, and Kyoto-Varanasi channel.

(x) There was a commitment between India and Japan to develop strategic partnerships and work to realize it.

Mr. Shinzo Abe, Prime Minister of Japan, paid an official visit to India at the invitation of Prime Minister Narendra Modi, from 11 to 13 December 2015.

Expressing satisfaction at the direction of bilateral engagement, the two Prime Ministers resolved to transform the India-Japan Special Strategic and Global Partnership—a key relationship with the largest potential for growth—into a deep, broad-based, and action-oriented partnership, which reflects a broad convergence of their long-term political, economic, and strategic goals.

Joint Statement on India and Japan: Vision 2025

The main points of the Joint Statement on India and Japan Vision 2025: Special Strategic and Global Partnership Working Together for Peace and Prosperity of the Indo-Pacific Region and the World (12 December 2015), are given below:[3]

1. The people of India and Japan are guided by common cultural traditions including the heritage of Buddhism, and share commitment to the ideals of democracy, tolerance, pluralism, and open society. India and Japan two of the largest and oldest democracies in Asia having a high degree of congruence of political, economic, and strategies interests, view each other as partners that have responsibility for and are capable of responding to global and regional challenges.
2. The two Prime Ministers reiterated their unwavering commitment to realize a peaceful, open, equitable, stable and rule-based order in the Indo-Pacific region

and beyond. India and Japan uphold the principles of sovereignty and territorial integrity; peaceful settlement of disputes; democracy, human rights and the rule of law; open global trade regime; and freedom of navigation and over flight. They pledged to work for peace, security, and development of the Indo-Pacific region towards 2025, underpinned by these principles.

3. The two Prime Ministers underlined the need for closer coordination and effective communication, bilaterally and with partners, to address existing and emerging challenges relating to security, stability and sustainable development. They underlined their determination to expand cooperation with other partners, to enhance connectivity in the Indo-Pacific region. India and Japan will work to strengthen regional economic and security forums and coordinate their actions to tackle global challenges including the reform of the United Nations, climate change as well as terrorism.
4. The two Prime Ministers viewed that imperatives of a stronger bilateral strategic partnership require deep and broad-based cooperation and concrete actions in defence, security, economic, and cultural fields. The future-oriented partnership between India and Japan raises our collaboration to a new level in areas of infrastructure, manufacturing and high technology, including advanced transportation systems, civil nuclear energy, solar power generation, space, biotechnology, rare earths, and advanced materials.
5. The two Prime Ministers welcomed Japan's participation in the India-US Malabar Exercises on a regular basis, as it would help create stronger capabilities to deal with maritime challenges in the Indo-Pacific region including through enhanced disaster response and mitigation capacity. They reaffirmed their desire to further develop dialogue and exchanges between the two countries in the security and defence fields including through the full utilisation of '2+2 Dialogue', Defence Policy Dialogue, Military-to-Military Talks, and Coast Guard to Coast Fuard cooperation. The two

Prime Ministers appreciated the decision to begin Air Force-to-Air Force Staff Talks.

6. Recognising the importance of people to people exchanges and cultural ties, the two Prime Ministers resolved to boost opportunities for study, tourism, youth exchanges and educational collaboration to deepen broad-based and diversified engagement between the two peoples.
7. With the view to realise the objectives of India and Japan Vision 2025, the two leaders decided to develop a comprehensive and concrete medium and long-term action plan.
8. The two Prime Ministers welcomed the conclusion of the Agreement concerning the Transfer of the Defence Equipment and Technology and the Agreement concerning Security Measures for the Protection of Classified Military Information, which further strengthens the foundation of deep strategic ties. Taking note of the Agreements, they reaffirmed their commitment to continue discussions to deepen the bilateral defence relationship including through two-way collaboration and technology cooperation, co-development, and co-production. The two Prime Ministers expressed their intention to explore potential further projects on defence equipment and technology cooperation such as US-2 amphibian aircraft.
9. Highlighting the need to leverage their excellent bilateral relations to promote trilateral dialogues and cooperation with major partners in the region, the two Prime Ministers welcomed the holding of the Japan-India-U.S. Trilateral dialogue among the Foreign Ministers of the three countries in New York in September 2015. They noted with satisfaction the efforts of the three countries to seek closer cooperation in such areas as humanitarian assistance and disaster relief, regional connectivity as well as maritime security. The two Prime Ministers expressed satisfaction on the inaugural Japan-India-Australia Trilateral dialogue. They were of the view that these dialogue mechanisms

could contribute to regional efforts to evolve an open, inclusive, stable, and transparent economic, political and security architecture in the Indo-Pacific region.

10. Seeking the synergy between India's "Act East" policy and Japan's "Partnership for Quality Infrastructure", the two Prime Ministers decided to develop and strengthen reliable, sustainable and resilient infrastructures that augment connectivity within India and between India and other countries in the region. The two Prime Ministers pledged to advance industrial networks and regional value chains with open, fair, and transparent business environment in the region. They recognised the importance of enhancing their cooperation and coordination bilaterally and with other stakeholders to realise this strategic initiative.
11. The two Prime Ministers welcomed the agreement reached the two Governments on the Agreement between the Government of Japan and the Government of the Republic of India for Cooperation in the Peaceful Uses of Nuclear Energy, and confirmed that this Agreement will be signed after the technical details are finalised, including those related to the necessary internal procedures.

Investing in the Future

12. The two Prime Ministers noted that India's railways modernization and expansion plans would open up commercial opportunities for Japanese companies in high speed rail, station re-development and rolling stock manufacturing. They welcomed the signing of memoranda on technological cooperation, and R&D collaboration in the railways sector.
13. The two Prime Ministers welcomed the signing of the Memorandum of Cooperation on introduction of Japan's High Speed Railways (HSR) technologies (the Shinkansen system) to Mumbai-Ahmedabad route. Prime Minister Modi appreciated Japan's consideration of providing highly concessional yen loan for the HSR on Mumbai-Ahmedabad route. Both sides will explore

further strengthening of their partnership in high speed railways, which is a high technology area having potential to transform India's transportation sector.

14. The two Prime Ministers stressed the need for further actions for investing in the future. Prime Minister Abe commended Prime Minister Modi's strong initiatives such as "Make in India", "Digital India", "Skill India", "Clean India" and "Smart City". Prime Minister Abe also expressed his intention to support India's efforts by sharing its advanced skills and technologies and through active mobilization of Japanese public and private sector involvement, including Official Development Assistance (ODA).
15. The two Prime Ministers welcomed the steady progress to realize 3.5 trillion yen of public and private financing to India in five years under the "Japan-India Investment Promotion Partnership" announced during the last annual summit meeting.
16. The two Prime Ministers welcomed the progress in the flagship such as the western Dedicated Freight Corridor (DFC), and reaffirmed the determination to expedite the Delhi-Mumbai Industrial Corridor (DMIC) projects. The two PMs further concurred to take the Chennai Bengaluru Industrial Corridor (CBIC) project to the next stage of concrete implementation including by utilising ODA loan schemes and other facility measures. Indian side expressed a hope to attract US $5.5 billion of investment and other support.
17. Prime Minister Modi welcomed the "Japan-India Make-in-India Special Finance Facility" up to 1.5 trillion Yen by Nippon Export and Investment Insurance (NEXI) and Japan Bank for International Cooperation (JBIC), which aims to promote direct investment of Japanese companies and trade from Japan to India, to support their business activities with their counterparts in India, including development of necessary infrastructure, and to help materialize Make in India policy of the Government of India. Prime Minister Abe expressed his expectation on further enhancement of reform

measures including in the financial sector. The two Prime Ministers decided to deepen mutual cooperation regarding the Make in India policy.

18. The Indian side appreciated Japan's support to Skill India Initiative through training at Industrial Training Institutions (ITIs), skills development for managers, curriculum development and the Skills Evaluation System Promotion Program. Both countries will further advance their cooperation by providing Indian trainees with opportunities to acquire industrial skills in Japan, including under the Technical Intern Training Program.

19. The two PMs recognised the invaluable role played by Japan's ODA in broadening, deepening and strengthening bilateral relations. Appreciating that India is one of the largest recipients of Japan's ODA, PM Modi thanked the people of Japan for their contribution to the building of social and physical infrastructure in India that is key to the country's development and modernisation.

    (a) PM Modi welcomed the Japanese ODA loans of about 100 billion Yen for the metro projects both in Chennai and Ahmedabad.

    (b) PM Able expressed Japan's intention to provide ODA loans for the improvement of road network connectivity in northeastern states of India, the peripheral ring road surrounding Bengaluru, and the horticulture irrigation in Jharkhand.

    (c) PM Modi welcomed ongoing surveys regarding Mumbai Trans Harbour Link and the modernisation of ship recycling yards in Gujarat, and an expected survey for tuticorin outer Harbour.

The two PMs also confirmed the importance of securing appropriate implementation of ODA projects.

20. The two PMs reaffirmed the intention to develop "Japan Industrial Townships (JITs)", with investment incentive for companies that would not be lower than under the prevailing policy framework such as Special Economic Zone (SEZ), and National Investment

and Manufacturing Zone (NIMZ). Moreover, both sides will work toward evolving special packages for attracting Japanese investment in the Japanese Industrial Townships in India. The two PMs reaffirmed to further deepen bilateral economic and financial cooperation.

21. The two PMs positively appraised the work of "Japan Plus" and expressed strong hope that investment-related assistance, guidance, and support extended by "Japan Plus" will become even more effective and efficient through enhancing coordination with stakeholders. PM Abe appreciated creation of "Core Group" chaired by Cabinet Secretary to coordinate and closely monitor the process to ensure that investments from Japan as envisaged in India-Japan Investment Promotion partnership are facilitated.

22. The two PMs stressed the importance of expansion in the two-way investment between Japan and India.

    The Japanese side expressed the intention of establishing a new mechanism, "Japan-India IoT Investment Initiative", to promote investment in Internet of Things (IoT) related areas from India to Japan.

23. The two Prime Ministers recognised the importance of close collaboration in the electricity and energy sector through such measures as use of high-efficiency and environmentally friendly coal-fired power generation technology, and Clean Coal Technology (CCT) including Integrated Gastification Fuel Cell (IGFC) once developed, and renewable energy and promotion of energy efficiency. PM Abe lauded India's effort to enhance contribution of renewables to its overall energy mix.

24. India and Japan, as two countries seeking to transform into knowledge-based societies, expressed satisfaction to the continuous strengthening of their institutionalised Science and Technology cooperation. They shared their intention to raise the level of their ambition through the establishment of joint research laboratories; enhanced exchanges between young scientists and those under

"Japan-Asia Youth Exchange Program in Science"; the establishment of joint research centres in India in the field of ICT; stem cell research collaboration; and the joint fellowship Programme for young researchers.

25. Acknowledging the importance of cooperation in the education sector, the two PMs welcomed the institutionalised exchange of doctoral and post-doctoral research fellows, and encouraged movement of professors and faculty between India and Japan. They invited their universities and academic institutions to further expand cooperation.
26. The two loaders welcomed the priorities for action in the Sendai framework for Disaster Risk Reduction 2015-2030, and noted the importance of measures to mitigate the risk of disaster arising from earthquake, cyclone and tsunami, including flood control and early warning systems.

On 12 December 2015, India and Japan signed 16 agreements in the fields of high-speed trains, defence equipment and technology, security, infrastructure, education and economy, including civil nuclear energy. The agreements were signed after the delegation-level talks between Prime Minister Narendra Modi and his Japanese counterpart Shinzo Abe. These agreements are listed below:[4]

(i) Memorandum concerning the agreement on cooperation in the peaceful uses of nuclear energy. Both sides confirmed they have reached agreement on such cooperation.

(ii) Pact on high-speed trains—confirming cooperation in developing Mumbai-Ahmedabad high-speed rail corridor using Japanese high-speed rail technologies and financial and technical assistance.

(iii) Agreement concerning transfer of defence equipment and technology—providing a framework to enhance defence and security cooperation by making available to each other defence equipment and technology necessary to implement joint research, development and/or production projects.

(iv) Agreement concerning security measures for the protection of classified military information—ensuring reciprocal protection of classified military information transmitted to each other, provided that the terms of protection are consistent with the national laws and regulations of the receiving party.

(v) Agreement on amending protocol of double taxation avoidance—amending the convention between India and Japan for the avoidance of double taxation and the prevention of fiscal evasion with respect to taxes on income, signed in the year 1989.

(vi) Memorandum of Cooperation (MoC) between India's Ministry of Railways and Japan's MLIT (Ministry of Land, Infrastructure, Transport and Tourism)—establishing areas for comprehensive technological cooperation, including sharing of information and best practices; exchanges of officials and technicians; facilitating the participation of other institutions, organizations and ministries; conducting joint research and studies.

(vii) Pact on technological cooperation between India's Research Designs and Standards Organization (RDSO) and Japan's Railway Technical Research Institute (JRTRI)—proposing cooperation in the areas of safety in train operations; advanced techniques of maintenance; and use of environment-friendly technologies.

(viii) Letter of Intent on the strategic international cooperation programme between India's Department of Science and Technology (DST) and the Japan Science and Technology Agency (JSTA)—promoting and supporting collaborative activities such as joint research projects, joint research laboratories and hub, joint seminars, symposia and other meetings between the research institutes and researchers supported by JSTA and DST.

(ix) Letter of Intent towards establishing a young researcher's exchange programme between the DST of India and the Japan Society for the Promotion of Science—intending to establish reciprocal fellowship programme for capacity building and Human Resource Development in frontier areas of Science & Technology.

(x) MoC between India's Central Drugs Standard Control Organization and Japan's Ministry of Health, Labour and Welfare—establishing the medical products regulation dialogue and cooperation framework to facilitate a constructive dialogue in areas pertinent to raw materials for pharmaceutical use, biological products and medical devices.

(xi) MoC in the field of education between India's Ministry of Human Resource Development and Japan's Ministry of Education, Culture, Sports, Science and Technology—encouraging development of contacts and cooperation between the educational institutions of the two countries and possible support for exchange of aspiring students between India and Japan.

(xii) Statement of Intent between NITI Aayog and Institute of Energy Economics, Japan (IEEJ)—laying down the broad mission of promoting cooperation between NITI Aayog and IEEJ for the purpose of analyzing issues related to energy sector in order to examine and understand various energy sector-related issues in the world.

(xiii) Pact on cooperation between State Government of Andhra Pradesh and Toyama Prefecture—strengthening existing bonds between Andhra Pradesh and Toyama by facilitating mutual collaboration between their governments, institutions, and companies.

(xiv) MoU between State Government of Kerala and Lake Nakaumi, Lake Shinji and Mt. Daisen area Mayors Association—under which Kerala and the Sanin region, Japan, agree to develop trade, investment and economic relations between the business circles with particular focus on small and medium enterprises.

(xv) MoU between Indian Institute of Management-Ahmedabad (IIM-A) and Japan's National Graduate Institute for Policy Studies (GRIPS)—promoting collaboration between the two institutions to enrich the intellectual environment of both.

(xvi) MoC between India's Ministry of Environment, Forest and Climate Change and Japan's Ministry of Agriculture, Forestry and Fisheries—endeavoring to enhance cooperation in Human Resource Development and institutional exchange between training institutes, sustainable forest management, enhancement of forest conservation and forest disaster prevention.

Modi's visit to Japan has been the most fruitful one as heads of both the nations agreed to many modernization and expansion plans, open up commercial opportunities for Japanese companies in high speed rail, station re-development, and rolling stock manufacturing.

With Japan agreeing to give support to Skill India Initiative through training at Industrial Training Institutions (ITIs), skills development for managers, curriculum development and the Skills Evaluation System Promotion Program, the initiatives brought by Modi are expected to get a boost.

2. France

Prime Minister Narendra Modi visited France on 10-11 April 2015 at the invitation of the President of the French Republic, Mr. François Hollande. The two leaders held wide-ranging and fruitful discussions on bilateral, regional and global issues. They reaffirmed their commitment to the strategic partnership and agreed to further deepen and strengthen bilateral ties based on shared principles and values relating to democracy, freedom, rule of law and respect for human rights. Some of the important agreements and commitments made by the two leaders are mentioned below:[5]

1. As global partners, India and France reiterated the need for urgent reform of the United Nations, including its Security Council, through an expansion in both categories of membership, to make it more representative of the contemporary world. France reaffirms its support for India's candidature for a permanent membership of the UN Security Council without further delay.

2. France and India share common concerns and objectives in the field of non-proliferation of weapons of mass destruction. In a further effort to strengthen global non-proliferation and export control regimes, France and India committed to continue to work jointly towards India's accession to the multilateral export control regimes, namely the Nuclear Suppliers Group (NSG), the Missile Technology Control Regime (MTCR), the Australia Group, and the Wassenaar Arrangement.
3. Tackling the issue of climate change is of vital importance for the sake of today's world and future generations. Prime Minister Narendra Modi extended his full support to France for a successful outcome of CoP 21 to UNFCCC, Paris, 2015. The leaders expressed confidence that the Paris Conference will finalize a historic agreement for the post-2020 period. This will further strengthen the resolve and the efforts of the international community to address the profound challenge of climate change, to facilitate access to a low carbon pathway and resilient sustainable development for all whilst keeping the global temperature rise below 2°C. The two leaders underlined the importance of enhancing Indo-French cooperation on joint research and development and technology innovation as well as diffusion of clean energy and efficiency solutions that will help in transitioning towards a climate resilient and low carbon economy.
4. Smart Cities development is a key area to foster sustainable development solutions. France welcomed India's offer to be a partner of the Smart Cities development scheme and is ready to implement its best technological solutions and share its experience in the field of integrated sustainable cities, in particular in urban planning, urban grids, water and sanitation, sustainable mobility and digital technologies.
5. The two PMs reiterated their strong support for ongoing efforts aimed at defeating terrorism. They called for dismantling of the terrorist infrastructure,

denying safe havens to terrorists, bringing perpetrators and conspirators of terrorist attacks to justice and to strengthen international frameworks to forge closer cooperation in this areas, including through supporting initiatives in the framework of the UN, such as the draft Comprehensive Convention of International Terrorism.

6. President Hollande confirmed the target of AFD (Agence Française de Développement) credit line of one billion Euros over the next three years for sustainable infrastructure and urban development in India and conveyed the commitment of France to partner with India in the implementation of the following projects launched by India for development of renewable sources of energy.
   (a) Extension of credit facility by AFD for India's Energy Efficiency Services Limited (EESL) promoting use of LED lighting in select Indian municipalities.
   (b) Arrangement on renewable energy cooperation between the Indian Ministry of New and Renewable Energy and the French Ministry of Ecology, Sustainable Development and Energy.
7. The two countries agreed to commence bilateral dialogue to discuss ways and means of enhancing their cooperation in the maritime domain, in particular in the Indian Ocean Region (IOR). India welcomed closer engagement of France in the affairs of the Indian Ocean Rim Association and will continue to work closely with France in realization of the objectives enshrined in the Charter of the Association.
8. The leaders stressed the importance of joint military exercises between their Armies, Navies, and Air Forces and welcomed the participation of the French Carrier Battle Group in the naval exercise in the Indian Ocean. The two leaders underlined the long history of cooperation between France and India in the defence sector and acknowledged the strong commitment of

French companies to manufacturing in India under the Make in India programme.

9. President Hollande welcomed Prime Minister's Make in India initiative, aimed at transforming India into a global manufacturing hub. The two leaders noted with satisfaction a number of new and ongoing projects of French companies in keeping with the Make in India policy.
10. In the field of transport, the leaders looked forward to cooperating in areas such as modernization of the Railways and in high speed and semi-high speed rail projects, in urban transportation and in roads and welcomed the development of the cooperation between Indian and French railways through the agreement between Indian Railways and the French National Railways (SNCF) to co-finance an execution study by SNCF for a semi-high speed project on upgradation of the Delhi-Chandigarh line to 200 kmph and for redevelopment of Ambala and Ludhiana railways stations.
11. France is already supporting India's efforts to secure its energy supply and develop its sources of renewable energy, including solar power. India welcomed the target set by French companies aimed at developing 8 to 10 GW of solar energy in India by 2020-22. France is also willing to support other renewable sources of energy in India, such as wind, biomass and hydropower.
12. The two leaders noted with satisfaction the forward movement on the following:
    (a) Cooperation in Human Resource Development and skill building by establishing a knowledge partnership to exchange expertise and best practices, aimed at developing nationwide skill standards and institutional structures to support skill development.
    (b) Signing of a Memorandum of Understanding (MoU) for knowledge partnership and cooperation in the

area of qualification registers between National Skill Development Agency (NSDA), under the Ministry of Skill Development and Entrepreneurship of India and Commission National de la Certification Professionnelle (CNCP) of France.

The French President Francois Hollande visited India on 24-26 January 2016. During his visit, the two countries sealed 19 deals, including 13 Memorandums of Understanding (MoUs), which are enumerated below:[6]

1. Indian Space Research Organisation (ISRO) and Centre National D'études Spatiales (CNES) implementation arrangement on hosting Argos-4 payload on board India's Oceansat-3 satellite.
2. ISRO and CNES implementation arrangement on a future joint Thermal Infrared earth observation mission.
3. Letter of Intent on CNES, French participation in ISRO's next Mars Mission.
4. Shareholding agreement on the joint venture between Alstom and Indian Railways for the production of 800 electric locomotives in Madhepura, Bihar.
5. Agreement between Indian Railways and SNCF, French Railways for the joint feasibility study for the renovation of Ludhiana and Ambala railways stations.
6. MoU between Food Safety and Standards Authority of India (FSSAI) and Agencenationale de Sécurité Sanitaire de L'alimentation (ANSES) in food safety.
7. A partnership agreement between Ministry of Personnel and Public Grievances and French on cooperation in public administration.
8. Declaration of intent for conducting next round of Namaste France (Indian festival) in 2016 and Bonjour India (French festival) 2017.
9. Cultural exchange programme for the period 2016-18.
10. Arrangement for the establishment of an Indo-French Ministerial-level Joint Committee on Science and Technology.

11. MoU for Industry Sponsored Ph.D. fellowship between IIT Mumbai and Thales Systemes Aeroportes.
12. A cooperation agreement between IISER, Pune and ENS de Lyon (France) for joint research, teaching, exchange of personnel, etc.
13. Agreement of cooperation between CNRS, TB, UBO, UBS, ENSTA Bretagne, ENIB (French universities) and IIT Mumbai in the field of higher education and research.
14. MoU for the purchase of 36 Rafale Fighter jets.
15. A solar alliance between France and India with the foundation of International Solar Alliance (ISA).
16. Joint cooperation between India and France to prevent off-shore tax evasion and steps to strengthen the exchange of information between both countries.
17. Agreement between Mahindra Aerospace and Airbus Group for the manufacture helicopters.
18. Three MoUs under the "Smart City" scheme between French Development Agency and the State Governments of the cities of Chandigarh, Nagpur, and Puducherry.
19. A joint venture between Indian SITAC group and EDF Energie Nouvelles signed to acquire 50% stake in the renewable energy business in Gujarat. The JV will invest 155 million Euros in 2016 and generate 142 MW power. Its objective will also be to produce one gigawatts of wind energy over five years.

France announced US$ 10 billion (₹ 67,540 crore) investment in India over the next five years, which will largely cater to the industrial sector in the country.

With Modi's visit to France, the relations between the two countries were further strengthened. There were agreements on counter-terrorism, intelligence sharing and cyber-security issues in addition to the original nuclear, space and defence related matters. The Joint Statement also covered a wide range of other areas of cooperation such as climate change and sustainable development, economic cooperation, urban development, Human Resource Development, heritage preservation, and cultural cooperation.

3. United States of America

Prime Minister Narendra Modi signed a number of MoUs/ agreements with President Obama as part of the implementation of the decisions taken during his visit to USA from 26 to 30 September 2014. The Vision statement for the US-India strategic partnership was "Chalein Saath Saath: Forward Together We Go". The major MoUs/agreements are listed below:[7]

1. Arrangement between the Multi-Agency Centre/ Intelligence Bureau of the Government of India and the Terrorist Screening Center of the Government of the United States of America for the exchange of Terrorist Screening Information.
2. Memorandum of Understanding between the Government of India and the Government of the United States of America to enhance cooperation on Energy Security, Clean Energy and Climate Change.
3. Memorandum of Understanding between Government of India and Government of the United States of America to enhance co-operation on Wildlife Conservation and Combating Wildlife Trafficking.
4. Memorandum of Understanding between Consular, Passport, and Visa Division of the Ministry of External Affairs, Government of India and US Customs and Border Protection, Department of Homeland Security of the United States for the Development of an International Expedited Traveler Initiative (the Global Entry Programme).
5. Technical Arrangement between the Indian Navy and the United States Navy concerning Unclassified Maritime Information Sharing.
6. Memorandum of Understanding between the Ministry of Petroleum and Natural Gas, Government of India and the Department of Energy of the United States of America for Cooperation in Gas Hydrates.
7. Information Exchange Annex (IEA) between the Ministry of Defence, Government of India and the Department of Defence of the United States of America

to the Master Information Exchange Agreement concerning Aircraft Carrier Technologies.

8. Logistics Exchange Memorandum of Agreement between the Ministry of Defence, Government of India and the Department of Defence of the United States of America.
9. Implementing Agreement between the National Aeronautics and Space Administration (NASA) and Indian Space Research Organisation (ISRO) to conduct the joint NASA-ISRO Synthetic Aperture Radar (NISAR) mission.

The President of the United States of America, Barack Obama visited India during 25-27 January 2015. Noting that the multifaceted partnership between the US and India is rooted in shared values of democracy and strong economic and people-to-people ties, President Obama and PM Modi elevated the bilateral relationship through their endorsement of a new India-US Delhi Declaration of Friendship, which builds on their 30 September 2014. Vision Statement by articulating tangible principles to guide ongoing efforts to advance mutual prosperity, a clean and healthy environment, greater economic cooperation, regional peace, security and stability for the larger benefit of humankind.

India-US Delhi Declaration of Friendship is based on "Sanjha Prayaas, Sabka Vikaas; Shared Effort, Progress for All". Recognizing the important role that both countries play in promoting peace, prosperity, stability and security in the Asia-Pacific and Indian Ocean Region, and nothing that India's 'Act East Policy' and the United States' rebalance to Asia provide opportunities for India, the United States, and other Asia-Pacific countries to work closely to strengthen regional ties, the Leaders announced a Joint Strategic Vision to guide their engagement in the region.

1. The PM Modi and the President Obama acknowledged and expressed satisfaction at the qualitative reinvigoration of strategic ties and the intensity of substantive interactions since the PM's visit to US in September 2014. The appreciated the focused action

and accomplishments by both sides on the decisions taken during September 2014 visit.

2. Reaffirming that India's rise is also in the interest of the United States, regional and global stability, and global economic growth, President Obama reiterated the United States' readiness to partner with India in this transformation. The two leaders pledged to translate their commitment of "Chalein Saath Saath" (Forward Together We Go) of September into action through "Sanjha Prayaas; Sabka Vikaas" (Shared Effort; Progress For All).
3. Both the leaders agreed to continue to strengthen their broad-based partnership for development through stronger trade, technology, manufacturing, and investment linkages between the two countries and triangular cooperation with partner countries, and that continued efforts to maintain labour standards as per domestic law and agreed international norms will make these linkages more durable. They also committed to continuing to cooperate on the finalization of the Post-Bali Work Programme in the spirit of the Doha mandate.
4. Both the leaders committed to explore areas of collaboration in skill development ranging from establishing quality assurance systems for skilling certification standards, setting up of skill development centres, nurturing and promoting social entrepreneurship and strengthening the innovation and entrepreneurship ecosystem.
5. Both the leaders agreed to collaborate in the implementation of India's ambitious Digital India programme and expand commercial cooperation, including by encouraging investment engagement in the Information and Communication Technology (ICT) sector.
6. Acknowledging the potential for technological cooperation in the rail sector in augmenting and optimizing India's rail infrastructure, the leaders agreed to facilitate US Trade and Development Agency

and Indian Railways technical cooperation that will assist Indian Railways' efforts to modify its leasing and public-private partnership frameworks to attract private sector funding.

7. Noting the importance of ongoing cooperation in higher education, the President and Prime Minister welcomed ongoing efforts to extend a knowledge partnership for supporting the Indian Institute of Technology at Gandhinagar through USAID. They also pledged to collaborate through India's Global Initiative of Academic Networks (GIAN), to facilitate short-term teaching and research programmes by up to 1000 visiting US academics in Indian universities.
8. Both the leaders agreed to expand the India-US Health Initiative into a Healthcare Dialogue with relevant stakeholders to further strengthen bilateral collaboration in health sectors including through capacity building initiatives and by exploring new areas, including affordable healthcare, cost saving mechanisms, distribution barriers, patent quality, health services information technology, and complementary and traditional medicine.
9. Both the leaders welcomed the efforts made by both sides to expand bilateral defence cooperation in areas of mutual interest and reaffirmed their commitment to continue to work towards deepening the bilateral defence relationship. They acknowledged bilateral military ties as the foundation of the defence relationship and encouraged their respective militaries to pursue additional opportunities for engagement through exercises, military personnel exchanges, and defence dialogues.
10. Both the leaders also acknowledged the need for the two-way defence engagement to include technology cooperation and collaboration, co-production and co-development. To this end, the President and the Prime Minister emphasized the ongoing importance of the Defence Technology and Trade Initiative (DTTI) in developing new areas of technology cooperation in the

defence sector including through co-development and co-production and the Prime Minister welcomed the US Defence Department's establishment of a dedicated rapid reaction team focused exclusively on advancing DTTI. They expressed confidence that continued DTTI collaboration will yield additional joint projects in the near future.

11. Both the leaders reiterated their strong condemnation of terrorism in all its forms and manifestations with 'zero tolerance' and reaffirmed their deep concern over the continued threat posed by transnational terrorism and called for eliminating terrorist safe havens and infrastructure, disrupting terrorist networks and their financing, and stopping cross-border movement of terrorists.
12. Both the leaders exphasized the critical importance of expanding clean energy research, development, manufacturing and deployment, which increases energy access and reduces greenhouse gas emissions. They announced actions to advance India's transition to low carbon economy. India intends to increase the share of use of renewable in electricity generation consistent with its intended goal to increase India's solar target to 100 gigawatts by 2022. The US intends to support India's goal by enhancing cooperation on clean energy and climate change.
13. Both the leaders agreed to expand their efforts to assist other developing countries and address global development challenges for the benefit of the wider region and the world and they lauded ongoing triangular assistance, which may involve US-India collaboration to address development challenges in third countries in areas including health, energy, food security, disaster management, and women's empowerment. They noted that this collaboration, which is active with Afghanistan, East and West Africa, may be expanded to additional third countries.
14. Understanding the importance of implementing infrastructure projects to enhance connectivity and

enable free-flow of commerce and energy in the region, the two leaders agreed to develop additional areas in which both sides could work together, including on India's initiatives to enhance its connectivity with the South and South East Asian region. They also stressed the importance of the economic and transport connectivity between Central and South Asia and the need to promote a secure, stable, and prosperous Afghanistan as part of a secure, stable, and prosperous region.

15. Both the leaders pledged to strengthen their efforts to forge a partnership to lead global efforts for non-proliferation of WMDs, to reduce the salience of nuclear weapons in international affairs, and to promote universal, verifiable and non-discriminatory global nuclear disarmament. They supported negotiations on a fissile material cut-off Treaty on the basis of the Shannon Mandate in the Conference on Disarmament.
16. To strengthen global non-proliferation and export control regimes, both the leaders committed to continue to work towards India's phased entry into the Nuclear Suppliers Group (NSG), the Missile Technology Control Regime (MTCR), the Wassenaar Arrangement, and the Australia Group. The President Obama reaffirmed India's early application and eventual membership in all four regimes.
17. Both the leaders acknowledged the Internet is a central element of the information society and a powerful enabler of global economic and social progress. They also noted that the growth of the Internet in the coming decade would be from developing countries, of which India would be a significant contributor, especially in the context of its "Digital India" programme.

Prime Minister Modi again paid a visit to the United States of America from 6-8 June 2016, during which the following six agreements were signed:[8]

1. Arrangement between the Multi-Agency Centre/ Intelligence Bureau of the Government of India and the Terrorist Screening Center of the Government of the

US for the exchange of terrorist screening information. The arrangement would enhance the counter terrorism cooperation between India and the US.

2. Memorandum of Understanding (MoU) between the Government of India and the Government of the US to enhance cooperation on energy security, clean energy and climate change. This will promote sustainable growth.
3. Memorandum of Understanding (MoU) between Government of India and Government of the United States of America to enhance co-operation on wildlife conservation and combating wildlife trafficking.
4. Memorandum of Understanding (MoU) between Consular, Passport and Visa Division of the Ministry of External Affairs, Government of India and US Customs and Border Protection, Department of Homeland Security of the United States for the development of an International Expedited Traveler Initiative (The Global Entry Programme). After joint scrutiny and clearance by both countries, the approved Indian travelers will be extended the facility of expedited entry into the US through automatic kiosks at select airports.
5. Technical Arrangement between the Indian Navy and the United States Navy concerning unclassified maritime information sharing. This will provide a framework for mutually beneficial maritime information.
6. Memorandum of Understanding (MoU) between the Ministry of Petroleum and Natural Gas, Government of India and the Department of Energy of the United States of America for cooperation in gas hydrates. This will enhance understanding of the geologic occurrence, distribution, and production of natural gas hydrates along the continental margin of India and in the US.

President Obama welcomed the start of preparatory work on six nuclear reactors in India, a key step in closing the first deal stemming from a US-India civil nuclear accord struck over a decade ago. The two leaders said in a joint statement that India and the US Export-Import Bank intends to work together toward a competitive financing package for the project and will work to finalize contractual agreements by June 2017. When completed, the project would be among the largest of its kind, fulfilling the promise of the US-India civil nuclear agreement and demonstrating a shared commitment to meet India's growing energy needs while reducing reliance on fossil fuels.[9]

Prime Minister Narendra Modi and President Obama reviewed the deepening strategic partnership between the United States and India rooted in shared values of freedom, democracy, universal human rights, tolerance and pluralism, equal opportunities for all citizens, and the rule of law. They pledged to pursue new opportunities to bolster economic growth and sustainable development, promote peace and security at home and around the world, strengthen inclusive, democratic governance and respect for universal human rights, and provide global leadership on issues of shared interest.[10]

4. Canada

Prime Minister Modi visited Canada on 14-16 April 2015. It was the first visit by an Indian Prime Minister in 42 years to Ottawa, Toronto and Vancouver. Prime Minister Modi and Canadian Prime Minister Stephen Harper held detailed discussions to assess the full spectrum of bilateral relations and exchanged perspectives on a range of regional and international issues of mutual interest. They noted the historic significance of Modi's visit to Canada in advancing bilateral ties to a new level marked with "New Vigour New Steps". The two PMs agreed to elevate their bilateral relations to a strategic partnership. Modi's visit generated business worth more than 1.6 billion Canadian dollars, according to official figures released by the Harper Government.

According to Press Trust of India, sixteen commercial agreements and announcements were made by Canadian and Indian companies and organizations during Modi's visit. The areas covered included aerospace and defence education, energy, mining, infrastructure, sustainable technologies, information and communications technology.

According to the statement, "One commercial agreement involving Saskatchewan-based Cameco will see the company supply India with over seven million pounds of uranium over the next five years. This deal was made possible due in part to the Canada-India Nuclear Cooperation Agreement negotiated by our government."

Some of the main agreements made by the two leaders are mentioned below:

1. MoU between ISRO and the Canadian Space Agency concerning cooperation in the field of space.
2. MoU between the Ministry of Railways and Department of Transport of Canada on technical cooperation in Rail transportation.
3. MoU between Ministry of Civil Aviation and Department of Transport of Canada on deepening cooperation in Civil Aviation.
4. Letter of intent between Department of Biotechnology, Ministry of Science and Technology and Grand Challenges Canada for the implementation of collaboration in disease elimination and Saving Brain Initiative.
5. An agreement between the Indian Department of Atomic Energy and Cameco of Canada for long-term supply of uranium to India.
6. The two leaders agreed to take concrete measures to expand bilateral cooperation in key areas including the economy, trade and investment, civil nuclear cooperation, energy, education and skill development, agriculture, defence and security, science, technology, innovation and space, culture, people-to-people ties, and regional and global issues.
7. The two leaders reaffirmed the need to elevate two-way trade and investment linkages to their full potential. They agreed to pursue specific measures to diversify and deepen bilateral trade and investment cooperation to increase the two way flow of goods and services.
8. The two leaders welcomed the agreement on a road map to expeditiously conclude a progressive, balanced,

and mutually beneficial Comprehensive Economic Partnership Agreement as a basis for significantly expanding two-way trade and investment and directed the negotiators to prioritise its finalisation.

9. The two leaders expressed support for bilateral partnerships for urban transformation and smart city development which would leverage Canadian expertise in a number of relevant fields including, public-private partnerships, intelligent transportation systems, civil engineering and urban planning, water and wastewater management, pre-cast wood construction, energy technology and efficiency and affordable housing.
10. The two leaders agreed to establish a Finance Ministers Dialogue for the purpose of deepening the India-Canada economic and financial relationship.
11. The two leaders agreed to encourage a collaborative programme to leverage their industries' respective strengths in the field of Pressurised Heavy Water Reactor technology for mutual benefit, as well as for the benefit of global nuclear energy needs. They also encouraged closer cooperation in civil nuclear energy between their companies and welcomed the setting up of the India Nuclear Insurance Pool with potential participation of foreign companies as a positive step towards facilitating such cooperation.
12. The two leaders noted the socio-economic opportunities inherent in India's ambitious goals of skills development. In this regard, they welcomed the 13 MoUs between the National Skill Development Council of India and 13 Canadian colleges, institutes, and Sector Skills Councils in the fields of agriculture, apparel and textiles, automotive, aviation, construction, green economy, healthcare, hydrocarbons, IT, telecom and electronics, sports sector, and water. They agreed to renew the Canada-India MoU on Higher Education on a rolling basis.
13. The two leaders noted interest from both countries to hold discussions to negotiate a bilateral organic equivalency arrangement. They welcomed the setting-

up of the Plant Health Technical Working Group, as a subgroup of the MoU on agriculture cooperation to promote trade in plants, plant products and other regulated articles by facilitating science-based discussions related to sanitary and phyto-sanitary issues.

14. The two leaders agreed to intensify bilateral engagement and exchange perspectives on emerging threats to national security, including in the cyber domain. In this context, they welcomed the signing of the MoU between the Indian Ministry of Communications and Information Technology and the Department of Public Safety and Emergency Preparedness of Canada an cooperation in the Area of Cyber Security. Recognising the importance of a free, open, and secure internet they welcomed the commitment to a broader framework for future dialogue on cyber issues.
15. The two leaders recognised defence cooperation as an important element of the overall bilateral security cooperation. To this end, they agreed to explore cooperative possibilities in diverse fields including cold climate warfare, peacekeeping, and participation in respective Defence Staff College training. They also agreed to explore further cooperation in enhancing naval linkages, and staff exchanges. They also welcomed the signing of the Statement of Intent between Defence Research and Development Organisation of India and Defence Research and Development Canada, aimed at exploring potential cooperative initiatives in defence and security science and technology.

Canada has expressed interest in various initiatives launched by the Indian Government, including the "Smart Cities" initiative, affordable housing for all by 2022 and, most importantly, the "Make in India" initiative. These provide the two nations with opportunities for collaborative ventures that could build the promising economic relations. Canada has prioritized India in its Global Market Action Plan. Through the plan, the Government of Canada concentrates its efforts on the markets that hold the greatest promise for Canadian business.

It is also an expansion of the concept of "economic diplomacy" of the Government of Canada. India has been identified for the key opportunities that it provides in such sectors as aerospace, agriculture, sustainable technology and railways, among many others.

The "Make in India" initiative, which aims to develop India as a manufacturing hub, provides Canada with an opportune moment to partner with India. With large firms setting up manufacturing units in India, it would provide India's youth population, a large segment of which is shifting from rural to urban areas, with employment, while for the industry, it would provide cheap labour and a stable economic environment to work in. India's large youth population is not just seeking job opportunities, but is also aspiring for better education to bring about higher standards of living.

Modi's visit to Canada was important from the energy point of view for India. It is being viewed as the start of a new 'energy' relationship between the two nations. Canada which is the world's second largest producer of uranium agreed to a long-term supply of uranium to India to meet its energy needs.

5. China

Narendra Modi went on a three-day visit to China on 14-16 May 2015. His visit generated a tremendous amount of interest in both countries. India and China signed 24 agreements/MoUs worth over 10 billion dollars during this visit. Prime Minister Narendra Modi held talks with Chinese Premier Li Keqiang. Business was the main focus of PM Modi's three-day visit to China. The agreements/MoUs are listed below:[11]

1. Protocol between India and China on the establishment of consulates-general at Chengdu and Chennai and the extension of the consular district of the consulate general of India in Guangzhou to include Jiangxi province. It would facilitate enhanced trade and economic engagement, people-to-people exchanges, tourism and would help in providing quicker consular assistance to the nationals of the two countries.

2. MoU between the Ministry of Skill Development and Entrepreneurship of India and the Ministry of Human Resources and Social Security of China on cooperation in the field of vocational education and skill development. Under this MoU, India and China will work towards capacity development and delivery of vocational education in India, including the setting up of vocational training institutes in India.
3. Action plan on cooperation in setting up of the Mahatma Gandhi National Institute for Skill Development and Entrepreneurship in Ahmedabad/ Gandhinagar in Gujarat. India will provide for the land and construct the Institute, and China will cooperate as the key knowledge partner for the Institute and cooperate in the development of curriculum in various trades/industry sectors.
4. MoU between India and China on consultative mechanism for cooperation in trade negotiations. It aims to strengthen and develop cooperation between the two countries in the field of multilateral trade negotiations at the WTO.
5. MoU on cooperation between the Ministry of External Affairs of India and International Department of the Central Committee of the Communist Party of China.
6. Action plan between the National Railway Administration of China and the Ministry of Railways of India on enhancing cooperation in the railway sector (2015-16).
7. MoU on education exchange programme. It will encourage the governmental departments and the educational institutions of the two countries to enhance the contacts and cooperation in the field of education. It will also provides for scholarships to students from the two countries in each others' educational institutions.
8. MoU between the Ministry of Mines of India and the Ministry of Land and Resources of China on the cooperation in the fields of mining and minerals sector.

9. Space Cooperation Outline (2015-20). It provides specific programmes that the two sides plan to cooperate on during 2015-2020. The themes selected for cooperation include cooperation on remote-sensing missions, space-based meteorology, lunar and deep-space exploration, piggy-back launching, satellite navigation, components and education and training.
10. Protocol on health and safety regulations on importing Indian rapeseed meal between the Export Inspection Council, Ministry of Commerce and Industry of India and the General Administration of Quality Supervision, Inspection and Quarantine. It will pave the way for export of rapeseed meal from India to China.
11. MoU between Doordarshan and China Central Television on cooperation in the field of broadcasting.
12. Agreement between the Ministry of Tourism of India and the National Tourism Administration of China on cooperation in the field of tourism.
13. MoU on establishing India-China think-tanks forum. It will bring together Indian and chinese scholars to deliberate on contemporary issues of regional and international significance. Thus, it will serve to enhance exchanges in the fields of area studies, security, economics, strategic thought and demographics.
14. MoU between India's Niti Aayog and the Development Research Centre, State Council of China. It seeks to create cooperative relations between the two institutions, with the broad objective of furthering cooperation and understanding on strategic macroeconomic and policy issues. It will establish a basis for exchange of research information, visits, joint workshops, and joint research.
15. MoU between India's Ministry of Earth Sciences and the China Earthquake Administration concerning cooperation in the field of earthquake sciences and earthquake engineering. The broad objective of the cooperation is to enable the exchange of information between the two countries, personnel and technical

knowledge, and to support the improvement and development of programmes in Earthquake Sciences and Services.

16. MoU between India's Ministry of Earth Sciences and the State Oceanic Administration of China on cooperation in the field of ocean science, ocean technology, climate change, polar science and cryosphere. It will enable exchange of scientific resources, personnel and technical knowledge, and cooperative activities in scientific areas of mutual interest.
17. MoU on scientific cooperation between Geological Survey of India, Ministry of Mines of India and the China Geological Survey, Ministry of Land and Resources of China in Geo-sciences.
18. MoU between the Ministry of External Affairs of India and Chinese People's Association for Friendship with Foreign Countries on the establishment of states/provincial leaders' forum. It will lay ground for development and strengthening of exchanges and cooperation at the State/Provincial and city/municipality level between India and China. This will also enable cooperation in the fields of trade and investment, agriculture, skill development, smart cities, urban planning, clean energy, education, culture, tourism, people to people exchanges.
19. Agreement on the establishment of sister-state/province relations between State Government of Karnataka and Provincial Government of Sichuan of China. It will enhance people-to-people exchanges fostering greater mutual understanding.
20. Agreement on the establishment of sister-city relations between Chennai and Chongqing of China.
21. Agreement on the establishment of sister-city relations between Hyderabad and Qingdao of China.
22. Agreement on the establishment of sister-city relations between Aurangabad and Dunhuang of China.
23. MoU between the Indian Council for Cultural Relations and Fudan University on the establishment of a centre

for Gandhian and Indian studies. The center will focus on research on Gandhian thought and practice, Indian politics, economy, language, religion and culture, Buddhism and ancient India-China contacts. Academic exchanges, promotion of teaching of Indian languages are also envisioned by the MoU.

24. MoU between Indian Council for Cultural Relations and Yunnan Minzu University on the establishment of a yoga college. It will provide a framework for the establishment of a yoga college at YMU in Kunming. Under this MoU, ICCR will assist YMU in planning, training, promotion and coordination of yoga education, therapy and research, while YMU will provide physical infrastructure and other facilities for yoga college in Yunnan.

Earlier, China's President Xi Jinping visited India on 17-19 September 2014. Prime Minister Narendra Modi received Jinping in Ahmadabad. It was for the first time that agreements were signed at the regional (Gujarat state) level on sister cities, sister states and development related issues. This has been the trend recently after Tamil Nadu, West Bengal, Andhra Pradesh and other states pushed the envelope of diplomacy by engaging with others in the economic field.

Following agreements/MoUs were signed during the State visit of Chinese President Xi Jinping to India:

1. MoU between the Ministry of External Affairs of India and the Ministry of Foreign Affairs of China on opening a new route for Indian Pilgrimage to the Tibet Autonomous Region of China. It will provide for conducting the annual Kailash Mansarovar Yatra through Nathula Pass in Sikkim addition to the existing Lipulekh Pass in Uttarakhand. The route through Nathula will augment the capacity and reduce the hardship and journey time enabling many more pilgrims in particular aged pilgrims to undertake the yatra.
2. MoU between Ministry of Railways of India and the Government of People's Republic of China on strengthening cooperation in Railways. Both sides have

agreed to enhance cooperation in the Railway sector in the following areas—(i) speed-raising, (ii) studying feasibility of cooperation in High-Speed Railways, (iii) Heavy-Haul transportation training of Indian Railway personnel, (iv) Redevelopment of Railway stations, (v) setting up of a Railway University in India.

3. Action plan between Ministry of Railways of India and the National Railway Administration of China on strengthening cooperation in Railways. It will provide specific projects for cooperation in railway sector.
4. Five year Trade and Economic Development Plan between Indian Ministry of Commerce and Industry and Chinese Ministry of Commerce. It will lay down a medium term road map for promoting balanced and sustainable development of economic and trade relations between China and India, on the principle of equality and mutual benefit. The main objectives of the plan are—(i) reduction of bilateral trade imbalance; (ii) strengthen investment cooperation to realize US$ 20 billion investment from China in 5 years; (iii) a transparent, stable and investor friendly business environment; and (iv) enhanced cooperation between chambers of Commerce and financial sectors.
5. Agreed Minutes of the Tenth Session of India-China Joint Economic Group. The tenth session of the India-China Joint Group on Economic Relations, Trade, Science and Technology was held in Beijing on 2nd September 2014. Both sides held detailed discussions on issues to promote broad and deep bilateral trade and economic cooperation between India and China and agreed to undertake measures to achieve sustainable and balanced trade. Specific measures to enhance market access to Indian products such as agricultural, pharmaceutical and export of services will be expedited.
6. MoU between Indian Space Research Organisation and China National Space Administration on cooperation in the peaceful use of space. It will enable both sides to encourage exchange and cooperation in

the exploration and use of outer space for peaceful purposes, including research and development of scientific experiment satellites, remote sensing satellites and communications, satellites.

7. Work plan on Drug Administration and Cooperation between China Food and Drug Administration and Ministry of Health and Family Welfare of India. Under the work plan, the two sides will carry out cooperation in fields of drug standards, traditional medicine and drug testing, etc. Both sides will exchange delegations to enhance cooperation in this area.
8. Agreements on establishing Sister City relationship between Mumbai and Shanghai; Ahmedabad and Guangzhou. It will enhance people-to-people exchanges fostering greater mutual understanding.
9. Agreement on establishing Sister Province/State relationship between Gujarat and Guangdong.
10. MoU between Maharashtra Industrial Development Corporation and Beiqi Foton Motor Co. Ltd. on supporting the setting up of industrial parks in Maharashtra. It will lead to setting up of a 1250 acre Industrial Park near Pune, providing cluster-type development and generation of employment for a large number of people.
11. MoU between China Development Bank Corporation and iNDEXTb on supporting the setting up of industrial parks in Gujarat.

Modi's visit to China yielded no breakthroughs on the border or on how to bridge the trade gap. Neither was it expected to bring a turnaround in the issues, given their complicated nature. Therefore, the two sides came up with some non-controversial 'doable' taking into account their complementarities—China being called the factory of the world and India the global back-office. Modi also spoke to Chinese CEOs about his key "Make in India" programme.

Pending a resolution to their boundary dispute, India and China have decided to set up a hotline between the military headquarters of the two countries. It was also agreed that there will also be an increase in the number of meetings between border personnel and commanders at all sectors of the India-China border areas.

The agreements in the area of cooperation in skill development, railways, mining and minerals, broadcasting, tourism, ocean studies, establishing sister city relations and consulates in Chennai and Chengdu were also welcome steps.

6. Russia

Prime Minister Narendra Modi visited Russia on 23-24 December 2015 for the 16th India-Russia Annual Summit. At the summit, Prime Minister Modi and President Putin reviewed the relationship between India and Russia to strengthen it further and held discussions on regional and global issues. India and Russia agreed to put the government's flagship "Make in India" programme at the centrestage of their strategic relationship, as the two countries decided to build nuclear reactor components and military helicopters in India. Besides, the agreement is expected to lead to the construction of 12 atomic plants with the involvement of Indian firms.

Russia was the first country to have agreed to take the initiative under the "Make in India" umbrella in two key strategic sectors—nuclear energy and defence.

After bilateral talks with Russian President Vladimir Putin in Moscow, Prime Minister Narendra Modi said, "The Inter-Governmental Agreement on the manufacture of Kamov-226 helicopters in India is the first project for a major defence platform under the Make in India mission. It is, rightly, with our most important defence partner."

During Modi's visit, the two sides inked 16 pacts, including those on the nuclear and defence sectors. On defence, a joint statement said, "The sides took note of achievements in the field of joint design, development and production of high-technology military equipment. Both sides reaffirmed their intention to expand the scope of such cooperation and to avail of the opportunities provided by the Make in India initiative in the defence sector and directed the concerned agencies to finalize such projects between relevant entities and enterprises of the two countries at the earliest." According to a joint statement, "The two countries agreed to actively work towards localization of manufacturing in India under the aegis of Make in India and in tandem with the serial construction of nuclear power plants."[12]

Following Agreements/MoUs were signed during the visit of Prime Minister Modi to Russia.

1. Protocol amending the agreement between India and Russia on simplification of requirements for mutual travels of certain categories of citizens of the two countries.
2. Protocol amending agreement between India and Russia on mutual travel regime for holders of Diplomatic and Official Passports of 3 December 2004.
3. Agreement between India and Russia on cooperation in the field of Helicopter Engineering.
4. Plan for cooperation between the Federal customs Service of the Central Board of Excise and Customs, Department of Revenue, Ministry of Finance of India and the Russian Federation for combating Customs violations in 2015-17.
5. Programme of Action agreed between the Department of Atomic Energy of India and the Russian State Atomic Energy Corporation "Rosatom" for localization of manufacturing in India for Russian-Designed Nuclear Reactor Units.
6. MoU between the Ministry of Railways of India and the Joint Stock company "Russian Railways" on technical cooperation in railway sector.
7. MoU between Solar Energy Corporation of India and Russian Energy Agency regarding construction of solar energy plants in India.
8. MoU for cooperation between HEC and CNIITMASH for upgradation and modernization of HEC's manufacturing facilities.
9. MoU for cooperation between HEC and CNIITMASH for development of Centre of Excellence for heavy engineering design at HEC.

10. MoU between Prasar Bharati and Digital Television Russia on cooperation in the field of Broadcasting.
11. Tripartite MoU between Centre for Development of Advance Computing (C-DAC), Indian Institute of Science (IISc) Bangalore and Lomonsov Moscow State University (MSU).
12. Tripartite MoU between Centre for Development of Advance Computing (C-DAC), OJSC "GLONASS" and GLONASS Union.
13. MoU in the field of investment cooperation in the Russian Far East between the Tata Power Company Limited and Ministry for Development of the Russian Far East.
14. MoU for cooperation for geologic survey, exploration and production of hydrocarbons onshore and on the continental shelf of the Russian Federation.
15. Confirmation of successful completion of the first stage pre-completion actions in relation to the creation of a Joint Venture in JSC VankorNeft.
16. MoU for cooperation for geologic survey, exploration and production of hydrocarbons onshore the Russian Federation between Rosneft Oil Company, Oil India Limited and Indian Oil Corporation Limited.
17. Agreement between Central Council for Research in Ayurvedic Sciences, India and Peoples' Friendship University of Russia (PFUR) on cooperation in the field of Ayurveda.

Reflecting their continued emphasis on further enhancing bilateral economic and commercial relations, President Putin and Prime Minister Modi jointly addressed CEOs of leading Russian and Indian Companies. A number of important agreements in diverse fields of bilateral cooperation, including several commercial agreements between Russian and Indian companies, were signed during the visit.

7. The United Kingdom

Prime Minister Narendra Modi visited the UK on 12-13 November 2015. David Cameron, then Prime Minister of UK, and Modi celebrated the growing strength, breadth, and depth of the relations between the two countries. They emphasised that the enduring connection between India and the UK plays a vital role in safeguarding and promoting the security and prosperity of both the countries. India's economic development and rise as a global power affords opportunities to further deepen and extend this partnership to foster economic growth and inclusive development, update and strengthen the rules based international system, and counter global threats. For it, the two PMs endorsed a "Vision Statement" setting out the fundamental principles on which the UK-India partnership is built, and outlining a road map for deepening cooperation. They resolved to hold financial PM-level summits to advance the partnership. They also agreed on a new Defence and International Security Partnership which will intensify cooperation on defence and security, including cyber-security, counter-terrorism and maritime security. Addressing climate change and promoting secure, affordable and sustainable supplies of energy, they agreed to endorse a Joint Statement on Energy and Climate Change. The two PMs also agreed to scale up bilateral cooperation to a global partnership for development through a "Statement of Intent on Partnership for Cooperation in Third Countries", which will facilitate working together to benefit third country partners by assisting them in addressing their development challenges in a wholly demand driven manner.

India and the UK have made following commercial announcements during the visit of PM Modi.

1. OPG Power Ventures of the UK has agreed to add to its existing investment in India by a total of 2.9 billion to a total of 3.4 billion. It will create 4200 MW of new power capacity in India, of which 1000 MW will be solar power and 3200 MW will be thermal and renewable power in Tamil Nadu.
2. King's College Hospital NHS Foundation Trust and Indo-UK Healthcare Pvt Ltd. have signed an agreement to open King's College Hospital in Chandigarh. This is the first of a proposed eleven new UK-Indo Institutes for Health that will be developed across India, which, when fully implemented, would amount to a £ 1 billion

investment into India's healthcare system, accompanied by strategic clinical and training partnerships with UK's finest NHS organisations, universities and private sector companies.

3. Merlin Entertainments announced its first business in India—a Madame Tussauds wax attraction scheduled to open in New Delhi. It is also looking to roll out several more of its iconic global 'Midway' attraction brands such as SEA LIFE and LEGOLAND Discovery Centres in key cities across India, and expects to invest up to £ 50 million over the next ten years.
4. Genus ABS agreed to invest £ 1 million in India, providing the latest dairy genetics and constructing a state-of-the-art facility near Pune in Maharashtra.
5. Light source, the largest Solar PV generator in the UK and Europe, has agreed to invest £ 2 billion in India. It will design, install and manage around 3 gigawatts of solar power infrastructure in India over the next five years.
6. The UK's Kloudpad Mobility Research has announced a £ 100 million investment in South India to "Made in India" the next generation of smart watches, wearables and tablets.
7. Vodafone has announced a range of further investments in India totalling £ 1.3 billion to support the Government of India's campaigns on "Digital India" and "Made in India". It will invest £ 800 million to enhance, upgrade and expand its country-wide network coverage; £ 300 million in its high-end technology centres in Pune and Ahmedabad. A further £ 100 million will be invested to create a first of its kind, state-of-the-art Tier-4 data centre, providing customised communication services for enterprises and businesses. Demonstrating strong commitment towards the Government of India's Financial Inclusion initiative, Vodafone has announced another £ 100 million investment to create a payment bank focused on serving the unbanked and under banked and to accelerate India's journey towards cashless economy.

8. Standard Life, Bupa and Aviva have committed to invest a combined total of £ 238 million of FDI in their Indian Joint Ventures.
9. E-commerce cloud platform provider, cloudBuy, has signed a contract with the confederation of Indian Industry (CII) for an online business to business marketplace. CII members and other businesses in India will have a new gateway to global supply chains, with the ability to access partners and providers across the world, do business online, and boost their exports. Over the next five years the platform is projected to facilitate transactions worth £ 3.5 billion and increase trade further between traditional business partners India and the UK.
10. Intelligent Energy, the UK technology company, has signed an agreement to acquire the energy management business of Indian company GTL, to provide efficient, clean and economical energy to 27,400 telecoms towers in India, with a total contract value of £ 1.2 billion over ten years.
11. Holland and Barrett International has signed a deal worth £ 20 million with Apollo Hospitals to open 1000 Holland and Barrett outlets in India over the next five years.
12. London Stock Exchange Group and Yes Bank have signed a MoU to faster joint collaborations on bond and equity issuance, with a strong focus on Green Infrastructure Finance.
13. State Bank of India and London Stock Exchange Group announced to create the "FTSE-SBI India Bonds Indices" to be used initially by a new investment fund run by SBI. These indices will facilitate investment into India's bond markets and support market liquidity and pricing.
14. HSBC announces the launch of its 'Skills for Life' initiative in India, a programme to skill 75,000 disadvantaged young people over five years. HSBC Skills for Life programme will focus on nine sectors—retail, transportation and logistics, beauty and

wellness, tourism, hospitality and travel, IT and IT enabled services, electronic and IT hardware; healthcare, banking, financial services and insurance, and education.

Speaking at a news conference, the then Prime Minister David Cameron said London wanted to support Modi in his vision to transform India with improved infrastructure and education: "We want to become your number one partner for supporting the finance needed for Modi's ambitious plan, making London the world's centre for offshore rupee trading with the issue of over £ 1 billion in bonds including the first government backed rupee denominated bond", he said.

Narendra Modi's visit to UK gave a greater thrust to political and cultural relations between the two countries and a boost to bilateral trade and investment.

The two Prime Ministers agreed to have deals worth US$ 13.7 billion. Modi emphasized India's outsized economic stake in the United Kingdom and highlighted the fact that India invests more in the UK than in the rest of the European Union. The economic deals during Modi's visit concerned India's creative and retail sectors, logistics, financial services, energy, information technology and cyber, healthcare, and education.

8. Australia

The Prime Minister of India, Narendra Modi, paid an official visit to Australia from 16-18 November 2014, following the G-20 Summit. Prime Minister Tony Abbott and Prime Minister Modi agreed to unlock the vast potential of the economic relationship, especially in priority areas such as resources, education, skills, agriculture, infrastructure, investments, financial services, and health. They expressed satisfaction at the increase in investment while recognizing the tremendous untapped potential in both directions. Indian investment in the resource sector in Australia promises to create jobs and value for the Australian economy, while Australian investment in cold chain storage, energy, infrastructure and other sectors can help the growth of Indian economy.

Earlier, Australian Prime Minster Abbott had paid a two-day visit to India. India and Australia sealed a long-awaited nuclear deal during Abbott's visit. Arguing that India and Australia were bound by "strongly convergent" trade and strategic interests, Abbott announced the finalization of a deal that would allow Australia to export uranium to India. Australia holds 40 percent of the world's uranium.

During Prime Minister Modi's visit to Australia, the two leaders agreed to cooperate on clean coal technologies and welcomed the intention to explore opportunities for partnership between Australian institutions and the Indian School of Mines in Dhanbad.

Prime Minister Modi and Prime Minister Abbott decided to extend defence cooperation to cover research, development and industry engagement. They agreed to hold regular meetings at the level of the Defence Minister, conduct regular maritime exercises and convene regular Navy to Navy, Air Force to Air Force and Army to Army staff talks.

Australia and India are working together more closely to build a safe and prosperous region, including through key regional forums such as the East Asia Summit. Both countries value their engagement with ASEAN, are strongly committed to building up the Indian Ocean Rim Association (IORA)[13], and support regional efforts to create stronger humanitarian and disaster relief capabilities, combat malaria and boost regional trade, including through the Regional Comprehensive Economic Partnership.

Australia and India have deepened both defence and economic ties signing a new security pact and committing to an unlikely one-year time-line to sign a free trade agreement. A trade deal with India would give Australian exporters access to a market of 1.3 billion people, including an increasingly affluent middle-class burgeoning towards 500 million people in coming years.

Following Agreements/MoUs were signed during the visit of Prime Minister Modi to Australia on 16-18 November 2014.

1. Agreement on Social Security—To strengthen the people-to-people contracts and facilitate and regulate the regulations between the two countries with respect to social security benefits and coverage. It will provide for social security and superannuation benefits for those who have been residents of the other country on basis of equality of benefit, export of benefits and avoidance of double coverage. It will lead to greater economies and promote the flow of professionals.
2. Agreement concerning transfer of sentenced persons—To enhance cooperative efforts in law enforcement and administration of justice and to cooperate in the enforcement of penal sentences. It will facilitate, regulate and lay down procedures for the transfer of sentenced persons and enable rehabilitation and reintegration of sentenced persons into society.
3. MoU on combating Narcotics Trafficking and Developing Police Cooperation—To address concerns regarding illicit trafficking and drug abuse. It places priority on tackling illicit trade, diversion of precursors, asset forfeiture and drug money laundering. It will promote capacity building and help develop strategies and procedures for operations to disrupt and dismantle transnational narcotic related threats.
4. MoU on cooperation in the Field of Arts and Culture—To enhance cultural relations between the two countries in pursuance of the Cultural Agreement of 1971. It will promote cooperation through exchange of information, professional expertise, training and exhibitions in the field of culture. It will deepen understanding between the people, institutions and art genres and promote sound and sustainable artistic and cultural activities.
5. MoU in the field of Tourism—To enhance the bilateral cooperation and strengthen the friendly between the people. It will encourage cooperation in tourism policy, information exchange, interaction between tourism stakeholders, training and investments in hospitality sector and promote the importance of the tourism sector in economic development and employment generation.

9. South Korea

Prime Minister Narendra Modi visited South Korea on 18-19 May 2015. There was a broad consensus across political circles in India about the need for a strong relationship with Seoul so that there is a steady growth in the country just as has been the case in South Korea. In January 2014, South Korean President Park Geun-hye had a reasonably successful visit to India, where she was the guest of honour at the Republic Day. The main highlight of Park's visit was a memorandum of understanding signed between the Export-Import Bank of Korea and India Infrastructure Finance Co. Ltd for the funding of infrastructure projects. Key issues were also discussed, including South Korea's strategic initiatives in East Asia, among them trust-building on the Korean Peninsula and the Northeast Asia Peace and Cooperation Initiative. An agreement was also signed to share information about the nuclear activities of Pakistan and North Korea.

According to Narendra Modi, India-Korea partnership can play an important role in his "Make in India" vision. In areas like shipbuilding, as well as in rail and other infrastructure development, there is great scope for further cooperation.

South Korea is a democratic country like India and has made tremendous progress in its infrastructure, technology, and economy at large. In a 2013 speech, before he became Prime Minister, Modi had referred to that progress, saying, "South Korea also gained independence at the same time. It is the size of Gujarat. Now, in this short span, it is among the developed nations. Such a small country hosts Olympics. Through sports, it has established a position in the world."

It is pertinent to mention here that South Korea was one of the first countries that sought to increase economic engagement with India after latter's initiation of its "Look East" policy in the 1990s. South Korean investment in India has increased over the past two decades, to an estimated US$ 3 billion. This is notwithstanding the challenges investors have had to face, with one of the biggest setbacks to the relationship being the apparent scrapping of the POSCO Project, which would have been a major investment.

During Prime Minister Narendra Modi's visit to South Korea, the two countries inked seven agreements, which are briefed below:[14]

(i) Agreement for the avoidance of double taxation and the prevention of fiscal evasion with respect to taxes on income: It was signed in line with the Double Taxation Avoidance Convention (DTAC) signed between both nations in 1985. The agreement revises previous convention with a view to avoiding the burden of double taxation on taxpayers in the two countries, and will provide confidence to business houses that are importing goods and services from or exporting the same to South Korea.

(ii) Cooperation in audio-visual co-production: It will boost opportunities for collaboration between both countries in film industry sector and facilitate collaboration, exchange and co-production of films, animation and broadcasting programmes. With the advancement of technology, there has been phenomenal spread of animation, video games, filmmaking, and there is a large market for these.

(iii) MoU for cooperation between India's National Security Council Secretariat and Korea's Office of National Security: It will formalize consultations between the structures of National Security Council of both the nations in a number of areas.

(iv) MoU between the Ministry of Power of India and the Ministry of Trade, Industry and Energy of the Republic of Korea concerning cooperation in the field of electric power development and new energy industries: It envisages cooperation in areas of electric power development and new energy industries. It inter alia includes areas such as smart grids and power information and technology, renewable energy, transmission and distribution of electric power, energy efficiency and storage system.

(v) MoU between the Ministry of Youth Affairs and Sports of India and the Ministry of Gender Equality and

Family of the Republic of Kora on cooperation in youth matters: It will encourage and strengthen cooperation on youth matters through participation. It will basically enhance participation in events and activities through international conferences, exchanges, youth camps, seminars, festivals, among other such activities.

(vi) Framework of cooperation in the field of road transport and highways between the Ministry of Road Transport and Highways of India and the Ministry of Land, Infrastructure and Transport of the Republic of Korea: It envisages cooperation in areas such as road policies, design and construction, road operation, road management and safety, electronic toll collection systems and intelligent transport systems.

(vii) MoU between the Ministry of Shipping of India and the Ministry of Oceans and Fisheries of the Republic of Korea on cooperation in the fields of maritime transport and logistics: It aims to enhance cooperation between the two countries in the fields of maritime transport and logistics. It will include sharing of information, technologies and experiences, exchange of experts and port operations, training of seafarers, etc.

Bilateral trade has consistently increased over the past two decades, but at an estimated US$ 17 billion, it is still far below its potential of US$ 40 billion, which both countries have targeted. PM Modi's visit was a major fillip for the projects that he promised to deliver during his 2014 General Elections campaign as well as for the initiatives he brought after becoming India's Prime Minister, like Smart Cities, Digital India and others as Korea promised more investment in India.

10. United Arab Emirates

Prime Minister Narendra Modi visited United Arab Emirates (UAE) on 16-17 August 2015. No Indian Prime Minister had visited the UAE in the last 34 years. Modi's visit has had a huge political implication, as it came ahead of the National Security Adviser (NSA) level meeting between India and Pakistan (on August 23-24) during which the two South Asian neighbours discussed issues like state-sponsored terrorism and the current security scenario in the region. India sent a strong signal to Pakistan by securing the UAE's backing in its fight against terrorism.

Narendra Modi and Crown Prince of the UAE Mohamed Bin Zayed Al Nahyan urged the global community to reject the use of terrorism and bring the perpetrators of violence to justice. The two leaders issued a joint statement, condemning efforts to use religion for justifying, supporting and sponsoring terrorism against other countries. The statement clearly stated that all 'terrorism infrastructure' should be dismantled in order to ensure global peace and prosperity.

India and the UAE, despite enjoying robust economic relations, have so far engaged in limited co-operation on security and counter-terrorism measures. The joint statement underscores the need to do something concrete to root out terrorism which has become the bane of civilized societies everywhere in the world.

Crown Prince Mohamed Bin Zayed Al Nahyan and Prime Minister Narendra Modi agreed to seize this historic visit of opportunity and shared responsibility to chart a new course in their partnership for the 21st century. The two leaders agreed on the following.

1. Elevation of the India-UAE relationship to a comprehensive strategic partnership.
2. Coordinating efforts to counter radicalization and misuse of religion by groups and countries for inciting hatred, perpetrating and justifying terrorism or pursuing political aims. The two sides will facilitate regular exchanges of religious scholars and intellectuals and organise conferences and seminars to promote the values of peace, tolerance, inclusiveness and welfare that is inherent in all religions.
3. Opposing terrorism in all forms and manifestations, wherever committed and by whomever, calling on all states to reject and abandon the use of terrorism against other countries, dismantle terrorism infrastructures

where they exist, and bring perpetrators of terrorism to justice.

4. Enhancing cooperation in counter-terrorism operations, intelligence sharing and capacity building.
5. Working together for the adoption of India's proposed comprehensive convention on International Terrorism in the United Nations.
6. Working together to control, regulate and share information on flow of funds that could have a bearing on radicalization activities and cooperating in interdicting illegal flows and take action against concerned individuals and organizations.
7. Strengthening cooperation in law enforcement, anti-money laundering, drug trafficking, other trans-national crimes, extradition arrangements, as well as police training.
8. Promoting cooperation in cyber security, including prevention on use of cyber for terrorism, radicalization and disturbing social harmony.
9. Establishing a dialogue between their National Security Advisors and National Security Councils. The National Security Advisors, together with other high level representatives for security from both nations, will meet every six months. The two sides will also establish points of contract between their security agencies to further improve operational cooperation.
10. Cooperate to strengthen maritime security in the Gulf and the Indian Ocean region, which is vital for the security and prosperity of both countries.
11. Promoting collaboration and inter-operability for humanitarian assistance and evaluation in natural disasters and conflict situations.
12. Strengthening defence relations, including through regular exercises and training of naval, air, land and Special Forces, and in coastal defence.
13. Cooperation in the manufacture of defence equipment in India.

14. Working together to promote peace, reconciliation, stability, inclusiveness and cooperation in the wider South Asia, Gulf and West Asia region.
15. Supporting efforts for peaceful resolution of conflicts and promoting adherence to the principles of sovereignty and non-interference in the conduct of relations between nations and settlement of disputes.
16. Call on all nations to fully respect and sincerely implement their commitments to resolve disputes bilaterally and peacefully, without resorting to violence and terrorism.
17. Establishing a Strategic Security Dialogue between the two governments.
18. Recognising that India is emerging as the new frontier of investment opportunities, especially with the new initiatives by the government to facilitate trade and investment, encourage the investment institutions of UAE to raise their investments in India, including through the establishment of UAE-India Infrastructure Investment Fund, with the aim of reaching a target of US$ 75 billion to support investment in India's plans for rapid expansion of next generation infrastructure, especially in railways, ports, roads, airports, and industrial corridors and parks.
19. Facilitating participation of Indian companies in infrastructure development in UAE.
20. Promoting strategic partnership in the energy sector, including through UAE's participation in India in the development of strategic petroleum reserves, upstream and downstream petroleum sectors, and collaboration in third countries.
21. Promoting trade between the two countries, and using their respective locations and infrastructure for expanding trade in the region and beyond; and with the target of increasing trade by 60% in the next five years.
22. Strengthening cooperation between UAE's increasingly sophisticated education institutions and India's

universities and higher research institutions. Promoting scientific collaboration, including in the areas of renewable energy, sustainable development, and agriculture, desert ecology, urban development and advanced healthcare.

23. Promoting cooperation in Space, including in Joint development and launch of satellites, ground-based infrastructure and space application. Prime Minister Modi welcomed UAE's plan to set up the West Asia's first Space Research Centre at Al Ain and plans to launch a Mars Mission in 2021.
24. Cooperate in peaceful uses of nuclear energy including in areas like safety, health, agriculture and science and technology.
25. The finalization of the post-2015 Development Agenda with elimination of poverty by 2030 as its core objective was a welcome development.
26. People-to-People were at the heart of India-UAE relations and both governments will continue to nurture these relations and ensure the welfare of their citizens, especially the workers, in each other's country, as also work together to prevent human trafficking.

11. Iran

Prime Minister Narendra Modi visited Iran on 22-23 May 2016. During the visit PM Modi held talks on a wide range of subjects of mutual interest with the President of the Islamic Republic of Iran Dr. Hassan Rouhani. India and Iran share longstanding civilisational ties. Iran is situated in India's extended neighbourhood and the two countries have significant overlap in their economic and security space. The visit of PM Modi to Iran was in the direction of building on these commonalities by focussing on specific cooperation in regional connectivity and infrastructure, developing energy partnership, boosting bilateral trade, facilitating people-to-people interaction in various spheres and promoting peace and stability in the region.

Following Agreements/MoUs were signed between India and Iran during PM Modi's visit on 22-23 May 2016.

1. India-Iran Cultural Exchange programme—It aims at extending the CEP for the period 2016-2019 covering the areas of culture and art; radio, TV, mass media and cinema; and relevant general and financial terms.
2. MoU between the Ministry of External Affairs (MEA) of India and the Ministry of Foreign Affiars (MoFA) of Iran on Policy Dialogue between Governments and Interaction between Think Tanks—It seeks to create a Joint Secretary/Director General policy dialogue as well as encouraging new institutional mechanisms between think tanks on both sides.
3. MoU between Foreign Service Institute, MEA and the School of International Relations, Iran's MoFA—It intends to enhance cooperation between the two parties for training of diplomats and exchange of eminent speakers.
4. Implementation Protocol between Department of Science and Technology, Ministry of S&T and Iran's Ministry of Science, Research and Technology on Cooperation in the Fields of Science and Technology—the IP fleshes out the specific cooperation between the two sides pursuant to the 2003 MoU and covers areas like exchange of experiences, seminars, conferences, etc.
5. MoU between Indian Council for Cultural Relations and Islamic Culture and Relations Organisations of Iran—It provides for institutional mechanisms for cooperation between ICCR and ICRO and lays down the modalities for the cooperation.
6. Bilateral contract on Chabahar Port for port development and operations between India Ports Global Private Limited (IPGPL) and Arya Banader of Iran—It envisages development and operation for 10 years of two terminals and 5 berths with cargo handling (multipurpose and general) capacities.
7. MoU between EXIM Bank and Iran's Ports and Maritime Organization (PMO) on current specific terms for the Chabahar Port project—It intends for

the purpose of credit of US$ 150 million for Chabahar Port.

8. Confirmation Statement between EXIM Bank and Central Bank of Iran—It confirms the availability of credit up to ₹ 3000 crore for the import of steel rails and implementation of Chabahar Port.
9. MoU between Export Credit Guarantee Corporation (ECGC) of India and the Export Guarantee Fund of Iran (EGFI)—It seeks to establish a framework of cooperation between ECGC and EGFI in supporting and encouraging foreign trade and foreign investment between India and Iran and, where appropriate, the supply of goods and services from their respective countries as part of a project to a third country.
10. MoU between National Aluminum Company Limited (NALCO) and the Iranian Mines and Mining Industries Development and Renovation Organisation (IMIDRO)—It aims to jointly explore the possibility of manufacturing aluminium metal by setting up of a smelter on joint venture basis of Iran and/or entering into tolling arrangements with smelters in Iran or any other form of business collaboration including sale of alumina, etc.
11. MoU between IRCON and Construction, Development of Transport and Infrastructure Company (CDTIC) of Iran—It will enable IRCON to provide requisite services for the construction of Chabahar-Zahedan railway line which forms part of transit and transportation corridor in trilateral agreement between India, Iran and Afghanistan. Services to be provided by IRCON include all superstructure work and financing the project which is around US$ 1.6 billion.
12. MoU for cooperation between the National Archives of India and the National Library and Archives Organisation of Iran—It aims to facilitate exchange of information and knowledge in the field of archival matters through exchange of manuals, guidelines, rules, publications and other special literature on archival topics.

In recent times, China and Pakistan have aimed to develop a US$ 46 billion China-Pak Economic Corridor, snaking its way from Kashi in China through the length of Pakistan, terminating at Gwadar Port on the Arabian Sea in Pakistan's restive province of Balochistan.[15]

The Chabahar port will make way for India to bypass Pakistan in transporting goods to Afghanistan through sea route. The port will give momentum to the International North-South Transport Corridor of which both Iran and India are initial signatories along with Russia. The port entails the ship, rail and road routes for moving freight between India, Russia, Iran, Europe and Central Asia.

The deal with Iran is considered to be Modi's master stroke as it would counter Chinese presence in the Arabian sea aimed to support Pakistan in developing Gwadar port. It can be used to station security vessels for merchant ships off the African coast apart from giving the country a foothold in Western Arabian sea which is important as most of the energy imports pass through this route.[16]

12. Saudi Arabia

Prime Minister Narendra Modi visited the Kingdom of Saudi Arabia on 2-3 April, 2016. During the visit, PM Modi held discussions with King Salman Bin Abdulaziz Al-Saud on bilateral, regional and multilateral issues of mutual interest. India and Saudi Arabia share friendly relations based on close people-to-people contracts. The strategic partnership established through Riyadh declaration in 2010 envisions a deeper engagement in political, economic, security and defence areas. Saudi Arabia has become 4th largest partner of India with bilateral trade exceeding US$ 39 billion in 2014-15. Saudia Arabia is also India's largest crude oil supplier accounting for about one-fifth of India's total imports.

India's relations with Saudi Arabia, one of the world's leading oil producers, have been on an upswing over the last two decades based on burgeoning energy ties. There are nearly three million Indian nationals working in Saudi Arabia, the largest expatriate community in the country, and both countries looked to move beyond buyer-seller relationship in the sector and go for joint ventures and investment in refineries and oil fields.

Saudi Arabia plans to invest US$ 1 trillion in infrastructure development over the next five years and PM Modi is likely to pitch for participation of Indian companies in the projects.

India and Saudi Arabia signed the following agreements during Modi's visit to that country:[17]

(i) A pact on cooperation in the exchange of intelligence related to money laundering, terrorism financing and related crimes. The two countries agreed to enhance cooperation in counter-terrorism operations, intelligence sharing and capacity-building and to strengthen cooperation in law enforcement.

(ii) Agreement on labour co-operation between the Ministry of Labour of the Kingdom of Saudi Arabia and Ministry of External Affairs of India for recruitment of general category workers.

(iii) Technical cooperation agreement between the Bureau of Indian Standards (BIS) and the Saudi Standards, Metrology and Quality Organization (SASO).

(iv) MoU between Export Promotion Council for Handicraft (EPCH) of India and Saudi Commission for Tourism and National Heritage to promote cooperation in the field of handicrafts.

(v) Agreement on preparing a framework for Investment Promotion Cooperation between Invest India and the Saudi Arabian General Investment Authority (SAGIA).

Modi's visit to Saudi Arabia was important for a number of reasons. Saudi Arabia was a key source for India's energy needs and is host to three million Indians. Several thousand Indians visit the two holy mosques in Mecca and Medina for Hajj every year. Besides, India is also looking for Saudi investments in its infrastructure development and the PM's "Make in India" programme. The country also has strategic importance. The civil war in Syria and Yemen, and the rise of the Islamic State have posed threat to many countries in the region. The successful conclusion of the nuclear deal between Iran and the Western powers has only enhanced the feeling of a stronger Shia-Sunni rivalry for domination in this region. A realignment has begun among key countries in the area—all of whom, especially Iran, Israel and Saudi Arabia—leaders of the Gulf countries, are important partners of India. Engagement with all of them, especially the Saudi leadership, therefore becomes crucial for India.[18]

13. Brazil

Prime Minister Narendra Modi went to Brazil on 15-16 July 2014 for his maiden summit meeting of the BRICS nations. India and Brazil decided to expand trade and investment flows while deepening collaboration in the fields of renewable energy, defence and cyber security as they signed three pacts including one on cooperation in the environment sector. PM Modi and Brazilian President Dilma Rousseff also agreed to intensify their cooperation in international forums and multilateral institutions including the G-20.

The Ministry of External Affairs said Modi and Rousseff agreed to take steps to further expand and diversify trade and investment flows and deepen cooperation in agriculture and dairy science, conventional and renewable energy, space research and application, defence, cyber security and environment conservation. Three agreements were signed in the presence of Modi and Rousseff related to cooperation in the fields of environment, space and in the establishment of a consultation mechanism on mobility and consular issues.

Brazil is one of the BRICS countries—an association of five major emerging national economies: Brazil, Russia, India, China and South Africa. These are all leading developing or newly industrialized countries and are distinguished by their large, sometimes fast-growing economies and significant influence on regional affairs. Bilateral relations among BRICS nations have mainly been conducted on the basis of non-interference, equality, and mutual benefit.[19]

Thus, Modi's visit to Brazil holds significance as it was his first summit meeting of the BRICS nations there. There were discussions to address the current problems and advance global economic stability. The visit gave a fillip to India's relations with other BRICS members, especially Brazil.

14. African Nations (Mozambique, South Africa, Tanzania and Kenya)

Prime Minister Narendra Modi visited Mozambique, South Africa and Tanzania, besides Kenya from 7 to 11 July 2016. This was Modi's first visit to the African mainland.

The visit aimed to bolster and sustain ties between India and energy- and resource-rich Africa. The main takeaways from Modi's Africa tour are the following:[20]

1. India signed a long-term agreement for the import of pulses from Mozambique during Modi's visit, the first by an Indian Prime Minister to the southeast African State in three decades. The pact will help India tide over shortage of pulses in the country that has led to a spurt in prices over the last one year and a half. India's Cabinet had cleared in June 2016 a proposal to enter into an agreement with Mozambique for importing 100,000 tonnes of pulses in 2016-17 with an option to scale it up to 200,000 tonnes by 2020-21. India and Mozambique have also signed MoU on drug demand reduction and prevention of illicit trafficking in narcotic drugs, psychotropic substances and precursor chemicals and related matters.
2. Modi invited defence businesses to set up a manufacturing base in India, which could service the domestic requirements of India and South Africa as well as for export to other countries. During the visit, the following Agreements and MoUs were signed between India and South Africa.
   (a) MoU on Information Communication Technologies (ICT).
   (b) MoU on the establishment of grassroots innovation in the area of Science and Technology.
   (c) MoU on Tourism and Cultural cooperation.
3. Modi invoked India's past links with Africa and shared experience of struggle against colonial powers. Modi

also laid out blueprints for future cooperation in the face of competition from China. In Mozambique, Modi offered to share India's expertise in agriculture infrastructure. He also noted that healthcare was a sector where India's capabilities would match the needs of Mozambique. In Tanzania, Modi offered US$ 500 million of concessional credit for water supply connections to 17 cities in addition to an existing US$ 100 million.

4. Prime Minister Narendra Modi offered assistance in public health with the supply of medicines and equipment. In South Africa, he sought a partnership between the businesses of the two countries which he thought can give a new shape to the India-Africa partnership and drive it to new levels.
5. Modi addressed meetings of the Indian community in all four countries, emphasizing the links between Africa's East coast and India's West coast and their common connect across the Indian Ocean.
6. Guided by the necessity to establish a solid framework to facilitate engagement between India and Kenya, the following bilateral instruments were concluded during the visit.
   (a) MoU on the Defence Cooperation.
   (b) MoU on the Cooperation in the field of National Housing Policy Development and Management.
   (c) Agreement for the avoidance of double taxation and the prevention of Fiscal Evasion with respect to taxes on income.
   (d) MoU between Bureau of Indian. Standards and Kenya Bureau of Standards.
   (e) Agreement on exemption of Visa for holders of Diplomatic Passports.
   (f) Line of Credit Agreement for US$ 15 million to IDB Capital Limited, for development of small and medium enterprises (SMEs).

(g) Line of Credit Agreement for US$ 29.95 million to the Government of Kenya for upgrade of Rift Valley Textiles Factory (RIVATEX).

Modi's visit to the four African nations is the third high-level visit to Africa after the visits by President Pranab Mukherjee and by Vice-president Hamid Ansari in the preceding six months. The visits are part of India's efforts to consolidate gains made at the third India-Africa summit that took place in New Delhi in October 2015. According to the Ministry of External Affairs, these four countries are our maritime neighbours and are gateways to the African mainland. The focus of Modi's visit to Mozambique was on energy as it is world's third largest exporter of natural gas after Qatar and Australia, and food security as India is importing large number of food items particularly pulses from it. In view of the sharp rise of prices of pulses in India, it was a highly necessary move.

15. Sri Lanka

Prime Minister Narendra Modi visited Sri Lanka on 13-14 March 2015. This was Modi's first tour to the island country in which he met Lankan President Maithripala Sirisena and discussed bilateral issues and issues of regional importance. The following were the key takeaways of the visit:

(i) The two leaders agreed to boost bilateral trade by reducing non-tariff barriers.

(ii) India committed to help Trincomalee to become a petroleum hub and announced that New Delhi will provide a fresh Line of Credit of up to US$ 318 million for the railways sector in Sri Lanka.

(iii) The Reserve Bank of India and the Central Bank of Sri Lanka have agreed to enter into a Currency Swap Agreement of US$ 1.5 billion to help keep the Sri Lankan rupee stable.

According to Institute for Defence Studies and Analyses, Modi's Sri Lanka visit is significant for three reasons. The first and most important is political. India's neighbours have come to believe that Indian leaders do not consider their countries as important enough places to visit. Further, of even the little attention that India deigns to give to the neighbourhood, a disproportionate percentage goes to Pakistan. Against this backdrop, Modi's successive visits to Bhutan, Nepal and then Sri Lanka within a year of assuming office is being considered as a significant departure and an important political statement.[21]

Moreover, considering the growing dominance of China in the region and its alliance with Pakistan, which is hostile towards India as ever, it is necessary to develop stronger relationships with our other neighbours to maintain a balance of power. It goes to Modi's credit that he is well aware of this fact and paid a visit to Sri Lanka.

16. Switzerland

Prime Minister Narendra Modi visited Switzerland on 5-6 June 2016. There were discussions on many important issues.[22]

(i) Switzerland expressed its support for membership in the Nuclear Suppliers Group (NSG), welcoming the latter's contributions to non-proliferation of nuclear arms.

(ii) Both the countries agreed to support each other for our respective bids for the non-permanent membership of the UN Security Council.

(iii) The two nations also discussed the issue of black money and stated that combating the menace of black money and tax evasion was also their shared priority.

(iv) The two sides discussed clean technology, energy security, clean air and sustainable development.

(v) Modi invited Swiss business leaders to invest in India, saying, "Within my country I need to create two or three Switzerlands. So the scope for partnership is immense." "We want to have manufacturing of global standards. Hence, the Swiss model of skill development is very relevant for us", the Indian Prime Minister added.

17. Mexico

Prime Minister Narendra Modi visited Mexico on 8 June 2016. President of the United Mexican States Enrique Pena

Nieto himself backed India's NSG bid during the Indian PM's visit. The two countries also issued a joint statement during this brief visit by the Indian PM which included, among others, the following:

(i) Opportunities to define the path of the India-Mexico Privileged Partnership for the 21st century that allows the growth of bilateral relations in economic field, in science and technology and in the most important issues of the global agenda reflecting a broad convergence of long-term political, economic and strategic goals.

(ii) Detailed exchange of views on regional issues of mutual interest, including the political and economic developments in Latin America, the CELAC and the Pacific Alliance, as well as the current situation in the Asia-Pacific region.

(iii) Promotion of investment and the use of solar energy. The two sides agreed to explore ways and means to boost objectives of the International Solar Alliance.

(iv) Offer opportunities by the convergence between the National Digital Strategy of Mexico and the Digital India Initiative, which share common objectives.

The agreements will go a long way in extending cooperation between the two countries, further strengthening the relations between the two countries.

18. Vietnam

Prime Minister Narendra Modi visited Vietnam on 2-3 September 2016. He signed 12 agreements with Vietnam after meeting his Vietnamese counterpart Nguyen Xuan Phuc. The leaders of the two countries also held delegation level talks. PM Modi announced a new line of credit of US$ 500 million for Vietnam to facilitate deeper defence cooperation. Following are the agreements signed between India and Vietnam:

1. Framework Agreement on Cooperation in the Exploration and Uses of Outer Space for Peaceful Purposes.
2. Protocol for amending the Agreement on Avoiding Double Taxation.

3. Program of cooperation in UN Peacekeeping Matters.
4. Protocol between the Ministry of Foreign Affairs of Vietnam and the Ministry of External Affairs of India on Celebrating 2017 as the "Year of Friendship".
5. MoU on Health Cooperation.
6. MoU on cooperation in Information Technology.
7. MoU on cooperation between the Vietnam Academy of Social Sciences and the Indian Council of World Affairs.
8. MoU on cooperation in Cyber Security.
9. MoU between the Bureau of Indian Standards and Directorate for Standard, Metrology and quality for cooperation in the fields of Standardization and Conformity Assessment.
10. MoU on the establishment of the Centre of Excellence in Software Development and Training.
11. Technical Agreement on sharing of White Shipping Information.
12. Contract for offshore high speed Patrol Boats.

Along with setting a bilateral trade target of US$ 15 billion by 2020, the Prime Minister Modi sought facilitation of ongoing Indian projects and investments in Vietnam. India also committed to grant US$ 5 million to set up a software park in the country. According to the Ministry of External Affairs, "The 12 MoUs and agreements signed and Prime Minister Modi's visit will set a new benchmark for India-Vietnam ties which will take our relationship to a new level."

Prime Minister Modi inspected a guard of honour by the three armed forces of the host country, and said: "We wish to forge a strong economic relationship with Vietnam that can mutually benefit our citizens. Strengthening the people-to-people ties will also be my endeavour during the Vietnam visit."[23]

19. Laos

Prime Minister Narendra Modi went to Vientiane, Laos on 7-8 September 2016 to attend two important meetings—the 14th Indo-ASEAN Summit and the East Asia Forum.

Indo-ASEAN Summit is the third summit between India and the 10-nation grouping that Modi attended. The ASEAN countries—Myanmar, Singapore, Malaysia, Laos, Vietnam, Cambodia, Indonesia, Brunei, the Philippines and Thailand—have a combined GDP of US$ 2.5 trillion and an annual economic growth rate of 4.6 percent. They are central to India's Act East policy.

The cooperation between India and ASEAN bloc can be broadly divided into political, economic, security and cultural categories. The ties became a strategic partnership in 2012. At present, there are 30 official and seven ministerial meetings between India and the ASEAN. The total India-ASEAN trade is US$ 6,404 billion. The security ties encompass maritime security, counter terrorism and cyber security. Many ASEAN countries have territorial disputes with China over South China Sea and they believe that the rise of China is not good for them.[24]

East Asia Summit consists of leaders of ten ASEAN countries plus China, Japan, South Korea, New Zealand, Australia, India, Russia and the US. As a bloc, the East Asia Summit forum accounts for 55% of the global population and 55% of the global GDP. India is closely associated with the grouping in a number of fields of cooperation and it includes the setting up of Nalanda University.

Developing more cooperation and better understanding with ASEAN nations is very important for India considering the fact that China is trying to increase its influence and power in the region and claims almost all of the South China Sea, through which US$ 5 trillion in shipping trade passes annually. But, the waters of the sea approach the coasts of the Philippines and other Southeast Asian nations as well.

The Philippine Government released some surveillance pictures of Chinese coast guard ships and barges at a disputed shoal in the South China Sea, though the charge was dismissed by the Chinese Government. India's better relations with other members are expected to keep China's excursions in the sea at will in check.

Modi has paid a visit to a number of countries after becoming India's Prime Minister. In 2015, he visited as many as 26 countries. In 2016 too he visited several countries holding discussions with the respective state heads and other important people. He addressed the Indian people settled abroad. His visits have not only strengthened India's relationships with other countries, but also endeavored to build a common consensus on issues of concern like terrorism, environmental pollution, slow trade, inadequate energy sources, hindrances in the way of peaceful use of nuclear energy, and disputes in sharing water, among others. Modi visits to ASEAN countries like Laos and Vietnam aim to enhance cooperation between India and the ASEAN bloc in political economic and security areas. Entering into important agreements with other countries, signing the Memorandums of Understanding (MoUs) and issuing joint statements, Narendra Modi has exhibited a high level of active diplomacy not hitherto reached by any earlier Indian Prime Minister. One can expect good results in the time to come.

Notes

1. https://www.quora.com/What-are-the-benefits-of-Modis-foreign-visits
2. "PM Narendra Modi's Japan Visit: 10 Key Takeaways." ET Bureau & Agencies. 2 Sept. 2014.
3. http://www.dnaindia.com/money/report-here-are-19-republic-day-deals-between-india-france-2170403
4. *Business Standard*. 12 December 2015.
5. www.mea.gov.in
6. www.indiandefensenews.in/2016/01/here-are-19-deals-signed-between-india.html
7. http://indianexpress.com/article/india/india-news-india/india-us-ink-six-agreements-including-climate-change-and-terrorism-2841485/
8. *Ibid.*
9. http://mea.gov.in/Images/pdf1/List_of_MOUs_26_02_2015.pdf
10. http://www.pmindia.gov.in/en/news_updates/india-us-joint-statement-during-pms-visit-to-usa/
11. *The Times of India*. 15 April 2015.
12. www.firstpost.com

13. The Indian Ocean Rim Association (IORA), formerly known as the Indian Ocean Rim Initiative and Indian Ocean Rim Association for Regional Cooperation (IOR-ARC), is an international organization consisting of coastal states bordering the Indian Ocean. The IORA is a regional forum, tripartite in nature, bringing together representatives of Government, Business and Academia, for promoting cooperation and closer interaction among them. It is based on the principles of Open Regionalism for strengthening Economic Cooperation, particularly on Trade Facilitation and Investment, Promotion as well as Social Development of the region.
14. http://currentaffairs.gktoday.in/india-south-korea-sign-7-agreements-enhance--bilateral-relations-05201522854.html
15. *The Quint*. 24 May 2014.
16. *The Economic Times*. 23 May 2014.
17. hindustantimes.com
18. http://www.governancenow.com/news/regular-story/key-takeaways-pm-modis-saudi-arabia-visit#sthash.IZjV4qid.dpuf
19. "The Sino-Brazilian Principles in a Latin American and BRICS Context: The Case for Comparative Public Budgeting Legal Research." *Wisconsin International Law Journal*. 13 May 2015.
20. http://www.brics-info.org/narendra-modis-africa-visit-key-takeaways/
21. Smruti S. Pattanaik. "Modi's Visit will Herald a New Chapter in India-Sri Lanka Relations." Institute for Defence Studies and Analyses. 12 March 2015.
22. www.the quint.com
23. *Hindustan Times*, 2 September 2016.
24. *Hindustan Times*, 7 September 2016.

CHAPTER 10

Narendra Modi's Foreign Policy

Ever since Narendra Modi took charge as India's 14th Prime Minister in May 2014, he has made foreign policy a cornerstone of his administration. Among his first decisions as head of government was an unconventional act of diplomacy—inviting eight foreign leaders of neighbouring countries to attend his swearing in ceremony. While many commentators claimed before his election that Modi would be a nationalist hardliner, a foreign affairs novice, or simply more of the same on external affairs, the PM instead proved more active and more pragmatic than many had expected. Travelling frequently across the globe, he has managed to infuse a personal enthusiasm into India's staid diplomatic establishment. In last three years, he has displayed an instinctive understanding of power in the conduct of world affairs, and he has also benefited from being less politically hamstrung than his predecessor Manmohan Singh, with whose worldview he in fact shares much in common.

Modi has given the impression that he aspires to be a great foreign policy PM, perhaps greater than—Jawaharlal Nehru, who left an indelible imprint and legacy; Indira Gandhi; who blended Nehru's idealistic vision with realpolitik; Narasimha Rao, who adopted policy to cope with the post-Cold War world; and Atal Bihari Vajpayee, who made India a nuclear weapons state.

According to Lord Palmerstone, a British statesman who served twice as Prime Minister in the mid-19th Century, a nation has neither "eternal allies" nor "perpetual enemies". It has only "eternal and perpetual" interests. Foreign policy, a medium to promote national interest, is moulded by the interplay of national, regional and global factors. In its 2014 general election manifesto, BJP committed itself to ensuring that "a resurgent India" got its "rightful place in the comity of nations and international institutions". It articulated a vision to fundamentally reboot and reorient the foreign policy goals, content and process. Judging by Modi Government's record so far, it seems that the PM understands foreign policy well and enjoys being the nations and chief diplomat. The past three years indicate that Modi's external policy five key elements.

1. India plans to be 'a leading power' rather than a mere 'balancing power'.
2. Diplomacy should be deployed to accelerate the nation's socio-economic transformation.
3. South Block should have a 360° global view and matching ability to influence the world through a web of international friendships and a balance of power favourable to India.
4. While increasing defence capability and economic strength, India must also utilize its abundant soft power.
5. Nurturing ties with the Indian diaspora and helping Indians in distress abroad is a priority.

In adopting these five approaches, Modi has borrowed from his predecessors, especially ex-PM Manmohan Singh, since the basic foreign policy framework remains unchanged. But variations through re-prioritisation, emphasis and nuance, sharper communication, strategic boldness, vigour and activism that Modi has, can hardly be ignored. The public articulations, combined with the nature, outcomes, and timings of Modi's diplomatic activities, offer a clear picture of India's priorities and strategic objectives. They are essentially five-fold:

1. Prioritizing an integrated neighbourhood—"Neighbourhood First".

2. Leveraging international partnerships to promote India's domestic development.
3. Ensuring a stable and multipolar balance of power in the Indo-Pacific—"Act East".
4. Dissuading Pakistan from supporting terrorism.
5. Advancing Indian representation and leadership on matters of global governance.

These are the yardsticks against which the international activities of Modi Government or any Indian government should be measured. In each case, it is important to assess the progress made, the setbacks experienced, and the long-term or structural challenges that will continue to confront India. Management of foreign relations is a complex business and the results take a long time to materialize. Yet we small try to analyse the Modi Government's foreign policies for the last three years.

A highlight of Modi's first years was his outreach to the United States. In September 2014, Washington rolled out the red carpet for a leader it had once publicly shunned, and Modi reciprocated by inviting Barack Obama to India's Republic Day celebrations on 26 January 2015, a first for a U.S. President. But beyond normalizing and enhancing relations will the U.S., Modi's international priorities were quickly made evident. Within his first year, he embarked upon state visits to India's immediate neighbourhood, three crucial Indian Ocean island countries, important Asia-Pacific powers (China, Japan, and Australia), and eventually Western Europe. His second year followed in much the same fashion, with a ground-breaking visit to Bangladesh, a swing through Central Asia, a long overdue visit to Afghanistan, and a renewed focus on the Middle East or West Asia. It also included a surprise stopover in Pakistan, a trip no Indian prime minister had managed since 2004. In addition, Modi has in his first two years played host in India to most of the world's top leaders, including those of the United States, China, Russia, France, Japan, and Germany. He also hosted a landmark India-Africa Forum Summit that involved 41 heads of state and government. In the third year as Prime Minister, Modi visited Japan, China, Switzerland, Mexico, Qatar,

Afghanistan and many African countries such as South Africa, Kenya, etc.

At the think India dialogue forum in 2013 when he was declared BJP's prime ministerial candidate, Modi out-lined his first foreign policy outlook in the following points:

(i) His priority would be to improve the relations with India's immediate neighbours as peace and tranquility in South Asia is essential for realizing his development agenda.

(ii) There would be para diplomacy in India wherein each state and city would have liberty to forge special relation with countries or federal states or even cities of their interest.

(iii) The relations with most countries would be dominated by bilateral trade. However, with important global powers there would be strategic partnerships.

Approaches of Permanent Members of UN Security Council towards India

When Narendra Modi formed the new government in May 2014, important world leaders expressed their willingness to work with him to strengthen their relations with India as it provides them a big market. The five permanent members of UN Security Council (UNSC), the US, UK, France, Russia and China sent their envoys to India within the first 100 days of forming the government by Modi, which is significant given India's long standing bid to get a permanent membership at UNSC.

China was first to send its envoy to India after Modi Government came into power. Chinese Foreign Minister Wang Yi visited new Delhi on 8 June 2014 and held bilateral talks with his counterpart and also called on PM Modi. China also indicated a willingness to reach a final settlement over border disputes with India.

Russian Deputy Chairman Dmitry Rogozin visited India on 18-19 June 2014. The two sides discussed the cooperation in joint defence production which is one of Modi's top agenda.

French Foreign Minister Laurent Fabius made an official visit to India from 29 June to 2 July 2014. He held talks with Prime Minister Modi and External Affairs Minister Sushma Swaraj. Strategic and defence cooperation was top on Fabius's agenda and he expressed hope of speedy completion of Dassault Rafate Jet deal as part of the much delayed Indian MMCRA project under the new government.

British Foreign Secretary William Hague visited India on 7-8 July 2014. During his meeting with Modi he pressed for Eurofighter Typhoon as an alternative for Dassault Rafale.

The US Secretary of State John Kerry emphasized the importance of US-India partnership in twenty-first century and he borrowed "Sabka Saath, Sabka Vikaas" a Hindi slogan from Modi's campaign meaning "together with all, development for all" and said that America shared this goal and was willing to work in full cooperation with the new government to realize it. Kerry arrived in New Delhi on 1 August 2014 and held bilateral talks with his Indian counterpart to make the groundwork ready for Modi's upcoming USA visit and also bided a strong lobby to gain support from India for sanctions on Russia amidst the 2014 Ukraine crisis. But the reply he received from External Affairs Minister Sushma Swaraj was: "There is no change in our policy. We think that foreign policy is in continuity. Foreign policy does not change with the change in the government."

Act East Policy (AEP)

India switched from the 'Look East Policy', which was formulated during PM Narasimha Rao's Government in 1992 for better economic engagement with its eastern neighbours, to 'Act East Policy', with a promise to widen the policy's scope and focus on action. The purpose of this shift was to show greater intent in realising what had long been an aspiration for India, i.e., to become an integral past of Asia. The greater urgency implicit in the shift in terminology is largely an outgrowth of Indian concerns regarding China's rise and the upsetting of Asia's delicate balance of power. In addition to the development of military and dual use Chinese infrastructure in India's neighbourhood and the Indian Ocean, India's concerns are three-fold—the risk of Chinese assertiveness on the disputed border, the possibility of Chinese primacy in the Indo-Pacific region, and an uneven economic playing field. Therefore, the primary objective of 'Act East Policy' is to promote economic cooperation, cultural ties and develop strategic relationship with countries in the Asia-Pacific region through continuous engagement at bilateral, regional, and multilateral levels thereby providing enhanced connectivity to the States of North Eastern Region including Arunachal Pradesh with other countries in our neighbourhood. The North East of India has been a priority in the Act East Policy (AEP) as it provides an interface between North East India including the state of Arunachal Pradesh and the ASEAN region. Various plans at bilateral and regional levels include steady efforts to develop and strengthen connectivity of Northeast with the ASEAN region through trade, culture, people-to-people contacts and physical infrastructure (road, airport, telecommunication, power, etc.). Some of the major projects include Kaladan Multi-modal Transit Transport Project, the India-Myanmar-Thailand Trilateral Highway Project, Rhi-Tiddim Road Project, the Bay of Bengal Initiative for Multi-Sectoral Technical and Economic Cooperation, etc.

In terms of the broader strategic context in Asia, India's AEP has three distinct facets—institutional, commercial, and security-related. The first has largely been successful, mostly as by-product of two decades of Indian economic growth. Barring the Asia-Pacific Economic Cooperation (APEC) forum, India has been integrated into Asia's multilateral networks, most notably the apex East Asia Summit. However, the conclusion of the Trans-Pacific Partnership agreement, the largest trade pact in history, threatens to affect India's commercial ambitions in the region, possibly costing India as much as 0.1 percent of GDP.

The India-ASEAN Plan of Action for the period 2016-20 has been adopted in August 2015 which identifies concrete initiatives and areas of cooperation along the three pillars of political-security, economic and socio-cultural. India continues with stepped up efforts to forge closer partnership with concerned regional and multilateral organization such as ASEAN, ARF, EAS, BIMSTEC, ACD, MCG, and IORA. On the civilization front, Buddhist and Hindu links could be energised to develop new contacts and connectivity between people. On connectivity, special efforts are being made to develop a coherent strategy, particularly for linking ASEAN with North East of India. Measures, including building transport infrastructure, encouraging airlines to enhance connectivity in the region, contacts between academic and cultural institutions and underway. India's economic engagement with ASEAN has been stepped up regional integration, and implementation of projects are priorities. The India-ASEAN Agreement on Trade in Service and Investments has entered into force for India and seven ASEAN countries from 1 July 2015. The India-ASEAN Trade Negotiating Committee has been tasked to undertake a review of the India-ASEAN Trade in Goods Agreement. India has also invited ASEAN member states to participate in the International Solar Alliance which it has co-launched with France on 30 November 2015 at COP-21. On strategic issues, India has increasing convergence on security interests with key partners both in bilateral and multilateral format. Closer cooperations in combating terrorism, collaborating for peace and stability in the region and promotion of maritime security based on international norms and laws are also being pursued.

However, bilateral economic relations with China offer a contradictory picture. On the one hand, India seeks to be a beneficiary of China's attempts at rebalancing its economy, and has become a destination for Chinese investment. The last two years saw a significant jump in Chinese foreign direct investment (FDI) from ₹ 767 crores in 2013-2014 to ₹ 3066 crores a year later. In fact, those two years also have accounted for over 70 percent of Chinese FDI ever into India.

But, now geopolitical realities in the region have been redefined, especially with the rise of an assertive China. The focus of all the countries in the region is to protect themselves from China's growing economic influence and military might. The major powers in the world, notably America and Eurozone, are trying to find new and better alliances to cope with the rise of China. These developments have necessitated a greater need for strengthening India's ties with ASEAN. That's why India's top leaders have visited nine out of ten ASEAN states during the last two years, discussing issues of importance with the respective state heads and extending cooperation and signing trade and other agreements. As a result, the relations are getting a renewed vitality.

India has focused to promote connectivity with other ASEAN states through Myanmar and Thailand. In November 2015, Modi allocated US$ 1 billion for promoting connectivity at the India-ASEAN Summit in Kuala Lumpur, which brought the primacy of "connectivity, culture, and commerce" to the fore. Modi government recognizes the fact that the success of AEP will be determined by its contribution to security and economic development of Northeast India.

India's relations with ASEAN countries have become multi-faceted as per the prevailing needs and circumstances, covering security concerns, strategic points, political affairs, terrorism threat, bilateral trade and defense collaboration, among others. Under Modi Government, India's relations with ASEAN states have not only advanced but also covered many more issues which were not covered earlier. India is also playing a more proactive role in the region.

Modi Government has aimed to rejuvenate India's ties with countries that have been neglected in recent years. Australia saw the first visit by an Indian Prime Minister in 28 years; Fiji saw the first visit in 33 years and Mongolia was visited by the first time ever by an Indian Prime Minister. Thus, the Act East Policy has also taken initiatives to expand India's focus beyond ASEAN to include other countries like Japan, Australia, Pacific Island nations, South Korea, and Mongolia.

As part of its extended Act East Policy, India is actively promoting good relations with smaller islands nations of the South Pacific, along with heavyweights in the region, and is seeking as well as providing cooperation on several issues, including blue economy (ocean based economy), oil and natural gas, mining, IT, health care, fishing and marine research, among others. Space collaboration with Pacific countries are of vital importance for India as they provide ISRO, India's space administration, an eye to monitor launch of their rockets.

Modi announced to convene international conference on blue economy in New Delhi in 2016 and invited all the experts from the island nations to set up Space Application Center, in partnership with ISRO, in any of the 14 countries and assured that there will be friendly port calls by the Indian Navy. Pacific leaders expressed their concerns over climate change and its effect on their respective counties and sought each other's cooperation in this regard. India voiced their concerns at the 2015 United Nations Climate Change Conference (COP 21) in Paris. In return all the 14 visiting heads of state/government reiterated their support to India's bid for permanent memberships at the reformed United Nations Security Council.

Thus, India's Act East Policy focuses on strengthening collaboration with the ASEAN. Partnerships with neighbouring countries aim at promoting economic revival through implementation of India-ASEAN FTA in services and investment and strategic cooperation to fight terrorism, freedom of navigation, maritime security and defence cooperation. Modi's use of soft power such as Buddhism, tourism, people-to-people contacts, and cultural ties with the region must also be harnessed. Beyond ASEAN, India is working to strengthen ties with East Asia, particularly Japan and Republic of Korea and Australia, which are both relevant for India's strategic and economic interests. Continuous engagement with China too is necessary to expand cooperation, particularly on the economic front. With India being the second largest shareholder of the Asian Infrastructure Investment Bank (AIIB) and an equal partner in the National Development Bank (NDB), the forthcoming decades must ensure that areas of conflict are minimised and economic integration for the benefit of both nations are fully leveraged.

Neighbourhood First Policy

Signals may not speak as loudly as actions, but they go a long way in diplomacy. Modi Government's decision to host all South Asian heads of state (and Mauritius) to Modi's swearing-in ceremony signaled that the neighbourhood would be central in its foreign policy. The excellent beginning was followed by another notable feat—Modi's visit to all SAARC countries, except Maldives, in his first 19 months. The list also includes Pakistan, which his predecessor could not visit even once during his 10-years tenure. This approach of "Neighbourhood First" of Modi Government is meant to indicate four things.

(a) New Delhi's willingness to give political and diplomatic priority to its immediate neighbours and the Indian Ocean island states.

(b) To provide neighbours with support, as needed, in the form of resources, equipment, and training.

(c) Greater connectivity and integration, so as to improve the free flow of goods, people, energy, capital, and information.

(d) To promote a model of India-led regionalism with which its neighbours are comfortable.

The new diplomatic priority on the region is evident in Modi's visits to all of India's neighbouring countries (barring the Maldives), as well as regular leadership meetings in India and on the sidelines of multilateral summits. Modi's first state visit was to neighbouring Bhutan, where he promised assistance with hydroelectric power projects; next was Nepal, where no Indian Prime Minister had visited in almost two decades. Modi signed a land-swap deal with Bangladesh resolving a 70-year old political and humanitarian issue involving thousands of people stuck in pockets of land belonging to one country within the other's territory. In Sri Lanka, where the Rajapaksa Government chose to get closer to China at significant strategic cost to India, recovery of lost ground seemed imminent with the election of the new President Maithripala Sirisena.

India has become more forthcoming in providing support and in capacity building, whether concluding its biggest ever defence sale to Mauritius, or in providing humanitarian assistance to Nepal or Sri Lanka. With Bangladesh, the completion of the Land Boundary Agreement, improvements in energy connectivity, and steps taken towards accessing the port of Chittagong have all been crucial developments that help to set a positive tone for a region long defined by cross-border suspicion and animosity. India's focus on connectivity is also gradually extending outward, whether to Chabahar in Iran or Kaladan in Myanmar.

Although India will continue investing in the South Asian Association for Regional Cooperation (SAARC) as an institutional vehicle, it has also expressed a willingness to develop issue-specific groupings that are not held hostage to consensus—a "SAARC minus X" approach. For examples, Bangladesh-Bhutan-India-Nepal (BBIN) grouping meant to advance motor vehicle movement, water power management, and inter-grid connectivity; and the common SAARC Satellite, which India has decided to proceed with despite Pakistan's objections.

Modi's "neighbourhood first" approach, however, encompasses more than South Asia and follows a "proactive foreign policy" in the extended neighbourhood. It aims not just to react to events unfolding in Asia but to shape them. Modi has developed personal relationships via high-level visits—24 of his 37 trips through 2015 were to Asian countries. The visits have been followed by proposals for cooperation in areas of mutual interest in the economic and strategic domains.

These concerted efforts have so far had mixed results. Bangladesh and Bhutan have clearly been positive responses for India. Ties with Sri Lanka have proved a mixed bag, despite the electoral loss of former president Mahinda Rajapaksa, who had testy relations with New Delhi. However, President Maithripala Sirisena remains well-disposed and personally invested in better relations with India. The Maldives has proved more difficult. India has continuing concerns about the fate of former president Mohamed Nasheed, although several defence agreements were concluded during the visit to India of incumbent Abdulla Yameen.

Despite efforts, Modi has failed to make a breakthrough in Pakistan. The relationship seems stuck in the same vicious circle, as a terrorist attack in an Indian airbase days after Modi's seemingly spontaneous visit to Pakistan has once again raised questions about the prospects of meaningful dialogue. India's approach to Nepal floundered when a constitution that India finds inadequately representative was promulgated. India was accused of enforcing an unofficial economic blockade, and its image in Nepal has deteriorated rapidly. Considering that the neighbourhood focus comes after years of neglect and ambivalence, the policy will need time to yield results. Many of the issues affecting India's immediate neighbourhood have domestic motivations and offer little scope for India to intervene.

With respect to all of its neighbours including Nepal, Modi's visits were guided by three objectives—maximizing security, expanding India's sphere of influence, and securing economic growth; and in this direction India has taken concrete steps over the past three years to promote goodwill and deepen economic and social connectivity. But nationalist sentiments in all these countries—often directed against India as the region's predominant power—will continue to present a challenge. Anti-Indian sentiments will also, paradoxically, drag India further into these countries' domestic politics, suggesting that undulating highs and lows in its neighbourhood relationships will now be the norm. Furthermore, for all of India's neighbours, China is now prepared to step in to provide financial, military, infrastructural, and even political assistance and act as a potential alternative to India. This new development is something India will have to carefully monitor and appropriately respond to particularly if Indian security interests are seriously compromised. As the status quo power in its neighbourhood, India will have to constantly play defence in its own backyard.

Addressing Indian space scientists at the Satish Dhawan Space Centre is Sriharikota after the successful launch of PSLV C23 rocket, the Prime Minister Modi said that the fruits of India's space missions should reach other developing nations, especially India's neighbours. He told the scientists that they should develop a SAARC satellite. He said, "We should dedicate this satellite to our neighbourhood as India's gift.... India is rooted in our age-old ethos of 'Vasudeva Kutumbakom'. Our space science reflects that we should share the fruit of this with our neighbouring countries." Modi is a strong believer in SAARC and is hopeful of its potential in strengthening regional cooperation and developmental activities. He is giving more importance to SAARC as confirmed by *New York Times*: "SAARC has so far failed to serve its purpose as compared to ASEAN and other regional groupings, and even the bloc has failed to hold summits at regular interval. Now, the Indian policy-makers started focusing again on its role in building and nourishing institution like SAARC to strengthen regional cooperation."[1]

Modi Government's neigbourhood policy has been criticized by some people saying that through it India is interfering in the internal matters of some countries like Nepal, Sri Lanka, Bangladesh and Maldives. But, it has brought some economic progress in the region. Bangladesh has high economic hopes as it steps into a low middle income status. The recent agreements signed between India and Bangladesh complement Dhaka's quest to get integrated into the world economy, especially through better connectivity by land and sea. Many of these agreements will go a long way in improving connectivity through roads and rail, easing the time and cost of transport. Signing of the landmark Bangladesh, Bhutan, India, Nepal (BBIN) Motor Vehicles Agreement (MVA) for the Regulation of Passenger, Personnel and Cargo Vehicular Traffic is a significant step. After its implementation the agreement is said to have the potential to increase intra-regional trade within South Asia by almost 60 percent and with the rest of the world by over 30 percent.

Thus, Modi's neighbourhood first policy shows economic promise, but it needs a proper mechanism in place to adequately respond to political and security situations in South Asia.

India's Issues with China

India's relations with China have always been complex. It is an open secret that the ties between China and India have a long and chequered history. The two neighbours fought a short border war in 1962 and since then a sense of mistrust has prevailed and dogged their bilateral ties. Despite visits of leaders and other delegates to each other's country and assurances of cooperation from both sides, there are many unresolved issues. China has not supported India's pitch for permanent membership of the United Nations Security Council and is the only one of the P5 members trying to thwart India's bid. However, economic complementarity draws the two countries closer together, while political and strategic divergences pull them apart. India needs Chinese investment, China needs India's market; but neither seems to agree on sensitive political issues, viz., border question, terrorism, Pakistan, India's bid for membership of UN Security Council, Nuclear Suppliers Group, etc. Yet, they find ways to work together on numerous platforms such as RIC, Shanghai Cooperation Organisation and BRICS.

Narendra Modi realized the importance of maintaining good relations with China. Many efforts were initiated by him, immediately after becoming India's Prime Minister. In July 2014, India's Army Chief Bikram Singh went to Beijing for a three-day trip. Later that month, Modi met General Secretary of the Communist party of China, Xi Jinping for the first time during the BRICS summit in Brazil. The two leaders met for almost 80 minutes, where the latter said, "When India and China meet, the world watches us."

In September 2014, Xi visited India, and Modi, breaking protocol, received him in Ahmedabad. China promised US$ 20 billion worth of investments in India over the next five years.

When US President Barack Obama visited India in January 2015 for the second time, Modi reportedly spent some 45 minutes with him talking about China. Both the leaders expressed concern about Beijing's expansionist stance, especially in the South China Sea.

In February 2015, External Affairs Minister Sushma Swaraj visited Beijing and met President Xi, who said, "I have full confidence on the future of China and India relations and I believe that good progress will be achieved in the growth of bilateral relations...."

The relations between these two Asian giants warmed up in the aftermath of the visit of the Chinese President Xi Jinping to India in September 2014 and the visit of the Indian Prime

Minister Narendra Modi to China in May 2015, but the relations have once again hurtled downhill as they went in pursuit of their respective foreign policy agendas.

The unresolved issues between India and China include border disputes, Chinese military incursions into Indian territory, established military infrastructure along border areas by both the countries, China's strong strategic bilateral relations with Pakistan, and its claim over the entire South China Sea. Although, much was agreed between the two nations during Modi's visit to China, no concrete response has come from China.

India's bid to enter the Nuclear Suppliers Group (NSG)—the exclusive group that controls global nuclear commerce, was scuttled by China in June 2016 insisting that India sign the nuclear Non-Proliferation Treaty (NPT) before gaining admission. China's stance put a question mark on cooperation between China and India in international fora.[2]

The Indian Ocean region is India's nautical backyard, but of late it is turning into a hotspot due to growing Chinese strategic presence over the region's numerous strategically located archipelagos.[3] In order to counter the recent moves made by China in the name of President Xi's pet Maritime Silk Road project, India has started to reach out its maritime neighbours in the Indian Ocean region with proposals of enhanced economic and security cooperation.[4]

The whole world knows that Pakistan has been harbouring terrorism and India has warned it a number of times and asked it to stop it. China, despite knowing fully well Pakistan's clandestine plans against India, is not supporting India's fight against terrorism. China put a "technical hold" over India's attempts to designate the Jaish-e-Mohammed chief, Maulana Masood Azhar, as a terrorist at the United Nations committee. Azhar was the mastermind behind a host of terror attacks in India.

But, Narendra Modi has created huge pressure on Pakistan through meetings and talks with the leaders of other countries, notably the United States, United Kingdom, France and Russia, and has been able to isolate Pakistan. There is hardly any support for Pakistan, except from China and Korea—the states that are infamous for nuclear proliferation.

China continues to help Pakistan. Beijing has announced that it will invest US$ 46 billion in the China-Pakistan Economic Corridor, which will connect Kashgar in China's Xinjiang province with the port of Gwadar in Pakistan.

Gwadar is a deep-sea port situated in the Arabian Sea at Gwadar in the Balochistan province in Pakistan. It has featured prominently in the China-Pakistan Economic Corridor (CPEC) plan, and is considered to be a crucial link between the ambitious One Belt, One Road and Maritime Silk Road projects.[5]

In May 2016, Indian Prime Minister Narendra Modi and Iranian President Hassan Rouhani signed a series of twelve agreements in Tehran, in which India Ports Global Pvt. Limited will refurbish a 640-meter long container handling facility, and reconstruct a 600-meter long berth at the Port of Chabahar. According to *The Economic Times*, the deal is a part of India's larger geo-strategic calculations to begin access to Middle East and Central Asia and counter China-Pakistan's plan to develop Gwadar port.[6] *Global Times* also expressed a similar opinion saying "...what interests New Delhi more is a comprehensive scheme that can reshape India's geopolitics to the northwest and extend its influence further into the Middle East, Central Asia and the trans-Caucasus. Although, New Delhi ostensibly highlights economic considerations...its larger geo-strategic calculations and ambitions are obvious."

Although, the direct gateway through Pakistan is the shortest route, considering its animosity with India, Pakistan will not grant India access. Therefore India is developing a sea-land route bypassing Pakistan. With this new route, India is likely to take further advantages of its ties with Iran and Afghanistan, and reduce Pakistan's political and economic influence in the region. It goes to Narendra Modi's credit that he has taken this step to counter China-Pakistan alliance. The future will show how the three defining characteristics—cooperation, competition and desire to avoid confrontation—shape the relationship between India and China that will determine Asia's destiny.

Pakistan—Engagement and Isolation

Pakistan's relative importance for India has declined significantly over the past three years. The development of nuclear weapons by both countries has ensured an uneasy peace, while Pakistan, despite Indian entreaties, has refused to open up economically. Terrorism by entities based in Pakistan, and supported by the country's military and intelligence agencics, continues to be directed at India, although certain measures have helped reduced the number of infiltrations and severity of attacks. Still Pakistan is a political hot button issue, and India-Pakistan relations dominate the political discourse in India.

It is well-known fact that Pakistan supports terrorism in India. But India's options are limited. For all the talk about retaliating against Pakistan, particularly militarily, such steps risk an escalation to the nuclear level. Containing Pakistan is not a possibility either. India's economy is not yet large enough, it is limited by geography, and Pakistan continues to find support in the Gulf, the United States, and China. Any attempt of India's responding "in the same coin" is unnecessary as Pakistan is doing a perfectly good job destabilizing itself. Nor can Pakistan be ignored. Indian passiveness is exactly what Pakistan wants, for it would invite third-party intervention, something a rising sovereign India would naturally resent.

After several attempts by Modi Government at setting the terms of engagement over the past three years, India has had to settle upon a two-track policy. The first is to continue keeping lines of engagement open, as long as terrorism tops the agenda and that dialogue is strictly bilateral in nature. This has resulted in a peculiar ping-pong—inviting Nawaz Sharif to Delhi in 2014 resulted in Pakistan trying to involve the Hurriyat, a coalition of Kashmiri separatists, and Pakistani shelling along the Line of Control with India. The 2015 Ufa Declaration was heavily criticised in Pakistan and led to Islamabad calling off the national security advisor talks under rather farcical circumstances. Modi's Lahore stopover in December 2015 was followed soon after by the Pathankot attack. And the response to India allowing Pakistani investigators access to the Pathankot site was Pakistan producing an alleged Indian spy, whom India insists is an innocent former Navy Officer kidnapped from Iran. But India has repeatedly tried to renew talks in good faith, only for elements in Pakistan to make brazen attempts at sabotaging the process. India's constant willingness to engage has kept the United States and others from interjecting themselves in the region.

Indian Government is not satisfied with simple bilateral engagement, but has had to take countermeasures and steps to delegitimise state support for terrorism. New Delhi's critical response to the U.S. decision to supply Pakistan with F-16 fighter planes and prime ministerial visits to Saudi Arabia, the United Arab Emirates, and Afghanistan have all been part of an attempt to isolate Pakistan, to slowly compel its deep state to reconsider its priorities. It cannot be expected that the U.S. or Saudi Arabia will change their policies for Pakistan overnight, but both now have the ability to dehyphenate their subcontinental relationships. Of greater concern in this respect is China's decision to go forward with the ambitious, multi-billion dollar China-Pakistan Economic Corridor. While India has expressed its concerns, dissuading Beijing from this path will be a severe challenge, since much of China's historical support for Pakistan has been driven by its desire to balance against India.

Prime Minister Modi's efforts with Pakistan have not yet borne results. A statemate continues. The only difference now is that India's Pakistan Policy has assumed a certain consistency and that it is playing the chessboard with white, rather than black pieces, seizing control of the momentum and initiative. The process of both engaging the isolating Pakistan despite repeated provocations will be long, frustrating, and politically unpopular at home. However, as long as domestic pressures can be navigated, India's continuing bilateral engagement with Pakistan, its efforts at internationally isolating it, and its offering a viable alternative model of South Asian engagement remain the only real prospect for resolving the Pakistan problem on India's terms. Therefore, India clearly has to do a much better job remaining vigilant in its own neighbourhood, managing or proactively addressing the domestic political fallout of its Pakistan policy, and better coordinating external outcomes with internal development, all the while raising its ambitions and improving its ability to follow through.

Indo-US Strategic Moves

Victory of the BJP in the May 2014 elections bringing in a single party government under the leadership of Narendra Modi seemed to have opened new avenues for restoring the momentum in the evolving strategic partnership between India and the US. Restored thrust was amply mirrored in three cabinet level officials of the Obama Administration—Secretary of State, John Kerry; Secretary of Commerce, Penny Pritzker; and Secretary of Defence, Chuck Hagel—visiting India in quick succession and generating scepticism over the future of India-US relations. However, these apprehensions were soon laid to rest with Modi's visit to the US in September 2014 and Obama's visit to India as chief guest on India's Republic Day in January 2015. These visits signalled the tenacity, which Indo-US ties had come to acquire and the significance that each accords the other. Prime Minister Modi held his first summit with the US President in Washington in September 2014, having met him 2 months earlier at the BRICS Summit at Fortaleza, Brazil. Modi's visit to the US was hailed as a landmark development that paved the way for setting in motion many stalled dialogues on energy, technology transfer, trade, security and other issues. The visit saw the US President foregoing protocol and even penning a joint Op Ed in the Washington Post, a leading US newspaper.

On the economic front, robust ties with the US are very essential for economic development of India. India's fiscal deficit stood at 4.5 percent of India's GDP in 2013-14 and its economy grew only by 4.7 percent. Close economic relations with the US is considered ideal for the Modi Government's vision of ensuring an economically strong India. The US is keen on increasing ties with India on matters of trade and investment, and it aims to take bilateral trade from $100 billion to $500 billion. Modi has sought investment from the Indian Diaspora and business community in the US, has touted for foreign direct investment, and promoted his "Make in India" concept to make India a manufacturing hub. Discussions in the India-US Trade Policy Forum (TPF), which were since 2010 were resumed in 2014 with a special emphasis on resolving the IPR issue. In October 2014, the Indian Ministry of Commerce and Industry announced the formation of a think tank to review India's extant IPR framework. Despite these encouraging signs, there has been some concern regarding the trajectory of the India-US economic ties. For example, regarding Modi's ability to attract the $35 billion investment from Japan and $20 billion investment pledge from China made many commentators observe that there was no such investment forthcoming from the US. But Modi's economic diplomacy during his visit to the US was successful in attracting potential investment to the tune of $41 billion in the next three to four years from corporate America.

Apart from boosting economic relations, there have been certain distinct advances in the defence relations of India and the US. The US has welcomed the Modi Government's initiatives to carry out reforms in defence procurement and allow the private sector to have a larger share in design and production of defence equipment. Modi has allowed FDI up to 49 percent in the defence sector without any mandatory transfer of technology. Modi Government's major achievement in the defence arena has been the incorporation of co-production of weapons in India, along with transfer of technology through the Defence Trade and Technology Initiative (DTTI) in the renewed Indo-US ten-year Defence Framework Agreement. It shows India's attempts at diversifying its sources of arms production and procurement as well as the coming of age of Indo-US defence relations.

China's missile capabilities include a missile network capable of credibly threatening US forces deployed in China's maritime periphery and forms the foundation of its anti-access and area-denial (AZ/AD) capabilities. The American response has been development of a concept known as the Air-Sea Battle concept, which creates a force that can attack targets even in a prohibitive anti-access environment. As these scenarios may play out in India's immediate vicinity, and given China's less than acquiescent relations with India, especially on security issues, close cooperation with the US on defence would be prudent diplomacy.

With regard to nuclear issues relating to India's nuclear liability act and Washington's support for Delhi's membership of the NSG, it was reported that the two sides found innovative ways to prevail over the impasse allowing the leaders to proclaim a "breakthrough understanding" on the nuclear issues. The US appears determined to retain its military and economic presence in the Asia Pacific/Indo-Pacific region. A stronger partnership with India could enable the US to prop India as a balancer to a rising China in the region. India has been viewed as the "linchpin" of Washington's strategic rebalancing towards the Asia-Pacific, and US Vice-President Joe Biden has described India's "Look East" policy as complimentary to the US' rebalancing toward Asia, which has been further bolstered with the change in nomenclature from Look East to Act East under the Modi Government.

A rising China has united the US and India, fostering strategic cooperation between them. In a first of its kind, the US and India released a joint statement on the Asia-Pacific and Indian Ocean Region in 2015. It explicitly spells out the importance accorded by both countries to safeguarding maritime security and ensuring freedom of navigation and flight, especially in the South China Sea. India has also been favourably disposed towards the US administration's New Silk Route and the Indo-Pacific Economic Corridor as alternatives to China's Maritime Silk Road. In addition, India is keen to revive the India-US-Japan trilateral relations and the Quadrilateral Security Dialogue (QSD).

Despite advances in areas like co-production of defence items, differences between the US and India remain. For example, there is no advancement on the issue of climate change; save Modi's articulation that India is willing to cooperate closely with America to conclude a global climate agreement. Moreover, India comprehends that the US would not abandon Pakistan as its strategic ally despite the mention of "joint and concerted efforts" for dismentling safe havens of terrorists and criminal networks. The US is also aware of the importance of Iran and

Russia to Indian interests. Other contentions issues relate to IPR, trade and investment barriers, among others. Notwithstanding these contentions, cooperative relations between India and the US have become the mainstay of their relations in the Post-Cold War era and the Modi Government seems keen to further bolster the ties. India hopes to get US support to emerge as an economically, technologically and militarily vibrant country and the US views India as a valued partner, which can further the American vision of a stable Asia. Steps taken by Modi and Obama, however incremental, are symptomatic of the leaders' understanding that India and the US have stakes in shaping the Indo-Pacific region in particular and the world in general in terms favourable to them, which will be best achieved through cooperation between the two nations.

Fast Track Diplomacy

While hard power and soft power are necessary attributes of sustainable power projection by nation states, smart and fast power can help nations, big and small, find their way through or adapt to complex and rapidly changing strategic environments. By acting "fast", Modi Government has more than neutralized, in a short period of time, the negative impact of its predecessor's months of inaction. The "fast-tract diplomacy" the Modi Government draws attention to four different categories of diplomatic engagement by Modi and Swaraj—first, with South Asian neighbours; second, with East and West Asian neighbours; third, with five permanent members of the United Nations Security Council (P-5); and finally, India's most important economic and strategic partners, led now by Japan and including Australia, Brazil, South Africa and Singapore. Within its first 100 days in office, the Modi Government has engaged all. After taking charge as India's External Affairs Minister, Sushma Swaraj held round-table meeting with all Indian heads of missions to the SAARC region, ASEAN region and Middle East separately as a follow up measure to carry forward the leads gained by high-profile visits and exchanges.

Modi's fast track diplomacy over the last three years has taken him and his ministerial colleagues to a number of countries while he himself has averaged about one trip each month, visiting many world capitals.

Modi listed his priorities as soon as he took over as the Prime Minister of India. The directive were clear—act east, link west, re-integrate South Asia, and do business with affluent nations. His itinerary is therefore carefully planned by keeping his priorities in mind. Over 100 foreign dignitaries have met him, because he enjoys a certain level of curiosity in foreign capitals. During his tours, particularly to China, Japan, US and Canada, he has got commitments of nearly US$ 100 billion in investments.

It has often been questioned why Modi has not been taking External Affairs Minister Sushma Swaraj on most of his trips, which is an unnecessary departure from established diplomatic practice, not only in India but the world over. The former Foreign Secretary Shyam Saran believes Modi has introduced some fresh nuances and pursued foreign policy objectives with a vigour and determination that was missing in the past few years. There is also a difference in leadership style of Modi and Sushma Swaraj. Modi being more dynamic and more influential, he believes in being direct and discusses most issues with the leaders of the host countries himself. Modi takes most of the decisions himself. On crucial decisions like granting e-visas to Chinese and purchasing 32 ready-to-fly Rafale aircraft, the home and defence ministers were not consulted. And there are many instances, where even Sushma Swaraj has been bypassed, critics have pointed out.[7]

Paradiplomacy

The term "constituent diplomacy" or "paradiplomacy" was coined in 1990 by the American scholar John Kincaid, who outlined a foreign policy role for local and regional governments within a democratic federal system. With the growing policymaking capacity of sub-state entities paradiplomacy can be employed by states, provinces and even cities both in federal as well as unitary states for solving diplomatic issues. Economic paradiplomacy related to trade and investment in particular has become an institutionalised practice across the world.

Paradiplomacy can be employed with a variety of aims which can range from bringing in a decentralised dimension to international debates to internationalisation of domestic issues by bringing regional issues on the global stage, promoting trade, tourism, cultural ties and even post-conflict reconciliation to local political activism being sought for international support. Subnational relations can also be conducted to promote and attract investments seeking region-specific economic advantages. In more ways than one, paradiplomacy owes its origins to globalisation. As the world economy has become increasingly global and increasingly integrated in a variety of ways, sub-national units, such as regions, states, provinces and even cities, find their functions and activities circumscribed by the global system. Federalism is also a key contributor to the growth of paradiplomacy. Sub-national actors such as states and provinces which have a formal legal personality are necessarily more likely to engage in international activities designed to promote and protect local and international interests and prerogatives.

The credit of introducing the concept of paradiplomacy in India's foreign policy goes to Prime Minister Narendra Modi. As globalisation has eroded traditional boundaries, the Central Government by itself is not well-equipped to meet the challenges posed by new political, economic and social forces. It is here that sub-national involvement in international affairs can help push forward India's stand on key issues. In a country as sizeable as India, there is a definitive need for decentralisation of foreign policy implementation and in selected areas of diplomacy. It is argued that states are often better equipped than the Central Government to undertake diplomatic measures in areas of trade, commerce, foreign direct investment, education, cultural exchanges and also outsourcing of business. Another factor that brings the importance of paradiplomacy to the surface is that there might be cases where the Central Government will differ with state governments on ideological and political grounds, which makes it likely that some judgements of New Delhi may not be viewed in the best interest of states and vice versa. In addition, given India's size, provincial governments are often better placed to enhance diplomatic relations with other governments in their neighbourhood because of geographical, cultural, historical and economic reasons. For example, West Bengal can have more successful paradiplomatic relations with Bangladesh and Bhutan than an MEA official stationed at the country's capital. Similarly, Kerala has vested interests in engaging in diplomatic relations with the Gulf countries as a large number of the state's residents find jobs in those countries.

Modi has also propagated the term "city diplomacy", which has gained increased usage and acceptance, particularly as a strand, if not a variant, of paradiplomacy and public diplomacy. Town twinning, as it's more commonly called, is a concept where cities develop their own foreign relations based on cooperative agreements. These pairings can be conducted for cultural or economic exchanges, which, is turn are beneficial to both cities/ towns. While such city-to-city relationship or the twinning model is not entirely new to India, there is a need for India to substantially increase its engagements with other nations at the subnational level. Paradiplomacy has the potential to not only strengthen the federal structure of the Indian state but also radically alter the trajectory of Indian foreign policy by helping regional governments to realise their potential in the conduct of cross border relations.

During the visit of Chinese President Xi Jinping, there were Town Twinning agreement between Mumbai and Shanghai, Ahmedabad and Guangzhou, and Sister States' agreement between Gujarat and Guangdong province of China. Earlier Varanasi signed a partnership agreement with Kyoto, Japan.

West Asia Policy

India has interests in economic, political, security and strategic fields with the West Asian nations as they supply's two thirds of our energy needs, employ over 6 million Indians and account for over 110 billion dollars of trade. Modi Government's 'Link West' policy indicates India's emerging economic and strategic relations with countries of West Asia in order to boost its energy security and a counterbalance to the strategic influence of other major powers in the region.

India has always shared a special relation with its West Asian neighbours and that India had emerged as the second largest trading partner, after the US, of Gulf Cooperation Council (GCC) member countries Saudi Arabia, Oman, the United Arab Emirates, Kuwait, Bahrain, and Qatar. India given its uniqueness with a fully functioning democracy, a multi-religious, multi-ethnic and multi-lingual pluralist society is also being viewed by many as a model to the societies in West Asia. Indeed this possible role of a model can very well be taken advantage of to serve the mutual interests of the countries in the region and that of India. The Prime Minister Modi's new Foreign Policy efforts are also able to break the conventional dichotomy of Arab-India relations and Israel-India relations. Both Arab countries and Israel want stronger and greater engagement with India. Neither Arab nations, nor Israel is forcing Delhi to select between them.

The PM Modi's visit to the UAE shows Delhi's intention to get more close with West Asian countries. An Indian Prime Minister has visited the UAE over 34 years, the country that contains 2.6 million Indian workers and Delhi's third largest economic partner with approximately 60 billion bilateral trade. Modi's visit covered multi issues, including trade, terrorism, and outreach to Indian diaspora, especially the blue-collared Indian workers. Modi proposed to the UAE's investors for investing in the infrastructure projects and both countries planned to reach a target of US$ 75 billion to support infrastructure investment in India with the help of the UAE-India Infrastructure Investment Fund. India and the UAE are serious on the issue of terrorism. The joint statement says that the two countries shall coordinate efforts to counter radicalization and misuse of religion by groups and countries by inciting hatred, perpetrating and justifying terrorism or pursuing political aims. Further, the statement says, "on all states to reject and abandon the use of terrorism against other countries, dismantle terrorism infrastructures where they exist, and bring perpetrators of terrorism to justice".

One of the most important development in India's "Link West" policy is the defence ties between India and the Kingdom of Saudi Arabia, which is not only significant for both countries, but for the whole conflict ridden Arab region. The Indian Air

Force made a visit to Saudi Arabia which has brought a new high in the Indo-Saudi defence relations. This visit of IAF is not new in the field of military and defence relations between New Delhi and Riyadh. The first major bilateral partnership between India and Saudi Arabia was the Delhi Declaration of 2006, which was signed during King Abdullah's visit to India. The relationship further extends by Riyadh Declaration of 2010, which was signed between Indian Prime Minister Manmohan Singh and King Abdullah. This declaration is considered as a cornerstone of the strategic relationship between India and Saudi Arabia, and it boosts a roadmap for a closer New Delhi-Riyadh partnership. The first serious attempts about cooperation on defence and military issues was the first meeting of the India-Saudi Arabia joint committee in 2012 which was spearheaded by Saudi Chief of Armed Forces Operations, Major General Suleiman Sale al-Khalifa. The major outcomes of the meeting were promoting defence exchanges and increasing military-to-military contacts. The new boost in the defence cooperation came in early 2014 when Salman bin Abdulaziz al Abdulaziz al Saud, the contemporary crown prince, the deputy Prime Minister, and the defence minister of Saudi Arabia visited India. A memorandum of understanding (MoU) on defence engagement was signed between India and Saudi Arabia, which allows military training, education and exchange of defence-related information and many more related fields. The joint naval exercise of the Indian Navy and the Royal Saudi Navy (RSN) and the joint Air Force exercise of the Indian Air Force (IAF) and the Royal Saudi Air Force (RSAF) have built trust and confidence between both countries for further cooperation in the field of defence.

The West Asia region is in the process of re-settlement and re-alignment of regional politics due to the recent entry of Iran in the international arena through the historic nuclear deal. India's growing relations with Iran may be a bridge Saudi Arabia and Israel to Teheran. A trustful relation between regional powers only can bring peace and stability in the region. In the midst of these challenges, the West Asian nations and India should have good and trustful relations.

Indo-Brazil Relations

The relationship between India and Brazil is extensive and comprehensive covering every important segment of interaction as seen at all the three levels—bilateral, plurilateral in forum such as IBSA, BRICS, BASIC, G-20, G-4, and in the larger multilateral arena such as the UN, WHO, UNESCO, WIPO, etc. Bilateral relations between India and Brazil have acquired the dimension of a strategic partnership in the last decade under the leadership of former Brazilian President Luiz Inacio Lula da Silva. His successor President Dilma Rousseff's first ever visit to India in March 2012 provided greater commitment and content to this relationship.

On 16 July 2014, President Rousseff hosted Prime Minister Narendra Modi in Brasilia on the margins of the 6th BRICS summit. Although it was not a bilateral visit, President Rousseff, in a special gesture, received PM Modi with full military honours at the Presidential Palace before their meeting over breakfast. Modi described Brazil as a key global partner for India. He noted that as two democracies and major emerging economies, India and Brazil not only have vast potential for bilateral cooperation, but also to strengthen each other in international forums and advance the interests of the developing world at large. President Rousseff emphasised the special place this relationship enjoyed in Brazil's foreign policy, because of the potential for bilateral cooperation and the international significance of their partnership.

India and Brazil agreed to take steps to further expand and diversify trade and investment flows and deepen cooperation in agriculture and dairy science, conventional and renewable energy, space research and application, defence, cyber security, and environment conservation. They also agreed to intensify their cooperation in international forums and multilateral institutions, including the G-20. As leaders of G-4 countries, Prime Minister Modi and President Rousseff called urgent progress on reforms of the United Nations, including the Security Council. The two countries have also signed three agreements—MoU on Cooperation in the Field of Environment; Implementing Arrangement Establishing Cooperation in

Augmentation of a Brazilian Earth Station for Receiving and Processing Data from Indian Remote Sensing (IRS) Satellites; and MoU on Cooperation in the Establishment of a consultation mechanism on mobility and consular issues.

India and Brazil have strategic partnership in a wide range of fields such as Economic and Trade, Mining and Energy, Agriculture and Food Processing, Science and Technology, Environment and Sustainable Development, Technical Cooperation, Social and Health issues, Education, Culture, Tourism, Sports, Consular issues, and Regional and Multilateral issues. There have been two way investments between India and Brazil. While the Brazilian companies have invested in automobiles, IT, mining, energy, biofuels, footwear sectors in India, the Indian companies have invested in such sectors as IT, Pharmaceutical, Energy, agri-business, mining, engineering/auto sectors.

Indo-Canada Relations

In April 2015, Modi visited Canada, which was the first bilateral visit to that country by an Indian Prime Minister in 42 years. India made nuclear deal with the Canada's biggest producer of uranium, Cameco—signed a US$ 280 million, five-year deal to supply uranium to fuel Indian nuclear reactors. The Indo-Canada Chamber of Commerce (ICCC) stated that India-Canada relations are poised for a leap in the coming years. Prime Minister Narendra Modi's visit to Canada has put the growing bilateral ties on a fast track. ICCC President Sanjay Makkar said in an interview that Canada was not willing much to engage with India till a few years ago when it supported India in the Nuclear Suppliers Group in 2008. After that, things started moving and we signed the nuclear deal in 2010. During the past four-five years, our relationship has really taken off.

According to the Indo-Canada Chamber of Commerce president, "Modi's visit has started a new era in India-Canada relations. So much is now happening in our relations. Canadians are showing a lot more interest in India now. More top-level delegations have started visiting each others' countries to explore new areas of cooperation. A FICCI delegation is coming here later this month, with its focus on infrastructure investment, large projects, real estate, etc."

Because of new streamlined Canadian immigration rules, he said, more and more skilled Indians are able to come to Canada. "On the other hand, Canadian universities and colleges are rushing to India to tie up with Indian institutions and even set up campus there. Many of them have signed exchange programmes with their Indian counterparts. The number of Indian students in Canada has suddenly grown many fold—from a mere 3,000-4,000 just a few years ago to almost 30,000 now," said Mr. Makkar.

Modi held bilateral talks with Canadian Prime Minister Stephen Harper and signed various MoUs like in areas of cyber security, skill development, cooperation in the railways and civil aviation front.[8]

Relations with Europe

France

France is India's important strategic partner in Western Europe. Both India and France have endeavored to deepen collaboration in the cultural, economic, social, technological and military realms. Modi met French President Fransois Hollande at the 2014 G-20 Summit in Brisbane, and discussed bilateral strategic, space and defence issues besides committing to global cooperation against terrorism. Modi condemned the January 2015 Charlie Hebdo terror attack in Paris, and called Hollande to convey condolences on behalf of the people of India as well as express solidarity with the people of France. French Foreign Minister Laurent Fabius made several visits to New Delhi to move forward the stalled negotiations regarding Dassaulte Rafale fighter aircraft for Indian Air Force and the 9900 MW nuclear power plant in Jaitapur by the French firm Areva.

In April 2015, Narendra Modi went to Paris making it his first destination in Europe as part of his Link West outreach. His visit resulted in a government-to-government deal for 36 Dassault Rafale fighter aircraft in fly-away condition. India and France signed an initial agreement between Nuclear Power

Corporation of India and Areva regarding the setting up of Jaitapur nuclear power plant.

Modi went to see the aircraft assembly facilities of Dassault Aviation in Bordeaux and Airbus in Tolouse where he promoted the Make in India campaign by urging the aerospace giants to cultivate manufacturing opportunities in India. Airbus committed to increase its outsourcing from India from current level of US$ 400 million to US$ 2 billion by 2020.

India and France have good relations since India's independence, and these relations have become more warm under Narendra Modi.

As global strategic partners, India and France consult each other on all international matters in a spirit of mutual understanding, respect, trust, and support, taking into account their respective security interests. In the economic field, trade relations have developed over the years and French companies have been investing massively in India. With an investment stock of around 20 billion euros, French companies have invested heavily in India.

President François Hollande came on a state visit to India in January 2016, less than a year after the visit of Prime Minister Narendra Modi to France in April 2015, which helped further strengthen the dynamism of economic, scientific and cultural exchanges between the two countries.

Bilateral cooperation in the peaceful uses of energy between India is not new. An agreement in this regard came into effect in January 2010. It defined the framework of our cooperation in this field. Two agreements signed on 6 December 2010 completed its legal aspects. Modi Government is building on the cooperation. Several cooperation projects in the area of nuclear research and safety are in the process of being finalized. The project of building a nuclear power plant in Jaitapur now involves 6 EPRs (European Pressurized Reactors), with a total capacity of 9900 MW.

There is active cooperation between India and France in the field of defence. A number of collaborative projects are currently being considered. Our military contacts with France are also increasing through joint exercises.

In the defence sector, France and its defence industry are actively contributing to India's Make in India programme. The first conventional submarine, Scorpene, which started being built in India in 2008 with transfer of technology and support from DCNS, began sea trials in 2015. An agreement on India's acquisition of 36 Rafale fighter jets is currently being finalized. This will clear the way for more cooperation for the next four decades to come and enable India to develop its production capacities in this sector.

France and India have also set up a network of operational exchanges and joint actions between their respective intelligence and security forces. The first joint exercise between France's GIGN and India's NSG was held in 2016 as part of their cooperation.

France and India celebrated 50 years of their space cooperation in 2014. The April 2015 MoU signed between the French (CNES) and Indian (ISRO) space agencies has paved the way for undertaking new projects. A third, jointly-developed satellite for climate monitoring and a joint mission to be put in orbit for boosting the Argos system, which collects and processes environmental data via satellite are in the pipeline.

Bilateral trade between India and France has increased significantly over the past fifteen years. It increased by three times between 2000 and 2010. Moreover, the dynamism of Indo-French economic relations springs from the establishment of French companies in India. At present, more than 1000 French subsidiaries from a wide spectrum of sectors are present in India and employ a workforce of around 3,00,000 persons. The total investment stock of these companies in India stands at around 20 billion Euros.

United Kingdom

Former UK Prime Minister David Cameron and Prime Minister Modi met for the first time on 14 November 2014 on the sidelines of the G-20 leaders summit in Brisbane, where the former said that improving the relations with India was the top priority of UK's foreign policy.

Modi paid a state visit to the UK in the latter half of 2015, meeting Queen Elizabeth II and the then Prime Minister David Cameron. Modi addressed a rally at the New Wembley Stadium at Wembley Park, London. As many as 60,000 people, mostly British Indians, attended the rally.

Modi's visit to the UK has managed to radically reshape the contours of the India-UK partnership. Where the media was keen to highlight the controversies surrounding Modi, he has managed to redefine the India-UK relationship for the new century.

Though the two countries sealed UK£ 9 billion worth of commercial deals in the retail, logistics, energy, finance, IT, education and health sectors, it was the perceptual change in this bilateral tie-up that will have a much lasting impact on the future trajectory of a relationship which was seemingly headed nowhere before this visit.

Modi's visit came at a time when there were widespread doubts in the UK if India took the UK seriously at all despite British Prime Minister David Cameron's impressive outreach to India. Ever since he came to office, Cameron had made earnest endeavours to upgrade India-UK ties. In his first term, India, in fact, was at the top of the list of emerging powers but there was no appropriate response from the then UPA Government. It was one of the reasons why in Cameron's second term China got priority. Chinese President Xi Jinping's visit to the UK in 2015 resulted in two nations signing UK£ 40 billion worth of contracts, including for the project to build a nuclear power station in Britain. In one of the most significant shifts in British foreign policy in decades, the UK is trying to position itself as a key partner of China in Europe. It was Modi who recognized that it was time for him to reciprocate Cameron's investment in India.

Modi's 2015 visit to UK has managed to successfully put India-UK ties back on track and to redefine the terms of the relationship when India is no longer a supplicant but an emerging power, even providing jobs to the British economy. His visit to Jaguar Land Rover, which is owned by India's Tata Motors, was meant to underscore this changing dynamics. His outreach to the Indian diaspora also signalled the power of the British-Indian community in the UK politics.[9]

Modi's visit made UK-India relationship more forward-looking. The leaders of the two countries underscored their resolve "to work together to disrupt all financial and tactical support for terrorist networks, including ISIS, Al Qaeda, Lashkar-e-Tayyeba, Hizb-ul-Mujahideen, the Haqqanis and associated groups". This resolve is of great importance as civil societies all over the world are facing the menace of terrorism, and it needs joint effort to fight against it. In his speech to British Parliament, Modi stated that the UK and India were "two strong economies and two innovative societies" but their relationship "must set higher ambitions". Modi's visit succeeded in changing the course of India-UK ties considerably. It'll be now up to the two nations to build on its success.[10]

It is pertinent to mention here that according to Priti Patel, Britain's Minister of State for Employment, exiting the European Union will prove a "massive boost" to relations with India, and help develop stronger trade links that were allegedly hampered by EU laws. "Voting to leave the European Union would be a massive boost to UK-India relations. New opportunities for the UK and India to cooperate more closely and develop stronger trading links would emerge as the UK re-aligns its foreign policy and trade priorities", she said. As for Modi, he is continuing his efforts for a stronger relationship with UK after Britain left EU by means of a referendum held in June 2015. It is believed that India's rapidly growing economy could provide the U.K. with trade opportunities post exit from the EU.[11]

Russia

Russia has been India's long term strategic ally for more than half a century. The strategic cooperation that Russia has offered all along is unparalleled in India's foreign relations. It was erstwhile Union of Soviet Socialist Republics (USSR) that vetoed on 22 June 1962 and "smashed an Irish resolution" dealing a body blow to the West's aim to prize the disputed territory from India's control and hand it to Pakistan.[12]

Relations between India and Russia were upgraded from "strategic partnership" to "special and privileged strategic partnership" in 2010. Strong relations with Russia are a key pillar of India's foreign policy. Russia is a longstanding, time-tested, partner. Be it in the field of equipping our defence forces or industrialisation of the country or strategic support in the UN Security Council, Russia has always come to India's help. Relations between India and Russia have been based on defence acquisition, hydrocarbons, nuclear energy, space cooperation, trade and commerce, science and technology, culture and people-to-people ties.

After the end of Cold War the relation between the two countries experienced strain as India started diversifying its defence purchases from a totally Soviet dominated one and struck defence deals with America and some European countries.

Some major issues of dissonance have appeared between the two countries over the last few years. For example,

(a) The rapidly expanding ties between India and USA, which started with the India-US nuclear deal in 2008.

(b) The growing defence relationship between India and the USA.

India has so far been heavily dependent on Russian armaments with more than 70 percent of its weapons being sourced from Russia. However, in absolute terms Russia is still the largest supplier of defence equipment to India, its share in overall imports has progressively declined. India's reported decision to sign the three foundational defence agreements with USA, viz., Logistics Support Agreement (LSA), communications Interoperability and Security Memorandum of Agreement (CISMOA) and Basic Exchange and Cooperation Agreement (BECA) for Geo-spatial cooperation, has surfaced as a cause of serious concern for Russia. Russia feels that India is virtually entering into a military alliance with USA, which will severely restrict its ability to share sophisticated defence technology with India.

The frequency and comfort level in meetings between Modi and Obama were perceived to be higher than with Putin. Modi visited to USA four times in first two years after becoming Prime Minister in May 2014. Obama created history by visiting India twice in his term, as also to become the first US President to attend India's Republic Day celebrations as Chief Guest in January 2015. Also, Modi and Obama have interacted closely in several international fora like East Asia Summits, G-20 Summits, COP21, and others. As against this, meetings between Modi and Putin have been more formal and limited to two annual Summits and BRICS Summits.

According to *The Hindu*, with Putin and Modi, both with strongman image at their home country, at the helm of affairs in their respective foreign policy it is expected to get a push.[13] During the 20th India-Russia Inter-Governmental Commission on Trade, Economic, Scientific, Technological and Cultural Cooperation (IRIGC-TEC) held on 5 November 2014 in New Delhi, Modi met the Russian Deputy Prime Minister Dmitry Rogozin and reassured the visiting side that India will continue to attach very high importance to the time-tested and special strategic partnership with Russia. The annual commission meeting have identified new areas of cooperation including prioritising the International North South Corridor Project (INSTC), start negotiating on a Free Trade Agreement between India and the Eurasian Customs Union, focusing on enhancing economic partnership in areas like energy, civil aviation and diamond trade along with Russian participation in Modi's smart city project. Earlier on his first meeting with Putin, emphasising Russia's indispensable position in India's foreign policy Modi went on to saying that even a child in India considers Russia as its best friend.

During President Putin's visit to India on 11 December 2014, trade and energy cooperation dominated the talks as they set a target of US$ 30 billion of bilateral trade by 2025 with equal amount of investment in each other's economy. It is pertinent to mention here that in the backdrop of increasing Western sanctions, Putin had earlier signed a gas deal with China worth US$ 400 billion believed to be heavily tilted in China's favour.

India was also keen to strike an energy agreement on line of above. During the summit both sides agreed for a joint feasibility study of building gas pipeline through China. The two sides signed a total of 16 agreements and memorandum of understanding on various fields. Agreements on long term oil and gas cooperation were signed between ONGC Videsh and Essar Oil of India and Russia's Rosneft, Gasprom. Putin also vowed to install 10 more nuclear reactors in next 20 years including adding more units to Kudankulam plant. This will provide energy security to India.

Another important aspect of India-Russia relations is in the form of diamond trading. Russia is the largest producer of raw diamond, while India is the global hub of cutting and polishing raw diamonds. Russia has agreed to export raw diamonds to India directly instead of through mediators like Dubai and Belgium. Putin and Modi also attended a World Diamond Conference held in New Delhi.

The Crimean leader Sergey Aksyonov, who accompanied Putin in New Delhi, met many business delegations to discuss the opportunity in the Black Sea region though it was termed as unofficial. This has once again raised concerns in Washington, regarding India's stand on Crimea.[14]

According to some experts, it is surprising that Prime Minister Narendra Modi did not visit Russia, India's most important international partner, for 18 months after taking office.

Of course there had been earlier opportunities for Modi to meet with Russian President in Fortaleza in July 2014 during the BRICS summit, in Brisbane in November 2014 during the G-20 meeting, and then in Ufa in July 2015 during the BRICS and SCO conferences, but an official bilateral trip to Moscow has come slower than expected, considering India's special relationship with Russia for over half a century. In the same time, Modi visited France and the United States twice, indicating what can be seen as India's changed priorities and the new-found friends that come with it. Some experts have suggested that an increasingly powerful India no longer needs Russia's backup that it did during the Cold War period. A closer relationship with America, the sole superpower in the world will serve India's cause better than being closer to Russia.

India is buying weapons and conducting joint military exercises with Washington, Canberra, and Tokyo of late, and France is emerging as an important partner in defence, energy, and industry. Meanwhile sales of Russian weapons to India have also dropped and the only bright spot is the joint development of the Fifth Generation Fighter Aircraft (FGFA) between the two countries but even that has seen several setbacks of late. Even this deal has experienced certain setbacks like Russia's failure to meet delivery schedules, its tendency to increase costs, and the reluctance to transfer technology and supply spares, etc.

In November 2014, Russia agreed to sell Pakistan its Mi-35 attack helicopters and planned to hold its first joint military exercise with it. Moscow's relations with Beijing, too, have seen an upsurge in the wake of its rapidly deteriorating relations with the West over the conflict in Crimea. Of particular concern to India is the Russian sale of the S-400 Triumf and the advanced Su-35 air superiority fighter to China.[15]

However, all this should not be construed as India's shift away from Russia. Modi's visit, though it came later than expected, seems to have cleared many doubts. Reports suggest that the total value of the deals and MoUs signed between the two countries could be around US$ 150 billion, probably making Modi's visit the most valuable bilateral summit ever. The agreements included a second site for six Russian nuclear reactors in Andhra Pradesh and the manufacture of Russia's Kamov Ka-226T light helicopters under Modi's Make in India programme; negotiations are underway for India to seal the deal on the lease of another Akula-II class nuclear submarine, the acquisition of the S-400 air defence system, an order for three more Krivak-III class stealth frigates, and the FGFA.

The way things are at present, India-Russia relations are focused around arms sales and nuclear reactors. What India must realize that Russia's importance to India is much beyond the arms sale. Although, Russia is not as forceful as the erstwhile USSR, but it still possesses enviable diplomatic clout in the world affairs, advanced military-industrial technological complex, large deposits of natural resources, and a formidable military. Moscow played a positive role in India's successful conclusion of the nuclear negotiations with Iran of particular value of India is Russia's Veto in the United Nations Security Council, which Delhi has lobbied for before on throwing issues like Kashmir. The Kremlin's support for Indian entry into several technology regimes and political and economic groupings—MTCR, NSG, UNSC, SCO—is also something India counts on. Russia and India need each other in the long term to balance the rise of China.

Keeping this in mind, Modi does not discard the Russian relationship. Delhi has refrained from criticising Moscow in Ukraine or in Syria—in fact, it is not difficult to read silent support in between the diplomatic lines. Additionally, it is not possible for India to distance itself from Russia even if it so desires because of the dependencies it has built—70 percent of the Indian military uses Russian hardware and Delhi relies on Moscow to supply spare parts and other services. Modi understands this and his visit was partly an attempt to ameliorate the situation via the 'Make in India' programme.

The greatest transformation in India-Russia relations is an expansion of Indian trade from defence, and perhaps energy, to other sectors of the economy. Trade between the two countries stands at less than $10 billion today. So far, this has been because the Russian market was notoriously difficult to access for Indian firms but now, with Western sanctions against Russia and Russian sanctions against Turkey, there is an opening for aggressive Indian corporations to move into the space vacated by Western and Turkish firms in pharmaceuticals, agriculture, food products, fertilisers, textiles, furniture, and other areas.

Germany

India and Germany have a 'strategic partnership' since 2000, which has been further strengthened with two rounds of Intergovernmental Consultations (IGC) in New Delhi in May 2011, as well as in Berlin in April 2013. India was the Partner Country in Hannover Messe-2015 in April 2015. The two countries have several institutionalised arrangements to discuss bilateral and global issues of interest, viz. Strategic Dialogue, Foreign Office Consultations, Joint Commission on Industrial and Economic Cooperation, High Technology Partnership Group, High Defence Committee and Joint Working Group on Counter-Terrorism, Indo-German Consultative Group, etc. Germany and India cooperate closely on the issue of UN Security Council expansion within the framework of G-4. Both sides have regular consultation on foreign policy issues such as East Asia, Central Asia, UN issues, Disarmament and Non-proliferation, etc.

Bilateral relations between Germany and India one based on a sound foundation of mutual respect, understanding and support. The cooperation between both countries covers a wide range of areas from political action and growing economic exchange to landmark cultural events. It is complementary as India and Germany both contribute their particular and unique strengths to this truly strategic partnership. The Modi Government has launched a number of remodeling programmes, where Germany can bring in its expertise. Concepts of Vocational training, promotion of renewable energies, improved urban mobility and the rehabilitation of rivers are a part of these programmes. On the other hand, India has highly qualified IT-experts, who are also most interesting for the German industry. Apart from that the Indian market offers enormous growth potential. Back in May 2000 both countries adopted the 'Agenda for the Indo-German Partnership in the 21st century'. This includes regular meetings of both Heads of Government as well as annual meetings of the Foreign Ministers, if possible. In the following years both the countries directed the focus of further collaboration on future fields like energy, science, and technology as well as defence and adopted subsequent declarations.

In October 2015 German Chancellor Angela Markel visited New Delhi with members of her cabinet for the third Indo-German intergovernmental consultations. India keeps such a broad dialogue format at Government level only with Germany. Also, there has been a range of other political meetings between heads of states, government members and members of parliament of Germany and India. Together with German Chancellor Angela Markel, Prime Minister Narendra Modi opened the Hannover Fair in April 2015, which had India as partner country. The German-India parliamentary group of the German Bundestag (Parliament) visited India in February 2015 with a comprehensive political programme in New Delhi. The two countries agreed to a special exception for German companies seeking entry into the Indian market for setting up operations. Under a new bilateral agreement, German firms will receive fast-track approval to enter into the Indian market. Describing themselves as "strategic partners", both sides pledged to cooperate on the world stage. On the security front, India and Germany signed MoUs on aviation security, disaster management, and expressed their joint commitment to continue regular meetings of their joint working group on counter terrorism.[16]

The two countries also underscored the importance of freedom of navigation in international waters, the right of passage and other maritime rights in accordance with accepted principles of international law, including the UN Convention on the Law of the Sea. They called on "all parties concerned to seek peaceful and cooperative solutions in accordance with international law and practice." India also mentioned the South China Sea dispute in bilateral discussions.

The joint statement between the two countries included a statement on the crisis in Ukraine, where Russia-backed rebels were fighting a Western-backed government. Merkel and Modi "reiterated their full support for ongoing efforts to find a diplomatic solution to the conflict in eastern Ukraine," and "underlined their strong support to upholding the sovereign equality of all States as well as respect for their territorial integrity." India has followed an ambivalent line on Russia's actions in Ukraine, including the annexation of Crimea, while Germany, which has certainly been critical of Moscow, has been concerned by the threat of military force by NATO and Russia.[17]

The long list of economic MoUs speaks of the ongoing widening of the Indo-German relationship. The German Government, like many of Western states long frustrated by

India's foreign investor unfriendly economic environment, welcomed Modi's election victory in 2014 elections. With MoUs on manufacturing, fast-tracking registration for German firms in India, cooperation on railways, solar energy, and agriculture, among others, it is quite clear that the bilateral relationship is strengthening.

The relations between India and Germany still remain primarily focused on economic issues. Indeed, Germany, as the powerhouse economy at the heart of an economically beleaguered Europe, has much to gain from close ties with India, the world's fastest growing emerging economy.

Relations with Africa

Prime Minister Narendra Modi met the heads of state in four African countries from 7-11 July, 2016 in his first visit to the African continent. His visit took him to Kenya, Tanzania, Mozambique, and South Africa. His arrival in Mozambique marked the first time that an Indian Prime Minister has visited the East African nation in 34 years. Modi's visit to Africa signalled an extension of India's influence in the Indian Ocean region as well as deepening and strengthening of India-Africa partnerships and agreements. It provided a glimpse into the evolving principles of the Modi doctrine and its role in shaping India-Africa affairs.

The 2015 Africa-India Summit, where the focus was on increased diplomatic relations saw the largest representation of African heads of state since the summit began in 2008. The summit culminated in the 2015 Delhi Declaration, which outlined shared values and commitments between India and the African states.

A proposal for contract farming in Tanzania to buffer India's shortfall in grain production and maritime security agreements for co-operation on the safeguarding of India Ocean trade routes were high on the agenda of Modi's visit.

Since assuming the office of Prime Minister, Modi has embarked on several multi-country official state visits. This was his first tour of continental African countries. His earlier visits to

African nations included stops in Mauritius and the Seychelles as part of an Indian Ocean tour that successfully repaired relations with Sri Lanka. During the Mauritius portion of the journey, five agreements were signed on economic and security interests, including the India-Mauritius Tax Treaty and a trade agreement on agricultural products.[18]

Narendra Modi paid an official visit to the Republic of South Africa from 7 to 9 July 2016. President Zuma and Prime Minister Modi held discussions in the spirit of the strong friendship and historical links between the two countries. The two leaders expressed satisfaction with the current status of bilateral relations. However, they emphasized that there is still scope for the further strengthening and deepening of relations in the political, economic, scientific and socio-cultural spheres. It was therefore agreed that there should be frequent and sustained contact between the two countries in mutually identified areas as it will serve to maintain the momentum of the bilateral relationship.

In this regard, the comprehensive Strategic Partnership between South Africa and India, which was established through the Red Fort Declaration in March 1997, and reaffirmed in the Tshwane Declaration in October 2006, was hailed as an important mechanism that has contributed in the past to both South Africa and India achieving identified national objectives. According to Ministry of External Affairs, India and South Africa committed to elevate efforts in achieving the goals set out in the Declaration.

President Zuma and Prime Minister Modi also discussed intensified collaboration in the sectors of defence, energy, agro-processing, human resource development, infrastructure development as well as science, technology and innovation.

The leaders underlined the importance of strengthening cooperation between business entities of South Africa and India. They identified focus areas for deeper cooperation, including manufacturing, mines and minerals, IT, renewable energy, pharmaceuticals, tourism, S&T and financial services.[19]

South Africa President Zuma invited the private sector of India to invest in various sectors of South Africa's economy, while Prime Minister Modi called upon the South African private sector to consider investing in key economic sectors in India. South Africa took note of the many opportunities for the private sector available in the Make in India initiative, and the Indian side noted the invitation to take advantage of infrastructure development opportunities in South Africa and the Continent.

The two leaders expressed satisfaction at the steady pace of cooperation in defence sector encompassing a wide range of engagements, including defence production, joint collaboration, manufacturing research and development, training and joint exercises.

Both leaders noted that the proposed theme of the G-20 Summit, viz. "Breaking a New Path for Growth", was in line with the developmental plans of both countries. Prime Minister Modi took note of the request from South Africa for India's continued support for the proposals on the illicit financial flows, the Antimicrobial Resistance (AMR) and for the industrialization of Africa and Least Developing Countries (LDCs) as well as the G-20 Action Plan on the implementation of the Development Agenda 2030. The two leaders noted the progress made in implementing IMFs governance and quota reforms. They stressed that it should be reflective of relative weightage of IMF members in the global economy. In this regard, they highlighted the relevance of weightage to GDP on Purchasing Power Parity (PPP) in the new quota formula. Cognizant of the infrastructure-gap in developing countries, the leaders underscored the role that G-20 and the Multilateral Development Banks (MDBs) can play to bridge this gap through measures such as priority-lending, R&D, and technology transfers from the developed to developing countries.

The two leaders recognised G-20 as the premier Forum for coordination in international financial and economic matters. In this regard, they noted the continued sluggish recovery and deflationary-pressures on global economy. They called upon the world-community to utilise monetary, fiscal, and structural reforms to jump-start global economy.

Prime Minister Narendra Modi and President Zuma reiterated their support to WTO as the sole multilateral-mechanism on global-trade and commerce. They underscored the significance of centrality accorded to the development-agenda in the Doha Development Round. They agreed that the unfinished agenda for the Doha Development Round should be completed expeditiously and should lead to an outcome that is proportionate and significantly addresses the imbalances and inequities of the global system that impede development prospects for developing countries.

President Zuma noted that Indian Ocean Rim Association (IORA) gained new momentum when India took over as Chair and committed that it will be South Africa's objective to ensure that this momentum is sustained during its incoming Chairpersonship. Both leaders noted the importance of the Ocean Economy, growing interest by other countries to join the organization as dialogue partners, and the strategic nature the Indian Ocean can play in developing the Region.

Prime Minister Modi welcomed South Africa as the incoming Chair of IORA for 2017-19 when IORA commemorates its 20th anniversary. There was also speculation that part of the South Africa visit will include a request for support in India's efforts to join the Nuclear Suppliers Group (NSG).

A common theme that has emerged in Modi's strategy in Africa that his 2016 tours are located within the Indian Ocean sphere of influence with significant Indian diasporic populations. Modi's visits demonstrated an expansion of his initial forays into strengthening India-Africa partnerships in and around the Indian Ocean.

Modi's foreign policy strategy aims to increase assistance to developing countries and endeavor to establish linkages with the African continent for increased trade, access to agricultural land, and cooperation on maritime security, in part to buffer China's influence in the region. Both China and India have established roles as increasingly important powers in sub-saharan African trade and development. While India's trade with Africa has increased from $25 billion in 2006 to $70 billion; China-Africa trade was valued at an estimated $222 billion in 2014. As India's establishment as a global donor continues, greater development finance commitments feature prominently in Modi's Africa strategy, particularly in Tanzania, Kenya, and Mozambique. The visit shows a building of momentum of India's relations with Africa overlapping with Chinese interests.[20]

As India's economy has grown, its role as a global power and emerging donor have come to the fore in shaping 21st century geopolitics. Steered by the Modi doctrine, India's foreign policy has become more assertive in forging new relations with strategic partners while deepening and strengthening bilateral relations with African countries. Modi's visit formalised agreements to secure increased investment, bilateral trade, and south-south cooperation. Modi's tour demonstrated on evolving emphasis of India's foreign policy on south-south cooperation and the maturation of the Modi Doctrine in shaping world affairs.

India's Multilateral Engagements

BRICS Summit, Brazil

India is one of leading developing countries. It plays an active role in important multilateral forums for global governance like United Nations, World Trade Organization, G-20 Summit, East Asia Summit, BRICS Summit of emerging economies, and Commonwealth of Nations, among others. India is recognized as a "third world voice". In his maiden speech at the BRICS, in Brazil, Narendra Modi called for brotherhood among the member states saying that the entire world is one family, and it should unitedly face the global challenges.

Prime Minister Modi expressed India's keenness on the issue of equal shareholding for all members of the BRICS, viz., Brazil, Russia, India, China and South Africa. Modi said that India does not want a repeat of the distortions that had crept into Bretton Woods institutions like IMF, World Bank, and Asian Development Bank in which rich countries like US and Japan have a strangle hold.[21]

India together with its BRICS partner working toward launching of a financial institute rivalling the western dominated

World Bank and IMF which was first proposed during the New Delhi summit in 2012 by the then Indian Prime Minister Manmohan Singh. In the 6th BRICS summit held in Fortaleza, Brazil, the group have agreed to establish the bank with a corpus of US$ 100 billion. The bank would be named the New Development Bank as suggested by the Indian side but Modi Government has failed to bay the bank's headquarter for New Delhi which would be located in Shanghai, China.

United Nations General Assembly

Modi delivered his maiden speech in the 69th session of the United Nations General Assembly on 27 September 2014. He called for reform and expansion of United Nations Security Council (UNSC), and pressed for India's long standing demand of a permanent membership of the Security Council. Expressing his concern over continuation of the old setup of the UN in the 21st century, he stressed the need to evaluate UN's performance in the past 70 years. He also argued why UN should serve as 'G-All' for global governance instead of several parallel sub-groupings like G-7, G-20, etc.

In the wake of ISIS threat in West Asia and similar threat in other parts of the globe, Modi urged for immediate implementation of "Comprehensive Convention on International Terrorism" by the UN and offered India's proactive role in it, citing the fact that India has been a victim of terrorism for decades.

He along with External Affairs Minister Sushma Swaraj met UN Secretary General Ban Ki-moon and discussed UN governance relating issues. He vehemently put down Nawaz Sharif's demand of multilateral intervention on Kashmir problem and stated that his government is ready for bilateral talks with Pakistan provided Pakistan cultivates suitable environment for talks by giving up terrorism policy against India. Modi also commented on climate change and use of clean energy, and asked the governments to encourage people to use environment friendly practices.

At the sidelines, Modi held bilateral meetings with Bangladeshi Prime Minister Sheikh Hasina, Sri Lankan President

Mahinda Rajapaksa and Nepali Prime Minister Sushil Koirala, taking his Neighbourhood First policy forward even in New York. But there was no meeting with Pakistani Prime Minister Nawaz Sharif following Pakistan's terrorist activities. Later, he also met Israeli Prime Minister Benjamin Netanyahu, in a first meeting in 11 years between the two heads of government. The Israeli Prime Minister underscored the high potential of the bilateral relation.

ASEAN-India Summit

The 12th ASEAN-India Summit was held in Nay Pyi Taw, Myanmar on 12 November 2014, on the sidelines of 25th ASEAN Summit. The summit was attended by the President of Myanmar, Thein Sein, the Indian Prime Minister Narendra Modi and by all Heads of State/Government of ASEAN Member States. It was Modi's first appearance in an ASEAN meet. He called for greater connectivity with the Southeast Asian countries and mentioned that "India and ASEAN can be 'great partners'".[22] Stressing on the importance ASEAN commands in India's foreign policy, Modi said that his government has made relation with ASEAN a top priority and turned India's two decade old 'Look East policy' into 'Act East policy' which reflects a renewed momentum in India's approach toward ASEAN nations.

In the sidelines of ASEAN summit, Modi also held several bilateral meetings with his counterparts including Thai Prime Minister Gen Prayuth Chan-ocha, Singapore's Prime Minister Lee Hsien Loong, Sultan of Brunei Hassanal Bolkiah, Malaysian Prime Minister Najib Razak and South Korean President Park Geun-hye.[23]

ASEAN Regional Forum

Sushma Swaraj attended the 2014 ASEAN Regional Forum followed by the related East Asian Submit Foreign Ministers meeting, held on 8-11 August in Naypidaw, Myanmar. At the sidelines of the multilateral meetings, she held bilateral meetings with her counterparts from seven countries, including China, Australia, Canada, Vietnam, Philippines, Brunei, and Indonesia.

Regarding the controversy of territorial ownership in the South China Sea, a contentious issue impacting most ASEAN member states, where ONGC Videsh has investment in oil blocks, a spokesperson of the Ministry of External Affairs said, "India is not a party to the dispute in the South China Sea. We feel that the dispute should be resolved between those who are party to it in a peaceful manner and it should be in accordance with international law".

East Asia Summit

East Asia Summit (EAS) is an ASEAN led dialogue forum consisting of 18 countries, 10 core ASEAN nations along with Japan, China, South Korea, India, Australia, New Zealand, Russia and United States. It has become the most important multilateral body in the Asia-Pacific region for discussing security, trade and commerce, environment and others unlike APEC which is purely economic in nature. Modi participated in the ninth East Asia Summit in Nay Pyi Daw, Myanmar in November 2014 which was his second major multilateral event after BRICS in July. Describing the importance of the EAS in managing regional security, Modi stated that no other forum brings together such a large collective weight of global population, youth, economy and military strength like EAS. He underscored the fact that EAS is very critical for peace, stability and prosperity in Asia-Pacific and the world.

With a veiled reference of the issue of South China Sea, Modi asked the global community for respecting maritime norms and regulations and stressed on the importance of maintaining free and secured sea-lines of communication for regular trade and commerce. He also said that all the countries should follow international laws and norms and ensure peaceful passage for trade. This is necessary for peace and stability in South China Sea as well. Modi also said that EAS member countries should join hands to tackle the menace of terrorism in the region. The issue of Regional Comprehensive Economic Partnership (RCEP) was also discussed in detail during the summit.

G-20 Leaders Summit

The 2014 G-20 Brisbane summit was the ninth meeting of the G-20 heads of government/heads of state. The event was the largest ever peacetime police operation in Australia. India was represented by Prime Minister Modi.

The focus was on economic concerns, and plans were envisaged to increase global economic growth, create jobs, increase trade and reduce poverty. The communique set out a goal of increasing economic growth by an extra 2% through commitments made at the summit, and of increasing infrastructure investment through the creation of a four-year infrastructure hub, linking government, private sector, development banks and interested international organizations.

The 2015 G-20 summit was the tenth annual meeting of the G-20 heads of government/state. It was held in Antalya, Turkey on 15-16 November 2015. It was the second G-20 summit attended by Prime Minister Narendra Modi.

The summit mostly focused on political rather than economic issues due to the terrorist attacks in Paris, in which 132 people were killed. As an organization dealing with global issues of financial and economic cooperation, the G-20 decided to change the format of the session. According to the summit results, in addition to the pre-planned communiqué, the parties adopted a declaration on fighting terrorism.

The 2016 G-20 summit was the eleventh meeting of the G-20 heads of government/sate. It was held on 4-5 September 2016 in the city of Hangzhou, Zhejiang, China. The main themes of final communiqué of the summit were fight against tax evasion (asking the Organization for Economic Co-operation and Development for a black list of tax havens); facilitation of international trade and investments and opposition to protectionism; and innovation to boost economic growth; combating "populist attacks" against globalization; and strengthening support for refugees.

Prime Minister Narendra Modi not only attended the summit but also had bilateral meetings with top leaders of the world. He urged the international community to act in unity and respond against terrorism. He said a single nation (Pakistan) in South Asia was spreading agents of terror in the region and, therefore, called on the international community to isolate and sanction those indulging in the same.

South Asian Association for Regional Cooperation

Relations with the immediate neighbours in South Asia are a priority feature in Modi's foreign policy. He invited all the heads of states/governments of the neighbouring countries in his swearing in ceremony and then pushed for of an early summit to encourage cooperation in many regional issues like trade, connectivity, infrastructure, transit facility among the member states. In his maiden SAARC Summit in Kathmandu in November 2014, he focused on greater people-to-people contacts, better connectivity, and commercial linkages within the region.

The 19th SAARC Summit was scheduled to be held in Islamabad, Pakistan on 15-16 November 2016. It was to be attended by the leaders of the eight SAARC member states and representatives of observers and guest states. However, following the rising diplomatic tensions after the Uri terrorist attack, India announced to boycott the summit, alleging Pakistan's involvement in the same. Later, Bangladesh, Afghanistan, Bhutan and Sri Lanka also pulled out of the summit, leading to an indefinite postponement of the summit.

The Bangladeshi Foreign Ministry conveyed to the SAARC Chair Nepal that Pakistan's increasing interference in Bangladesh's domestic affairs was inimical to the interest of Bangladesh and under such circumstances it was not possible to participate in the summit at Islamabad. Afghanistan announced its withdrawal from the summit, stating, "Due to increased level of violence and fighting as a result of imposed terrorism on Afghanistan, (President) Ashraf Ghani with his responsibilities as the Commander-in-Chief will be fully engaged, and will not be able to attend the Summit." Bhutan stated that the recent escalation of terrorism in the region has seriously compromised the environment for the successful holding of the summit.[24]

The pressure created by India against Pakistan was responsible for this isolation of Pakistan. This is a significant achievement of Modi's foreign policy, but this pressure needs to be maintained to make Pakistan leave its evil designs against India.

Conclusion

There have been some changes in India's foreign policy under Narendra Modi. According to *The Hindu*, he made several interventions on foreign policy in the form of speeches, press releases, media interactions, and community receptions. He has addressed almost every major multilateral grouping in which India is a member, i.e., the United Nations, the East Asia Summit (EAS), the G-20 bloc, BRICS, the Shanghai Cooperation Organization (SCO), the India-Africa Summit and the Forum for India-Pacific Islands Cooperation. He has engaged with almost every major leadership in the world.

The Prime Minister's foreign policy interventions during this period reflect efforts to institutionalize the norms his government articulated in its first year, for example, the principle of "Asian solidarity" that has been a key theme in Modi's speeches. He has repeatedly defined this principle through three key markers, viz. the Regional Comprehensive Economic Partnership (RCEP), a cyber-security architecture for the ASEAN Regional Forum, and the settlement of disputes through multilateral rules. On maritime concerns in Asia, Prime Minister Modi has calibrated the Indian position, without straying too far from the traditional line. The India-Japan Joint Statement of December 2016 referred to the "Indo-Pacific", officially bringing this strategic phrase into India's foreign policy lexicon.

His second-year interventions indicate areas of foreign policy where the Modi Government is likely to invest political capital. Cyber-policy is one such theme, which is reflected in nearly a third of all of Modi's speeches. At intergovernmental venues like ASEAN, BRICS or the G-20, he has underscored the importance of securing "cyber networks" from state and non-state actors. At the East Asia Summit—markedly in the presence of China—he called for "norms of behaviour" in cyberspace. To the private sector, Modi has flagged "data privacy and security" as a key concern, notably during his visit to Silicon Valley in September 2015. These are norms that he has not broached at home, even in the context of the Digital India initiative.

Trade partnerships are another theme in Modi's foreign policy interventions. He has repeatedly called for an "early conclusion" of RCEP, while acknowledging the existence of the Trans-Pacific Partnership (TPP) agreement. This, however, is not a deviation from India's earlier position on the centrality of World Trade Organization (WTO) to international trade.

At the G-20 summit in Antalya, Modi asserted this clearly, warning that regional agreements "should not lead to a fragmentation of the global trading system." Renewable energy is another area of priority. His COP21 interventions skew the numbers, but the last six months have seen Modi consistently talk up India's renewable energy capacities.

These foreign policy themes are closely connected to three initiatives that the present Indian government has mooted: the Technology Facilitation Mechanism, a Comprehensive Convention on International Terrorism, and the International Solar Alliance.[25]

Narendra Modi has consistently highlighted the need for India's entry into export control regimes—the Missile Control Technology Regime, Wassenaar Arrangement and Nuclear Suppliers Group. This is indicative of the fact that India's special bilateral relationships cannot substitute for inclusive multilateral arrangements. Although, the prognosis of Modi's Government's foreign policy is optimistic, yet much will depend on India's economic performance in times to come and the influence it is able to have in the region and the world at large. There are also big challenges like containing the influence of China and building deterrence against the China-Pakistan alliance by being closer to the US and at the same time keeping a strong relationship with Russia and other countries of strategic and economic importance for India. So far Modi has done well by exhibiting active diplomacy. It is hoped that he will continue to do so in the remaining part of his regime.

Notes

1. *New York Times*, 7 June 2014.
2. *Live Mint*, 25 June 2016.
3. "The Small Islands Holding the Key to the Indian Ocean." *The Diplomat*, 24 February 2015.
4. "India: Mooring in foreign shores?" *Mid Day*, 3 March 2015.
5. Shyam Saran. "What China's One Belt and One Road Strategy Means for India, Asia and the World". The Wire, 10 September 2015.
6. *The Economic Times*, 7 June 2016.
7. *DNA*, 26 May 2015.
8. *The Times of India*, 6 September 2015.
9. www. dailymail.co. 16 November 2015.
10. *Ibid.*
11. *The Wall Street Journal*, 6 November 2016.
12. *Russia and India Report*, 1 November 2016.
13. "For a warmer Russian bear hug". *The Hindu*, 10 December 2014.
14. "US 'Troubled' By Crimean Leader's India Visit". *The Diplomat*, 3 December 2014.
15. http://m.firstpost.com/
16. *The Diplomat*, October 6, 2015.
17. *Ibid.*
18. *Ibid.*, 7 July 2016.
19. Ministry of External Affairs, Government of India, 8 July 2016.
20. *The Diplomat*, 7 July 2016.
21. *The Economic Times*, 14 July 2014.
22. *Ibid.*, 12 November 2014.
23. *Ibid.*
24. "SAARC summit collapses after India and three other members pull out." *Hindustan Times*, 28 September 2016.
25. *The Hindu*, 16 December 2015.

CHAPTER 11

Crackdown on Black Money

Black Money

Black money is a term used to money that is not fully legitimate in the hands of owner. The term "black money" is not defined per se in the tax laws of the Government of India. However, a definition of black money was adopted in the White Paper issued on Black Money by Government of India in May 2012. According to this report, 'black money' is defined as assets or resources that have neither been reported to the public authorities at the time of their generation nor disclosed at any point of time during their possession. This definition of black money is in consonance with the definition used by the National Institute of Public Finance and Policy (NIPFP) in its 1985 report on Aspects of Black Economy, where it defined 'black income' as "the aggregates of incomes which are taxable but not reported to the tax authorities". Further, black incomes or unaccounted incomes are "the extent to which estimates of national income and output are biased downwards because of deliberate, false reporting of incomes, output and transactions for reasons of tax evasion, flouting of other economic controls and relative motives". Thus, in addition to wealth accumulated through illegal means, the term black money also includes legal income that is concealed from public authorities:

(a) to evade payment of taxes, such as income tax, excise duty, sales tax, stamp duty, etc.;

(b) to evade payment of other statutory contributions;

(c) to evade compliance with the provisions of industrial laws such as the Industrial Dispute Act 1947, Minimum Wages Act 1948, Payment of Bonus Act 1936, Factories Act 1948, and Contract Labour (Regulation and Abolition) Act 1970; and/or

(d) to evade compliance with other laws and administrative procedures.

Black money is both an economic and a social problem. In the latter context, it is perceived as a problem with adverse sociological effects on society, such as social inequalities, social deprivation, etc. and in the former context, it is perceived as a parallel economy, an underground economy, or an unofficial economy that is the consequence of the economic policies of government and has damaging effects on country's economy and nation's planning for development. While a problem like poverty affects those who are poor, unemployment affects those who are unemployed, alcoholism and drug abuse affect those who consume them, black money is a problem which does not affect those who have black money but it affects the common man in the society.

Factors Leading to Generation of Black Money

Black money could arise broadly due to two possible reasons. The first is that the money may have been generated through illegitimate activities not permissible under the law of land, such as crime and corruption which have an underlying anti-social element. The 'criminal' component of black money may include proceeds from a range of activities including racketeering, trafficking in counterfeit and contraband goods, smuggling, cheating and financial fraud, illegal trade in arms, etc. Some of these offences are included in the schedule of the Prevention of Money Laundering Act 2002. Money laundering, as defined by Financial Action Task Force (FATF), is the processing of these criminal proceeds to disguise their illegal origin. The 'corrupt' component of black money could stem from bribery and theft by those holding public office, such as by grant of business, leakages from government social spending programmes, speed money to circumvent or fast-track procedures, black marketing of price-controlled services, and altering land use regularizing unauthorized construction. All these activities are illegal per se and a result of human greed combined with declining societal values and inability of the state to prevent them. Factors leading to their generation are both social and administrative.

The second and perhaps more likely reason is that the wealth may have been generated and accumulated by failing to pay the dues to the public exchequer in one form or other. In this case, the activities undertaken by the perpetrator could be legitimate and otherwise permissible under the law of the land but he has failed to report the income so generated, or comply with the tax requirements, or pay the dues to the public exchequer, thereby converting such income into black money. The failure to report or disclose such activities or income may be with the objective of evading taxes or avoiding the cost of compliance related to such reporting or disclosure. It may also be the result of non-compliance with some other law. For example, a factory owner may under-report production on account of theft of electricity which in turn leads to evasion of taxes. Normally, a high burden of taxation, either actual or perceived, provides a strong temptation to evade taxes and generate black money. Sometimes the procedural regulations can be such that complying with them may increase the probability of further scrutiny and thereby the incidence of the burden of compliance, creating a perverse incentive not to report at all and remain outside the reported and accounted proportion of the economy. Cultural and social practices also play a vital role in deciding the preferences of citizens between tax compliance and black money generation. In a society where tax evasion and under-reporting of activities and income is perceived to be very common or the norm, such activities may be considered acceptable and honest tax compliance and paying one's due share to the public fund may not be considered a virtue. Thus, countries with relatively poor implementation of regulations tend to have a higher share of unaccounted economy, whereas countries with properly implemented regulations and sound deterrence have smaller 'black' economies.

Generating Black Money by Manipulation of Accounts

One of the methods of generating black money is the crude approach of not declaring or reporting the whole of the income or the income or the activities leading to it. This is the likely approach in all cases of criminal, illegal, and impermissible activities. The sophistications in such an approach mostly get introduced subsequently for laundering the money so generated with the objective of making it accountable and converting it into legitimate reported wealth that can be openly possessed and used. The same approach of not declaring or reporting activities and the income generated there from may also be followed in cases of failure to comply with regulatory obligations or tax evasion on income from legitimate activities. Thus, a more sophisticated approach for generation of this kind of black money is often preferred, involving manipulation of financial records and accounting. The best way of classifying and understanding the various ways and means adopted by taxpayers for the generation of black money would be the financial statement approach, elaborating different means by which the accounts prepared for reporting and presenting before the authorities are manipulated to misrepresent and under disclose income, thereby generating unaccounted, undeclared, and unreported income that amounts to black money.

Out of Book Transactions—It is one of the simplest and widely adopted methods of tax evasion and generation of black money. Transactions that may result in taxation of receipts or income are not entered in the books of account by the taxpayer. The taxpayer either does not maintain books of account or maintains two sets or records partial receipts only. This mode is generally prevalent among the small grocery shops, unskilled or semi-skilled service providers, etc.

Parallel Books of Accounts—It is a practice usually adopted by those who are obliged under the law or due to business needs to maintain books of account. In order to evade reporting activities or the income generated from them, they may resort to maintaining two sets of books of account—one for their own consumption with the objective of managing their business and the other one for the regulatory and tax authorities. The second set of books of account, which is maintained for the purpose of satisfying the legal and regulatory obligations of reporting to different authorities, may be manipulated by omitting receipts or falsely inflating expenses, for the purpose of evading taxes or other regulatory requirements.

Manipulation of Books of Account—When books of accounts are required to be maintained by taxpayers under different laws, it may become difficult for these taxpayers to indulge in out of books transactions or to maintain parallel books of accounts. Such parties may resort to manipulation of the books of accounts to evade taxes.

Manipulation of Sales/Receipts—A taxpayer is required to pay taxes on profit or income which is the difference between sale proceeds or receipts and expenditure. Thus, manipulation of sales or receipts is the easiest method of tax evasion. Other innovative means may include diversion of sales to associated enterprises, which may become more important if such enterprises are located in different tax jurisdictions and thereby may also give rise to issues related to international taxation and transfer pricing.

Under-reporting of Production—Manipulation of production figure is another means of artificially reducing tax liability. It may be resorted to for the purpose of evading central excise, sales tax, or income tax.

Manipulation of Expenses—Since the income on which taxes are payable is arrived at after deducting the expenses of the business from the receipts, manipulation of expenses is a commonly adopted method of tax evasion. The expenses may be manipulated under different heads and result in under-reporting of income. It may involve inflation of expenses, sometimes by obtaining bogus or inflated invoices from the so-called 'bill masters', who make bogus vouchers and charge nominal commission for this facility. Any number of more sophisticated versions of manipulation of expenses can also be resorted to by those intending to generate black money. Sometimes it can also involve 'hawala' operators, who operate shell entities in the form of proprietorship firms, partnership firms, companies, and trusts. These operators may accept cheques for payments claimed as expense and return cash after charging some commission. There have been instances of claims of bogus expenses to foreign entities. The payments can be shown to foreign entities in the form of advertisement and marketing expenses or commission for purchases or sales. The funds may be remitted to the account of the foreign taxpayer and the money can either be withdrawn in cash or remitted back to India in the form of non-taxable receipts. Such money may also be accumulated in the form of unaccounted assets of the Indian taxpayer abroad.

Manipulation by Way of International Transactions through Associate Enterprises—One of the methods of manipulating accounted profits and taxes payable thereon involves using of associated enterprises in low tax jurisdictions through which goods or other material may be passed on to the concern. Intercorporate transactions between these associate enterprises belonging to the same group or owned and controlled by the same set of parties may be arranged and manipulated in a way that leads to evasion of taxes. This can often be achieved by arrangements that shift taxable income to the low tax jurisdictions or tax havens, and may lead to accumulation of black money earned from within India to another country.

Manipulation of Capital—The capital of the taxpayer is the accumulated wealth which is invested in the form of assets or as working capital of the business. Manipulation of capital can be one of the ways of laundering and introduction of black money in books of accounts.

Manipulation of Closing Stock—Suppression of closing stock both in terms of quality and value is one of the most common methods of understating profit. More sophisticated versions of such practice may include omission of goods in transit paid for and debited to purchases, or omission of goods sent to the customer for approval. A more common approach is undervaluation of inventory (stock of unsold goods), which means that while the expenses are being accounted for in the books, the value being added is not accounted for, thereby artificially reducing the profits.

Manipulation of Capital Expenses—Over-invoicing plant and equipment or any capital asset is an approach adopted to claim higher depreciation and thereby reduce the profit of the business. Increase in capital can also be a means of enabling the businessman to borrow more funds from banks or raise capital from the market. It has been seen that such measures are sometimes resorted to at the time of bringing out a capital issue. At the same time, under-invoiced investments, indicating entry of undeclared wealth, may imply introduction of black money.

Generation of Black Money in Some Vulnerable Sections of the Economy

While the source of generation of black money may lie in any sphere of economic activity, there are certain sectors of the economy or activities, which are more vulnerable to this menace. These include real estate, the bullion and jewellery market, financial markets, public procurement, non-profit organizations, external trade, international transactions involving tax havens, and the informal service sector.

Land and Real Estate Transactions—Due to rising prices of real estate, the tax incidence applicable on real estate transactions in the form of stamp duty and capital gains tax can create incentives for tax evasion through under-reporting of transaction price. This can lead to both generation and investment of black money. The buyer has the option of investing his black money by paying cash in addition to the documented sale consideration. This also leads to generation of black money in the hands of the recipient.

Bullion and Jewellery Transactions—Cash sales in the gold and jewellery trade are quite common and serve two purposes. The purchase allows the buyer the option of converting black money into gold and bullion, while it gives the trader the option of keeping his unaccounted wealth in the form of stock, not disclosed in the books or valued at less than market price.

Financial Market Transactions—Financial market transactions can involve black money in different forms. Initial public offers (IPOs) offering equity shares to the public at large are also vulnerable to various manipulations that can generate black money for the promoters or operators. Rigging of markets by the market operators is one such means. This may involve use of shell companies and more sophisticated versions of such manipulation may involve offshore companies or investors in foreign tax jurisdictions who invest in shares offered by the IPO and through manipulated trading escalate their price artificially, only to offload them later at the cost of ordinary investors.

Public Procurement—It also gives birth to black money. It has grown phenomenally over the years in volume, scale, and variety as well as complexity. It often includes sophisticated and hi-tech items, complex works, and a wide range of services. The Organisation for Economic Cooperation and Development (OECD) estimate puts the figure for public procurement in India at 30 percent of the GDP whereas the World Trade Organisation (WTO) estimate puts this figure at 20 percent of the GDP. The Competition Commission of India had estimated in a paper that the annual public sector procurement in India would be of the order of ₹ 8 lakh crore while a rough estimation of direct government procurement is between ₹ 2.5 and 3 lakh crore. This puts the total public procurement figure for India at around ₹ 10 to 11 lakh crore per year.

Non-profit Sector—Taxation laws allow certain privileges and incentives for promoting charitable activities. Misuse of such benefits and manipulations through entities claimed to be constituted for non-profit motive are among possible sources of generation of black money.

Informal Sector and Cash Economy—The issue of black money is related to the magnitude of cash transactions in the informal economy. The demand for currency is determined by a number of factors such as income, price levels, and opportunity cost of holding currency. Factors like dependence on agriculture, existence of a large informal sector, and insufficient banking infrastructure with large un-banked and under-banked areas contribute to the large cash economy in India.

External Trade and Transfer Pricing—More than 60 percent of global trade is carried out between associated enterprises of multinational enterprises (MNEs). Since allocation of costs and overheads and fixing of price of products/services are highly subjective, MNEs enjoy considerable discretion in allocating costs and prices to products/services and geographical jurisdictions. Such discretion enables them to transfer profit/income to no tax or low tax jurisdictions. Differing tax rates in different tax jurisdictions can create perverse incentives for corporations to shift taxable income from jurisdictions with relatively high tax rates to jurisdictions with relatively low tax rates as a means of minimising their tax liability. The illicit money transferred outside India may come back to India through various methods such as hawala, mispricing, foreign direct investment (FDI) through beneficial tax jurisdictions, raising of capital by Indian companies through Global Depository Receipts (GDRs), and investment in Indian stock markets through Participatory Notes.

Trade-based Money Laundering (TBML)—It is the process of disguising the proceeds of crime and moving value through the use of trade transactions in an attempt at legitimising the illicit origins. Factors that facilitate such manipulation include the enormous volume of international trade flow, the complexity associated with financing arrangements and currency exchanges as well as limited recourse to verification procedures between countries.

Tax Havens—The Organisation for Economic Cooperation and Development (OECD) has defined tax havens as being characterized by no or very low taxes, lack of effective exchange of information, and lack of transparency about substantial activities. It listed 35 countries/jurisdictions as tax havens in the year 2000.

Offshore Financial Centers—According to the IMF, 'Offshore Financial Centers' are centers where the bulk of financial sector transactions on both sides of the balance sheet are with individuals or companies that are not residents, where the transactions are initiated elsewhere, and where majority of the institutions involved are controlled by non-residents. Some of the old tax havens have adopted the more benign designation of 'Offshore Financial Center' (OFC) and tend to describe themselves as financial centers specializing in non-residential financial transactions. However, with their array of secrecy provisions that lack regulation, the zero or near zero taxation imposed by them, and lack of adequate capital controls, they are logical extensions of the traditional tax havens. The OFCs have the following characteristics:

(a) Jurisdictions that have financial institutions engaged primarily in business with non-residents;

(b) Financial systems with external assets and liabilities out of proportion to domestic financial intermediation designed to finance domestic economic; and

(c) More popularly, centers which provide some or all the following opportunities—low or zero taxation; moderate or light financial regulation; banking secrecy and anonymity.

International organizations including the BIS and IMF began to use the term OFC in a more restrictive manner to describe financial services that were evolving in tax havens.

Investment through Innovative Derivative Instruments— With increasing sophistication of derivative instruments, new opportunities for investing and making profits without being subjected to taxes and regulations are also opening up. Such innovative means can also be misused by unscrupulous parties to generate unaccounted income. Some such instruments like participatory notes may not be adequately covered by regulatory mechanisms and their oversight and hence have potential for misuse.

Estimates of Black Money Generated in India

There are no reliable estimates of black money generation or accumulation in India, neither is there an accurate well-accepted methodology for making such estimation. Since the black money cannot be accounted for, all attempts at its estimation depend upon the underlying assumptions made and the sophistication of adjustments incorporated.

By its very definition, black money is not accounted for, thus all attempts at its estimation depend upon the underlying assumptions made and the sophistication of adjustments incorporated. Among the estimates made so far, there is no uniformity, unanimity, or consensus about the best methodology or approach to be used for this purpose. There have also been wide variations in the figures reported, which further serves to highlight the limitations of the different methods adopted. Let us discuss some of the methods of estimation of black money in India.

(a) Analysis of individual methods used for estimation of black money has some limitations. One such method is the input/output method. It consists of using the input/output ratio along with the input to calculate the true output. It estimates black money as the difference between the declared output and the output expected on the basis of the input/output ratio. This is a simple method and may have some utility if applied to a uniform industry or a specific sector of the economy; but it is not of much help if applied to economy as a whole as it ignores structural changes in the economy including those related to technology.

(b) The second method adopted by the monetarists is based on the fact that money is needed to circulate incomes in both the 'black' and accounted for economies. As the official economy is known, the difference between that amount and the money in circulation could be assumed to be the circulating 'black' component. An estimate of the velocity of money enables an estimation of income circulated annually. A comparison of that with the income obtained in the National Accounting System (NAS) gives the difference income which could be estimated as the black money in the economy. But it cannot be assumed that the NAS represents accounted incomes accurately, because large proportions of income, such as those falling in the unorganized sector, are not accurately captured in the national accounting system, thus there may be upward bias in the estimate of black money so derived.

(c) The survey approach is also one of the methods of estimation of black money wherein sample surveys are carried out. It may be on the consumption pattern of a representative population sample, which is then compared to the total consumption of the country. In this method, the problems consist in getting a truly representative sample, unambiguous set of questions, and the willingness of persons in the sample size to reveal true facts.

(d) The 'fiscal approach' method for estimating black income considers the economy as comprising several sectors, each having its own sets of practices. The contribution of these sectors to black money generation is separately worked out, which when added would give the size of the 'black' economy. However, the manner of identifying the 'black component' in these sectors and the assumptions suffer from inherent subjectivity of the researcher and lack of uniform standards.

(e) In the past also, it had been attempted to quantify 'black' money generation in India. The estimates made so far have followed two distinct approaches— (i) Kaldor's approach of quantifying non-salary incomes above the exemption limit of income tax; and (ii) The Edgar L. Feige method of working out transaction income on the basis of currency-deposit ratio and deriving from it the 'black' income of the economy. Kaldor estimated non-salary income on the basis of the break-up of national income into— (i) Wages and salaries, (ii) Income of the self-employed, and (iii) Profit, interest, rent, etc. Excluding wages and salaries from the contribution to net domestic product, total non-salary income can be derived. An estimate of the actual non-salary income assessed to tax was made for each sector in order to arrive at the total non-salary income assessed to tax. The difference between the estimated non-salary income above the exemption limit and the actual non-salary income assessed to tax measures the size of 'black' income.

The Direct Taxes Enquiry Committee, also known as Wanchoo Committee, followed the method adopted by Kaldor with some modifications. It estimated assessable non-salary income for the year 1961-62 at ₹ 2686 crore and non-salary income actually assessed to tax to be of the order of ₹ 1875 crore. Accordingly, the income which escaped income tax was of the order of ₹ 811 crore. After making rough adjustments for exemptions and deductions, the Wanchoo Committee found that "the estimated income on which tax has been evaded (black income) would probably be ₹ 700 crore and ₹ 1000 crore for the years 1961-62 and 1965-66 respectively". "Projecting this estimate further to 1968-69 on the basis of percentage increase in national income from 1961-62 to 1968-69, the income on which tax was evaded for 1968-69 was estimated as ₹ 1800 crore."

Dr. D.K. Rangnekar, a member of the Wanchoo Committee, dissented from the estimates made by the Wanchoo Committee. According to him, tax-evaded income for 1961-62 was of the order of ₹ 1150 crore as compared to the Wanchoo Committee's estimate of ₹ 811 crore. For 1965-66, it was ₹ 2,350 crore against the ₹ 1000 crore estimated by the Wanchoo Committee. The projections for 1968-69 and 1969-70 were ₹ 2833 crore and ₹ 3080 crore respectively.

Noted economist O.P. Chopra published several papers about unaccounted income. He prepared a series of estimates of unaccounted income for a period of 17 years, i.e., 1960-61 to 1976-77. Chopra's methodology marked a significant departure from the Wanchoo Committee approach and, as a consequence, he found a larger divergence in the two series from 1973 onwards when income above the exemption limit registered significant increase.

The finding of Chopra's study was that after 1973-74, the ratio of unaccounted income to assessable non-salary income went up, whereas the Wanchoo Committee assumed this ratio to have remained constant. As a consequence, after 1973-74 there was wide divergence between the estimates of the

Wanchoo Committee and those of Chopra. Chopra's estimates corroborated the hypothesis that tax evasion was more likely to be resorted to when the rate of tax was comparatively high. His findings also supported the hypothesis that increase in prices lead to an increase in unaccounted income. Further, he gave a significant finding that funds were diverted to the non-taxable agriculture sector to convert unaccounted (black) income into legal (white) income. Chopra's study estimated unaccounted income to have increased from ₹ 916 crore in 1960-61, i.e., 6.5 percent of gross national product (GNP) at factor cost, to ₹ 8098 crore in 1976-77, 11.4 percent of GNP. According to Suraj B. Gupta, a noted economist, the amount of black money in our country was ₹ 3,034 crore in 1967-68 and ₹ 40,867 crore in 1978-79. According to his estimate, black money which constituted 9.5 percent of the GNP in 1967-68 swelled to nearly 49 percent in 1978-79. He estimated black money at 42 percent of GDP for the year 1980-81 and 51 percent for the year 1987-88.

The National Institute of Public Finance and Policy (NIPFP) estimated the quantum of black money in Indian economy in 1985 at around ₹ 1,00,000 crore or about 20 percent of the national income. The Planning Commission study, however, estimated it to be in the range of ₹ 70,000 crore. Further, it is generated at the rate of ₹ 50,000 crore per year. In 1996, the estimated black money in India was believed to be more than ₹ 4,00,000 crore. Prof. Arun Kumar of Center for Economic Studies, JNU (Delhi), has estimated the black money equivalent to 35 percent of the GDP for 1990-91 and 40 percent for the year 1995-96, out of which 32 percent is in the legal sectors (business and professionals like doctors, film-stars, etc.) and 8 percent in the illegal sector (narcotics, etc.).

The last official study for estimating black money generation was conducted at the behest of the Ministry of Finance by the NIPFP in 1985. The studies carried out for estimating the extent of black money in the economy have followed different methods and have been criticized for their numerous assumptions and approximations. Further, they have arrived at different figures of black money even for the same year. There have also been media reports in recent years that have extended several estimates of black money, especially the unaccounted money held abroad by Indians.

Estimates of Black Money Stashed Abroad—According to an e-mail, which first started circulating on the Internet in early 2009, Indians have more money in the Swiss Banks than all other countries combined. It reveals that as per a Swiss Banking Association report in 2006, bank deposits in the territory of Switzerland by nationals of a few countries are as—India, US$ 1456 billion; Russia, US$ 470 billion; UK, US$ 390 billion; Ukraine, US$ 100 billion; and China, US$ 96 billion. But it is now evident that there is no organization by the name of Swiss Banking Association, although there is a Swiss Bankers Association (SBA). According to James Nason, Head of International Communications of the SBA, the SBA had never published any such report and that the story about Indian deposits was a complete fabrication. Thus, these figures appear to be a figment of the imagination and the email circulating them baseless and mischievous in intent.

According to the 2008 report of Global Financial Integrity (GFI), Indian nationals held around US$ 1.4 trillion abroad in illicit external assets. However, in its November 2010 report, it accepted that the back-of-the-envelope method used to derive the figure was flawed—the figure was based on GFI's estimated average illicit outflows of US$ 22.7 billion per annum (over the period 2002-06) multiplied by the 61 years since independence and it is erroneous to apply annual averages to a long-time series when illicit flows are fluctuating sharply from one year to the next.

However, it is useful to mention here one estimate of the amount of deposits by Indian nationals in Swiss Banks. According to the spokesperson of the Swiss National Bank, at the end of 2010, the total liabilities of Swiss Banks towards Indians were around 1.945 billion Swiss Francs (i.e., about ₹ 9295 crore). The Swiss Ministry of External Affairs confirmed these figures when a reference was made by the Indian Ministry of External Affairs to them. From the information provided by the Swiss Bank, it can be seen that bank deposits of Indian nationals have decreased from ₹ 23373 crore in 2006 to ₹ 9295 crore in 2010. The deposits of Indian nationals in Swiss Banks constitute only 0.13 percent of the total bank deposits of citizens of all countries in 2010.

Illicit Money Transferred Outside India—According to an IMF study, the flight of capital from India during the period 1971-86 was at US$ 20-30 billion, or US$ 1-2 billion every year. This estimate was later revised in 2001-10 to US$ 88 billion over the 1971-97 period, a sum that is equivalent to 20 percent of net real debt disbursements to the economy from 1971 to 1997. In other words, for every dollar of external debt accumulated by India from 1971 to 1997, private Indian residents accumulated 20 cents of external assets. The method followed to arrive at these estimates was the World Bank residual method, which estimates capital flight as:

Capital Flight = Change in External Debt Outstanding + Current Account Surplus + Change in Official Reserve + FDI

The underlying rationale of the method is that the sources of funds exceeding recorded use of funds reflect unrecorded outflows, which may involve capital earned through legitimate means such as the profits of a legitimate business or it may involve capital earned through illegitimate business. The capital flight is adjusted through trade mis-invoicing which arises when transactions are reinvoiced when goods leaving the country of export under one invoice are reported under a different invoice in the country of import. The underlying rationale is that residents can acquire foreign assets illicitly by over-invoicing imports and under-invoicing exports. Thus, the adjusted capital flight was estimated at US$ 87881 million.

Illicit Return of Transferred Money from Abroad—In 'The Drivers and Dynamics of Illicit Financial Flows from India: 1948-2008', Global Financial Integrity (GFI) has estimated that from 1948 to 2008 a total of US$ 213.2 billion has been shifted out of India through illicit outflows. It has also estimated that after taking into consideration the rate of return on external assets, the adjusted gross transfer of illicit assets by residents of India amounted to about US$ 462 billion as of end-December 2008.

Now the question is whether such an amount is stashed abroad in offshore bank accounts or whether this money has at least partly already returned to India. The FDI statistics point to this fact. As per data of the Department of Industrial Policy and Promotion (DIPP), from April 2000 to March 2011, FDI from Mauritius was 41.80 percent of the entire FDI received by India. The two topmost sources of the cumulative FDI inflows from April 2000 to March 2011 were Mauritius (41.80 percent) and Singapore (9.17 percent). Singapore and Mauritius with their small economies cannot be the sources of such huge investments and it is apparent that the investments are routed through these jurisdictions for avoidance of taxes and/or for concealing the identities from the revenue authorities of the ultimate investors, many of whom could actually be Indian residents, who have invested in their own companies, through a process known as round tripping.

Investment in the Indian Stock Market through Participatory Notes (PNs) is another way in which the black money generated by Indians is re-invested in India. Participatory Notes or Overseas Derivative Instruments (ODIs) are issued by Foreign Institutional Investors (FIIs) against underlying Indian securities, which can be equity, debt, derivatives, or even indices. The investor in PNs does not hold the Indian securities in his own name. These are legally held by the FIIs, but he derives economic benefits from fluctuations in prices of the Indian securities, as also dividends and capital gains, through specifically designed contracts. Thus, through the instrument of PNs, investment can be made in the Indian securities market by those investors who do not wish to be regulated by Indian regulators due to a variety of reasons such as not meeting the eligibility criteria for investment in Indian securities market, cost and time considerations, or the desire to keep their identity anonymous, which is possible also for the reason that PNs/ODIs can be freely traded and easily transferred without disclosing the identity of the actual beneficiaries. The PNs can only be issued to persons who are regulated by an appropriate foreign regulatory authority and after satisfying know your customer (KYC) norms. Further, the FIIs are required to report to SEBI on a monthly basis, the name and location of the person to whom the PNs/ODIs have been issued. However, in view of the fact that the jurisdictions in which the persons to whom PNs are issued are not only countries such as the UK or USA but also well-known OFCs such as the Cayman Islands, British Virgin Islands, Switzerland, and Luxembourg, it is possible to hide the identity of the ultimate beneficiaries through multiple layers which is also evident by going through the orders passed by SEBI in some cases. The ultimate beneficiaries/investors through the PN Route can be Indians and the source of their investment may be black money generated by them.

Charitable organisations, Non-government Organisations (NGOs), and associations receiving foreign contributions are required to file an annual return to the Ministry of Home Affairs, where only the name and address of the foreign donors are mentioned, with no further details of the beneficial owners. It is possible that in many such cases, the black money generated by Indians is being routed back to India.

Misuse of Corporate Structure—Corporate structuring is a legitimate means of bringing together factors of production in a way that will facilitate business and enterprise and help the economy. However, an artificial personality can also be created of a corporate entity to conceal the real beneficiaries. Opaque structuring through creation of multiple entities that own each other and the secrecy granted by certain jurisdictions facilitate such misuse. For example, the Vodafone tax case provides an instance of the misuse of corporate structure for avoiding the payment of taxes. In this case, the Hutchison Group had made investments in India from 1992 to 2006 through several subsidiaries having 'separate corporate personality' but which were essentially post box companies based in the Cayman Islands, British Virgin Islands, and Mauritius. The Hutchison Group sold its entire business operation in India in February 2007 to the Vodafone Group for a total consideration of US$ 11.2 billion and the same was effected through transfer of a solitary share of a Cayman Islands Company. When the tax authorities requested the accounts of the said company, the answer given was that as per Cayman Islands law, the company was not required to prepare its accounts. With increasing realisation about the harmful effect of ownership being concealed behind complicated corporate ownership structure, such structure is coming under scrutiny. In the Indian context, it is one of the reasons for the fact that tax authorities are not able to act in cases where money is prima facie brought back to India through round tripping and other legitimate means.

PM Modi's Surgical Strikes against Black Money

The issue of 'Black Money' has become a political agenda in India and the promise to bring back trillions of dollars stashed in foreign banks has helped the BJP to increase its credibility and outreach among people. While accusing the previous UPA Government of not being serious on the issue of black money, PM Modi promised to get back every penny stashed in foreign banks. He has said that bringing back black money from outside the country is an "article of faith" for him and nothing will be lacking in his efforts to do so.

The Modi Government is hell-bent on cracking down on black money and undisclosed income of Indians within the country and safely stowed away abroad. While there is no proper estimation of the actual amount of black money in the economy, several studies including one done by Indian Institute of Finance estimate it is around US$ 2 trillion.

Recent media reports quoted Zurich-based Swiss National Bank saying that money held by Indians in Swiss banks had dropped by nearly one-third. According to Minister of State for Finance Santosh Kumar Gangwar, a sectoral analysis of the admission of undisclosed income during searches conducted by the Income Tax Department in FY16, revealed that the main sectors that is generating black money are—manufacturing (31%), real estate (29%), trading (8%), educational institutions (7%), contractors (6%), services (5%), gems & jewellery (4%). The Modi Government has taken the black money issue, both foreign and domestic, very seriously. The government has announced several measures to clamp down on black money, both, within the country and outside it. These involve policy-level initiatives, more effective enforcement action on the ground, putting in place robust legislative and administrative frameworks, systems and processes with due focus on capacity building, and integration of information and its mining through appropriate use of information technology. While the currency revamp may have come across as a surprise move, PM Modi has been preparing for the move ever since he came in power. Following are some of the major initiatives taken by the Modi Government to eradicate the black money from the Indian economy.

Constitution of Special Investigation Team (SIT) on Black Money

In its very first Cabinet meeting in May 2014, the newly elected Narendra Modi Government constituted a Supreme Court-monitored Special Investigation Team (SIT) on black money stashed abroad by evading taxes or generated through unlawful activities. This clearly establishes the positive intent of the government to deal with the menace of black money. The SIT on black money was constituted under Chairmanship and Vice-Chairmanship of two former judges of the Supreme Court—the team is headed by the former Supreme Court Judge M.B. Shah, known for the swiftness he showed in the cases about illegal mining, and is co-headed by another former Supreme Court Judge Arijit Pasayat. Both are known for their objectivity, boldness, and transparency. The other members of SIT include the most elite officers of ten different investigative and enforcement agencies to ensure that no loopholes may perpetuate. They include Secretary of the Department of Revenue, a Deputy Governor of Reserve Bank of India (RBI), IB Director, Director of Enforcement Directorate, Director of the Central Bureau of Investigation (CBI), CBDT Chairman and Director General of the Narcotics Control Bureau. Besides, D.G. of Directorate of Revenue Intelligence, Director of Financial Intelligence Unit, Secretary of Research and Analysis Wing (RAW), and a Joint Secretary of Foreign Tax and Tax Research are also the members of the SIT.

The 21-member SIT constituted to trace, track and retrieve the black money has acted very swiftly to chart out the roadmap of how to proceed for bringing this wealth of the nation, illicitly held abroad, in its very first meeting, held within a week of its constitution on 2 June 2014. According to the terms of reference for the SIT, it will investigate all matters with respect to unaccounted monies being stashed in foreign banks by Indian nationals or other entities operating in India, and would also prepare a comprehensive plan, including creation of the institutional structure that will enable the country to fight the battle against unaccounted money. It will have jurisdiction in cases where investigations have begun, are pending or waiting to be initiated and that which have been completed.

The Black Money (Undisclosed Foreign Income and Assets) and Imposition of Tax Act, 2015

The Undisclosed Foreign Income and Assets (Imposition of Tax) Bill, 2015 has been introduced in the Parliament on 20 March 2015. The Bill provides for separate taxation of any undisclosed income in relation to foreign income and assets. Such income will henceforth not be taxed under the Income Tax Act but under the stringent provisions of the proposed new legislation.

The Bill will apply to Indian residents and seeks to replace the Income Tax (IT) Act, 1961 for the taxation of foreign income. It penalizes the concealment of foreign income, and provides for criminal liability for attempting to evade tax in relation to foreign income. It came into force on 1 July 2015 to specifically and more effectively deal with undisclosed income in foreign countries and tax havens. It was launched to bring back black money stashed abroad and its compliance window ended on 30 September 2015. While the total disclosures under this scheme were underwhelming, the Act also has various stringent provisions for penalty and prosecution of foreign black money holder's unearthed during future investigation by tax department.

The salient features of the Undisclosed Foreign Income and Assets (Imposition of Tax) Act, 2015 are:

(a) **Scope of the Act**—The Act will apply to individual resident in India. Provisions of the Act will apply to both undisclosed foreign income and assets, including financial interest in any entity.

(b) **Tax Rate**—Undisclosed foreign income or assets shall be taxed at the flat rate of 30 percent. No exemption or deduction or set off of any carried forward losses which may be admissible under the existing Income-tax Act, 1961, shall be allowed. This would apply from 1 April 2016 onwards.

(c) **Income to be Taxed**—The total undisclosed foreign income and asset of an individual would include the income from a source located outside India, which has not been disclosed in the tax returns filed; the income from a source outside India for which no tax returns have been filed; and the value of an undisclosed asset, located outside India.

(d) **Penalties**—Violation of the provisions of the proposed new legislation will entail stringent penalties.

 (i) The penalty for non-disclosure of income or an asset located outside India will be equal to three times the amount of tax payable thereon, i.e., 90 percent of the undisclosed income or the value of the undisclosed asset. This will be in addition to tax payable at 30 percent.

 (ii) If a person who has filed tax returns does not disclose his foreign income, or submits inaccurate details of the same, has to pay a fine of ₹ 10 lakh. This will not apply to an asset, with a value of five lakh rupees or less.

 (iii) Any person, who continues to default in paying tax that is due, would be liable to pay an amount equal to the amount of tax arrears.

 (iv) If a person fails to abide by the tax authority in answering questions, signing off on a statement, or attending or producing relevant documents, he will have to pay a fine between ₹ 50,000 to ₹ 2 lakh.

(e) **Prosecutions**—The Act proposes enhanced punishment for various types of violations.

  (i) The punishment for willful attempt to evade tax in relation to a foreign income or an asset located outside India will be rigorous imprisonment from three years to ten years, in addition to a fine.

  (ii) Failure to furnish a return in respect of foreign assets and bank accounts or income will be punishable with rigorous imprisonment for a term of six months to seven years. The same term of punishment is prescribed for cases where although the assessee has filed a return of income, but has not disclosed the foreign asset or has furnished inaccurate particulars of the same.

  (iii) Abetment or inducement of another person to make a false return or a false account or statement or declaration under the Act will be punishable with rigorous imprisonment from six months to seven years. This provision will also apply to banks and financial institutions aiding in concealment of foreign income or assets of resident Indians or falsification of documents.

(f) **Safeguards**—The principles of natural justice and due process of law have been embedded in the Act by laying down the requirement of mandatory issue of notices to the person against whom proceedings are being initiated, grant of opportunity of being heard, necessity of taking the evidence produced by him into account, recording of reasons, passing of orders in writing, limitation of time for various actions of the tax authority, etc. Further, the right of appeal has been protected by providing for appeals to the Income-tax Appellate Tribunal, and to the jurisdictional High Court and the Supreme Court on substantial questions of law. To protect persons holding foreign accounts with minor balances which may not have been reported out of oversight or ignorance, it has been provided that failure to report bank accounts with a maximum balance of up to ₹ 5 lakh at any time during the year will not entail penalty or prosecution.

(g) **One-Time Compliance Opportunity**—A one-time compliance opportunity to persons who have any undisclosed foreign assets which have hitherto not been disclosed for the purposes of income tax, will be provided for a limited period. Such persons would be permitted to file a declaration before the specified tax authority within a specified period, followed by payment of tax at the rate of 30 percent and an equal amount by way of penalty. Such persons will not be prosecuted under the stringent provisions of the new Act. However, it should be noted that this is not an amnesty scheme as no immunity from penalty is being offered. It is merely an opportunity for persons to come clean and become compliant before the stringent provisions of the new Act come into force.

(h) **Amendment of Prevention of Money Laundering Act (PMLA)**—The new Act also proposes to amend PMLA (2002) to include offence of tax evasion under the proposed legislation as a scheduled offence under PMLA.

Thus, the Modi Government is committed to take focused action on black money front, and for it an unprecedented and multi-pronged attack has been launched to root out the menace of black money.

Renegotiation of Tax Treaties and Automatic Information Exchange Agreements with Tax Havens

The Modi Government has taken certain measures that will make it much harder to hide cash abroad as well as round tripping of funds to India. It has been collaborating with foreign governments to facilitate and expand the exchange of information. For this, the Double Taxation Avoidance Agreements (DTAAs) has been signed with tax havens like Mauritius and Cyprus. India has also joined with global efforts to combat tax evasion and black money by joining the Multilateral Competent Authority Agreement (MCAA) in respect of

Automatic Exchange of Information (AEOI) and having an information sharing arrangement with the US under its Foreign Account Tax Compliance Act (FATCA). The government is also trying to automate information exchange with several countries, including Switzerland, to clamp down on black money. For this both India and Switzerland have agreed to speed up work on the AEOI and make it possible by 2018.

The Modi Government has renegotiated the Double Tax Avoidance Agreement (DTAA) with Mauritius to impose Capital Gains Tax if such Capital Asset is situated in India. Agreements on the above pattern are also being negotiated or renegotiated with other tax jurisdictions and tax havens. From 2017, Organisation of Economic Cooperation and Development (OECD) countries have agreed to share information on foreign account holders with their home countries.

Income Disclosure Scheme, 2016

The Income Declaration Scheme, 2016, as incorporated in the Finance Act 2016, is like a one-time amnesty-like compliance window for citizens who have not declared income correctly in earlier years to come forward and declare their undisclosed income. Under this scheme, such income as declared by the eligible persons, would be taxed at the rate of 30 percent plus a *Krishi Kalyan Cess* of 25 percent on the taxes payable and a penalty at the rate of 25 percent of the taxes payable, thereby totaling to 45 percent of the income declared under the scheme.

The Income Disclosure Scheme was in force for a period of four months from 1 June 2016 to 30 September 2016 for filing of declarations and payments towards taxes, surcharge, and penalty had to be made latest by 30 November 2016. Declarations could be filed online or with the jurisdictional Principal Commissioners of Income Tax across the country. The salient features of this scheme were:

(a) It was for undisclosed income whether in the form of investment in assets or otherwise, pertaining to Financial Year 2015-16 or earlier.

(b) Where the declaration was in the form of investment in assets, the Fair Market Value of such asset as on

1 June 2016 was deemed to be the undisclosed income under the scheme. However, foreign assets or income to which the Black Money Act 2015 applied were not eligible for declaration under the scheme.

(c) Assets specified in the declaration were exempted from Wealth Tax.

(d) No scrutiny and enquiry under the Income Tax Act or the Wealth Tax were undertaken in respect of such declarations.

(e) Immunity from prosecution under the Income Tax Act and Wealth Tax Act was also provided along with immunity from the Benami Transactions (Prohibition) Act, 1988 subject to transfer of asset to actual owner within the period specified in the Rules.

(f) Non-payment of total taxes, surcharge and penalty in time or declaration by misrepresentation or suppression of facts rendered the declaration void.

(g) The circumstances in which the scheme did not apply or where a person was held to be ineligible were specified in Section 196 (Chapter IX) of the Finance Act, 2016.

(h) Non-declaration of undisclosed income under the scheme would render such undisclosed income liable to tax in the previous year in which it was detected by the Income Tax Department. Other penal consequences would also follow accordingly.

Thus, the attraction of this scheme for black money holders was that it had given them immunity from prosecution. Through this scheme, the Modi Government had given the last and final opportunity for tax evaders to come clean in the eyes of law.

Benami Transaction (Prohibition) Amendment Bill, 2015

The Benami Transaction (Prohibition) Amendment Bill, 2015 came into force from 1 November 2016, with the intent of bringing unaccounted money into the system, as well as seizing benami property and prosecuting those indulging in such activities. It is predominately an anti-black money measure with the three-fold objectives—amending the definition of benami transactions, establishing adjudicating authorities and setting up an Appellate Tribunal to deal with benami transactions, and specifying the penalty for entering into such transactions. It is the amended version of the Benami Transaction (Prohibition) Act, 1988, and will give more teeth to the authorities to curb benami transactions.

The new Act defines a benami transaction as:

(a) a transaction or an arrangement where a property is transferred to, or is held by, a person, and the consideration for such property has been provided, or paid by, another person; and the property is held for the immediate or for the future benefit, direct or indirect, of the person who has provided the consideration, except when the property is held by

(i) a Karta or a member of a Hindu undivided family, as the case may be, and the property is held for his benefit or benefit of other members in the family and the consideration for such property has been provided or paid out of the known sources of income of the Hindu undivided family;

(ii) a person standing in a fiduciary capacity for the benefit of another person towards whom he stands in such capacity and includes a trustee, executor, partner, director of a company, a depository or a participant as an agent of a depository under the Depositories Act, 1996 and any other person as may be notified by the Central Government for this purpose;

(iii) any person being an individual in the name of his spouse or in the name of any child of such individual and the consideration for such property has been provided or paid out of the known sources of income of the individual;

(iv) any person in the name of his brother or sister or lineal ascendant or descendant, where the names of brother and sister or lineal ascendant or descendant and the individual appear as joint-owners in any document, and the consideration for such property has been provided or paid out of the known sources of income of the individual.

(b) a transaction or an arrangement in respect of a property carried out or made in a fictitious name.

(c) a transaction or an arrangement in respect of a property where the owner of the property is not aware of, or, denies knowledge of, such ownership.

(d) a transaction or an arrangement in respect of a property where the person providing the consideration is not traceable or is fictitious.

Under the new Act, an authority to acquire benami properties was to be established by the rules. The Act seeks to establish four authorities to conduct inquiries or investigations regarding benami transactions—Initiating Officer, Approving Authority, Administrator, and Adjudicating Authority. If an Initiating Officer believes that a person is a benamidar, he may issue a notice to that person. The Initiating Officer may hold the property for 90 days from the date of issue of the notice subject to permission from the Approving Authority. At the end of the notice period, the Initiating Officer may pass an order to continue the holding of the property. In such case, the Initiating Officer will refer the case to the Adjudicating Authority who will examine all documents and evidence relating to the matter and then pass an order on whether or not to hold the property as benami. Based on an order to confiscate the benami property, the Administrator will receive and manage the property in a manner and subject to conditions as prescribed. The Act also seeks to establish an Appellate Tribunal to hear appeals against any orders passed by the Adjudicating Authority. Appeals against orders of the Appellate Tribunal will lie to the High Court.

Under the old Act, the penalty for entering into benami transactions was imprisonment up to three years, or a fine, or both. However, the new Act seeks to change this penalty to rigorous imprisonment of one year up to seven years, and a fine which may extend to 25 percent of the fair market value of the benami property. It also specifies the penalty for providing false information to be rigorous imprisonment of six months up to five years, and a fine which may extend to 10 percent of the fair market value of the benami property.

Penalty on Real Estate Transactions Undertaken in Cash Exceeding ₹ 20,000

It is a well-known fact that real estate is the pit where people hoard black money from the eyes of tax officials. In order to curb the generation of black money by way of dealings in cash in immovable property transactions, Section 269SS of the Income-tax Act has brought out some changes for the realty sector. As per the new tax law by Central Board of Direct Taxes (CBDT), which is effective from 1 June 2015, any transaction in real estate, including agricultural land, shall be required to be made through account payee cheque or real time gross settlement (RTGS) or electronic funds transfer if the amount exceeds ₹ 20,000. If transaction is done in cash then penalty of an amount equal to such cash transaction will be imposed on seller who accepts cash or refund of advance is made in cash by the seller of the property. This move of the Modi Government would ensure more transparency in the real estate businesses and wrong doers earning crores of unaccounted money involved in the litigation process will come to an end.

However, this new rule of transaction is not applicable to farmers if both the parties involved in a transaction have agricultural income only and not any other income chargeable to income tax, for instance, both of them should not have any income like interest or rent or salary, etc., even of one rupee, i.e. they should not have even income of one rupee other than the agricultural income.

Besides property transactions, so many other rules have been changed with effect from 1 June 2015. To name a few, existing Section 269SS provides that, subject to specified exceptions, a person shall not take or accept any loan or deposit from any other person otherwise than by the prescribed banking channels that is by an account payee cheque or account payee bank draft or by use of electronic clearing system through a bank account so that the aggregate of loan or deposit from one person together with aggregate of existing loans and deposits from such person is ₹ 20,000 or more. Also, bank or cooperative bank and post office recurring deposits (RD) interest will be liable to tax deduction at source (TDS), if it is more than ₹ 10,000 per year. If PAN number is not given, the TDS will be 20 percent. The purchase transactions in consumer products like fridge, TV, car, jewellery, etc. can be made in cash or cheque but if it is more than ₹ 1 lakh, the PAN number of buyer will have to be quoted. In case of purchase of jewellery of more than ₹ 5 lakh value is made, then TDS will be one percent. Contravention of the above provision attracts penalty under the provisions contained in Section 271D of Income-tax Act, which provides that the person will be liable to pay by way of penalty a sum equal to amount taken or accepted in contravention of Section 269SS. The above provisions are not applicable inter alia in a case when the accepter of the loan or depositor as well as the person giving the loan or deposit have agricultural income and neither has any income chargeable to income tax. By the Finance Bill, 2015, it has been proposed to expand this provision by adding the sums received in relation to transfer of immovable property whether as advance or otherwise and whether or not ultimately the contemplated transfer takes place or not.

Tax Collection at Source on Cash Sales Exceeding ₹ 2 Lakh

The Modi Government has taken one more important measure to curb high value cash transactions and create an audit trail by imposing tax collection at source at a nominal rate of one percent on cash purchases exceeding ₹ 2 lakh. Thus, in order to curb the cash economy, Finance Act, 2016, has amended Section 206C of the Income-tax Act to provide that the seller shall collect tax at the rate of one percent from the purchaser on sale in cash of certain goods or provision of services exceeding two lakh rupees.

Section 206C of the Income-tax Act, 1961, prior to amendment by Finance Act, 2016, provided that the seller shall collect tax at source at specified rate from the buyer at the time of sale of specified items such as alcoholic liquor, tender leaves, mineral being coal or lignite or iron ore, etc. It also provided for collection of tax at source at the rate of one percent on sale in cash of bullion exceeding ₹ 2 lakh and jewellery exceeding ₹ 5 lakh. In order to reduce the cash transactions in sale of goods and services, Finance Act, 2016, has expanded the scope of Section 206C(1D) to provide that the seller shall collect tax at the rate of one percent from the purchaser on sale in cash of any goods (other than bullion and jewellery) or providing of any services (other than payment on which tax is deducted at source under Chapter XV II-B) exceeding ₹ 2 lakh. So far as sale of bullion and jewellery is concerned, the provisions of sub-section (1D) of Section 206C prior to its amendment by the Finance Act, 2016, shall continue to apply.

Also, with a view to bring high value transactions within the tax net, it has been provided in sub-section (1F) of Section 206C of the Act that the seller who receives consideration for sale of a motor vehicle exceeding ₹ 10 lakh, shall collect one percent of the sale consideration as tax from the buyer.

Any person who obtains in any sale, the goods of the nature specified in sub-section (1D) or (1F) of Section 206C is a buyer. The seller for the purposes of collection of tax under Section 206C shall be—a Central Government or a State Government; any local authority, or corporation or authority established under any Central, State or Provincial Act; any company, firm or cooperative society; and an individual or Hindu undivided family who is liable to audit as per provisions of Section 44AB during the financial year immediately preceding the financial year in which the goods are sold or the services are provided.

The amendments brought in Section 206C by Finance Act, 2016 are applicable from 1 June 2016.

Demonetization

All cash transactions are not corrupt, but every corrupt transaction is in cash, and high denomination notes are assumed to be the currency of corruption. If we want to challenge root and branches of corruption, we cannot merely trim the branches periodically to appease public opinion. We must have to attack the curse at the roots. Corruption is the mechanism through which a section of our elite has poisoned the credibility of our nation's political and economic edifice. Governments have been either complicit or helpless as high end individuals, buoyed by the arrogance of unaccounted wealth, began to believe that they were above the law or beyond the reach of coercive instruments. That comfort zone has been wrecked by the announcement of Prime Minister Narendra Modi on 8 November 2016, at 8 p.m. address to the nation, that the currencies in the denominations of ₹ 500 and ₹ 1000 shall be invalid from the midnight of that day, i.e. from 9 November 2016, they shall not be the legal tenders for transactions. He also announced the introduction of new notes in denominations of ₹ 500 and ₹ 2000 with higher security features.

Behind demonetization Modi had two rationales. His first stated rationale was to cut down the black money market economy, which sustains illegal activities like tax evasion, bribery, counterfeiting, and terrorist finance. These goals are in line with Modi's campaign promises to deliver transparency and fairness. And the second rationale was to make India a cashless society. Thus, the demonetization is Modi's attempt to reduce bribery and the black economy so that India may shift towards digitalized money transfers, which are more traceable and taxable. Only 2.89 percent of Indians filed any income taxes in 2013, compared with 45 percent of US citizens. Although the majority of Indian's incomes are probably below the tax threshold in the first place, there is no doubt that India's black market is huge—according to the World Bank estimate it was 23.2 percent of the total economy in 2007. In other words, Modi's initiative can be marked as an important step toward cutting off funding for terrorism, reducing corruption, eliminating black money, and accelerating India's transition towards a 21st century cashless economy. As a result, taking Modi's exhortations for 'sacrifice' and 'patriotism' to heart, the populace lined up at banks and ATMs for several weeks to exchange their old currency for new notes.

A Remarkable Step: Historically, 'demonetizations' or radical recalls/replacements or redenominations of currencies by governments have been in response to hyperinflations. There are many such cases of outright withdrawal of notes from circulation being resorted to, when normal means to suck up excess liquidity in the system have failed. The underlying purpose has always been to control runaway inflation and the accompanying loss of faith in the domestic currency, both among investors and the larger public.

But the Modi Government's demonetization of ₹ 500 and ₹ 1000 banknotes—constituting over 86 percent of the total value of currency in circulation—is remarkable because it has not been undertaken in response to any hyperinflation or loss of confidence in the rupee. The rupee has actually been quite strong, both in terms of its internal and external value. Annual consumer price inflation was just 4.2 percent in October, while the rupee has held steady at ₹ 66 to ₹ 68 against the dollar for the last one year and more. In real effective terms, against a basket of 36 currencies after adjusting for inflation differentials vis-à-vis the countries concerned, the rupee's average trade-weighted exchange rate in October was the strongest since July 2011. Thus, the Modi Government's demonetization does not follow the conventional logic of a currency 'stabilisation' measure as the Indian economy is hardly suffering from any hyperinflation or run on the rupee today to even remotely warrant such an action. It has, instead, been projected as a 'structural reform', targeted at reshaping public attitudes towards currency with a view to move towards a cashless economy.

In India, most of the economic transactions take place in cash outside recorded market channels and hence go largely untaxed. This, apart from fostering a parallel 'black' economy with security implications, prevents the government from investing sufficiently in public goods to pursue long-term growth and equity objectives. Through demonetization Modi has given a clear message that cash is no longer cool; and demonetization should also be seen with the other planned big reform of instituting a nationwide goods and services tax regime, which is also ultimately aimed at raising the country's abysmally low tax-GDP ratio.

Although intended as a 'reform' measure, demonetization is likely to have more of a 'stabilisation' impact, with the difference that we are talking of an economy which was far from overheated and experiencing hyperinflation or a speculative attack on its currency. On the contrary, the Indian economy was already in slowdown mode and starved of investments, forcing even the Reserve Bank of India (RBI) to significantly loosen its monetary policy stance of late. Demonetization had led to unprecedented monetary tightening, with nearly ₹ 15 lakh crore worth of currency being withdrawn overnight from circulation. This untimely, and probably unintended, stabilization had the potential to convert a slowdown into a full-blown recession.

The Modi Government had said that the withdrawn ₹ 500 and ₹ 1000 denomination notes would be replaced with new currency with enhanced security features. But that was not so easy. To start with, printing itself, the total demonetized banknotes numbered 2300 crore pieces, might take five to six months, according to various estimates. Even after printing, the new currency notes had to be delivered to bank branches and ATMs in every nook and cranny of the country.

There is an additional aspect that needs to be highlighted. Out of the ₹ 17.54 lakh crore worth of outstanding notes in circulation as on 28 October, only ₹ 4.84 lakh crore, or 27.6 percent, was held by scheduled commercial banks as cash in hand and balances with RBI. The remaining amount would have been mostly with the public, repeatedly changing hands, and with each transfer resulting in a good or service getting produced or exchanged. 86 percent of such circulating money being suddenly immobilized was a huge thing, especially when every ₹ 500 or ₹ 1000 note got used for not one, but several transactions. If the whole cycle is considered—from printing and transporting the new currency across the length and breadth of the country, to its being actually withdrawn by people—it could take at least a year for liquidity, expressed as both quantity of money and velocity of circulation, to regain its pre-demonetization levels.

Although India scrapped its currency notes to curb tax evasion and terrorism in 1946, and again in 1978, Modi's demonetization move is unique, never attempted before—not for stabilization, but as reform.

Pros and Cons of Demonetization: Every move of the government has certain advantages and certain disadvantages. Some of the assumed advantages of the historic demonetization move are:

(a) **Will reduce the amount of black money in the economy**—After demonetization, people who have black money, which is more than 20 percent of the total economy, shall have to either abandon their money or move it to white by bringing it to the system.

(b) **Will increase the inflow of money in the economy**—Since people will have to put their money into bank, it will result in huge increase of inflow of cash in to the banking system and, thus, into the economy.

(c) **Will hit the counterfeiting of currency notes**—Crores of counterfeited money are being pumped by ISI and Pakistan to Indian economy, which will be hit by the demonetization move badly.

(d) **Funding of terror-related activities will get reduce**—Most of the illegal works and terror-related activities are being funded through fake currency and earning from the fake currency business. As the fake currency business will be hit badly by the demonetization, so it will lead to stop terror funding for the time being, which will result in a decrease in the terrorist activities.

(e) **Funding of naxal will go in vain**—Naxal and other illegal mafia have accumulated a huge amount of money with them, which they have earned through their illegal activities. That money will be useless, neither they can deposit it in the banks nor they can use it further.

(f) **Political funding will be hit**—As almost all political parties are themselves the biggest hoarders of the black money, their economy will be hit badly.

(g) **Will increase the GDP**—Government is expecting to get ₹ 10 trillion to be deposited in the banks after demonetization, which will very positively impact the Indian economy and improve the GDP by at least 1.5 percent.

(h) **Will increase public expenditures**—More tax will be collected, which will give leverage to the government to spend more on public expenditures like infrastructure, health, and education.

(i) **Will increase job opportunities**—As government will increase the public funding, the job opportunities in the fields of health sector, education sector, banking sector, and infrastructural sector will increase.

(j) **Poor people will be more benefited**—Government will have more money to spend for the welfare of the poorest of the poor population of the country. It will take more and more work for the upliftment of the poor.

There may be some short-term and some long-term problems due to demonetization. Some of the assumed disadvantages of the historic demonetization move are:

(a) **Problems in exchanging old notes**—Since about 85 percent of the total money in circulation was in the denomination of ₹ 500 and ₹ 1000 notes, it was very tough task both for the government and for the people to exchange old notes.

(b) **Public inconvenience**—It might be very inconvenient for public. Many people had medical emergency and health issues; there was wedding season around the corner. So, it was very inconvenient situation for the common people.

(c) **Lack of banking structure**—Banking structure, especially in rural India, is not so sound, which could support the huge economic transition. 50 days' time period given by the government for such a big economic transition was very short.

(d) **May not stop the corruption and hoarding**—If certain steps are not followed properly like reducing a discretionary power of tax officer, making tax policy easier, increasing the exemption limit and reducing the tax rate, it is assumed that people will again start hoarding money and evading tax. So, the whole marathon exercise of demonetization will go in vain.

(e) **Has Hit the economy for two quarters at least**—As 90 percent of the Indian economy was on cash, the crunch of cash situation would have hit the economy for two quarters at least if not more. Service sector, which generates 50 percent of the revenue, would have been worst hit by the cash crunch.

(f) **Has hit the agriculture sector**—It was high activity period for agriculture sector. Farmers did not have cash to buy seeds, fertilizers, etc. which might have hit the production of many important items, which would further impact the economy.

(g) **Inflation might return**—Normally, inflation should go down after demonetization. However, if the farm production gets hit by demonetization, it will further result in inflation and high prices of food grains.

Thus, despite the initiative's bungled execution and the attendant damage to the economy, demonetization may prove beneficial in the long-term.

Chapter 12

An Assessment of Modi Government's Achievements

On 26 May 2014, the National Democratic Alliance Government under Prime Minister Narendra Modi assumed charge of the country. For the first time in 30 years, the BJP came to power with an absolute majority and the swearing-in ceremony gave a hint that Team Modi was ready with a game-changing plan for the country. It is a good time to undertake an assessment of how Modi has fared so far. Have the promises he made been realized or not?

Most people think that the commitment of "*achhe din*" for Indians has not been met. The level of energy and enthusiasm that was unleased by Modi during 2014 Lok Sabha elections seems to have been all but dissipated. So, has Modi failed? This would be a harsh and sweeping judgment. His critics cite the losses in State elections in Delhi and Bihar to say that the Modi magic has evaporated. But, again a great win in the UP, Uttarakhand, and Goa Assembly elections in 2017 shows the dominance of Modi magic. Thus, Modi continues to be the most popular leader in the country, with none of the other leaders coming anywhere near him.

While making a fair and balanced assessment of Modi's performance, it should be recognized that expectations from Modi at the time when he took office were totally unrealistic. People wanted immediate results for their all sorts of problems whether it was providing jobs, lowering prices, improving agriculture, promoting business and industry, etc. No leader, even with the best of intentions and a majority in both Houses of Parliament, could have met these expectations considering the fractious policy, complexity, and magnitude of challenges confronted by the country.

Modi won the 2014 Lok Sabha elections on the twin planks of "development" and "good governance". It will be instructive to see how he has performed on these two fronts.

On development front, the Modi Government has taken several significant decisions in the economic field, resulting in initiatives such as Make in India, Swachh Bharat, Clean Ganga, Skill India, Jan Dhan Yojana, Crop Insurance Program, and many more. All these initiatives need to be implemented with determination so that their results become evident quickly. It is most essential to increase the share of manufacturing in the economy so that more jobs are created, to promote cleanliness so that productivity increases and expenditure on health care declines, to equip people with the right skills and training so that challenge of providing one million jobs every month can be met, and to increase the productivity and well-being of farmers and villages. It is also vital to provide suitable training to youths to reap the full dividend of the demographic advantage.

However, the economy has faced certain challenges as well. Although overall inflation has been arrested, the prices of food items have soared to a very high level. This is one of the biggest shortcomings of the Modi Government. Another is its failure to provide jobs to the youths. Macro-economic indicators like FDI, inward remittances, and a high-level GDP growth of 7.5 percent do not mean much unless they are translated into lower prices for essential commodities and more jobs for young people. Also, India's exports have declined continuously because of contracting international demand. On the other hand, the government has taken good advantage of ebbing energy prices and simultaneously moved to hike its target of renewable energy to 175 GW over the next 10 years. Significant progress has been made in vital areas of railways, roads, power, and other infrastructure.

On good governance front, the government has permitted itself to be put on the back foot by its opponents. Its commitment on "*sabka saath, sabka vikas*" has not been translated into action so far. In several areas like so-called *love-jihad*, *ghar wapsi*, and the beef ban, the government has permitted fringe fundamentalist elements in the party to hold center stage. This has encouraged the opposition to regroup under a banner of rising intolerance and paint the government in an unflattering light. Mishandling of student protestors at Hyderabad University, Jawaharlal Nehru University, and Jadavpur University could cost Modi dearly be depleting his voter support among the youths of the country. However, a big success for the government is that there is not a whiff of any huge corruption scandal or scam over its ministers.

On external affairs, the Modi Government has scored high marks in formulating and implementing foreign policy. Some analysts tend to term Modi's initiatives as a failure because of India's difficult and tense relations with its neighbours like Pakistan, China, Nepal, and Maldives. But fractious relations with Pakistan and China have existed for a long time. Initiatives by the Modi Government have put India in a stronger position, although they might not have necessarily helped in improving bilateral relations. Under Modi, India has sought to diminish the significance of Pakistan in its foreign policy formulation and establish strategic partnerships with countries like the US and Japan to enhance New Delhi's maneuverability to deal with the increasingly assertive behaviour of China. Difficult and stressed relations with Nepal and the Maldives, meanwhile, are due to India being sucked into the vortex of domestic politics in these countries. Modi's vision, energy, and infectious enthusiasm in strengthening relations with big and medium powers like the US, Germany, Japan, Russia, France, ASEAN, the UK, Australia, South Korea, Central Asia, and West Asia have been productive as he has made foreign policy a significant element in India's domestic economic development. Modi has used India's soft power like yoga, culture, and philosophy, to good effect as well. He has also actively and effectively reached out to the Indian diaspora to make them active partners in India's progress and development.

Although Modi's achievements have been substantial, they might not measure up to the impossible hype and hope of "*achhe din*". In the coming year, Modi and his colleagues will need to ensure that macro policies get implemented efficaciously and that their impact is felt by the people. On the governance side, it will be necessary to rein in the extremist elements who tend to take the focus away from development.

Foreign Policy: The Shiniest Diamond in Modi Government's Crown

Foreign policy has been the most visible dimension of the Modi Government's term so far. Modi's international visits have been the most visible manifestation of the BJP Government's foreign policy. His first year in office kicked off with an invitation to the leaders of SAARC countries (and Mauritius) to his swearing-in ceremony. The manifesto of the BJP had clearly indicated that "in our neighbourhood we will pursue friendly relations" and Modi began with a 'neighbourhood first' policy, making Bhutan his first foreign destination and Nepal his third, with the little matter of a Brazilian sojourn for the BRICS Summit sandwiched in between. Visits to Sri Lanka and Bangladesh, which came slightly after the one year mark, followed and an emphasis on India's neighbourhood was clear. While the signing of the Land Border Agreement between India and Bangladesh was a high point of the government's neighbourhood policy, the breakdown of India-Nepal relations in the context of the latter's new Constitution was a major low point. The other focus of the first year was the series of high-profile interactions with the permanent members of the UN's Security Council (China, US, UK, Russia and France) and BRICS countries (Brazil, China, and Russia). The Modi Government was sending out the message that India's 'rightful place' was as much with its neighbours, as with the upcoming world powers and indeed, the established global powers.

Modi wrote to heads of all nations claiming that a permanent seat in the UN Security Council is India's right. After that UN has adopted written resolution for UN Security Council reforms. As far as Pakistan is concerned, India is tackling it on

Doval policy—if Pakistan troubles Kashmir, then threaten to disturb Baluchistan. Till now, Pakistan Government used to talk peace thereby getting in good books of international community and Pakistan Army used to create problems in Kashmir. India had no choice but to continue talking because of international pressure. Now, what Modi has done is that when Pakistan Army does something in Kashmir, India in exchange gives it back disproportionately somewhere within Pakistan. So, it is Pakistan Government which is under pressure to continue talking to India.

On China, India has been cozying up to US, Japan, Australia, and getting high tech defence systems from them. Still, India has aligned with China wherever its interest match, such as on BRICS Bank and New Development Bank. Modi has visited all important countries and built a good future relationship with their leaders. India has built a dependable big brother image in SAARC—exploring a bridge connecting India to Sri Lanka from Rameswaram, Nepal wooed with aid, Bhutan was the first country Modi visited, Bangladesh boundary settlement. Due to motor vehicles accord passed by India, Nepal, Bhutan and Bangladesh, time of commute between West Bengal and North East will get reduced by 1000 km. India has expedited construction of highway linking West Bengal to Thailand. India has also got berthing rights in Chittagong port due to which time for goods to reach Bangladesh has reduced by nine days.

India is moving closer to ASEAN with Act East policy and, also, getting closer to Central Asia. India has become full time member of SCO. India has taken Chabahar port development in Iran and now will have direct access to Afghanistan and Central Asia through that—thereby countering China's Gwadar. India has also entered the Missile Technology Control Regime (MTCR), thereby placing it on high league of world nations.

One of the biggest success stories of India's foreign policy has been the speed with which New Delhi-Washington relations have improved and more importantly, deepened. The process began with the thaw in India-US ties brought about by former PM Manmohan Singh and former President George W Bush in 2005. However, it was the Modi Government that pushed the relationship to a new level, promoting President Barack Obama to term it one of the "defining partnerships of the 21st century".

Thus, it not surprising that the foreign trips Modi has undertaken, the majority have arguably been focused on molding the global environment to India's benefit. Whether this has involved shoring up ties with key neighbours such as Afghanistan, Bhutan or Bangladesh, or reaching out to states historically neglected by India, such as Mongolia, or strengthening links with nations that are critical for Indian economic success, such as Germany, or renewing ties with those Asian countries important for India's strategic interests, such as Australia, Japan or Singapore, and further transforming relations with the US, Modi has invested time and attention not merely in building personal ties with their leaders but also in persuading them to engage with India in ways that redound to its gain. Beyond these geostrategic aims, Modi has focused at least a third of his foreign travels on advancing Indian economic aims. For the most part, these have concentrated on attracting foreign investment to India. By addressing complaints about the ease of doing business and by removing obstacles to investments, Modi has attempted to woo investors in countries as disparate as China, Japan, the United Arab Emirates, the United Kingdom, Ireland, Canada, and the US, not to mention the myriad middle powers in continental Europe.

Modi has realized that India does not save enough domestically to generate high single-digit growth rates consistently over a long horizon. This constraint, which affects everything from employment to investment, can be mitigated by external investment. Modi has attempted to use a small but growing proportion of his time abroad to highlight India's desire to contribute to the production of global public goods as well as to spotlight the contributions of peoples of Indian origin. Benefiting from India's new ascendency as one of the world's fastest growing major economies consistent with his own vision of India as a "leading power", Modi has sought to burnish India's reputation as a good international citizen by increasing its contributions to everything from mitigating climate change to supporting nation and state building activities to promoting nuclear security to enhancing peace and stability in the Indian Ocean.

The issues like the Land Boundary Agreement with Bangladesh, and the nuclear deal with Japan and Australia are legacy issues on which considerable progress had already been made when the Modi Government assumed power in May 2014. It can be recalled that the India-Bangladesh Land Boundary Agreement, otherwise known as the Indira-Mujib Accord, was signed in 1974. None of the previous governments including UPA I or II (in power for 10 years) or even the Rajiv Gandhi Government, which had a 400-plus majority in the Lok Sabha, could manage to get Parliament to ratify the accord. It goes to Modi's credit that he got the agreement ratified unanimously by both Houses of Parliament. This move went a long way to enhance India's prestige and credibility not only in Bangladesh, but in the entire neighbourhood. This has set the stage for rapid growth in bilateral political, security, commercial and economic ties with Bangladesh including connectivity through Bangladesh with India's Northeast region.

The relation with Japan has witnessed a sharp upward trajectory because of the energy and focus that Modi has imparted to this partnership. Discussions on the bilateral civilian nuclear deal were meandering aimlessly for several years for well-known reasons. With Japan's formal entry into the India-US Malabar maritime exercises—which turned into a trilateral initiative aimed at ensuring peace, security and freedom of navigation in the Indo-Pacific region—Modi lifted the relationship with Japan from being economic and transactional to one that was a strategic partnership. An agreement on trilateral ministerial dialogue between India, US, and Japan has given a further impetus to this partnership.

Regarding Pakistan, things began warmly enough—as can be seen in swearing-in ceremony and the garment exchange that ensured, but soon degenerated into the calling-off of diplomatic talks. However, the bilateral relationship saw a reboot marked memorably by Modi swinging by Lahore to meet Nawaz Sharif on Christmas Day. And since then, while India and Pakistan have engaged in a lot more dialogue, the usual hostilities remain and New Delhi has conveyed its displeasure to Islamabad often enough, which is a fairly acceptable result.

Modi succeed to reach out in a meaningful way to African countries. South Africa is a BRICS member, Nigeria is an important trade partner, Kenya and Tanzania are home to a large Indian diaspora, and so on. Inviting the entire lot of African leaders to one mega-summit was nothing more than a start. It is time to start engaging with them on a deeper level, particularly considering the opprobrium rightly being heaped on India by African envoys in light of the treatment of Africans in India. Modi was also able to secure membership of crucial dual-technology denial regimes (Nuclear Suppliers Group, the Australia Group, the Wassenaar Arrangement and Missile Technology Control Regime) as well as on regional organisations like the SCO. Membership of these groups has moved India closer to its goal of getting a permanent seat in the UNSC.

Now, another goal of Modi is to collect a chunk of the investments that the countries he visited have committed to India. For example, Japan has assured an investment of US$ 35 billion over the five years, South Korea US$ 10 billion, China US$ 20 billion, France US$ 2 billion and more.

Thus, Modi's foreign policy achievements have been outstanding. He has imparted unexpected vigour, dynamism, and vision to conceptualizing, articulating and pursuing India's foreign policy. He has expanded the political, security, and economic outreach of Indian diplomacy. He travelled extensively, visited significant countries that had been neglected so far, conveyed a message of confidence in India's future, provided innovative ideas on issues of strategic import, offered economic opportunities, promoted ease of doing business to potential investors, and wooed Indian diaspora in an unprecedented manner. More than anything else, it signals India's return to a sensible activism in fashioning the world about it and, just as important, is driven boldly by the imperative of securing India's interest first. For all the above reasons, it would not be an exaggeration to posit that Modi's foreign policy is exceptionally successful.

Achievements in the Field of National Security

Domestic security and foreign policy play a key role in the country's overall security. On internal security and home affairs, Modi Government's performance had been on a par with that in the previous regimes. Though some incidents did take place which were "communal killings", especially like that of a man lynched in Dadri for consuming beef, the situation is similar to that in the previous regimes.

The Maoist movement remains a potent threat to the peace and stability in many districts of India as it had during the previous regimes. The only way to neutralize this menace is mainstreaming the Maoists who are misled about the nature of the Indian state.

Modi Government has not found any solution to Kashmir problem as yet. Narendra Modi rejected foreign "advice and analysis" on disputed Kashmir as authorities and said that India would instead follow former Prime Minister Atal Bihari Vajpayee's doctrine "to address Kashmir's problems".

"On Kashmir, I don't need anyone's advice or analysis. There can't be a better message than what Vajpayee offered," Modi said in his address to hundreds of supporters in the summer capital, Srinagar. "Vajpayee talked about Kashmir's pluralistic ethos, democracy and humanity to solve the issues. India will consolidate these three pillars in Kashmir." Vajpayee had offered to settle the Kashmir dispute in a spirit of "humanity" and friendship with Pakistan during his 2003 visit to the region.

Modi also offered a financial package of US$ 12 billion to the restive region, marred by a low-intensity conflict since 1989. "The major issue in Kashmir is unemployment. India will address it", he said. However, as Pakistan continues to harbor terrorism and terrorist activities, including attacks on Indian army camps, such as in Uri in September 2016, which took the lives of 18 Indian soldiers, Narendra Modi has adopted a hard line against Pakistan and mounted a global campaign to isolate it.

The Modi Government has been keen on the kind of vigour and agility that it has brought to the foreign policy discourse.

Modi himself has visited a number of countries ever since he became India's Prime Minister and met with state heads and other important people. However, the institutional capacity regarding the number of diplomats and missions to different countries has been a limiting factor. Also, the kind of depth regarding research and expertise which is needed is missing. This is where a systematic improvement concerning capability and numbers is required. Modi Government, to its credit, has touch based with 130 countries in the two years but this will have to be substantiated with ongoing processes and engagements rather than one-off meetings.[1]

India has signed agreements with France and Japan on defence and deals with some other countries for supply of latest and advanced defence equipment. China is posing threat to the region by continuing its policy of intimidation, but with India having defence pacts with a number of countries, the situation has remained under control.

Prime Minister Narendra Modi's visit to the US yielded tangible results with India entering the elite missile technology group and achieving sizeable progress in defence. The two countries finalized a deal that allows their militaries to help each other with crucial supplies, and the US formally recognized India as a "major defence partner". This will make it easy for India to access sophisticated US weaponry and technology to modernize its army and defence-manufacturing sector.

It has been disclosed that India had cleared all hurdles to become a member of the 34-member Missile Technology Control Regime (MTCR), a non-proliferation regime of which China is not a member. This will give India access to high-end missile technology from across the world and will allow India to purchase top-of-the-line missile systems. The MTCR will also pave the way for India to sell its supersonic BrahMos cruise missiles, which it developed jointly with Russia, to third countries. It's a feather in Modi's cap that the development will make India a significant arms exporter for the first time.[2]

In defence, 74 percent FDI has been allowed. Navy targets to have 200 ships by 2027, of which most ships will be built in

India. Aircraft acquisition and manufacture has been expedited. The government is thinking of getting a foreign partner for Tejas.

Another achievement of Prime Minister Modi was that India and America entered into an agreement that they can use land, naval and air bases of each other to counter an aggressive China. Although the agreement says that India and the US can use each other's land, air and naval bases for repair and resupply, in any serious eventuality, they will help each other beyond just repair and resupply. This is a major step towards reinforcing defence ties between the two countries as they seek to counter the rise of China.

The US also agreed to elevate defence trade and technology sharing with India to a level commensurate with its closest allies and partners, said a joint statement after the pact was signed. US Defence Secretary Ash Carter, and India's Defence Minister Manohar Parrikar said that the agreement would allow the Indian and US navies to have an easier time supporting each other in joint operations and exercises and when providing humanitarian assistance. The agreement is seen as a milestone in the India-US defence relationship because of the huge political importance it carries. But both leaders made it clear that the logistics agreement did not allow the basing of US troops in India.

The signing of the agreement will "make the logistics of joint operations so much easier and so much more efficient", said Mr. Carter. Washington's desire for deeper security cooperation with India had been complicated without the signing of the logistics agreement as well as two other pacts that would allow secure communications and the exchange of nautical and other data.

According the 'World News', "the US military has made clear it wants to do more with India, especially in countering China, which US officials say is risking stoking conflict through its claims in the South China Sea, a vital trade waterway."

Some experts have called the agreement the worst nightmare for China, as American presence in the region is certainly bad news for China and its policy of intimidating its neighboring countries and of claiming the wide South China Sea as under its sole jurisdiction, much beyond its territorial waters. Pakistan too is likely to feel in a precarious position despite China's backing because India plus America are a formidable and unconquerable combination, militarily as well as politically.

But there is more to it diplomatically, than just being a defence agreement. Despite regular meetings and joint military training, the United States and India are not allies in any formal sense. Officially, India was non-aligned in the Cold War, though it had closer relationships with the erstwhile USSR. The US at that time backed India's arch-rival Pakistan.

There is, according to *The National Interest*, "a slow yet historic is realignment underway. First of all, the United States and India are both growing warier of China's rise as a major regional military power. Second, the US-Pakistani relationship has deteriorated during the course of America's decade-and-a-half-long war in Afghanistan. Meanwhile, Pakistan is the world's top recipient of Chinese weapons."[3]

Things have changed over the last decade or so. India has come closer to the US, and Pakistan, after having taken all sort of help and support from the US, has moved towards China. The US which is concerned about the rising power of China is also against China-Pakistan alliance and has been forced to reconsider its relations with Pakistan.

In an April 2016 profile in *The Atlantic*, Jeffrey Goldberg wrote that US President Barack Obama "privately questions why Pakistan, which he believes is a disastrously dysfunctional country, should be considered an ally of the US at all."

And now the land, sea and air agreement has been signed which would enhance cooperation between the US and Indian militaries to an unprecedented level. It goes to Modi's credit that he has made India's defence impregnable with the aforesaid agreement with the US.

Assuaging Russia's concern that India has been tilting towards the US in terms of defence deals and military-to-military ties over the last decade, further reinforced by the recent inking of the bilateral logistics pact, India has reassured Russia that their traditional strategic partnership will continue on its upward trajectory.[4]

According to Defence Ministry sources, negotiations for mega defence projects with Russia like joint development of the futuristic fifth generation fighter aircraft (FGFA) and Kamov Ka-226T light utility helicopters were well on track now after being stalled for some time. Similarly, major defence deals with Russia, ranging from the ₹ 39,000 crore acquisition of five S-400 Triumf advanced air defence missile systems to the US$ 1.5 billion lease of a second nuclear-powered submarine, are also in the offing. It will provide security to India's key installations.

Thus, Modi Government is trying to strike a fine balance in maintaining relationship with the two erstwhile Cold War rivals. And so far, it has been successful. The defence deals with the US have made India's rivals Pakistan and China fear that India is not only itself a strong nation militarily, but also has the world's strongest nations—US and Russia supporting it.

The "*Yudh Abhyas*" exercise between US troops from Fort Louis and Madras Regiment soldiers was held at Chaubatia in Uttarakhand from September 14 to 27. The "Indra" exercise between Russian soldiers and Kumaon Regiment troops was held at Vladivostok from September 22 to October 2.

This is also a big development towards strengthening India's security and a deterrence to China and Pakistan. The deal with Russia is also important considering the fact that Russia has always been India's all-weather friend and we must keep up the relationship.[5]

Achievements in Social Sector

The Modi Government has scored big on giving high priority to not just launching but also ensuring execution of various welfare and social security schemes it launched. The size and scale of each project has drawn international attention and the international community is closely watching India's success achieved in both implementation and impact of these schemes.

Entitlements vs Empowerment: When the Modi Government rode to power in May 2014, many had expected (with anticipation or trepidation) that the government would radically alter the architecture for welfare. Indeed, early into its term, the government set about the task of distinguishing (and distancing) itself from the United Progressive Alliance's (UPA) rights-based welfare approach by positioning its approach to social policy as "empowerment" in opposition to the UPA's "entitlement" approach. Replacing the leaky and inefficient welfare delivery system with the deceptively elegant cash transfer model was a critical component of the empowerment narrative. To do this, the government's first task was to scale up the direct benefit transfer (DBT) pilots with the Jan Dhan, Aadhaar, Mobile (JAM) trinity as its foundation.

However, there has been slow progress. For 2014, the target was for DBT to cover 536 schemes across 65 ministries and departments. By December 2016, only 84 schemes across 17 departments and ministries were using DBT. Moreover, the pace of money transfers through DBT has slowed down. By December 2016, only 45 percent of the 2016-17 Government of India allocation for LPG subsidies and 62 percent for the National Social Assistance Program were transferred through DBT. And while the government is struggling to roll out the DBT, the PM has turned to the UPA's "entitlement" programs to respond to post-demonetisation shocks to the rural economy. The PM has committed his government to implement the maternity benefits program, a key provision of the National Food Security Act. Adding to this, the MGNREGA, which was given a new lease of life by the Modi Government, has received a supplementary grant on account of the increased demand. By early January 2017, the Centre had released ₹ 55076 crore for MGREGA, the highest allocation so far since the program was launched.

The most important reason for the Modi Government's reliance on the "entitlement approach", despite the rhetoric of "empowerment" through cash is the lack of consensus even within the BJP on what a credible alternative to the current welfare framework could be. Even as candidate Modi had campaigned from a center-right, less state intervention position with slogans like "maximum governance, minimum government", but the BJP's position on welfare was very much a continuation of the UPA's entitlement approach. Not unlike the UPA, the BJP manifesto promised to implement the right to food, a national health assurance program, and increase expenditure on education. Also, BJP-ruled states have done a better job of implementing the UPA's entitlement schemes than many Congress-ruled states. For example, Chhattisgarh under Raman Singh Government has become the poster child of PDS reform. With these successes, replacing entitlements like the PDS with cash transfers just does not make political sense.

The lack of political consensus also exposes the limitations of the cash argument. The push to cash transfers stems from the belief that cash transfers are a solution to the state's continued failure to deliver services. Yet, as the DBT experience is beginning to reveal, cash is not a substitute for a failed state system. Getting the cash architecture right requires negotiating complex governance tasks like getting right target, adapting to market fluctuations, dealing with supply constraints, and building a solid banking system. Rather than being a substitute, effective cash transfers require a sophisticated and capable state machinery to support it. The failure to recognize this, especially as calls for a universal basic income grew louder, and investment in building state capacity is Modi Government's greatest error. The UPA had left most of its entitlement schemes, including the MGNREGA, in urgent need of improved implementation. Rather than focusing on rightly implementation of the programs, the contradictory messages from the government have further weakened these programs. Wage payment under MGNREGA is a good example of this. In 2016-17, at a time when the government needed MGNREGA to perform, 53 percent of payments were delayed by between 15 to 90 days.

Health and Education: In line with government's recommendations of the 14th Finance Commission, which increased the allocation of states from 32 percent to 42 percent of the divisible funds, the government was seen shifting the responsibility more on the states. This is a welcome step but the problem still pertains to the capability of the states to understand and have the capacity to use the funds for health and education.

In the health care domain, the challenges have increased with changing disease patterns, especially with the coming of lifestyle diseases like diabetes and high blood pressure. Modi Government is fully aware of the fact that the aim of a productive population can only be fulfilled in a disease-free society. In this context, the *Swachh Bharat Abhiyan* was a positive step. However, how much of an impact it has had on people littering on the streets and the municipalities in maintaining cleanliness is not yet very well understood. However, the government's role here to facilitate preventive health care must be appreciated.

Considering India's large population and its high rate of growth, there is shortage of doctors, nurses, therapists and other health care professionals. Modi Government has taken some measures in this regard. It has initiated a new centrally-sponsored scheme for setting up a National Institute of Allied Health Sciences (NIAHS), eight Regional Institutes of Allied Health Sciences (RIAHS) and to support State Government medical colleges for conducting allied health courses to augment the supply of skilled health workforce.

Modi Government has come up with new AIIMS-like institutions in all states and increased medical seats over the last one year. The Prime Minister announced expansion of India's Universal Immunization Programme (UIP) to cover four more diseases—Rotavirus, Rubella, Polio and Japanese Encephalitis. This will cover 2.7 crore children and give momentum to India's aim of achieving Millennium Development Goals (MDG-4) targets that include reducing child mortality.[6]

Modi Government has also promoted alternative systems of medicine. A separate ministry, known as AYUSH, has been formed for this, and a health authority has also been established for centralizing records of all patients. The government has done a commendable job in terms of controlling spread of Ebola virus in the country. Heightened surveillance and tracking systems were put in place at air and sea ports. However, the authorities have failed to control the spread of diseases caused by mosquitoes, especially in New Delhi where dengue, chikungunia, etc. have become recurring feature every season.

In the 2016 budget, a new health insurance scheme was announced. A year later, this is still to be implemented. And while the Modi Government's rhetoric suggests a shift in priority toward insurance, there is no debate on how to tackle complex issues of regulation and quality. On the other hand, the National Health Mission (NHM), the current flagship program for strengthening primary health systems, which still accounts for 50 percent of the Center's health budget, is floundering. And despite growing evidence of a serious crisis in the quality of primary care, from doctor absenteeism to low effort, lack of use of treatment protocols, over-medication and maltreatment of patients, the government has no urgency to reform the NHM. The current crisis in health care is not the making of the Modi Government. However, the lack of a coherent vision and strategy on how to tackle the present crisis, especially in the context of the rhetoric of empowerment, is a serious failure.

The Modi Government has given somewhat better attention to elementary education. The need to urgently tackle the low learning levels in India's elementary schools has now widely been recognized and even though the National Education Policy has been deferred to yet another committee, the commitment to improve learning outcomes has been clearly stated. Now, the effort is focused on measuring learning. The NITI Aayog is in the process of launching a school quality index while the education ministry is preparing to undertake a learning census. Measurement is necessary but its usefulness hinges on the system's ability to use measurement as a diagnostic tool to reform the teaching-learning process. For the moment, there is little clarity from the government on how it intends to use these assessments. The problem is complicated by the fact that the current planning and budgeting process is not designed to give priority to learning. Planning continues to be based on school infrastructure goals and learning focused programs receive very little financing. For example, in 2014-15, 78 percent of the Sarva Shiksha Abhiyan (SSA) budget was allocated to infrastructure and salaries for teachers. The innovation and learning enhancement programs received less than one percent of the SSA budget. This is the one area that has seen the most cuts—in 2014-15 only 13 percent of funds requested for these activities were approved. This increased to 25 percent in 2015-16. Many state governments are now beginning to experiment with different ways of changing classroom practices to improve learning. These should to be supported, studied, and scaled. But, the absence of resources and the continued focus on school infrastructure in plans and budgets is a serious impediment.

Swachh Bharat and Co-operative Federalism: No discussion on the Modi Government's social policy approach is complete without mentioning two issues on which the PM has staked significant political capital—Swachh Bharat and Co-operative Federalism.

The high-level political commitment has made sanitation top priority across the country. But, the basic design and approach of the Swachh Bharat Mission (SBM) is flawed. As is widely acknowledged, total sanitation is only achieved when communities recognize the need for sanitation and demand sanitation services. Building awareness for sanitation and creating demand through sustained community engagement is thus critical and local governments are the appropriate institutional mechanism to achieve this. Rather than strengthen local governments, the SBM is designed as a top-down program implemented by bureaucrats. Consequently, even as money is being spent on toilet construction—98 percent of the 2016-17 Swachh Bharat Mission-Gramin (SBM-G) expenditure has been on toilet construction—the real challenge of behavioural change remains. There are separate figures for SBM-U (urban), which are even worse off in terms of spending and implementation.

The Modi Government has spent very less on awareness raising. In 2016-17, only ₹ 56 crore, which is one percent of the total expenditure on the scheme, had been spent for awareness raising activities. And in the face of pressure to meet targets toilets are being constructed mostly by coaxing citizens through orders threatening to withhold ration and electricity supplies if toilets are not constructed, imposing fines and withholding payments.

For social policy, the cooperative federalism agenda began to unfold in 2015 with the implementation of the Fourteenth

Finance Commission (FFC) recommendation to enhance tax devolution to states from 32 percent to 42 percent. In the 2015 budget, this increased tax devolution was accompanied by the rationalisation of Centrally Sponsored Schemes (CSS), the primary mechanism for Central Government financing for social sectors. It was now for states to enhance social sector spending as they saw fit. Moreover, states were required to contribute 40 percent of the total share of CSS funds. But, even as the burden of financing shifted to states, on the larger question of the role that the Central Government ought to play in this new financing architecture, the government has been silent.

In August 2016, the Government of India accepted the recommendations of the NITI Aayog's chief ministers' sub-group on Centrally Sponsored Schemes (CSS). This led to an effort to restructure CSS into 28 umbrella schemes. But, a closer look at this restructuring reveals that little has changed. Most old schemes continue to function with budgetary allocations, but have been grouped under a common name. Moreover, CSS continue to function in a top-down, one-size fit all model, where state budgets for CSS continue to reflect Central Government's priorities. For example, in the National Health Mission, in 2016, 76 percent of state proposals for communicable diseases were approved for funding while 90 percent of state proposals for immunisation and infrastructure were approved. Adding to this, expenditure, even at the grassroots, is linked to orders from Delhi and state capitals.

The one fundamental and potentially transformational shift that the Modi Government is well positioned to institutionalise in social sector funding is a shift to outcomes-based financing. By all accounts, the NITI Aayog has initiated a process of creating an outcome focused measurement index to rank states on key social sector indicators. If designed right, this outcomes index could be used to design a performance based inter-governmental transfer system. In this model, Central funding could be given to states in two windows. The first window would be an untied block grant, so states are not dependent on the whims and fancies of Central Government budget approvals. The second would be a performance-based financing window linked to progress on the outcomes index measured by NITI Aayog. The primary role for the center in this model would be to support states in designing and implementing their plans while at the same time encouraging competition and incentivizing states to innovate for improved outcomes.

Pradhan Mantri Jan Dhan Yojana (PMJDY): One of the largest initiatives ever undertaken anywhere for financial inclusion was launched in India to bring into the banking system a large section of people who remained outside it all these years. In the shortest span of one year, over 15 crore bank accounts have been opened. The significance lies in the government's plan to implement direct cash transfer to the beneficiaries of various government welfare schemes and programs. Unfortunately, many remain with zero balance till date. However, once the cash transfers begin, it is expected to inculcate a habit of banking in a large section of people who never had access to this facility.

Pradhan Mantri Suraksha Bima Yojana (PMSBY): This Accidental Death and Disability scheme is available for a nominal premium of ₹ 12 per person per annum. With this, the individual gets an accidental death insurance cover of ₹ 2,00,000 and permanent partial or full disability cover of ₹ 1,00,000. Its low premium and high returns are attractive options for those with no cover at all.

Pradhan Mantri Jeevan Jyoti Bima Yojana (PMJJBY): This scheme provides a cover of ₹ 200,000 in case of death against a single installment premium of ₹ 330 per annum that is auto debited to the policyholder's bank account. The scheme is open to everyone between 18 and 50 years of age.

Atal Pension Yojana (APY): This scheme provides a guaranteed pension to the scheme holder and spouse, ranging from ₹ 1,000 to ₹ 5,000. The corpus is returned to the nominees after 60 years of age along with the monthly pension. The Government's co-contribution is 50 percent of the total contribution amount or ₹ 1,000 per annum, whichever is lower, for a period of five years. There is some concern on whether this scheme will be attractive enough to sustain long-term investment interest of the account holder. The scopes and coverage of this scheme is vast and the government is earnest in making the schemes successful.

Mudra Bank: To address the vast majority of youth who wish to be self-employed and start small business ventures, the government has launched Mudra Bank. The bank will address the start-up capital needs as well as working capital needs of small traders, businessmen, service providers, etc. The bank is expected to give a major fillip to the youth who has the potential for self-employment but is unable to harness it due to lack of seed or working capital.

Clean Ganga Initiative: India's holiest river remains heavily polluted. Unlike previous government's half-hearted approach, the Modi Government initially allocated ₹ 2,037 crore to the project. The same has now been given a massive hike totaling ₹ 20,000 crore towards the Clean Ganga campaign and is being monitored at the highest level. Hopefully, the country will finally be able to reclaim its holiest river as it once was.

LPG Subsidy Reforms: Modi Government brought LPG subsidy reforms by barring gas subsidy to people whose annual income is more than ₹ 10 lakh. The amount saved has been used to give over five lakh new LPG connections to those who still use firewood or kerosene stoves for cooking. This will also serve the cause of environment as the families who have shifted to using LPG will no longer cut wood and many trees will be saved. As the LPG does not give out smoke, which burning of wood does, there will be less air pollution.

EPFO and ESIC Reforms: In February 2016, Modi Government initiated efforts to reform EPFO and ESIC for the benefit of employees in the organized sector. It planned to extend ESIC benefits as part of a larger scheme to upgrade facilities for medical education and specialized tertiary care.

The government introduced Universal Access Number (UAN) to all EPF holders to make transfer of PF accounts easy when switching jobs. A UAN has been allotted to over six crore workers as of February 2016, enabling portability of their EPF accounts. Further, the government proposed to expand coverage and offer additional facilities and services through the ESIC.

The wage ceiling for EPF benefits has been raised from ₹ 6500 to ₹ 15,000. An EPFO Mobile App has been launched for easier access to its services for both workers and employers. The Bonus Act has been amended to increase the ceilings for eligibility and bonus payable to ₹ 21,000 and ₹ 7,000 per month, respectively.

The government has created Shram Suvidha Portal for online services related to 16 labor laws, including administering a process of transparent and random inspections of businesses. A Labour Identification Number (LIN) has been issued to nearly one million employers, enabling them to process single online filings on eight labour laws.

The central labour laws has been simplified by consolidating the existing 44 laws into four labour codes—namely, on wages, industrial relations, safety and security, and health. This would considerably increase the ease of doing business and facilitate job creation, without compromising on the genuine protections and rights available for workers. The coverage of ESI scheme has been expanded from only the industrial and commercial clusters within a district to the entire district.

The ESIC has proposed to expand coverage by complementing its own services with Public Private Partnerships (PPP). Apart from cancer detection, cardiology treatment, and dialysis, the ESIC has proposed to offer in a phased manner pathological and X-ray facilities in all its dispensaries through PPPs. Besides allopathic treatment, ESIC hospitals will also provide AYUSH treatment in a phased manner.

The services offered by ESIC and EPFO have been integrated with the e-Bis portal of the Department of Industrial Policy and Promotion to promote ease of business and limit transaction costs. Further, it is proposed to promulgate new EPFO and ESIC Acts providing more choice, increased coverage among workers and employers, and better and expanded range of services for organized sector workers.[7]

A Yoga Day: India's lobbying got success when the United Nations declared June 21 as International Yoga Day. The mass yoga performance at Rajpath in New Delhi, which was led by

PM Modi himself, set the record of most number of people participating in such an event.

Mann Ki Baat: A first initiative in India where a top leader addresses millions, that too periodically. It has made Narendra Modi the most interactive Indian Prime Minister ever. In his radio programme "Mann Ki Baat", he addresses the people of the nation on radio, DD National and DD News. In his addresses broadcast so far, thousands of ideas have been received on the website and audio. Each month, some selected calls become a part of the broadcast.

The program was started in October 2014 and it aims to deliver the Prime Minister's voice to the general masses of India. Radio was chosen as the medium because television connection is still not available in many parts of India, especially in the isolated, rural, and less developed regions. It is estimated that 90 percent of the total Indian population is reachable over radio. Various private FM radio stations in the metropolitan cities of India are allowed to broadcast a recording of the show. Doordarshan's Direct to Home (DTH) service Free Dish relay feeds the 20-minute-long episodes, to television and radio channels.

Mann Ki Baat is a unique initiative of the Prime Minister Narendra Modi to reach the masses across the country through the radio. The Prime Minister through his address on the radio aims to connect with the common people on a regular basis and inform them about the initiatives of the government and also seeks the support of the common man in nation building and governance. It provides people the opportunity to become a part of Prime Minister's radio address by suggesting the areas and topics on which he should focus during his address and also brings to light the issues faced by common man so that they may be taken up during the address followed by subsequent action. It provides people the opportunity to connect, suggest and become part of participatory governance through the Prime Minister's radio address.[8]

In a democratic country like India where all the government policies and actions focus on the socio-economic development of society and its people, such interaction holds great significance. It apprises people about the plans and initiatives being envisaged and executed by the government and at the same time tells the government about what is in the mind of the people. Suggestions and ideas given by people also help the government to reshape its policies as per people's needs and expectations. Such a thing was not done by any previous government in India.

NITI Aayog: An Institution for Transforming India

The Modi Government, in keeping with its reform agenda, on 1 January 2015 constituted the National Institution for Transforming India, known as the NITI Aayog, to replace the Planning Commission instituted in 1950. This was done in order to better serve the needs and aspirations of the people of India. An important evolutionary change from the past, NITI Aayog is the premier policy 'Think Tank' of the Government of India, providing both directional and policy inputs, and acts as the quintessential platform of the Government of India to bring States to act together in national interest, and thereby fosters Cooperative Federalism. It also provides relevant technical advice to the Centre and States while designing strategic and long-term policies and programmes.

There are two hubs at the core of NITI Aayog's creation, which reflect the key tasks of the Aayog.

(a) Team India Hub—It leads the engagement of states with the Central Government.

(b) Knowledge and Innovation Hub—It builds NITI Aayog's think-tank capabilities.

Aayog is also developing itself as a State of the Art Resource Centre, with the necessary resources, knowledge and skills, that will enable it to act with speed, promote research and innovation, provide strategic policy vision for the government, and deal with contingent issues. Following are the key tasks of the Aayog.[9]

- To evolve a shared vision of national development priorities sectors and strategies with the active involvement of States in the light of national objectives.

- To foster cooperative federalism through structured support initiatives and mechanisms with the States on a continuous basis, recognizing that strong States make a strong nation.
- To develop mechanisms to formulate credible plans at the village level and aggregate these progressively at higher levels of government.
- To ensure, on areas that are specifically referred to it, that the interests of national security are incorporated in economic strategy and policy.
- To pay special attention to the sections of our society that may be at risk of not benefiting adequately from economic progress.
- To design strategic and long-term policy and programme frameworks and initiatives, and monitor their progress and their efficacy. The lessons learnt through monitoring and feedback will be used for making innovative improvements, including necessary mid-course corrections.
- To provide advice and encourage partnerships between key stakeholders and national and international like-minded think tanks, as well as educational and policy research institutions.
- To create a knowledge, innovation and entrepreneurial support system through a collaborative community of national and international experts, practitioners and other partners.
- To offer a platform for resolution of inter-sectoral and inter departmental issues in order to accelerate the implementation of the development agenda.
- To maintain a state-of-the-art Resource Centre, be a repository of research on good governance and best practices in sustainable and equitable development as well as help their dissemination to stakeholders.
- To actively monitor and evaluate the implementation of programmes and initiatives, including the identification of the needed resources so as to

strengthen the probability of success and scope of delivery.

- To focus on technology upgradation and capacity building for implementation of programmes and initiatives.
- To undertake other activities as may be necessary in order to further the execution of the national development agenda, and the objectives mentioned above.

NITI Aayog: A Universal Game Changer—It has taken the role of coordinating "Transforming our World: 2030 Agenda for Sustainable Development", also known as SDGs. Moving ahead from the Millennium Development Goals (MDGs), SDGs have been evolved through a long inclusive process for achievement during 2016-30. The SDGs cover 17 goals and 169 related targets resolved in the UN Summit meet during 25-27 September 2015, in which India was represented by the PM Narendra Modi. The SDGs will stimulate, align, and accomplish action over the 15-year period in areas of critical importance for the humanity and the planet. Thus, the task of NITI Aayog is not merely to periodically collect data on SDGs but to act proactively fructify the goals and targets not only quantitatively but also maintaining high standards of quality. The goals covered under SDGs are:

1. Ending poverty in all its forms everywhere.
2. Ending hunger, achieving food security and improved nutrition, and promoting sustainable agriculture.
3. Ensuring healthy lives and promoting well-being for all at all ages.
4. Ensuring inclusive and equitable quality education and promoting lifelong learning opportunities for all.
5. Achieving gender equality and empowering all women and girls.
6. Ensuring availability and sustainable management of water and sanitation for all.

7. Ensuring access to affordable, reliable, sustainable, and modern energy for all.
8. Promoting sustained, inclusive, and sustainable economic growth, full and productive employment and decent work for all.
9. Building resilient infrastructure, promoting inclusive and sustainable industrialization, and fostering innovation.
10. Reducing inequality within and among countries.
11. Making cities and human settlements inclusive, safe, resilient, and sustainable.
12. Ensuring sustainable consumption and production patterns.
13. Taking urgent action to combat climate change and its impacts.
14. Conserving and sustainably using the oceans, seas and marine resources for sustainable development.
15. Protecting, restoring, and promoting sustainable use of terrestrial ecosystems, sustainably managing forests, combating desertification, halting and reversing land degradation and halting biodiversity loss.
16. Promoting peaceful and inclusive societies for sustainable development, providing access to justice for all and building effective, accountable and inclusive institutions at all levels.
17. Strengthening the means of implementation and revitalizing the global partnership for sustainable development.

Ministry of Statistics and Programme Implementation (MoSPI) has undertaken a parallel exercise of interaction with the ministries to evolve indicators reflecting the SDG goals and targets. To achieve the target, the draft mapping of the goals and targets as an initial step on proposed Nodal and other Ministries has been carried out in consultation with MoSPI. The Centrally Sponsored Schemes (CSSs), including the 'core of the core', 'core' and 'optional' Schemes being implemented by the States have been mapped along with some of the recent initiatives undertaken by the Central Government. In addition, Ministries are implementing Central Sector Schemes and States are also implementing various State Schemes aligned with one or more SDGs.

The Major Achievements of NITI Aayog: The significant achievements of NITI Aayog over the years are:

(a) *Vision Document, Strategy and Action Agenda beyond 12th Five Year Plan*—Replacing the Five-Year Plans beyond 31 March 2017, NITI Aayog has prepared the 15-year vision document keeping in view the social goals set and/or proposed for a period of 15 years. A 7-year strategy document spanning 2017-18 to 2023-24 to convert the longer-term vision into implementable policy and action as a part of a "National Development Agenda" has also been worked upon. The 3-year Action Agenda for 2017-18 to 2019-20, aligned to the predictability of financial resources during the 14th Finance Commission Award period, has been completed and submitted before the Prime Minister. The main points of vision document are:

- Over the next 15 years economy will grow at 8 percent per annum.
- After 15 years, India's gross domestic product or the size of the economy will touch ₹ 469 lakh crore as compared with ₹ 137 lakh crore in 2015-16.
- States will use the government e-market place platform to reduce corruption and increase transparency in procurement.
- Move to less cash economy by use of technologies such as BHIM and Aadhaar.
- States will use District Mineral Fund, the Compensatory Afforestation Fund, Management and Planning Authority and the Construction Workers Welfare Fund for mobilizing resources.

(b) *Reforms in Agriculture Sector*—The Governing Council of NITI Aayog at its first meeting held under the chairmanship of PM Modi on 8 February 2015 decided to constitute a Task Force on Agriculture Development at NITI Aayog to suggest measures to reinvigorate agriculture in the country. The NITI Aayog has undertaken following reforms in the agriculture sector.

- *Model Land Leasing Law*—NITI Aayog has formulated a Model Agricultural Land Leasing Act, 2016 to both recognize the rights of the tenant and safeguard interest of landowners. A dedicated cell for land reforms was also set up in NITI Aayog. Based on the model act, Madhya Pradesh has enacted separate land leasing law and Uttar Pradesh and Uttarakhand have modified their land leasing laws. Some States, including Odisha, Andhra Pradesh and Telangana, are already at an advance stage of formulating legislations to enact their land leasing laws for agriculture.
- *Reforms of the Agricultural Produce Marketing Committee Act*—NITI Aayog has undertaken three critical reforms in the field of agriculture produce marketing. They are Agricultural Marketing Reforms; Felling and Transit Laws for Tree Produce Grown at Private Land; and Agricultural Land Leasing.
- *Agricultural Marketing and Farmer Friendly Reforms Index*—NITI Aayog has developed the first ever "Agriculture Marketing and Farmer Friendly Reforms Index" to sensitise states about the need to undertake reforms in the three key areas of Agriculture Market Reforms, Land Lease Reforms, and Forestry on Private Land (Felling and Transit of Trees). This index aims to induce a healthy competition between States and percolate

best practices in implementing farmer-friendly reforms.

- *Reforms through the e-National Agricultural Market (e-NAM)*—The existing agriculture marketing system in the country is constrained with serve institutional and infrastructural constraints. In order to overcome these impediments and create a unified national market for agriculture commodities, e-NAM, the e-trading platform for the National Agriculture Market was launched by the Modi Government in April 2016. Till date 21 mandis from eight States have joined e-NAM. The e-NAM would provide a platform to have a transparent and stable pricing mechanism at national level transforming the market into a competitive one and ultimately benefit the farmers. It will cover selected 585 regulated wholesale markets in States and Union Territories by 2017-18 and provide a single window service for all APMC related information and services. This will facilitate rapid direct interface between farmers and buyers by reducing number of intermediaries. It will also benefit the farmers in terms of better selling options, competitive returns, and reasonable and stable prices to the consumers. However, inter-state variations in the rates of taxes or levies and commissions add to the price differentials across states even for the same grade or quality product. Unless common taxes or levies are fixed throughout the country with free inter-state movement of commodities, physical integration of markets of the country would be difficult to realise. The items under the NAM include transparent sale transactions and price discovery, liberal licensing to intermediaries, one license for a trader valid across all markets in the State, harmonization of quality standards, and single point levy of market fees. The Centre will initiate dialogue with States to establish necessary infrastructure facilities and amend existing rules for successful implementation of the Scheme.

- *Pradhan Mantri Fasal Bima Yojana* (*PMFBY*)—It has replaced the existing two schemes, viz., National Agriculture Insurance Scheme (NAIS) as well as Modified NAIS (MNAIS), which had some inherent drawbacks. Under this scheme, the farmers' premium remains between 1.5 to 2 percent for food-grains and oilseeds crops and up to 5 percent for horticultural and cotton crops. It envisages in increasing the insurance coverage to 50 percent of the total crop area of 194.4 million hectare from the existing level of about 25 to 27 percent crop area. In it, there will not be a cap on the premium and reduction of the sum insured, 25 percent of the likely claim will be settled directly on farmers account and there will be one insurance company for the entire state as well as farm level assessment of loss for localized risks and post-harvest loss. Private insurance companies, along with the Agriculture Insurance Company of India Ltd., will implement the scheme. All claim liability will be on insurer and the government will give upfront premium subsidy. This scheme is significant as the country faces drought regularly due to poor monsoon rains and the government wants to enhance insurance coverage to more crop area to protect farmers from vagaries of monsoon.

(c) *Medical Education Reform*—The Parliamentary Standing Committee on Health in its 92nd Report has observed that Medical Council of India (MCI) has repeatedly failed all its mandates over the decades and urged the Central Government to usher in game changer reforms of transformational nature. A committee chaired by Vice-Chairman of NITI Aayog recommended scrapping of the MCI and suggested a new body for regulating medical education. The draft legislation for proposed National Medical Commission (NMC) has been submitted to the Government for further necessary action. The major features of the Draft NMC Bill are:

- Nominated regulator rather than elected regulators with some representation of non-medical experts.
- Separation of functions, such as UG & PG educations, Assessment & Rating, and Registration & Ethics, into autonomous Boards with overcharging NMC for policy coordination.
- A compact executive body (NMC) to facilitate quick decision-making.
- NMC autonomy from the Central Government; vested with power to make regulations without referring it to the government.
- Merit based admissions through a compulsory common entrance examination (NEET) to stamp out the pernicious practice of discretion based admission via the back door of Management/NRI quotas and/or capitation fees.
- Ensure uniform standards of medical professionals graduating from different medical institutions through a mandatory National Common Licentiate Examination.
- Transparent and pro-active disclosure by Medical institution with regard to fees.
- A mandatory assessment and rating of Medical colleges on annual basis to be carried out and published in order to enable prospective students to make an informed choice.

(d) *Digital Payments Movement*—In a transformative attempt to weed out black money and corruption from public life, the Modi Government has constituted a Committee of Officers to enable 100 percent conversion of Government-Citizen Transactions to the digital platform. The committee will identify and operationalize in the earliest possible time frame user-friendly digital payment options in all sectors of the economy. This is integral part of the governments strategy to transform India into a cashless economy. The aim of the committee is to identify various digital payment systems appropriate to different sectors of the economy and coordinate efforts to make them accessible and user-friendly. The committee will also identify and access infrastructural and bottlenecks affecting the access and utility of digital payment options. To achieve expeditious movement into the cashless, digital payments economy across all States and sectors, it will engage regularly with Central Ministries, regulators, State governments, district administration, local bodies, trade and industry associations, etc. to promote rapid adoption of digital payment systems. The attempt is to establish and monitor an implementation framework with strict timelines to ensure that nearly 80 percent of the transaction in India moves to the digital-only platform. The committee will also attempt to estimate costs involved in various digital payments options and oversee implementation of measures to make such transaction between government and citizens cheaper than cash transaction. The committee led by NITI Aayog will also implement an action plan on advocacy, awareness and handholding efforts among public, micro enterprises and other stakeholders. That apart, it will organize training and capacity building of various States/UTs, Ministries/Departments of the Government of India, representatives of States/ UTs, Trade and Industry Bodies as well as other stakeholders. NITI Aayog has taken following initiatives to boost up digital payment movements.

- An action plan on advocacy, awareness and co-ordination of handholding efforts among general public, micro enterprises, and other stakeholders was prepared. Appropriate literature in print and multimedia was prepared on the subject for widespread dissemination. Presentations/ interactions were organized by NITI Aayog for training and capacity building of various concerned departments as well as all stakeholders.

- The Aayog has also constituted a Committee of Chief Ministers on Digital Payments on 30 November 2016 with the Chief Minister of Andhra Pradesh, Chandrababu Naidu, as the convener to promote transparency, financial inclusion, and a healthy financial ecosystem nationwide. The committee submitted its interim report to PM in January 2017.
- To incentivize the States and UTs for promotion of digital transactions, Central assistance of ₹ 50 crore has been provided to the districts for undertaking information, education, and communication activities to bring 5 crore Jan Dhan accounts to digital platform.
- Cashback and referral bonus schemes were launched by the PM Modi on 14 April 2017 to promote the use of digital payments through the BHIM App.
- The Aayog also launched two incentive schemes to promote digital payments across all sections of society—the Lucky Grahak Yojana and the Digi Dhan Vyapar Yojana. Over 16 lakh consumers and merchants have won ₹ 256 crore under these two schemes.
- Digi Dhan Melas were also held for 100 days in 100 cities, from 25 December 2016 to 14 April 2016.

(e) **Atal Innovation Mission (AIM)**—It has been set up by the Modi Government with a view to strengthen the country's innovation and entrepreneurship ecosystem by creating institutions and programs that spur innovation in schools, colleges, and entrepreneurs in general. It primary objective is to serve as a platform for promotion of world-class innovation hubs, grand challenges, start-up businesses, and other self-employment activities, particularly in technology driven areas. It has two core functions—entrepreneurship promotion and innovation promotion. In 2016-17, the following major schemes were rolled out.

- *Atal Tinkering Labs (ATLs)*—It has been started to foster creativity and scientific temper in students. AIM is helping to establish 500 ATLs in schools across India, where students can design and make small prototypes to solve challenges they see around them, using rapid prototyping technologies that have emerged in recent years.
- *Atal Incubation Centres (AICs)*—AIM will provide financial support of ₹ 10 crore and capacity building for setting AICs across India, which will help startups expand quicker and enable innovation-entrepreneurship, in core sectors such as manufacturing, transport, energy, education, agriculture, water and sanitation, etc.

(f) **Indices for Measuring States' Performance in the Fields of Health, Education, and Water Management**—NITI Aayog has prepared indices to measure incremental annual outcomes in critical social sectors like Health, Education, and Water with a view to nudge the States into competing with each other for better outcomes, while at the same time sharing best practices and innovations to help each other—it is an example of competitive and cooperative federalism.

(g) **Sub-group of Chief Ministers on Rationalization of Centrally Sponsored Schemes**—Based on the recommendations of the sub-group of Chief Ministers, a Cabinet note was prepared by NITI Aayog which was approved by the Cabinet on 3 August 2016.

Among several key decisions, the sub-group led to the rationalization of the existing Centrally Sponsored Schemes in 28 umbrella schemes. Out of 28 umbrella schemes, 6 schemes have been categorized as Core of the Core schemes, 21 schemes are Core schemes and remaining one is Optional scheme. The existing funding pattern will continue for Core of the Core schemes. For Core Schemes, the funding pattern for the 8 North Eastern States and Himalayan States of Uttarakhand, Himachal Pradesh, and Jammu & Kashmir shall be Centre—90 percent and State—10 percent, whereas for the rest of the States this ratio shall be Centre—60 percent and State—40 percent. For Optional Schemes, the funding pattern for the 8 North Eastern States and Himalayan States of Uttarakhand, Himachal Pradesh and Jammu & Kashmir shall be Centre—80 percent and State—20 percent, whereas for the rest of the States this ratio shall be Centre—50 percent and State—50 percent. Ordinarily, no CSS will be sanctioned where the central share is less than percent. The flexi-funds available in each CSS has been raised from the current level of 10 percent to 25 percent for the States and 30 percent for the UTs of the overall annual allocation under each Scheme so that the implementation can be better attuned to the needs of individual State/UT.

(h) **Sub-group of Chief Ministers on Swachh Bharat Abhiyan**—Constituted by NITI Aayog on 9 March 2015, the sub-group has submitted its report to the PM in October 2015, and most of its recommendations have been accepted. So far, 24.05 lakh household toilets, 0.76 lakh seats of community toilets and 0.22 lakh seats of public toilets have been constructed out of mission targets of 66.42 lakh, 2.52 lakh and 2.56 lakh respectively. 100 percent door to door collection of solid waste in 39,571 out of 82,609 wards has been achieved. 405 cities have declared themselves Open Defecation Free. Waste to energy production and waste to compost production have reached to 88.4 Megawatt and 17000 tonnes respectively.

(i) **Sub-group of Chief Ministers on Skill Development**—Constituted on 9 March 2015, the report of the sub-group of Chief Ministers on Skill Development was presented before the PM on 31 December 2015. The recommendation and actionable points emerging from the report were approved by the PM and are in implementation by the Ministry of Skill Development.

(j) **Task Force on Elimination of Poverty in India**—Constituted on 16th March 2015, the report of the Task Force was finalized and submitted to the PM on 11 July 2016. The report of the Task Force primarily focusses on issues of measurement of poverty and strategies to combat poverty. Regarding estimation of poverty, the report of the Task Force states that "a consensus in favour of either the Tendulkar or a higher poverty line did not emerge. Therefore, the Task Force has concluded that the matter be considered in greater depth by the country's top experts on poverty before a final decision is made. Accordingly, it is recommended that an expert committee be set up to arrive at an informed decision on the level at which the poverty line should be set." With respect to strategies to combat poverty, the Task Force has made recommendations on faster poverty reduction through employment intensive sustained rapid growth and effective implementation of anti-poverty programs.

(k) **Task Force on Agriculture Development**—The Task Force on Agricultural development was constituted on 16 March 2015. The Task Force based on its works prepared an occasional paper entitled "Raising Agricultural Productivity and Making Farming Remunerative for Farmers" focusing on 5 critical areas of Indian Agriculture—(i) Raising Productivity; (ii) Remunerative Prices to Farmers; (iii) Land Leasing, Land Records & Land Titles; (iv) Second

Green Revolution—Focus on Eastern States; and (v) Responding to Farmers' Distress. After taking inputs of all the States on occasional paper and through their reports, the Task Force submitted the final report to the PM on 31st May 2016. It has suggested important policy measures to bring in reforms in agriculture for the welfare of the farmers as well as enhancing their income.

(l) Transforming India Lecture Series—As the government's premier think tank, NITI Aayog views knowledge building and transfer as the enabler of real transformation in States. To build knowledge systems for States and the Centre, NITI Aayog launched the "NITI Lectures: Transforming India" series, with full support of the PM Modi on 26 August 2016. The lecture series is aimed at addressing the top policy making team of the Government of India, including members of the cabinet and several top layers of the bureaucracy. It aims is to bring cutting edge ideas in development policy to Indian policy makers and public, so as to promote the cause of transformation of India into a prosperous modern economy. The Deputy Prime Minister of Singapore, Shri Tharman Shanmugaratnam, delivered the first lecture on the topic—India and the Global Economy. On 16 November 2016, Bill Gates, Co-Founder, Bill and Melinda Gates Foundation, delivered the second lecture in the series under the theme—Technology and Transformation.

GST: The Biggest Indirect Tax Reform After Independence

The introduction of Goods and Services Tax (GST) is a very significant step in the field of indirect tax reforms in India. By amalgamating a large number of Central and State taxes into a single tax, it has mitigated cascading or double taxation in a major way and paved the way for a common national market. After a very long time, the decks have been cleared for the introduction of the path-breaking GST in the country from 1 July 2017 with the Parliament approving four supplementary GST legislations. These are the Central GST (CGST), Integrated GST (IGST), Union Territory GST (UTGST), and the Compensation Law bills. The impressive acronyms for these bills indicate that the long awaited new tax is being introduced in a way that was not originally planned. Instead of a single level tax, it is in the form of several levies including an inter state tax and a state level tax. Initially it was envisaged as a single point tax replacing the multiplicity of levies existing currently. Even so, it means that the numerous layers of taxation currently being imposed will be replaced by only a few taxes.

The taxes that GST will replace are the Central Excise Duty, Additional Duties of Customs (commonly known as CVD), Special Additional Duty of Customs (SAD), and service tax which are currently levied and collected by the Central Government. It will also replace certain taxes levied by States such as State VAT, Central Sales Tax, Entertainment and Amusement Tax (except when levied by the local bodies) and taxes on lotteries, betting, and gambling. It will also replace the onerous octroi that makes trucks wait for hours on end while moving from one State to another. Thus, in effect, it makes India a large single market. Comparisons can be drawn with the European Union since in the Indian federal structure, States have been levying their own taxes which are numerous. This has pushed up the level of taxation on the citizens to a very high level. By replacing the plethora of Central and State Taxes with just a few levies, the burden of taxation on the people should come down in an ideal GST scenario. GST has different aspects for different stakeholders.

For Central/State Governments:

- A unified common national market to boost Foreign Investment and "Make in India" campaign.
- Boost to export/manufacturing activity, generation of more employment, leading to reduced poverty and increased GDP growth.

- Improving the overall investment climate in the country which will benefit the development of states.
- Uniform SGST and IGST rates to reduce the incentive for tax evasion.
- Reduction in compliance costs as no requirement of multiple record keeping.

For Citizens:

- Simpler tax system.
- Reduction in prices of goods and services due to elimination of cascading.
- Uniform prices throughout the country.
- Transparency in taxation system.
- Increase in employment opportunities.

For Trade/Industry:

- Reduction in multiplicity of taxes.
- Mitigation of cascading/double taxation.
- More efficient neutralization of taxes especially for exports.
- Development of common national market.
- Simpler tax regime-fewer rates and exemptions.

From the consumer point of view, the biggest advantage would be in terms of a reduction in the overall tax burden on goods, which is currently estimated to be around 25-30 percent. Introduction of GST would also make Indian products competitive in the domestic and international markets. Studies show that this would have a boosting impact on economic growth. Last but not the least, this tax, because of its transparent and self-policing character, would be easier to administer.

Goods and Services Tax Council (GSTC): The GSTC has been notified with effect from 12 September 2016. GSTC is being assisted by a Secretariat. Thirteen meetings of the GSTC have been held so far. The following decisions have been taken by the GSTC:

(a) The threshold exemption limit would be ₹ 20 lakh. For special category States enumerated in article

279A of the Constitution, threshold exemption limit has been fixed at ₹ 10 lakh.

(b) Composition threshold shall be ₹ 50 lakh. Composition scheme shall not be available to inter-State suppliers, service providers (except restaurant service) and specified category of manufacturers.

(c) Existing tax incentive schemes of Central or State Governments may be continued by respective government by way of reimbursement through budgetary route. The schemes, in the present form, would not continue in GST.

(d) There would be four tax rates namely 5 percent, 12 percent, 18 percent and 28 percent. Besides, some goods and services would be under the list of exempt items. Rate for precious metals is yet to be fixed. A cess over the peak rate of 28 percent on certain specified luxury and sin goods would be imposed for a period of five years to compensate States for any revenue loss on account of implementation of GST. The Council has asked the committee of officers to fit various goods and services in these four slabs keeping in view the present incidence of tax.

(e) The five laws namely CGST Law, UTGST Law, IGST Law, SGST Law and GST Compensation Law have been recommended.

(f) In order to ensure single interface, all administrative control over 90 percent of taxpayers having turnover below ₹ 1.5 crore would vest with State tax administration and 10 percent with the Central tax administration. Further all administrative control over taxpayers having turnover above ₹ 1.5 crore shall be divided equally in the ratio of 50 percent each for the Central and State tax administration.

(g) Powers under the IGST Act shall also be cross-empowered on the same basis as under CGST and SGST Acts with few exceptions.

(h) Power to collect GST in territorial waters shall be delegated by Central Government to the States.

(i) Formula and mechanism for GST Compensation Cess has been finalised.

(j) Four rules on input tax credit, composition levy, transitional provisions and valuation have been recommended. Further five rules on registration, invoice, payments, returns and refund, finalized in September 2016 and as amended in light of the GST bills introduced in the Parliament, have also been recommended.

Salient features of GST: Following are some of the salient features of GST:

- GST would be applicable on "supply" of goods or services as against the present concept of tax on the manufacture of goods or on sale of goods or on provision of services.
- GST would be based on the principle of destination-based consumption taxation as against the present principle of origin-based taxation.
- It would be a dual GST with the Centre and the States simultaneously levying it on a common base. The GST to be levied by the Centre would be called Central GST (CGST) and that to be levied by the States (including Union Territories with legislature) would be called State GST (SGST). Union Territories without legislature would levy Union Territory GST (UTGST).
- An Integrated GST (IGST) would be levied on inter-State supply (including stock transfers) of goods or services. This would be collected by the Centre so that the credit chain is not disrupted.
- Import of goods would be treated as inter-State supplies and would be subject to IGST in addition to the applicable customs duties.
- Import of services would be treated as inter-State supplies and would be subject to IGST.

- CGST, SGST/UTGST and IGST would be levied at rates to be mutually agreed upon by the Centre and the States under the aegis of the GSTC.
- GST would replace the following taxes currently levied and collected by the Centre—Central Excise Duty; Duties of Excise (Medicinal and Toilet Preparations); Additional Duties of Excise (Goods of Special Importance); Additional Duties of Excise (Textiles and Textile Products); Additional Duties of Customs (commonly known as CVD); Special Additional Duty of Customs (SAD); Service Tax; Cesses and surcharges insofar as they relate to supply of goods or services.
- State taxes that would be subsumed within the GST are—State VAT; Central Sales Tax; Purchase Tax; Luxury Tax; Entry Tax; Entertainment Tax (except those levied by the local bodies); Taxes on advertisements; Taxes on lotteries, betting and gambling; State cesses and surcharges insofar as they relate to supply of goods or services.
- GST would apply to all goods and services except alcohol for human consumption.
- GST on five specified petroleum products (crude, petrol, diesel, ATF and natural gas) would be applicable from a date to be recommended by the GSTC.
- Tobacco and tobacco products would be subject to GST. In addition, the Centre would continue to levy Central Excise duty.
- A common threshold exemption would apply to both CGST and SGST. Taxpayers with an annual turnover of ₹ 20 lakh (₹ 10 lakh for special category States as specified in Article 279A of the Constitution) would be exempt from GST. A compounding option (i.e. to pay tax at a flat rate without credits) would be available to small taxpayers (including to specified category of manufacturers and service providers) having an annual turnover of up to ₹ 50 lakh. The

threshold exemption and compounding scheme would be optional.

- The list of exempted goods and services would be kept to a minimum and it would be harmonized for the Centre and the States as well as across States as far as possible.
- Exports would be zero-rated.
- Credit of CGST paid on inputs may be used only for paying CGST on the output and the credit of SGST/UTGST paid on inputs may be used only for paying SGST/UTGST. In other words, the two streams of Input Tax Credit (ITC) cannot be cross utilized, except in specified circumstances of inter-State supplies for payment of IGST. The credit would be permitted to be utilized in the following manner—ITC of CGST allowed for payment of CGST and IGST in that order; ITC of SGST allowed for payment of SGST and IGST in that order; ITC of UTGST allowed for payment of UTGST and IGST in that order; ITC of IGST allowed for payment of IGST, CGST and SGST/UTGST in that order. ITC of CGST cannot be used for payment of SGST/UTGST and vice versa.
- Accounts would be settled periodically between the Centre and the State to ensure that the credit of SGST used for payment of IGST is transferred by the originating State to the Centre. Similarly, the IGST used for payment of SGST would be transferred by Centre to the destination State. Further the SGST portion of IGST collected on B2C supplies would also be transferred by Centre to the destination State. The transfer of funds would be carried out on the basis of information contained in the returns filed by the taxpayers.
- Input Tax Credit (ITC) to be broad based by making it available in respect of taxes paid on any supply of goods or services or both used or intended to be used in the course or furtherance of business.

- Electronic filing of returns by different class of persons at different cut-off dates.
- Various modes of payment of tax available to the taxpayer including Internet banking, debit/credit card and National Electronic Funds Transfer (NEFT)/Real Time Gross Settlement (RTGS).
- Obligation on certain persons including government departments, local authorities and government agencies, who are recipients of supply, to deduct tax at the rate of one percent from the payment made or credited to the supplier where total value of supply, under a contract, exceeds two lakhs and fifty thousand rupees.
- Refund of tax to be sought by taxpayer or by any other person who has borne the incidence of tax within two years from the relevant date.
- Obligation on electronic commerce operators to collect "tax at source", at such rate not exceeding one percent of net value of taxable supplies, out of payments to suppliers supplying goods or services through their portals.
- System of self-assessment of the taxes payable by the registered person.
- Audit of registered persons to be conducted in order to verify compliance with the provisions of Act.
- Limitation period for raising demand is three years from the due date of filing of annual return or from the date of erroneous refund for raising demand for short-payment or non-payment of tax or erroneous refund and its adjudication in normal cases.
- Limitation period for raising demand is five years from the due date of filing of annual return or from the date of erroneous refund for raising demand for short-payment or non-payment of tax or erroneous refund and its adjudication in case of fraud, suppression or willful mis-statement.

- Arrears of tax to be recovered using various modes including detaining and sale of goods, movable and immovable property of defaulting taxable person.
- Officers would have restrictive powers of inspection, search, seizure and arrest.
- Goods and Services Tax Appellate Tribunal would be constituted by the Central Government for hearing appeals against the orders passed by the Appellate Authority or the Revisional Authority. States would adopt the provisions relating to Tribunal in respective SGST Act.
- Provision for penalties for contravention of the provision of the proposed legislation has been made.
- Advance Ruling Authority would be constituted by States in order to enable the taxpayer to seek a binding clarity on taxation matters from the department. Centre would adopt such authority under CGST Act.
- An anti-profiteering clause has been provided in order to ensure that business passes on the benefit of reduced tax incidence on goods or services or both to the consumers.
- Elaborate transitional provisions have been provided for smooth transition of existing taxpayers to GST regime.

Benefits of GST: Following are some of the important benefits of GST:

For Make in India:

- Will help to create a unified common national market for India, giving a boost to foreign investment and "Make in India" campaign.
- Will prevent cascading of taxes as Input Tax Credit will be available across goods and services at every stage of supply.
- Harmonization of laws, procedures and rates of tax.
- It will boost export and manufacturing activity, generate more employment and thus increase GDP

with gainful employment leading to substantive economic growth.

- Ultimately, it will help in poverty eradication by generating more employment and more financial resources.
- More efficient neutralization of taxes especially for exports thereby making our products more competitive in the international market and give boost to Indian exports.
- Improve the overall investment climate in the country which will naturally benefit the development in the states.
- Uniform SGST and IGST rates will reduce the incentive for evasion by eliminating rate arbitrage between neighboring States and that between intra- and inter-state sales.
- Average tax burden on companies is likely to come down which is expected to reduce prices and lower prices mean more consumption, which in turn means more production thereby helping in the growth of the industries . This will create India as a "Manufacturing Hub".

For Ease of Doing Business:

- Simpler tax regime with fewer exemptions.
- Reductions in the multiplicity of taxes that are at present governing our indirect tax system leading to simplification and uniformity.
- Reduction in compliance costs. No multiple record keeping for a variety of taxes. So, lesser investment of resources and manpower in maintaining records.
- Simplified and automated procedures for various processes such as registration, returns, refunds, tax payments, etc.
- All interaction to be through the common GSTN portal, so less public interface between the taxpayer and the tax administration.

- Will improve environment of compliance as all returns to be filed online, input credits to be verified online, encouraging more paper trail of transactions.
- Common procedures for registration of taxpayers, refund of taxes, uniform formats of tax return, common tax base, common system of classification of goods and services will lend greater certainty to taxation system.
- Timelines to be provided for important activities like obtaining registration, refunds, etc.
- Electronic matching of input tax credits across India, thus, making the process more transparent and accountable.

For Benefit to Consumers:

- Final price of goods is expected to be lower due to seamless flow of input tax credit between the manufacturer, retailer, and service supplier.
- It is expected that a relatively large segment of small retailers will be either exempted from tax or will suffer very low tax rates under a compounding scheme-purchases from such entities will cost less for the consumers.
- Average tax burden on companies is likely to come down which is expected to reduce prices and lower prices mean more consumption.

Goods and Services Tax Network (GSTN): It has been set up by the government as a private company under erstwhile Section 25 of the Companies Act, 1956. It would provide three front end services, namely registration, payment, and return to taxpayers. Besides providing these services to the taxpayers, it would be developing back-end IT modules for 25 States who have opted for the same. The migration of existing taxpayers has already started from November 2016. The Revenue departments of both Centre and States are pursuing the presently registered taxpayers to complete the necessary formalities on the IT system operated by Goods and Services Tax Network (GSTN) for successful migration. About 60 percent of existing registrants have already migrated to the GST systems. GSTN has already appointed M/s Infosys as Managed Service Provider (MSP) at a total project cost of around ₹ 1380 crores for a period of five years. GSTN has selected 34 IT, and financial technology companies, to be called GST Suvidha Providers (GSPs). GSPs would develop applications to be used by taxpayers for interacting with the GSTN.

Suitable legislation for the levy of GST (Central GST Bill, UTGST Bill, IGST Bill and State GST Bills) drawing powers from the Constitution would be introduced in Parliament or the State Legislatures on the recommendations by the GSTC. Unlike the Constitutional Amendment, the GST Bills would need to be passed by a simple majority. The levy of the tax can commence only after the GST Law has been enacted by the respective legislatures. Also, unlike the State VAT, the date of commencement of this levy would have to be synchronized across the Centre and the States. This is because the IGST model cannot function unless the Centre and all the States participate simultaneously.

Impact of GST on Economy: Following are some of the important impacts of GST on Economy:

- Simplicity of operation for both industry and services producers. Manufacturers will find life much easier as they will only pay a single point tax instead of the numerous excise, octroy, and other levies that have to be paid at each tire of the production process.
- Ease of movement throughout the country as goods can be moved from State to State without having to stop to pay octroy.
- Services will become more expensive as these are now being taxed at a lower rate than the proposed new levy.
- The government revenues should rise as the simplicity of paying tax is an incentive to do so rather than evade or avoid levies.

- The ease of doing business will improve which should in turn lead to more investments and thereby give a push to economic growth.

Conclusion

Modi, according to *Wall Street Journal*, has turned out to be more of an economic policy tinkerer than the radical reformer some optimists had expected. However, Modis crackdown on black money with demonetization of 500 and 1000 rupee notes was a giant step at regulating the economy. He has also proved New Delhi's most business-friendly Prime Minister ever. No wonder that India's economy has been doing better relative to other countries. A look at 12 key indicators shows that India is now on much better footing than it was under the last government led by the Congress party and headed by Dr. Manmohan Singh. In the fiscal year ended March 31, 2015, India's gross domestic product rose 7.6 percent, helping it overtake China as the fastest-growing big economy in the world. That's up from 6.6 percent in the last full fiscal year when Congress was in power.[10]

It was apprehended by some experts that business, especially in the informal sector would suffer on account of Modi's demonetization move. The position will became clear after sometime when the effect of this more is seen.

India has now a Prime Minister who is strong, decisive and always available to the masses. He has a professional work style and has invigorated a new work culture in the government. He routinely conducts review meetings with ministers, top bureaucrats, and interacts with officials across the country via video conferences. He talks to people through "Mann Ki Baat", his monthly programme on radio.

It would be wrong however to say that whatever he and his government are doing or have done is right, as concerns remain in many areas. Many policies made by Modi and the initiatives taken by him are praiseworthy but their implementation has not been up to the desired level. Only time will tell what extent they are able to bring results. Time is also testimony to the fact that the political climate of India is highly volatile. People's mood changes with new events and developments. Many people are satisfied with what he has done so far, while many others are not. The remaining part of his term will be a test of his policies and claims and will decide his party's future as well as that of India politically.

Notes

1. economictimes.indiatimes.com
2. http://www.firstpost.com/world/india-emerges-as-a-major-defence-partner-for-us-scoops-billions-in-investment-2822984.html
3. http://nationalinterest.org/blog/the-buzz/chinas-worst-nightmare-us-india-military-alliance-brewing-16301
4. *Times of India*, 7 September 2016.
5. *Ibid.*
6. *India Today*, 5 May 2015.
7. *Business Standard*, 2 May 2016.
8. https://secure.mygov.in/group/mann-ki-baat/
9. http://niti.gov.in/content/functions
10. *The Wall Street Journal*, 25 May 2016.